Global Antitrust and Sustainability

Global Antitrust and Sustainability

Law, Economics, Enforcement

JULIAN NOWAG
Associate Professor in Competition Law, Lund University, Sweden
Associate Professor, University of Hong Kong, Hong Kong
Associate at the Centre for Competition Law and Policy, Oxford University, UK

OXFORD
UNIVERSITY PRESS

OXFORD
UNIVERSITY PRESS

Great Clarendon Street, Oxford, OX2 6DP,
United Kingdom

Oxford University Press is a department of the University of Oxford.
It furthers the University's objective of excellence in research, scholarship,
and education by publishing worldwide. Oxford is a registered trade mark of
Oxford University Press in the UK and in certain other countries.

Published in the United States of America by Oxford University Press
198 Madison Avenue, New York, NY 10016, United States of America.

British Library Cataloguing in Publication Data
Data available

Library of Congress Control Number: 2024936316

ISBN 9780192864505

DOI: 10.1093/9780191955013.001.0001

Printed and bound by
CPI Group (UK) Ltd., Croydon, CR0 4YY

MIX
Paper | Supporting
responsible forestry
FSC® C013604

The manufacturer's authorised representative in the EU for product safety is
Oxford University Press España S.A., Parque Empresarial San Fernando de Henares,
Avenida de Castilla, 2 – 28830 Madrid (www.oup.es/en or product.safety@oup.com).
OUP España S.A. also acts as importer into Spain of products made by the manufacturer.

Preface

This book covers the sustainability competition law debate. The exact start of this debate is difficult to determine, as a discussion about environmental protection and competition has been ongoing, certainly amongst academics, since the 2000s. However, a real interest in the interaction between sustainability and competition on the side of policy makers can be traced back to the 2019 Brussels conference on 'Sustainability and Competition Policy: Bridging Two Worlds to Enable a Fairer Economy'.[1] The event was in part co-organized by civil society[2] and marks the beginning of the involvement of national competition authorities, namely the Greek and Dutch agencies, with the matter. This engagement kickstarted a debate amongst policy makers which has since snowballed around the globe.

The idea of this book was conceived in 2020 following an OECD background paper I authored on Sustainability and Competition,[3] with a view to develop many of the ideas covered in the paper and broaden the context in the book. The idea is to distil the approaches and potential actions for competition authorities and courts globally and examine past efforts, current capabilities, and future possibilities, thereby serving as a comprehensive guide to best practices. Originally, the plan was to publish the book by the end of 2020. But with the Covid-19 pandemic, a first child, and, in the meantime, rapid developments in the field of sustainability and competition, the book took another four years to be completed.

In the process, I have received immense support and encouragement from many people, without whom the book would have never been fully written. In particular, I would like to acknowledge the support of numerous research assistants that helped with summarizing and collecting material and cases and proofreading drafts of this book and the OECD background paper. I would like to express my heartfelt thanks to Arletta Gorecka, Fabian Richter, Izel Naz Karahan, Kunwar Bir Singh, Rica Papa, Vasudha Verma, Vidhi Damani, Zhengmin Li, Shivi Sharma, Marco Chun Wing Chan, and Larry Ting Ho Cheung for their research assistance over a number of years, the reviewers of the book, and Teresa Orani for an in-depth read and comments. Heartfelt thanks also to my 'personal last minute proofreader', Yasmine El Masri.

[1] See <https://www.ucl.ac.uk/laws/events/2019/oct/conference-sustainability-and-competition-policy-bridging-two-worlds-enable-fairer> (accessed 14 December 2024).

[2] Organizers were the European Committee of the Regions, the European Economic and Social Committee, the Fair Trade Advocacy Office, the Global Competition Law Centre of the College of Europe, and the Centre for Economics, Law and Society at University College of London.

[3] 'Sustainability and Competition', OECD Competition Committee Discussion Paper (2020) available at <http://www.oecd.org/daf/competition/sustainability-and-competition-2020.pdf> (accessed 30 November 2023).

Moreover, I would like to recognize and acknowledge some of the active participants in this debate who challenged my thinking and generously shared their thoughts and new research in the area with me. In particular, I would like to thank Anna Gebrandy, Cento Veljanovski, Cristina Volpin, Dirk Middelschulte, Elias Deutscher, Grant Murray, Giorgio Monti, Hans Vedder, Ioannis Lianos, Johannes Persch, Juan David Gutiérrez, Klaudia Majcher, Leni Papa, Leonard Treuren, Maarten Pieter Schinkel, Marios Iocavides, Martijn Snoep, Maurits Dolmans, Nadine Watson, Nicole Kar, Roman Inderst, Simon Holms, Stavros Makris, Teresa Orani, and Suzanne Kingston.

The book attempts to cover global perspectives, by bringing in cases from jurisdictions around the globe. Nevertheless, I will inevitably have failed in this attempt. The book remains heavy on jurisdictions that currently lead the debate in the English language, and I remain limited to the languages I speak fluently. So, I encourage anyone who finds interesting cases and developments to contact me. Another limitation stems from my epistemological community which will have inevitably shaped my thinking as well as my view of the area.

Most importantly a comparative work like this one must always answer the difficult question of how the jurisdictions covered in it were chosen. The answer is in part already contained in the previous paragraphs. The jurisdictions were chosen firstly based on the accessibility of their material. Moreover, the second criterion was their engagement with the sustainability-related matters, which was further enriched by cases which provide for the possibility for such an engagement. The choice has also been influenced by the global relevance of the jurisdiction. This applies in particular to the USA, which has not seen much activity in the area, while those jurisdictions that have actively engaged with sustainability may have cases and policy documents that provide insights into many or even most aspects of the matters covered in this book. They are not always specifically mentioned or covered in detail. Instead, the examples that are presented in the different chapters are chosen for illustrative purposes. They represent particularly relevant instances that reflect interesting insights, a broad coverage, and a variety of voices.

The book is written in a way that is aimed to make it accessible to people who are not versed in every detail of the legal quirks of a specific jurisdiction. This accessibility point also implies some generalizations. For example, the book does not distinguish between unilateral, coordinated action, or mergers. While these concepts are occasionally addressed specifically, it is hoped that the overall lessons are relevant to all anti-competitive behaviour.

To make the book more engaging, I also included short stories at the beginning of each chapter and a matching answer at the end of each chapter. These stories not only made writing the book more fun, but I also hope they make the book a more enjoyable read, while also providing some practical insights. I have inserted these stories in separate boxes so they can easily be skipped, to focus on the core content.

In addition, I have also added text boxes throughout the book which contain details on cases, guidelines, or other material. These are supposed to enrich the main text by providing additional detail. But readers can easily skip these, as the main text and content is design to ensure that it can be understood without the content of the text boxes.

The book is designed to be useful for readers. Those with specific interests can be easily guided by the chapter subtitles to pick and choose those that are of most relevance to them.

Contents

Detailed Contents

Table of Cases

AUSTRALIA

BRAZIL

CHINA

EU

FRANCE

INDIA

JAPAN

SOUTH AFRICA

GERMANY

ITALY

NETHERLANDS

URUGUAY

US

UK

Table of Legislation

FRANCE

GERMANY

GREECE

HUNGARY

INDIA

JAPAN

KENYA

HONG KONG

TURKEY

US

SINGAPORE

SWITZERLAND

SOUTH AFRICA

SPAIN

THE PHILIPPINES 1987 CONSTITUTION OF THE REPUBLIC OF THE PHILIPPINES

ECUADOR

MEXICO

RUSSIA

Table of Guideline, Notice and Other Soft Law

HONG KONG

HUNGARY

JAPAN

SOUTH AFRICA

SINGAPORE

PORTUGAL

NETHERLANDS

US

UK

NEW ZEALAND

1

Introduction: scope and limits of sustainability and antitrust law

I. The interaction of sustainability and antitrust law

As the title suggests, in this book we will examine how antitrust or competition law[1] deals with sustainability matters in different jurisdictions across the globe. The book is not so much concerned with the limits of antitrust or competition law in terms of sustainability.[2] Rather, it focuses on what can be done to achieve a more sustainable future within the boundaries of the discipline. The discussion will show that a clear dividing line cannot be drawn between, on the one hand, competition concerns and competition law, and sustainability issues on the other. In other words, there is no clear distinction between a competition concern and a non-competition concern. The areas of competition law and sustainability overlap, and upon closer examination and comparison with other jurisdictions, previously imagined boundaries between them seem to shift.

Amongst competition agencies, the topic of sustainability has recently gained more attention. In 2021, the Hungarian competition agency conducted a survey on sustainability and competition law on behalf of the International Competition Network (ICN)[3]: the majority of competition agencies saw the interaction between sustainability and competition law as an important future trend.[4] Although currently, the number of case precedents is limited, the agencies also expected that sustainability questions will emerge more often in cases.[5]

Yet, the debate about sustainability and competition puts competition agencies in a difficult position. On the one hand, a clear message is needed that sustainability

[1] The terms are used interchangeably and here refer to the rules on anti-competitive conduct by means of joint or unilateral action, as well as merger regulation.

[2] In fact, sustainability and antitrust have often been (and are still) described as two separate spheres which should not mix. Thus, one might argue that the starting point is that antitrust is not and should not be supporting sustainability.

[3] An informal network of around 140 competition agencies from around the globe, available at <https://www.internationalcompetitionnetwork.org/> (accessed 23 December 2024).

[4] Hungarian Competition Authority, 'Sustainable Development and Competition Law—Survey Report (Special Project for the 2021 ICN Annual Conference)' (30 September 2021) available at <https://www.gvh.hu/pfile/file?path=/en/gvh/Conference/icn-2021-annual-conference/sustainability_survey_REPORT_3rdEd_2021_09_30_final_PUBLIC.pdf1&inline=true> (accessed 23 December 2024) 9.

[5] ibid 8.

Global Antitrust and Sustainability. Julian Nowag, Oxford University Press. © Julian Nowag 2025.
DOI: 10.1093/9780191955013.003.0001

cannot be used as a cover for cartelization or otherwise anti-competitive conduct (greenwashing). On the other hand, agencies may want to avoid the impression that they pursue their mission in a single-minded fashion. It would be disastrous for the legitimacy of agencies to be seen as disregarding the effects of their action on other values of the societies. Put differently, agencies want to avoid a situation where they are seen as obstructing sustainability initiatives or—even worse—protecting those that impose negative externalities on others in the form of unsustainable business practices.[6]

In any event, the interest of competition authorities is justified. We witness devastating effects on a global level. Two obvious examples are climate change and loss of biodiversity. The UN Environment Programme estimates the costs of adaptation to climate change alone are in the range of $140 to $300 billion per year by 2030, and between $280 to $500 billion by 2050.[7] Extreme weather phenomena attributable to climate change alone created costs of around $143 billion per year between 2000 to 2019.[8] In contrast to the increasing temperature, biodiversity is declining at a dramatic rate. For example, already in 2000 nearly one-third of the species (animals and plants) inhabiting the US were at risk of extinction.[9] The rate of decline will likely accelerate further due to feedback effects.[10] In light of the recent Covid-19 pandemic, we can also highlight the link between biodiversity, deforestation, and human expansion into remote natural habits. The decrease in biodiversity directly affects the chances of the emergence and spread of infectious diseases.[11] For instance, the expansion of humans into previously remote natural habitats, through deforestation and land use for farming, has reduced the physical distance between nature and human habitats. It thereby increases the risk of zoonotic diseases. These risks have also been further increased by the intensive use of pesticides for crop protection and antibiotics in animal production by fostering resistances of photogenes and their animal and plant vectors.[12] Thus, the reduction of deforestation combined with limiting the trade in wildlife is important in reducing the risk of such diseases.[13]

[6] At the same time, they must deal with the dangers of legitimate sustainability cooperation between businesses getting out of hand, as in the *Consumer Detergents* case (EU Commission decision of 13 April 2011, Case 39579 *Consumer Detergents*). The case started as an environmental initiative regarding laundry detergents but led to a cartel coordinating price increases.

[7] Anne Olhoff and others, 'The Adaptation Finance Gap Report' (2016) United Nations Environment Programme available at <https://www.unep.org/resources/adaptation-gap-report-2016> (accessed 23 December 2024).

[8] Rebecca Newman and Ilan Noy, 'The Global Costs of Extreme Weather that are Attributable to Climate Change' (2023) 14 *Nature Communications* 6103.

[9] Kevin Shear McCann, 'The Diversity–Stability Debate' (2000) 405 *Nature* 228–233.

[10] ibid.

[11] On this, see Felicia Keesing and others, 'Impacts of Biodiversity on the Emergence and Transmission of Infectious Diseases' (2010) 468 (7324) *Nature* 647–652.

[12] See Jason R Rohr and others, 'Emerging Human Infectious Diseases and the Links to Global Food Production' (2019) 2(6) *Nature Sustainability* 445–456.

[13] Andrew P Dobson and others, 'Ecology and Economics for Pandemic Prevention' (2020) 369 *Science* 379–381.

During the Covid-19 pandemic, the competition authorities were swift in providing 'temporary frameworks'[14] or special rules that dealt with potential antitrust risks in order to strengthen supply chain and address related issues. While the majority of sustainability challenges do not emerge suddenly or abruptly, they might still be termed crises and demand urgent attention.[15] In response, non-governmental organizations (NGOs) such as charities and also firms[16] are stepping up their attempts.[17] Action by firms is urgently needed as economic activity, in many cases by firms, is a major contributor to the crisis. In the context of climate change, for example, 70 per cent of emissions can be traced back to around 100 companies.[18]

We can observe various ways in which not only firms but also NGOs[19] or competition agencies might act to mitigate sustainability impacts, which may or may not be subject to antitrust law.[20] One example where sustainability concerns have interacted with competition law is the Indonesian Palm Oil Pledge.[21] This case, which we explore later,[22] concerns a commitment by palm oil producers to *not* sell palm oil from newly deforested land in Indonesia. Another example, possibly frequently observed, is supermarkets that may jointly decide to charge for the use of single-use plastic bags. Although such a case appears to be simple and straightforward, the outcome under competition law can vary dramatically around the world. While the Japanese competition authority[23] in such a case found that competition law was not infringed, the Uruguayan competition authority[24] found a restriction of competition and a serious violation of competition law. However, we have also seen numerous other cases that might potentially raise antitrust concerns, in particular with regard to climate change, where several companies have made (joint) public commitments. One example is European heavy vehicle producers,

[14] See eg EU Commission, 'Communication from the Commission Temporary Framework for Assessing Antitrust Issues Related to Business Cooperation In Response to Situations of Urgency Stemming from the Current COVID-19 Outbreak' [2020] OJ C 116I/7.

[15] See eg with regard to climate change David Archer and Stefan Rahmstorf, *The Climate Crisis: An Introductory Guide to Climate Change* (CUP 2010).

[16] Throughout the book the terms firm, business, company, and corporation will be used interchangeably, although the terms firm and business may also include non-incorporated economic actors like the self-employed, or even charities, where they operate on the market. See in this regard also Chapter 4, section III. 1. a).

[17] See below section IV for the different challenges that this brings about on the interaction between international law, constitutional law, and competition law.

[18] Paul Griffin, 'The Carbon Majors Database—CDP Carbon Majors Report 2017' (2017) CDP Report, available at: <https://cdn.cdp.net/cdp-production/cms/reports/documents/000/002/327/original/Carbon-Majors-Report-2017.pdf?1501833772> (accessed 23 December 2024).

[19] See with regard to whether actions by NGOs (or firms for that matter) are subject to competition law Chapter 4, section III 1. a).

[20] As explored in Chapter 3 and 4.

[21] For an overview see Ahmad Dermawan and Otto Hospes, 'When the State Brings Itself Back into GVC: The Case of the Indonesian Palm Oil Pledge' (2018) 9(S2) *Global Policy* 21–28.

[22] More details in Chapter 4.

[23] One notable point was that in the Japanese case the municipality took part in setting up the scheme; see OECD, 'Horizontal Agreements in the Environmental Context' (2010) DAF/COMP(2010)39, 149.

[24] Resolucion 330/2021 (*Plastic Bags Case*) (Comisión de Promoción y Defensa de la Competencia).

who agreed to phase out diesel trucks a decade earlier than had been planned.[25] Another example is attempts in the financial services and banking industry. In this area, there is currently a debate about the Climate Action 100+ initiative,[26] and whether the pledges made by institutional investors[27] should be seen as a violation of the Sherman Act.[28] In particular, the US has seen heated debates more recently in the context of the 'anti-woke backlash'. Under the banner of fighting 'woke capitalism', a number of Republican attorney generals and law-makers have tried to leverage antitrust laws to pressure companies over their Environmental, Social, and Governance (ESG) efforts.[29] A similar allegation is made against banks in New Zealand where around 40 per cent of the banks have committed to the UN-backed Net Zero Banking Alliance. The concern is that this would be discriminating farmers based on their CO2 emissions.[30]

II. Central argument, theme, and structure of the book

The mission of this book is to distil different approaches and potential actions in sustainability matters for competition authorities and courts globally. It examines past efforts, current capabilities, and future possibilities, serving as a comprehensive guide to best practices. By showcasing various methods for incorporating sustainability into competition law, it offers diverse examples that can be adapted to the legal frameworks of different countries. Essentially, it provides a comprehensive

[25] Peter Campbell, 'European Truckmakers to Phase Out Diesel Sales Decade Earlier than Planned' *Financial Times* (2020), available at <https://www.ft.com/content/7d49589b-ff50-444d-8eef-b8abe5691f91?segmentId=114a04fe-353d-37db-f705-204c9a0a157b> (accessed 23 December 2024).

[26] Available at <https://www.climateaction100.org> (accessed 23 December 2024).

[27] For an argument about how institutional minority shareholders can persuade portfolio companies in the fossil fuel industry to reduce emissions, and how a consequential reduction in output may be in line with their interests, see Madison Condon, 'Externalities and the Common Owner' (2020) 95 *Washington Law Review* 1–81.

[28] One (mainly Republican) group of state attorney generals (AGs) investigated them for a possible violation of the Sherman Act, while another group of AGs (mainly Democrats) wrote a letter expressing that there were no antitrust concerns. For a summary of the different AG actions in this regard see Latham and Watkins, 'ESG Initiatives Face Increased Pressure From Potential Antitrust Challenges' (15 May 2023) 3102 Client Alert available at <https://www.lw.com/admin/upload/SiteAttachments/ESG-initiatives-face-increased-pressure-potential-antitrust-challenges.pdf> (accessed 23 December 2024).

[29] See eg James Surowiecki, 'The War on "Woke Capital" Is Backfiring' *The Atlantic* (31 January 2024) available at <https://www.theatlantic.com/ideas/archive/2024/01/republicans-wokecapital-esg-investment/677294/> (accessed 23 December 2024); Cynthia Hanawalt and Denise Hearn, 'The Slippery Notion of Boycotts in the Anti-ESG Movement' *Climate Law* (14 June 2023) available at <https://blogs.law.columbia.edu/climatechange/2023/06/14/the-slippery-notion-of-boycotts-in-the-anti-esg-movement/> (accessed 23 December 2024); for a discussion with regard to antitrust law, see Maurits Dolmans, Wanjie Lin, and Jessica Hollis, 'Sustainability and Net Zero Climate Agreements—A Transatlantic Antitrust Perspective' (8 September 2023) available at <https://ssrn.com/abstract=4571804> (accessed 23 December 2024).

[30] Jonathan Milne 'Inquiry into Banks "Colluding" to Put Climate Ahead of Farmers' *Newsroom* (2024) available at <https://newsroom.co.nz/2024/08/19/crackdown-on-banks-colluding-to-favour-climate-ahead-of-farmers/> (accessed 23 December 2024).

menu from which authorities and scholars can draw inspiration, customizing the insights to meet their specific needs, limitations, and requirements.

Its central argument and theme are the overlap[31] between sustainability and traditional antitrust goals, such as consumer welfare. It shows how sustainability and competition are not necessarily two opposing values in antitrust analysis. Instead, they overlap. The various options presented in this book illustrate that competition authorities have multiple pathways to address sustainability issues. Whether they choose to do so is not a matter of feasibility but one of policy choice. A policy choice that is a political choice, but that will also be influenced by the general legal framework, as discussed below.[32]

While globally not all competition laws have consumer welfare as their expressed goal, the benefits from competition for consumers are an important *leitmotif* for nearly all jurisdictions.[33] Even in the USA,[34] the home of the consumer welfare standard, its relevance and appropriateness have come under fire. Some scholars (and even economists) have suggested that it should be abolished and that quantification requirements in competition law are misguided.[35] This book does not engage in the (endless) debate about what the goals of competition law are, or what they should be. Instead, it starts from the observation that consumer welfare is a relevant consideration. It explores the different spheres where competition law, or specifically consumer welfare as an antitrust goal, overlaps with sustainability. In fact, we might refer to this overlap as sustainable consumer welfare, and the overlap can take different shapes.

[31] Or integration, to use a different word.

[32] See section IV of this chapter.

[33] See for example OECD, 'The Consumer Welfare Standard—Advantages and Disadvantages Compared to Alternative Standards—Background Note' (2023) DAF/COMP(2023)4 available at <https://one.oecd.org/document/DAF/COMP(2023)4/en/pdf> (accessed 23 December 2024); International Competition Law Network, 'Competition Enforcement and Consumer Welfare—Setting the Agenda' (2011) available at <https://www.internationalcompetitionnetwork.org/wp-content/uploads/2019/11/SP_CWelfare2011.pdf> (accessed 23 December 2024).

[34] And likewise in Europe.

[35] See eg Tim Wu, *The Curse of Bigness: Antitrust in the New Gilded Age* (Columbia Global Reports 2018); Mark Glick, 'How Chicago Economics Distorts "Consumer Welfare"' (2019) 64(4) *Antitrust Bulletin* 495–513; Sandeep Vaheesan, 'The Profound Nonsense of Consumer Welfare Antitrust' (2019) 64(4) *Antitrust Bulletin* 479–494; Steven C Salop, 'Question: What Is the Real and Proper Antitrust Welfare Standard? Answer: The True Consumer Welfare Standard' (2020) 22(3) *Loyola Consumer Law Review* 336–353; Barak Y Orbach, 'The Antitrust Consumer Welfare Paradox' (2011) 7(1) *Journal of Competition Law & Economics* 133–164; Robert W Crandall, and Clifford Winston, 'Does Antitrust Policy Improve Consumer Welfare? Assessing the Evidence' (2003) 17(4) *Journal of Economic Perspectives* 3–26; Herbert Hovenkamp, 'Is Antitrust's Consumer Welfare Principle Imperiled?' (2019) 45 *Journal of Corporation Law* 101–130; Roger D Blair, and D. Daniel Sokol, 'Welfare Standards in U.S. and E.U. Antitrust Enforcement' (2013) 81(5) *Fordham Law Review* 2497–2541; Kati Cseres, 'The Controversies of the Consumer Welfare Standard' (2006) 3(2) *Competition Law Review* 121–173; Cristina Caffarra, '"Consumer Welfare Is Dead": What Do We Do Instead?—A Perspective from Europe' *ProMarket* (27 April 2023) available at <https://www.promarket.org/2023/04/27/consumer-welfare-is-dead-what-do-we-do-instead-a-perspective-from-europe/> (accessed 23 December 2024).

Occasionally, the overlap might involve balancing between traditional concerns, such as consumer welfare in the form of price and sustainability. Such balancing might for example occur where sustainability is a quality parameter of competition. In such a case higher (sustainability) quality would be balanced against the higher price of the product. However, such balancing—while possibly controversial—is rather the exception than the norm. Moreover, it is important to bear in mind that much of the application of the available tools depends on the (legal) interpretation of the existing tools. In other words, it affects how competition law treats specific arrangements and contexts such as (sustainability) standard-setting, whether certain areas, for instance agriculture, are excluded from the scope of competition law or otherwise treated differently in the competition law analysis. Thus, the overlap of competition law and sustainability is not only different between jurisdictions but might vary temporally within the same jurisdiction. Put differently, depending on the legal requirements (and political will) at a specific point in time, the interpretation and thus the overall overlap space between the two areas will be larger or smaller. Law, in a certain way, is never fixed.[36]

That said, competition laws across jurisdictions and time share multiple commonalities which allow the agencies and courts to explore how other jurisdictions have handled sustainability and competition law questions. It is in this space that this book hopefully will be a valuable source. The basic distinction[37] that seems inherent in all jurisdictions—and which structures this book—is the following: on the one hand, questions around enforcing competition law against unsustainable business practices (Chapter 3) and, on the other hand, questions as to how to apply the competition rules where private actors advance sustainability (Chapter 4). In situations where competition is beneficial for sustainability, we need to maintain such competition and ask to what extent unsustainable business practices are within the scope of competition law and thus prohibited. In these circumstances, the competition authorities become guardians of sustainability by enforcing the competition law prohibitions. Conversely, where private actors advance sustainability, all jurisdictions are faced with questions around two areas: first, whether such pro-sustainability actions are considered to be anti-competitive, and subject to their law (within the scope of the law). Within this framework, we may, for example, observe exclusions for de minimis restrictions of competition, sectoral exclusions, or exclusions for standard-setting activities and situations involving state action. Second, if actions are within the scope of the law, there will be questions as to whether and how harm to competition can be balanced with improvements in sustainability. Different frameworks might be applicable to such balancing. For

[36] On legal interpretation see eg William Baude and Stephen E Sachs, 'The Law of Interpretation' (2017) 130(4) *Harvard Law Review* 1079–1147.

[37] As developed in Julian Nowag, *Environmental Integration in Competition and Free-Movement Laws* (OUP 2017) 1–12 and Julian Nowag, 'Competition Law's Sustainability Gap? Tools for an Examination and a Brief Overview' (2022) *Nordic Journal of European Law* 150–152.

example, we might see 'abstract balancing' and 'competition-specific balancing'.[38] In the case of abstract balancing, the balancing may, for example, involve a general proportionality assessment as part of a public interest test. Competition-specific balancing, in contrast, will for example 'translate' competition harm and sustainability benefit into monetary terms and calculate the overall effect for affected consumers or society as a whole. All jurisdictions will have tools that can be used to balance competition and sustainability. Some will only have abstract balancing, some will only have competition-specific balancing, and others will have both.

Overall, this book focuses on the areas where an overlap between competition and sustainability can be identified, rather than exploring possibly unsolvable tensions or incommensurability.[39] The book is also in line with the empirical findings of the ICN's sustainability survey amongst competition agencies. The survey found that the majority of agencies believe that competition law can play a role in the sustainability debate, as sustainability and competition should not be seen as opposites, although regulation will usually be superior.[40]

This first chapter of the book sets the scene and explains the concept of sustainability and its significance for the debate about competition law and policy. Chapter 2 explores the economics of the interaction of competition and sustainability; its focus is distinct from that of the subsequent three chapters (Chapters 3–5), which focus on the law. In Chapter 3, the first of the law chapters, substantive competition law questions are considered, and it examines the extent to which competition authorities can become guardians of sustainability by enforcing the competition law prohibitions. In other words, the chapter studies how competition authorities can foster sustainability by enforcing competition rules against anti-competitive practices. Chapter 4 explores situations where firms foster sustainability. The question addressed in that chapter is how the antitrust rules can be applied so as to ensure that competition law does not unnecessarily prevent or limit the achievement of sustainability goals. This chapter also addresses one of the most contentious issues: how restrictions of competition and improvements in sustainability can be balanced. Chapter 5 moves the focus to procedural

[38] For details see Chapter 4. A similar distinction between the two forms of balancing is also drawn by Christopher Townley, *Article 81 and Public Policy* (Hart 2009) who in Part B of the book distinguishes between 'mere balancing' and 'market-balancing'.

[39] On an underlying conflict between the idea of output expansion and CO2 emission, see eg Johannes Persch, 'Pro-enforcement Perspectives on Competition Law and Sustainability' in Julian Nowag (ed), *Research Handbook on Sustainability and Competition* (Edward Elgar 2024) 235–248. This can also be linked to the critique of green growth vs degrowth; for an examination in competition law see Christos Vrettos and Marios C Iocavides, 'Green or Grey? EU Competition Policy, Sustainability, and the Grean Deal: the Degrowth Policy Agenda' (forthcoming, on file with the author). More generally on sustainable development and degrowth, see Yaryna Khmara and Jakub Kronenberg, 'Degrowth in the Context of Sustainability Transitions: in Search of a Common Ground' (2020) 267 *Journal of Cleaner Production* 122072.

[40] ICN report (n 4) 7, 19.

questions and enforcement tools. It covers the relevance of public and private enforcement actions in the pursuit of sustainability and how jurisdictions, and in particular, competition agencies have reacted to the sustainability challenge.

The seemingly dramatic shift in focus between the economics perspective (Chapter 2) and the legal perspective (in particular that of Chapter 4) is likely to reflect the divergence in interests and focus between economists and lawyers when they approach the topic. As Chapter 2 suggests, economists are often most interested in finding out what the general rule is, or should be, in a particular context. That is to say, they examine situations and try to extrapolate regularities, in other words, to define a rule that applies in the majority of cases. In contrast, lawyers work with an already existing rule. Sometimes smaller elements of the rule need to be clarified, but in general, lawyers seem more interested in the non-standard case—the exception to the rule.

III. Background: sustainability as a concept

Before we turn to the interaction between sustainability and competition from an economic perspective in the next chapter, we should gain a better understanding of the concept of sustainability and its different elements. This section, thus, explains the history of sustainability and the three basic tenets of sustainability: environmental sustainability, social sustainability, and economic sustainability. Finally, the section highlights the role of the private sector and firms in the pursuit of sustainability.

1. History and basic tenets of sustainability

In this book, as in many parts of modern scholarship, 'sustainability' and 'sustainable development' are often used interchangeably. In fact, when the book uses the broad term 'sustainability', it refers to what might be more precisely termed as 'sustainable development'.[41]

The term 'sustainability' is broader and is commonly applied in science[42] and refers to a capacity to sustain something (eg, a person, a system, a habit) for an

[41] This is a common approach, followed also in for example the seminal work of Kent E Portney, *Sustainability* (MIT Press 2015). However, we should acknowledge that this synonymous usage may not be without its problems. As Soini and Dessein point out, such a usage is not very helpful where one aims to narrow down the conceptual definitions of either terms, and it might hamper the creation of theoretical frameworks or even the operationalization of these concepts. See Katriina Soini and Joost Dessein, 'Culture-Sustainability Relation: Towards a Conceptual Framework' (2016) 8(2) *Sustainability* 1–12.

[42] In particular, it is known from the thermodynamic equilibrium, and relates to a permanent equilibrium.

indefinite period of time. The first use of sustainability in the way that is used in this book may be traced back to Thomas Robert Malthus. In 1798, he expressed in his work a concern for future generations. Humanity would grow faster than it could grow its means to maintain subsistence, hence future generations would suffer from malnutrition and famine.[43] This concern was later picked up prominently by the 'Club of Rome', who in 1972 published the famous report, *The Limits to Growth*.[44]

The definition of 'sustainable development' is different yet related to sustainability.[45] The most commonly used definition of sustainable development stems from the so-called Brundtland Report of the World Commission on Environment and Development.[46] It defines sustainable development as 'development that meets the needs of the present without compromising the ability of future generations to meet their own needs'.[47] We may therefore understand sustainable development as a 'universal goal to be achieved'[48] or a 'moral obligation that we are supposed to have for future generations'.[49]

The core of this definition is built upon environmental concerns[50] around the concept of 'eco-development'. This concept comes from the 1972 UN Stockholm Conference on Human-Environment. There, the impact of human society on the environment was discussed and attempts were made to reconcile economic development and environmental preservation.[51] The social dimension[52] was

[43] Thomas Malthus, *An Essay on the Principle of Population* (1798) available at <http://www.esp.org/books/malthus/population/malthus.pdf> (accessed 23 December 2024).

[44] Donella H Meadows and others, *The Limits to Growth: A Report for the Club of Rome's Project on the Predicament of Mankind* (1972) available at <https://collections.dartmouth.edu/teitexts/meadows/diplomatic/meadows ltg-diplomatic.html> (accessed 23 December 2024).

[45] The foundational principles for sustainable development are based on science, in particular studies of ecology and conservation science as well as economics. The earlier ideas of this concept seemed to appear in 1798. Then, the economist Thomas Malthus first theorized that the unabated growth of the human population would quickly deplete all the earth's resources necessary for human life, see Portney (n 41); Bâc Dorin Paul, *A History of the Concept of Sustainable Development: Literature Review* (2008) available at <https://www.researchgate.net/publication/242219096_A_history_of_the_concept_of_sustainable_development_Literature_review> (accessed 23 December 2024) 576–580; Ben Purvis, Yong Mao, and Darren Robinson, 'Three Pillars of Sustainability: in Search of Conceptual Origins' (2019) 14 *Sustainability Science* 681–695.

[46] The United Nations General Assembly organized the World Commission on Environment and Development (WCED) in 1987 to propose 'a global agenda for change' that can deal with issues of economic, environmental, and social development. The WCED then published *Our Common Future*, also known as the Brundtland Report, named after the head of the Commission, available at <https://sustainabledevelopment.un.org/content/documents/5987our-common-future.pdf> (accessed 23 December 2024)

[47] ibid 441.

[48] See Soini and Dessein (n 41).

[49] Robert M Solow 'Sustainability: An Economist's Perspective' in Robert N Stavins (ed), *Economics of the Environment* (WW Norton 1991) 180.

[50] For details, see below under section 2.

[51] See Purvis (n 45).

[52] For details, see below under section 3.

incorporated in the 1980s as it was recognized that war and poverty have devastating effects on the environment.[53]

An important milestone was the above-mentioned 1987 report by the UN World Commission on Environment and Development, *Our Common Future* (the Brundtland Report). The core contribution of the report was the acknowledgement that issues of environmental protection, social, and economic development are interdependent. This recognition marks a shift from focusing on environmental problems to their causes. This shift was highlighted in the report's acknowledgement that poverty is both 'a major cause and effect of global environmental problems'.[54] The report suggested focusing on the following areas:

- reviving growth;
- changing the quality of this growth;
- meeting essential needs for jobs, food, energy, water, and sanitation;
- ensuring a sustainable population level;
- conserving and enhancing the resource base;
- reorienting technology and managing risk;
- merging environment and economics in decision-making; and
- reorienting international economic relations.[55]

Overall, we can identify three 'pillars'[56] at the heart of the concept of sustainability: the environment, the economy, and the society.[57] Thus, sustainability is achieved through a balanced and simultaneous pursuit of all three components.[58] Although trade-offs might exist, the concept emphasizes that growth does not need to be balanced against environmental sustainability. It highlights that economic growth and environmental protection can co-exist, in particular as growth can foster ecological protection and social equity.[59]

[53] For instance, poverty and war have dramatic effects on humans. These will in turn negatively affect the natural environment and the social institutions.

[54] WCED (n 46) 8.

[55] ibid 46.

[56] Occasionally, culture is seen as a fourth component of sustainability. See Soini and Dessein (n 41) who argue that culture helps 1. by defining goals of preserving cultural capital (eg, art, heritage, knowledge, diversity), 2. by mediating between initiatives of economic, social, and ecological sustainability while protecting material and immaterial culture, and 3. by defining development as a cultural process, where all the pillars are shaped by the culture wherein they manifest.

[57] For a review paper on these, see Justice Mensah and Sandra Ricart Casadevall, 'Sustainable Development: Meaning, History, Principles, Pillars, and Implications for Human Action: Literature Review' (2019) 5(1) *Cogent Social Sciences* 1653531.

[58] The system effectively creates a 'balance of trade-offs' between economic growth, environmental protection, and social equity. See Purvis and others (n 45) 685.

[59] Portney (n 41) 6.

The currently applicable international law framework, the Agenda 2030,[60] aims to provide more concrete guidance on sustainable development. It was adopted in 2015 by the United Nations General Assembly as UN Resolution 70/1 entitled 'Transforming our world: the 2030 Agenda for Sustainable Development'. The Resolution establishes the UN Sustainable Development Goals (SDGs) and is a 'plan of action for people, planet, and prosperity'.[61] It sets out a roadmap towards sustainable development until 2030 with the aim of providing guidance to all nations' policies. It provides seventeen sustainable development goals on the economic, social, and environmental dimensions of sustainable development.[62] These sustainable development goals are presented in Table 1.1.

The resolution also contains 169 more concrete targets that are associated with these goals, aiming to promote economic growth through increased investments,[63] trade reform,[64] industrialization,[65] and the promotion of bank financing.[66]

This UN Resolution has been very influential in guiding countries' policies. For example, when the OECD in 2019 surveyed the influence of the SDGs in different countries, it showed that in 2018 only 9 per cent of the countries had not yet referred to the SDGs in their national development plans, and that over 74 per cent of countries had incorporated SDGs into their country-level strategies.[67]

[60] Before the Agenda 2030 was adopted, all UN member states had already committed to implementing the so-called Millennium Development Goals (MDGs). While MDGs promoted significant progress, it had been argued that the MDGs focused primarily on social improvements for developing countries. They thereby limited the participation of richer countries to financial and technological assistance; see Jeffrey D Sachs, 'From Millennium Development Goals to Sustainable Development Goals' (2012) 379(9832) *The Lancet* 2206–2211.

[61] UN, *Transforming our World: the 2030 Agenda for Sustainable Development* (2015), available at <https://sustainabledevelopment.un.org/content/documents/21252030%20Agenda%20for%20Sustainable%20Development%20web.pdf> (accessed 23 December 2024).

[62] The SDGs have not been without criticisms. It has for instance been argued that they did not assign sufficient importance to social equity, failed the most marginalized by neglecting their urgent needs, and they inadequately reflect the environment limits and the drawbacks of economic growth. See Erling Holden, Kristin Linnerud, and David Banister, 'The Imperatives of Sustainable Development' (2017) 25(3) *Sustainable Development* 213–226.

[63] SDG 2.a Increase investment, including through enhanced international cooperation, in rural infrastructure, agricultural research and extension services, technology development, and plant and livestock gene banks in order to enhance agricultural productive capacity in developing countries, in particular least developed countries.

[64] SDG 2.b Correct and prevent trade restrictions and distortions in world agricultural markets, including through the parallel elimination of all forms of agricultural export subsidies and all export measures with equivalent effect, in accordance with the mandate of the Doha Development Round.

[65] SDG 9.2 Promote inclusive and sustainable industrialization and, by 2030, significantly raise industry's share of employment and gross domestic product, in line with national circumstances, and double its share in least developed countries.

[66] SDG 8.10 Strengthen the capacity of domestic financial institutions to encourage and expand access to banking, insurance, and financial services for all.

[67] OECD, 'Sustainable Results in Development: Using the SDGs for Shared Results and Impact' (2019), OECD Publishing available at <https://doi.org/10.1787/368cf8b4-en> (accessed 23 December 2024).

Table 1.1 UN Sustainable Development Goals

Goal 1	End poverty in all forms everywhere
Goal 2	End hunger, achieve food security and improved nutrition, and promote sustainable agriculture
Goal 3	Ensure healthy lives and promote well-being for all at all ages
Goal 4	Ensure inclusive and equitable quality education and promote lifelong learning opportunities for all
Goal 5	Achieve gender equality and empower all women and girls
Goal 6	Ensure availability and sustainable management of water and sanitation for all
Goal 7	Ensure access to affordable, reliable, sustainable and modern energy for all
Goal 8	Promote sustained, inclusive, and sustainable economic growth, full and productive employment and decent work for all
Goal 9	Build resilient infrastructure, promote inclusive and sustainable industrialization and foster innovation
Goal 10	Reduce inequality within and among countries
Goal 11	Make cities and human settlements inclusive, safe, resilient, and sustainable
Goal 12	Ensure sustainable consumption and production patterns
Goal 13	Take urgent action to combat climate change and its impacts
Goal 14	Conserve and sustainably use the oceans, seas, and marine resources for sustainable development
Goal 15	Protect, restore, and promote sustainable use of terrestrial ecosystems, sustainably manage forests, combat desertification, and halt and reverse land degradation and halt biodiversity loss
Goal 16	Promote peaceful and inclusive societies for sustainable development, provide access to justice for all and build effective, accountable and inclusive institutions at all levels.
Goal 17	Strengthen the means of implementation and revitalize the Global Partnership for Sustainable Development.

2. Environmental sustainability

Core to sustainability is environmental sustainability.[68] The modern concern for the environment and possibly modern environmentalism can be traced back to

[68] On this see eg Torsten Krause, 'Environmental Sustainability' in Julian Nowag (ed), *Research Handbook Sustainability and Competition Law* (Edward Elgar 2024) 32–48.

1962 when Rachel Carson published her book *Silent Spring*.[69] In it, she described how the use of pesticides, seen as technological progress, had devastating effects on whole ecological communities, how it contaminated the food chain and thereby ultimately affected humans. She suggested that regulation was needed to curtail the drive for short-term economic gain to ensure long-term benefits and survival. This insight led to the enactment of the very first environmental laws regulating economic activity to protect the environment as such. The Club of Rome report of 1972, mentioned above, added to this understanding. It highlighted the finite nature of the planet's resources in light of the depletion rate that exceeds their replenishing rate. The report introduced the idea that our use of natural resources is creating an increasing deficit, leaving less for future generations. While national and international efforts at numerous international institutions have been made, we have still not reversed this trend. The commonly used 'ecological footprint'[70] is a tool that allows the tracking and compairing of resource use, both in a geographical and temporal manner.

Locally, many environmental problems can be identified, but only a small number of problems have a global impact.[71] These global problems are primarily climate change, deforestation and changes in land use, loss of biodiversity, and pollution.[72]

Climate change is an obvious example of a global environmental sustainability problem. Climate change increases the likelihood of extreme weather events such as droughts and floods but is also leading to sea level rises. It also harms ecosystems and species.[73] These impacts are caused by the unprecedented speed of climate change, which exceeds the capacity of both the natural systems and humans to adapt, thereby risking long-term survival.[74] The risks of climate change are further

[69] Rachel Carson, *Silent Spring* (Houghton Mifflin 1962).

[70] See <https://www.footprintnetwork.org/our-work/ecological-footprint/> (accessed 30 November 2023).

[71] For example, questions about local wildlife, local air quality, or noise pollution are typically more local concerns, yet they are still important matters.

[72] See eg Krause (n 68); Robert Goodland, 'The Concept of Environmental Sustainability' (1995) 26 *Annual Review of Ecology, Evolutions, and Systematics* 1–24.

[73] IPBES, 'Global Assessment Report on Biodiversity and Ecosystem Services of the Intergovernmental Science-Policy Platform on Biodiversity and Ecosystem Services.' (2019) available at <https://www.ipbes.net/global-assessment-report-biodiversity-ecosystem-services> (accessed 23 December 2024); IPCC, 'Climate Change 2022: Impacts, Adaptation, and Vulnerability, Contribution of Working Group II to the Sixth Assessment Report of the Intergovernmental Panel on Climate Change' (2022) available at <https://www.ipcc.ch/report/ar6/wg2/> (accessed 30 November 2023); Peter E Robins and others, 'Impact of Climate Change on UK Estuaries: a Review of Past Trends and Potential Projections' (2016) 169 *Estuarine, Coastal and Shelf Science* 119–135; Arie Staal and others, 'Hysteresis of Tropical Forests in the 21st Century' 2020 11(1) *Nature Communications*, 4978.

[74] IPCC, 'Climate Change 2022: Impacts, Adaptation and Vulnerability: Summary for Policymakers' (2022) available at <https://www.ipcc.ch/report/ar6/wg2/downloads/report/IPCC_AR6_WGII_SummaryForPolicymakers.pdf> (accessed 23 December 2024); Johannes Wessely and others, 'Habitat-based Conservation Strategies Cannot Compensate for Climate-Change-Induced Range Loss' (2017) 7(11) *Nature Climate Change* 823–827.

compounded by tipping points which initiate cascading effects, further increasing the speed of changes in the climate and ecosystems.[75]

A second global issue is deforestation and changes in land use, which in part is also linked to climate change. Deforestation increases carbon emissions in two ways: on one hand, by carbon emissions from the soil, and on the other hand, by releasing the carbon from burning the cut wood.[76] Moreover, deforestation also reduces biodiversity by destroying habitats, thereby affecting the income and food availability of people who rely on the forest for these.[77] Changes in land use often also lead to deforestation, for example, by making space for urban areas. Furthermore, such changes in land use have other impacts. For example, creating infrastructure, expanding urban areas, establishing mining businesses, draining wetlands, or turning grassland into agricultural land further increases carbon emissions and reduces biodiversity.[78]

The third issue connected to changes in land use and deforestation is the loss of biodiversity.[79] Human activity greatly impacts biodiversity. While the exact rate of biodiversity loss is difficult to calculate, it is between 100 and 1000 times higher than the natural biodiversity loss rate.[80] The loss of biodiversity has numerous implications for future generations, as it impacts ecological processes and interactions. An example is the overall decrease of insects, which have been impacted by numerous human activities but primarily by the use of pesticides and herbicides.[81] The worrying 75 per cent decrease in the number of insects in the last fifty years hinders pollination of plants across the globe and thereby impacts food security.[82]

The fourth, and sometimes also visible, environmental sustainability problem is pollution. The most visible form is solid waste pollution which results from a lack of

[75] Timothy M Lenton and others, 'Tipping Elements in the Earth's Climate System' (2008) 105(6) *Proceedings of the National Academy of Sciences* 1786–1793; Nico Wunderling and others, 'Interacting Tipping Elements Increase Risk of Climate Domino Effects Under Global Warming' (2021) 12(2) *Earth System Dynamic* 601–619.

[76] Timothy RH Pearson and others, 'Greenhouse Gas Emissions From Tropical Forest Degradation: An Underestimated Source' (2017) 12(1) *Carbon Balance and Management* 3; IPPC, 'Climate Change 2014: Mitigation of Climate Change. Contribution of Working Group III to the Fifth Assessment Report of the Intergovernmental Panel on Climate Change' available at <https://www.ipcc.ch/site/assets/uploads/2018/02/ipcc_wg3_ar5_full.pdf> (accessed 23 December 2024); James EM Watson and others, 'The Exceptional Value of Intact Forest Ecosystems' (2018) 2 *Nature Ecology & Evolution* 599–610.

[77] Watson, ibid.

[78] Alexandra Marques and others, 'Increasing Impacts of Land Use on Biodiversity and Carbon Sequestration Driven by Population and Economic Growth' (2019) 3 *Nature Ecology & Evolution* 628–637.

[79] See eg Tim Newbold and others, 'Has Land Use Pushed Terrestrial Biodiversity Beyond the Planetary Boundary? A Global Assessment' (2016) 353(6296) *Science* 288–291; Tim Newbold and others, 'Global Effects of Land Use on Local Terrestrial Biodiversity' (2015) 520(7545) *Nature*, 45–50.

[80] Eg IPBES (n 73).

[81] Tari Gunstone and others, 'Pesticides and Soil Invertebrates: A Hazard Assessment' (2021) 9 *Frontiers in Environmental Science* 1–21.

[82] Pedro Cardoso and others, 'Scientists' Warning to Humanity on Insect Extinctions' (2020) 242 *Biological Conservation* 108426; Sebastian Seibold and others, 'Arthropod Decline in Grasslands and Forests is Associated with Landscape-Level Drivers' (2019) 574(7780) *Nature* 671–674.

adequate waste management systems.[83] In recent years, we have witnessed greater attention to plastic pollution stemming from packaging and other disposable objects.[84] Plastics not only accumulate in the soil and aquatic systems, but also break down into micro and nano-plastics with numerous consequences (some unknown to us as of yet).[85] These residues can, for example, be found even in human lungs and blood.[86] Another invisible form of pollution is the contamination of habitats by toxins. Such toxins are, for example, released during production processes or used as pesticides and herbicides. They can be stable chemical compounds that accumulate in the environment and impact the health and DNA of humans and other organisms.[87] Finally, pollution occurs not only in the soil and aquatic system but also in the air. Air pollution has numerous sources and is affected by local and seasonal changes, but major sources are combustion processes in industry and private households, such as fossil fuel use or the burning of organic and non-organic products.[88] The health impacts are numerous[89] and outdoor air pollution alone leads worldwide to between 1.61 and 4.81 million premature deaths per year.[90]

3. Social sustainability

The second cornerstone of sustainability is social sustainability.[91] It broadly concerns human well-being in terms of wealth and access to basic services, justice in

[83] Subhasish Das and others, 'Solid Waste Management: Scope and the Challenge of Sustainability' (2019) 228 *Journal of Cleaner Production* 658–678.

[84] Stephanie B Borrelle and others, 'Predicted Growth in Plastic Waste Exceeds Efforts to Mitigate Plastic Pollution' (2020) 369(6510) *Science* 1515 1518.

[85] See eg Nsikak U Benson and others, 'Micro(nano)plastics Prevalence, Food Web Interactions, and Toxicity Assessment in Aquatic Organisms: A Review' (2022) 9 *Frontiers in Marine Science* 851281; Tânia Gomes and others, 'Ecotoxicological Impacts of Micro- and Nanoplastics in Terrestrial and Aquatic Environments' in Michael S Bank (ed) *Microplastic in the Environment: Pattern and Process* (Springer 2022); Ahmed M Elgarahy, Abdullah Akhdhar, and Khalid Z Elwakeel, 'Microplastics Prevalence, Interactions, and Remediation in the Aquatic Environment: a Critical Review' (2021) 9(5) *Journal of Environmental Chemical Engineering* 106224.

[86] Luís Fernando Amato-Lourenço and others, 'Presence of Airborne Microplastics in Human Lung Tissue' (2021) 416 *Journal of Hazardous Materials* 126124; Heather A Leslie and others, 'Discovery and Quantification of Plastic Particle Pollution in Human Blood' (2022) 163 *Environment International* 107199.

[87] Kevin Christopher Jones and Pim de Voogt, 'Persistent Organic Pollutants (POPs): State of the Science' (1999) 100 *Environmental Pollution* 209–221.

[88] See Claire Holman, 'Sources of Air Pollution' in Stephen T Holgate and others (eds), *Air Pollution and Health* (Academic Press 1999) 115–148.

[89] Frank J Kelly and Julia C Fussell, 'Air Pollution and Public Health: Emerging Hazards and Improved Understanding of Risk' (2015) 37(4) *Environmental Geochemistry and Health* 631–649.

[90] Which might double by 2050 in the business-as-usual scenario; see Jos Lelieveld and others, 'The Contribution of Outdoor Air Pollution Sources to Premature Mortality on a Global Scale' (2015) 525 *Nature* 367–371.

[91] On the interaction and challenges of social sustainability in the overall sustainability debate, see Magnus Boström, 'A Missing Pillar? Challenges in Theorizing and Practicing Social Sustainability: Introduction to the Special Issue' (2012) 8(1) *Sustainability: Science, Practice and Policy* 3–14; Kevin Murphy, 'The Social Pillar of Sustainable Development: a Literature Review and Framework for Policy Analysis' (2012) 8(1) *Sustainability: Science, Practice and Policy* 15–29.

the form of intra- and intergenerational equity and the power and abilities of individuals or social groups to shape and take part in decision-making on matters that affect them. Moreover, social sustainability is about rights, human rights in the broadest sense (for instance the right to life and freedom) but also rights of particular social groups (for instance indigenous peoples' rights), and it concerns the recognition of the needs of the individual.[92]

An important distinction can be drawn between the inter- and intra-generational justice aspects. Inter-generational aspects relate in particular to questions of how the use of natural resources today relates to the ability of future generations to fulfil their needs.[93] In this regard, it might be seen as closely linked to environmental sustainability[94] as it is about the ethical obligations to ensure that future generations are accounted for when making decisions about current resources.[95]

The more social focus in terms of social sustainability might be on intra-generational justice aspects. In this regard, we might mention poverty reductions and equity, as well as rights and freedoms,[96] or wellbeing more generally. Compared to poverty, and maybe even wellbeing, rights and freedoms are rather difficult to measure.[97] Targets in many areas were set by the UN at its Millennium Summit in 2000, which adopted the Millennium Development Goals to be achieved by 2015. These goals include, for example, targets for the reduction of poverty, hunger, child mortality, and disease burdens, and for increasing education, gender equality, and maternal health.[98] The UN's 2030 Agenda for Sustainable Development includes the reduction of poverty as well as inequalities, and improvement of the wellbeing of humans and their living conditions.[99]

Possibly two of the most well-known indices for measurement in the context of social sustainability are the Gini coefficient and the Human Development Index.[100] The Gini coefficient measures inequality in terms of income and wealth, and it

[92] Torsten Krause, 'Social Sustainability' in Julian Nowag (ed), *Research Handbook Sustainability and Competition Law* (Edward Elgar 2024) 34.

[93] See eg, Suresh Kumar, Anurag Raizada, and Hrittick Biswas, 'Prioritising Development Planning in the Indian Semi-Arid Deccan Using Sustainable Livelihood Security Index Approach' (2014) 21(4) *International Journal of Sustainable Development & World Ecology* 332–345.

[94] Krause (n 92) 12–13.

[95] Theo Henckens, 'Mineral Resources Ethics' in Theo Henckens (ed), *Governance of the World's Mineral Resources: Beyond the Foreseeable Future* (Elsevier 2021) 71–98.

[96] This includes matters such as access to safe drinking water, which can be seen as matters of right but are also impacted by inequality.

[97] Vasiliki Voukelatou and others, 'Measuring Objective and Subjective Well-Being: Dimensions and Data Sources' (2021) 11(4) *International Journal of Data Science and Analytics* 279–309.

[98] United Nations, 'United Nations Millenium Declaration' (2000) available at <https://www.ohchr.org/en/instruments-mechanisms/instruments/united-nations-millennium-declaration> (accessed 23 December 2024).

[99] United Nations (n 46).

[100] For an overview of the different indices, see World Bank, 'World Development Indicators' available at <https://datacatalog.worldbank.org/search/dataset/0037712> (accessed 23 December 2024).

increases where such inequalities are higher. The Gini coefficient only measures general inequality; other indices, such as the multidimensional poverty index,[101] provide further insights into how equality is distributed amongst different social or ethnic parts of the society. The Human Development Index brings together measurements of life expectancy, education, and income per capita. These indicators can be used to compare different countries, and also to track the development of countries over time.

The overall idea of social sustainability is, thus, that a more sustainable world should achieve social justice and equity,[102] which includes a fair distribution of the costs but also of the benefits[103] as well as meaningful rights to participate in the decision-making.[104] This challenging field of sustainability is highlighted by the highly unequal child mortality figures, the highly differentiated burden of disease, and the unequal access to safe drinking water and food.

4. Economic sustainability

The last of the three elements of sustainability is economic sustainability. This concept is possibly closest to the meaning used in traditional economics: the ability to sustain an economic activity. In the context of sustainable development, it relates to the ability to sustain such activity and development considering the environmental limits and the effects on humans which implies a different approach to parts of the economy and economic growth more generally.[105] At the same time, economic development in a certain form is crucial to achieve any of the sustainable development goals, in particular the social ones, like ending poverty. In other words, achieving economic sustainability could be described as green growth that delivers development but ensures that planetary boundaries are not exceeded.

[101] OPHI and UNDP, *Global Multidimensional Poverty Index 2021—Unmasking Disparities by Ethnicity, Caste and Gender* (UNDP and OPHI 2021) available at <https://ophi.org.uk/multidimensional-poverty-index/> (accessed 23 December 2024).

[102] Susan Chomba and others, 'Roots of Inequity: How the Implementation of REDD+ Reinforces Past Injustices' (2016) 50 *Land Use Policy* 202–213; James Konow, 'Fair and Square: The Four Sides of Distributive Justice' (2001) 46(2) *Journal of Economic Behavior & Organization* 137–164; Anil Markandya, 'Equity and Distributional Implications of Climate Change' (2011) 39(6) *World Development* 1051–1060; Thomas Sikor and others, 'Toward an Empirical Analysis of Justice in Ecosystem Governance' (2014) 7(6) *Conservation Letters* 524–532; Klara Helene Stumpf and others, 'The Justice Dimension of Sustainability: A Systematic and General Conceptual Framework' (2015) 7(6) *Sustainability* 7438–7472.

[103] Esteve Corbera, Katrina Brown, and W Neil Adger, 'The Equity and Legitimacy of Markets for Ecosystem Services' (2007) 38(4) *Development and Change* 587–613; Unai Pascual and others, 'Social Equity Matters in Payments for Ecosystem Services' (2014) 64(11) *BioScience* 1027–1036.

[104] Katrina Brown, 'Three Challenges for a Real People-Centred Conservation' (2003) 12(2) *Global Ecology and Biogeography* 89–92.

[105] In this regard see eg John Ikerd, *Essentials of Economic Sustainability* (Lynne Rienner 2012); Joachim H Spangenberg, 'Economic Sustainability of the Economy: Concepts and Indicators' (2005) 8(1/2) *International Journal of Sustainable Development* 47–64.

A very illustrative way of explaining the issue can be found in Kate Raworth's *Doughnut Economics*.[106] Raworth's model uses the shape of a doughnut to illustrate sustainable development and economic sustainability. The inner part (the hole of the doughnut) stands for a human existence without the basic necessities such as health, education, and fundamental rights. These basic human necessities are based on the UN's SDGs. The outer crust of the doughnut is set by the planetary boundaries. These boundaries ensure the protection of biodiversity, the climate, and the ozone layer, as well as healthy soils and water bodies (freshwater and saltwater). Economic sustainability helps developing humanity to move out of the inner hole of the doughnut to live 'in the doughnut' and not beyond its outer crust. In this way, everyone's needs are met.

5. Sustainability and corporate conduct

Having explored sustainability and its three basic tenets, we can now move on to reflect on the role of the private sector, and in particular firms, in the sustainability debate. Rooms for private actions exist for various reasons, for one, legislative vacuum.[107] The legislature does not regulate an area either because of a lack of understanding, lobbying to prevent such action, a lack of time to address every (however small) sustainability issue, or an explicit decision that the matter should be resolved by the private sector[108] instead of adopting laws.

In the 1990s, the debate on sustainability started to consider the impact of private actors and of free trade on sustainable development, particularly in the context of the North–South divide, where it became the focus.[109] More recently, in the US, there has been a heated debate triggered by the anti-woke backlash. Under the banner of fighting 'woke capitalism' a number of Republican attorney generals and law-makers have tried to use antitrust to put pressure on companies in the context of their ESG efforts.[110] The latest development is that a lawsuit by a number of Republican attorney generals has been brought against Blackrock, State Street, and Vanguard.[111] It alleges an antitrust violation by means of an agreement via Climate Action 100+ and the Net Zero Asset Managers Initiative to vote as shareholder

[106] Kate Raworth, *Doughnut Economics* (Penguin Random House 2017).

[107] See Giorgio Monti, 'Four Options for a Greener Competition Law' (2020) 11(3–4) *Journal of European Competition Law & Practice* 131.

[108] In this respect see, eg, European Commission, 'A European Strategy for Plastics in a Circular Economy' (2018) COM(2018)28 Final.

[109] See the 1992 United Nations Conference on Environment and Development, the so-called Rio Summit, which adopted the 'Agenda 21'.

[110] See eg Surowiecki (n 29)); Hanawalt and Hearn, (n 29); for a discussion with regard to antitrust law see Dolmans, Lin, and Hollis (n 29) '.

[111] See <https://www.texasattorneygeneral.gov/sites/default/files/images/press/States%20v%20BlackRock%20Complaint%20Filed.pdf> (accessed 23 December 2024).

in support of reducing the coal output and exchanging information to foster that goal. Concerns around antitrust have also appeared in the context of the UN's Race to Zero Campaign,[112] as academics have experienced issues with antitrust[113] when they suggested that new coal projects should be funded to achieve net zero.

We can identify three ways in which the private sector, and in particular businesses, are crucial in achieving sustainability.[114] The first is the 'green economy', which would not exist without businesses.[115] Second, even beyond the green economy, companies can improve their sustainability track record. They can, for example, reduce their environmental footprint or employ equitable management systems supporting social sustainability. In this regard, we could think of eco-friendly packaging, corporate social responsibility projects, and the use of the 'triple bottom line' approach in their annual reports.[116] The third pathway in which the private sector can get involved is the joint creation of new organizations by businesses and NGOs.[117] Such organizations, in contrast to traditional business lobbying organizations, advocate for enhanced sustainability in the private sector and governments. Some like Polman and Winston, even argue that business action is needed as governments cannot achieve sustainability alone.[118] Companies should become 'net positive' by embracing and addressing the company's impact on its customers, suppliers, employees but also communities and the environment. This approach offers business opportunities in terms of savings and innovation and brings about a more purpose-driven corporate culture that is 'more humane' and 'connected' while increasing long-term shareholder value.

In 2000, the UN also picked up on these options for corporate conduct and adopted the UN Global Compact on Corporate Sustainability.[119] Companies can sign the pledge and get involved. This non-binding pact to adopt more sustainable business practices is the most extensive non-binding global pact ever reached. It consists of over 13,000 companies and stakeholders and sets out 10 principles for

[112] See United Nations, 'United Nations Framework Convention on Climate Change' (Race to Zero) available at <https://racetozero.unfccc.int/system/race-to-zero/> (accessed 23 December 2024).

[113] See Thomas Hale, 'Corporate Pushback Against Climate Action Is Getting Desperate', *Climate Home News* (28 September 2022) available at <https://www.climatechangenews.com/2022/09/28/corporate-pushback-against-climate-action-is-getting-desperate/> (accessed 23 December 2024).

[114] Portney (n 41) 110–117.

[115] In other words, businesses and industries that provide services that improve the environment, and the jobs that support those businesses.

[116] This accounting technique reports not only on the financial but also on the social and environmental bottom line. In this regard see in particular, John Elkington, *Cannibals with Forks: the Triple Bottom Line of 21st Century Business* (New Society Publishers 1997).

[117] For example, the World Economic Forum (WEF), the World Business Council for Sustainable Development, or Ceres.

[118] Paul Polman and Andrew Winston, *Net Positive: How Courageous Companies Thrive by Giving More Than They Take* (Harvard Business Review Press 2021).

[119] Available at <https://www.unglobalcompact.org> (accessed 23 December 2024).

corporate conducts with regard to environment, human and labour rights, and anti-corruption. Companies pledge to:[120]

1. uphold human rights and not to be complicit in human rights violation (principles 1 and 2);
2. protect labour rights by respecting the freedom of association and recognise collective bargaining; by eliminating forced, compulsory, and child labour; by not producing under hazardous working conditions; and by ensuring non-discrimination in their employment practices (principles 3–6);
3. protect the environment by adopting the precautionary principles regarding environmental problems; by taking greater environmental responsibility; and by encouraging the development and diffusion of technology that is environmentally beneficial (principles 7–9);
4. not engage in or promote corrupt practices such as extortion and bribery (principle 10).

Subsequently, the 2030 Agenda also adopted the theme of business and sustainability. It stressed the need for business to adopt more sustainable practices, and SDG 12.6 specifically addressed firms with a focus on large and transnational companies. These companies should implement sustainable business practices, change their reporting practices, and integrate sustainability information.

Yet, business involvement in the sustainability agenda has not been without criticism, a theme that is picked up in the next chapter on the economics of sustainability and competition. The critique often relates to the sincerity of the businesses. In other words, private businesses are accused of abusing the concept of sustainability to improve the public image, ie, 'greenwashing'.[121] Similarly, companies have been criticized for lacking real motivation to contribute to sustainable development. They are accused of 'using' sustainability as a means for streamlining processes, ensuring more cost-effective business strategies, and increasing profit margins.[122]

6. Conclusions

In conclusion, sustainability has its roots in environmental protection, but it expanded its reach to take into account social and economic development. The essential idea is that environmental degradation and depletion of natural resources

[120] Available at <https://www.unglobalcompact.org/what-is-gc/mission/principles> (accessed 23 December 2024).
[121] Portney (n 41) 117.
[122] ibid 118.

will limit and reduce economic growth and social development. These, however, should take place within, rather than beyond, the planetary boundaries. Sustainable development aims to change the nature of growth. It incorporates forward thinking by ensuring the wellbeing of the large and still growing world population. As such, sustainable growth ensures that current developmental needs such as jobs, food, energy, clean water, and sanitation are provided without compromising future generations' needs. In terms of decision-making, sustainable development merges environmental considerations and economics. It thereby aligns technology and risk management to achieve sustainable growth while ensuring that the benefits of international economic relations are more widely shared.

The UN's 2030 Agenda is a good starting point with its seventeen sustainable development goals and its 169 associated targets that provide more detailed and measurable targets. For the purposes of this book, we highlight the need to encourage companies, especially large and transnational ones, to adopt sustainable practices and to integrate sustainability information into their reporting cycle.[123]

Overall, we can identify a focus of sustainable development on productive (using fewer resources) and dynamic efficiencies (innovation) whilst taking into account equity. Whilst the significance of environmental protection in sustainability is well-established, the role of equity may remain somewhat ambiguous. Although equity is acknowledged as a crucial component of sustainability, its theoretical integration continues to be a subject of debate. Yet, equity and fairness certainly are part of the international sustainability efforts, as poverty is a major driver of environmental degradation. The relevance of equity and fairness frequently comes to the fore in international debates on the extent to which the rich and the poor have the same responsibilities to ensure a sustainable future, for example, in the context of climate change.

Sustainability in the context of business activity can take different forms. It can specifically mean that companies are part of and promote the 'green economy'. More generally, it encourages sustainability innovation and/or ensures that existing business activities are evaluated to ensure they increase rather than decrease sustainability levels.

IV. Law and sustainability

We have explored the concept of sustainability and how it is anchored in international law and obligation under UN resolutions. Yet, whether and the extent to which competition law should take account of sustainability considerations[124]

[123] SDG 12.6, see also SDG 12.7 on sustainable procurement practices.

[124] Critical, eg, Edith Loozen, 'Strict Competition Enforcement and Welfare: a Constitutional Perspective Based on Article 101 TFEU and Sustainability' (2019) 56 *Common Market Law Review* 1265.

is a normative question. In other words, answering this question involves value judgement. It can be distinguished from the more technical questions[125] of how it can take such considerations into account. From a normative point of view, it has been suggested that the answer to the question is related to how we define the goals of competition law, and that competition law should move away from consumer welfare.[126] On the other side of this debate, the argument has been made that competition authorities should not make value judgements by deciding between competition and sustainability.[127] In between the two poles of opinion, we might identify what this book is concerned with: identifying pathways where the protection of competition—and possibly consumer welfare—overlap with sustainability.

Indeed, we might see it as problematic if bureaucrats who are not democratically elected make value judgements. Yet, where a normative question such as whether to take account of sustainability in competition law is encountered, the answer must take into account the specific legal context. In other words, the first point of reference to answer this question is the legal framework.[128] Hence, the answer to 'should competition law take account of sustainability considerations?' is not always the same. The answer depends on the legal framework of the jurisdiction where this question is posed. Every jurisdiction has its own specific answer to the question based on its legal, and, more specifically, constitutional setting.

The locally relevant norms may or may not require such a consideration of sustainability because competition law and policy are subject to different legal requirements and constraints in different jurisdictions.[129] The legal requirements and constraints are contained in the relevant competition law or other legal frameworks such as the constitution. The requirements might equally result from international law obligations and their domestic implementation. As such, the debate on the goals of competition law and policy is also relevant.[130]

Overall, the answer to the normative question of whether competition law and policy should take account of sustainability cannot be found in the abstract and for

[125] See in this regard the following chapters, in particular Chapter 3, 4, and 5.

[126] R Claassen and A Gerbrandy, 'Rethinking European Competition Law: From a Consumer, Welfare to a Capability Approach' (2016) 12(1) *Utrecht Law Review* 1–15.

[127] In terms of such value judgement and competition authorities see eg Okeoghene Odudu, 'The Wider Concerns of Competition Law' (2010) *Oxford Journal of Legal Studies* 13–14; Barbara Baarsma and Nicole Rosenboom, 'A Veritable Tower of Babel: On the Confusion between the Legal and Economic Interpretations of Article 101(3) of the Treaty on the Functioning of the European Union' [2016] *European Competition Journal* 402–425.

[128] For an analysis of law as a normative discipline see, eg, Panu Minkkinen, 'Why is Law a Normative Discipline? on Hans Kelsen's "Normology"' (2005) 11 *Res Publica* 235–249.

[129] See also Ariel Ezrachi, 'Sponge' (2017) 5(1) *Journal of Antitrust Enforcement* 49–75.

[130] On this debate see eg, OECD Global Forum on Competition, 'The Objectives Of Competition Law And Policy—Note by the Secretariat' (2003) CCNM/GF/COMP(2003)3; Daniel Zimmer (ed), *The Goals of Competition Law* (Edward Elgar 2012), Ioannis Lianos, 'Some Reflections on the Question of the Goals of EU Competition Law' CLES Working Paper Series 3/2013; Oles Andriychuk, *The Normative Foundations of European Competition Law: Assessing the Goals of Antitrust through the Lens of Legal Philosophy* (Edward Elgar 2019).

all jurisdictions. Instead, the answer is specific and found by examining the goals of competition law, the constitution, and other relevant legal sources such as international law and its status in that jurisdiction. In the following, we will explore how the requirement to foster sustainability can be found in numerous constitutions and other legal obligations, and then highlight how sustainability considerations have made inroads into the competition laws of some jurisdictions.

1. Constitutional and other obligations towards achieving sustainability

There are numerous jurisdictions across the world that oblige governments to consider sustainability matters.[131] The European Union (EU), for example, has such a requirement in Article 11 of the Treaty on the Function of the European Union (TFEU) and Article 37 of the EU Charter of Fundamental Rights. These provisions require the EU to 'integrate' environmental protection and sustainable development into its policies, including competition law.[132] Several EU member states also reference sustainability or environmental protection in their constitutions. These include, amongst others, Belgium, Finland, France, Greece, Germany, Hungary, Italy, Luxembourg, Netherlands, Malta, Portugal, Spain, and Sweden. The Greek constitution, for example, states in Article 24(1) that '[t]he protection of the natural and cultural environment constitutes a duty of the State and a right of every person. The State is bound to adopt special preventive or repressive measures for the preservation of the environment in the context of the principle of sustainable development.' The German constitution contains a similar clause in Article 20a which sets out that '[m]indful also of its responsibility toward future generations, the state shall protect the natural foundations of life and animals by legislation and, in accordance with law and justice, by executive and judicial action, all within the framework of the constitutional order.' Germany also adopted a Federal Climate Protection Act that requires that all '[b]odies discharging public duties shall give due consideration to the purpose of this Act and to the targets set for its implementation.'[133] Another example could be found in the Hungarian constitution, in which Article Q(1) mandates 'sustainable development of humanity' as an aim of the state. It also contains a right to a 'healthy environment' in Article XXI. These

[131] For an overview see eg, David Richard Boyd, *The Environmental Rights Revolution: A Global Study of Constitutions, Human Rights, and the Environment* (University of British Columbia Press 2012); Chris Jeffords and Joshua C Gellers, 'Constitutionalizing Environmental Rights: A Practical Guide' (2017) 9(1) *Journal of Human Rights Practice* 136–145.

[132] See for example on the history and the intended reach of Art 11 TFEU, Julian Nowag, 'The Sky Is the Limit: On the Drafting of Article 11 TFEU's Integration Obligation and its Intended Reach' in Beate Sjåfjell and Anja Wiesbrock (eds), *The Greening of European Business under EU Law: Taking Article 11 TFEU Seriously* (Routledge 2014) 15–30.

[133] S 13(1) Federal Climate Protection Act.

constitutional requirements shall according to Article 28 be used '[i]n the course of the application of law'.

Outside the EU, there are also numerous countries that require the consideration of sustainability. For example, the Turkish constitution in Article 56 states that '[e]veryone has the right to live in a healthy and balanced environment. It is the duty of the State and citizens to improve the natural environment, to protect the environmental health and to prevent environmental pollution.'[134] Similar provisions can also be found for example in Switzerland,[135] Russia,[136] Mexico, Brazil, the Philippines, Kenya, and Mexico. The Mexican constitution, for example, declares that: 'Any person has the right to a healthy environment for his/her own development and well-being. The State will guarantee the respect to such right.'[137] The Brazilian constitution asserts in Article 170 that

> economic order, [is] founded on the appreciation of the value of human work and on free enterprise, is intended to ensure everyone a life with dignity, in accordance with the dictates of social justice, with due regard for the following principles:
>
> ...
>
> IV—free competition;
>
> ...
>
> VI—environment protection, which may include differentiated treatment in accordance with the environmental impact of goods and services and of their respective production and delivery processes;
>
> VII—reduction of regional and social differences

This constitutional setup is further strengthened by Article 225 in the section on economic rights that sets out a right to an 'ecologically balanced environment'. The 1987 constitution of the Philippines in Article XII, section 1 also makes equitable distribution of income, wealth, and opportunities, as well as the improvement of the conditions of the underprivileged an aim of the state.[138] In the

[134] Emphasis added.

[135] Art 73 of the Swiss constitution: 'The Confederation and the Cantons shall endeavour to achieve a balanced and sustainable relationship between nature and its capacity to renew itself and the demands placed on it by the population.' See also Arts 74, 89, and 104.

[136] Art 58 of the Russian constitution: 'Everyone shall have a duty to preserve nature and the environment and to treat natural resources with care.' See also Arts 36 and 72.

[137] Art 4, see also Arts 2, 25, and 73.

[138] For how this affects the application of competition law, see Leni Papa and Raya Teston, 'Competition Policy, Poverty, Inequality: The Philippine Experience' in Julian Nowag (ed), *Research Handbook on Sustainability and Competition Law* (Edward Elgar 2024).

same vein, the Kenyan constitution imposes '[o]bligations in respect of the environment' in Article 69 and section 1 sets out that '[t]he State shall—(a) ensure sustainable exploitation, utilisation, management and conservation of the environment and natural resources, and ensure the equitable sharing of the accruing benefits'.

Possibly the most demanding duty can be found in the Ecuadorian constitution. It sets out in Article 15(1) that

> [t]he State shall promote, in the public and private sectors, the use of environmentally clean technologies and nonpolluting and low-impact alternative sources of energy. Energy sovereignty shall not be achieved to the detriment of food sovereignty nor shall it affect the right to water.

In Article 71–73(1) it goes further, explaining that

> Article 71
>
> Nature, or Pacha Mama, where life is reproduced and occurs, has the right to integral respect for its existence and for the maintenance and regeneration of its life cycles, structure, functions and evolutionary processes.
> All persons, communities, peoples and nations can call upon public authorities to enforce the rights of nature. To enforce and interpret these rights, the principles set forth in the Constitution shall be observed, as appropriate.
> The State shall give incentives to natural persons and legal entities and to communities to protect nature and to promote respect for all the elements comprising an ecosystem.
>
> Article 72
>
> Nature has the right to be restored. This restoration shall be apart from the obligation of the State and natural persons or legal entities to compensate individuals and communities that depend on affected natural systems.
> In those cases of severe or permanent environmental impact, including those caused by the exploitation of nonrenewable natural resources, the State shall establish the most effective mechanisms to achieve the restoration and shall adopt adequate measures to eliminate or mitigate harmful environmental consequences.
>
> Article 73
>
> The State shall apply preventive and restrictive measures on activities that might lead to the extinction of species, the destruction of ecosystems and the permanent alteration of natural cycles.

These are possibly the most far-reaching obligations that a constitution imposes on the state and the administration, including the competition authority. Yet, the aforementioned constitutional provisions in the other jurisdictions will equally have effects on the enforcement of competition law.

Moreover, depending on the national constitutional setup, obligations under international law such as the Paris Agreement or the 2015 UN Resolution 70/1 '2030 Agenda for Sustainable Development' can have a directly binding effect. The effect of international law obligation domestically depends primarily on whether a country is monist or dualist.[139] While dualist states require an implementation act, such acts are generally not needed in monist countries. In such countries, international agreements can be relied upon directly and national courts can use them as a standard of review. A recent example is the Dutch Supreme Court decision in the *Urgenda* case.[140] The Court held that the UN Climate Convention, in combination with the Dutch state's legal duties to protect life and well-being under the European Convention for the Protection of Human Rights and Fundamental Freedoms, meant that the Netherlands was required to reduce its greenhouse gas emissions by 25 per cent by the end of 2020.

Such legal requirements and obligations may also apply to competition law and policy in particular jurisdictions. Yet, we must note that respecting such legal requirements does not mean that the aims or goals of competition law change as such.[141] Moreover, we should note that where such requirements apply, it seems misguided to argue against the consideration of sustainability concerns in order to keep competition law 'apolitical', 'value judgement free', or 'pure'. Where the constitution requires consideration, it was the constitutional legislature that has imposed such requirements, and we should not second-guess these decisions in the name of purity.[142]

2. Competition laws

While a number of constitutions mandate the consideration of sustainability in competition law and policy, sustainability itself has made inroads into competition

[139] On the monist/dualist distinction and its effects see eg John Laws, 'Monism and dualism' (2000) 53(2) *La Revue Administrative* 18–22.

[140] Decision by the Dutch Supreme Court of 20 December 2019 in *De Staat Der Nederlanden v Stichting Urgenda* ECLI:NL:HR:2019:2006 (in English:ECLI:NL:HR:2019:2007).

[141] In the same way as the requirement to ensure due process, respect for the separation of powers, or the protection of fundamental rights, do not become aims of competition law, although competition law needs to take them into account. See Julian Nowag, 'Competition Law's Sustainability Gap? Tools for an Examination and a Brief Overview' (2022) *Nordic Journal of European Law* 163–164. For the view that sustainability cannot be squared with the aims of competition law, see, eg, Michał Derdak, 'Square Peg in a Round Hole? Sustainability as an Aim of Antitrust Law' (2021) 14(23) *Yearbook of Antitrust and Regulatory Studies* 39–67.

[142] ibid. But one can always argue for constitutional change.

laws. We will later[143] come back to such instances. Here, it should suffice to provide two examples.

In 2021, Austria changed its competition law. The changes were aimed at addressing the environmentally sustainable and carbon-neutral economy. The Competition Act now contains in section 2(1) a clarification that should guide authorities in the definition of consumer benefit. The provision states that:

> Consumers are also allowed a fair share of the resulting benefit, if the benefit derived from improving the production or distribution of goods or promoting technical or economic progress contributes significantly to an environmentally sustainable or carbon-neutral economy.

This definition is relevant in particular when the agency or court is considering whether an agreement that restricts competition can be exempted because of its consumer benefits.

The Hungarian competition law has a similar provision. Article 17 sets out that:

> An agreement is exempted from the prohibition pursuant to Article 11 [the prohibition of anti-competitive agreements] provided that
> (a) it contributes to a more reasonable organisation of production or distribution, the promotion of technical or economic progress, or the improvement of competitiveness or of the protection of the environment
> (b) it allows trading parties not participating in the agreement a fair share of the resulting benefit;
> (c) the concomitant restriction or exclusion of competition does not exceed the extent necessary to attain economically justified common goals; and
> (d) it does not enable the exclusion of competition in respect of a substantial proportion of the goods concerned.

These rules show that sustainability can also appear directly in competition laws of jurisdictions.

V. Conclusion

In this chapter of the book, we briefly introduced the interaction between sustainability and antitrust and then set out the central argument of the book: there are numerous areas where sustainability and orthodox competition law principles overlap. This overlap needs to be examined while taking into account economic

143 See Chapter 4, sections IV 1) and V.

and legal insights from different jurisdictions. This helps us to identify real conflicts and possible solutions. The comparative exercise of the book will provide a comprehensive set of best practices focused on existing efforts and future possibilities. It will, thus, provide food for thought for academics, policy-makers, and practitioners and help define the overlaps between consumer welfare and sustainability, in other words, sustainable consumer welfare.

The chapter also introduced the concept of sustainability and its historical development. We saw how sustainability is based on three key tenets: environmental, social, and economic sustainability. It also became clear how economic development—and thus productive and dynamic efficiency—is crucial in achieving social sustainability. Social sustainability in turn is crucial for ensuring environmental sustainability because it is rather difficult to ensure the protection of natural resources if people rely on them for their livelihood. Environmental sustainability, however, also sets the outer—planetary—boundary. To achieve sustainability, we need to stay within the planetary boundaries. These boundaries are being pushed against. It is, therefore, of paramount importance that we concentrate on climate change, deforestation and changes in land use, loss of biodiversity, and pollution. We also explored how the focus of the sustainability debate has shifted, starting in the 1990s. Since then, a greater emphasis has been put on corporate conduct and how firms can help or hinder the achievement of sustainability.

This led us to subsequently examine the extent to which sustainability and environmental concerns are reflected in constitutions around the world. This examination showed how many states require their government and thereby their administrations to consider sustainability concerns, whether through the constitutions, specific laws, or directly via international law. In some countries, sustainability has even found its way into the competition laws.

This introduction provides us with a background to examine competition policy in light of sustainability in the coming chapters. In the next chapter, we will examine how competition and sustainability interact from an economic point of view. These insights will provide us with the relevant theoretical foundation before we delve into the substantive competition laws and procedural questions in the following chapters.

2

The economics of competition and sustainability: good and bad competition

Felipe and the world of sustainability

Felipe studied economics and is now managing a company in a developing country that has been growing steadily in the last decade. It produces a range of wooden furniture and other wood-based goods, and it is also active in designing, selling, installing, and servicing such wood-based goods.

The company sells a large part of its goods and services to customers in its home base. Yet, with expansion it has also acquired a substantive consumer base in the US and in Europe.

Many of its consumers appreciate that the company offers quality goods and services at a good value-for-money ratio. Yet, many of its European and US costumers and also a growing number of consumers in Felipe's home market, are concerned about sustainability. The company's competitors are starting to change their behaviour in response to these demands.

Moreover, at the last shareholder meeting, some shareholders also asked Felipe and the board about sustainability and Felipe has—as many directors across the country—received the letter from the head of Blackrock,[1] a shareholder of the company.

Felipe feels he needs to engage in this emerging field, and he sets up a small focus group to look into sustainability and its interaction with market forces to identify ways in which the company can address consumer and shareholder demands in a cost-effective way.

[1] In his letters to the companies it invests in, Larry Fink, the CEO of BlackRock, in 2019 and again in 2022 highlighted the importance of stakeholder capitalism and sustainability. See Larry Fink, 'The Power of Capitalism', letter to CEOs (2022) available at <https://www.blackrock.com/ca/investors/en/2022-larry-fink-ceo-letter> (accessed 10 January 2025); Larry Fink, 'Purpose & Profit', letter to CEOs (2019) available at <https://www.blackrock.com/corporate/investor-relations/2019-larry-fink-ceo-letter> (accessed 10 January 2025).

Global Antitrust and Sustainability. Julian Nowag, Oxford University Press. © Julian Nowag 2025.
DOI: 10.1093/9780191955013.003.0002

I. Introduction

What does economics tell us about the interaction between competition and sustainability? Is competition good for sustainability or is it the driver of unsustainable business practices? What does the economic evidence suggest? Is engaging in sustainable business practices beneficial for companies like Felipe's? Should companies aim to address the issues alone, or should they see whether it makes sense to cooperate with other firms in the industry? Or should companies not bother with such delicate questions and leave them to states to regulate?

In this chapter we will explore some of the economics that underpin the debate about sustainability and competition law. We will examine what economics tells us about the general effects of competition on sustainability. As discussed in the previous chapter, sustainability highlights resource efficiency, innovation, and the role of the private sector in achieving the sustainability goals set by the UN. As such, economics provides us with valuable tools to understand the market forces at play and to determine whether they increase or decrease sustainability.[2] Moreover, this exploration of the economics of competition and sustainability assists in identifying pathways to consider sustainability within the orthodox economic framework applied in competition law.

The chapter shows not only the overlap between sustainability and competition, in other words, how competition drives sustainability, but also cases where less competition leads to increased sustainability. However, it is important to note that in the latter cases, the economic trade-off between competition and sustainability does not necessarily implicate trade-off in the context of law.[3] Before we delve deeper into the economics of competition and sustainability, a difference between what is discussed in this chapter and the following law-focused chapters needs to be noted. This chapter is not only different because it looks at economics and not law, but equally, because economists often take a different approach to their field of study than lawyers do. While economists most of the time examine situations and try to find out what the general rule is, in other words, what we expect to happen in the majority of cases, lawyers are most often focused on the opposite. Lawyers are more often interested in the non-standard cases. They are interested in the exception to the rule. For the standard case, the rule has typically already been established by the legislator.

This chapter in divided into two main sections. Section II explores markets and the extent to which they can deliver sustainable outcomes.[4] It discusses economic

[2] For a good overview of the economics debate on sustainability and competition, see Roman Inderst and Stefan Thomas, 'Competition Policy and the Environment' (2023) 15 *Annual Review of Resource Economics* 199–211.

[3] In this regard see Chapter 4.

[4] More generally on the morality of market, see eg Armin Falk and Nora Szech, 'Morals and Markets' (2013) 340 *Science* 707, and Björn Bartling, Roberto Weber, and Lan Yao, 'Do Markets Erode Social Responsibility?' (2015) 130 *Quarterly Journal of Economics* 219–266.

studies that examine the relationship between competition and sustainability, with a specific focus on efficiency. We will also investigate models that show how competition can very well produce sustainable market outcomes, as well as those exemplifying the contrary. In other words, the chapter looks at whether monopoly or cooperation between private actors is superior to competition in terms of sustainability and efficiency. We will specifically highlight the consequences as well as limitations of these models with particular regard to competition, sustainability, innovation, and the economics of sustainability standards. Further, this section seeks to provide an overview of empirical papers in the field and investigates how competition economics might adjust its measuring tools to capture sustainability benefits.

In the section III, we will briefly investigate the interaction between markets and states in delivering sustainability. This section focuses on the effectiveness and efficiency of private and public actions. First, we inspect different tools such as taxation, financial support, regulation, competition advocacy, and the enforcement of competition law. Then, we turn our attention to comparing state action that restricts competition to firms restricting competition, in particular in light of imperfect government. We will see in this chapter the answers are not always black and white and the results are context-dependent.

II. The markets delivering sustainability

In this section, we highlight and explore how markets can deliver sustainability and what economic theory has to say about whether a more or less competitive market is better at delivering such outcomes. This section first examines the theoretical foundations and what they tell us about the relationship between competition and monopoly[5] and its effects on sustainability. For example, increased intensity of competition may drive up demand for cheaper inputs that are more harmful from a sustainability perspective. Yet, where sustainability is valued by consumers, for instance a demand for greener products, competition can equally promote sustainability outcomes as these products provide a competitive edge. In the second part, we will move away from economic theory and look at more practical questions such as empirical studies or how to measure sustainability in a consumer welfare context.

[5] For example, achieved by means of agreements.

1. Economics: theory

Competition economists have only recently started to model and study the relationship between competition and sustainability.[6] Overall, the theoretical literature offers us two insights. Firstly, competition can foster sustainability when consumers care about sustainability. Yet, there are some situations where cooperation/monopoly provides more sustainable outcomes. Secondly, economists and competition lawyers both seem to agree that government regulation is the more efficient and appropriate tool to achieve sustainability. In this section, we will look at this theoretical literature and explain how competition increases sustainability. We also explore situations where some form of cooperation/monopoly might provide better outcomes. Subsequently, some consequences and limitations of these studies are highlighted. In the final two parts of this economic theory section, we will consider the relationship between competition and sustainability in the context of dynamic competition (sustainability innovation) and in standardization where so-called 'coopetition' exists.

a) Competition producing better sustainability outcomes in static analysis

There are now a number of papers that show how competition can increase sustainability outcomes. When categorizing these papers, one can distinguish[7] between papers that focus on demand-side questions, in other words, consumer preferences, and those that look at supply-side considerations, in particular workers' and financiers' preferences.

aa) Demand side

Demand-side papers on sustainability and competition economics take as a starting point that consumers value sustainability as a product feature. In this regard, Maarten Pieter Schinkel has done a substantial amount of work together with different co-authors to show how competition can produce more sustainable outcomes when compared to monopoly situations. In their first published paper, Schinkel and Spiegel examined, in the case of differentiated products, the outcome with regard to sustainability and consumer surplus under perfect competition and monopoly.[8] In their model, firms first decide on the level of sustainability of their product and then compete over the output. Competition between companies takes place while consumers also value sustainability. Schinkel and Spiegel then compare the outcomes when the firms either jointly or under competition set the level

[6] Publications on this issue remain scarce; many articles are still at the stage of working paper.

[7] See Leonard Treuren, 'The Potential and Limitations of Competition to Achieve Sustainability' in Julian Nowag (ed), *Research Handbook on Sustainability and Competition Law* (Edward Elgar 2024) 50–68.

[8] Maarten Pieter Schinkel and Yossi Spiegel, 'Can Collusion Promote Sustainable Consumption and Production?' (2017) *International Journal of Industrial Organization* 371–398.

of sustainability or production, or both. They found that when firms set the level of sustainability jointly but set production levels in competition, the level of investments in sustainability is lower, leading to a lower consumer surplus. Conversely, where the level of production is set jointly, investment in sustainability increases, but consumer surplus might be harmed. This results from the higher prices due to output coordination which can then be used to increase investment in sustainability. Moreover, one can imagine the sustainability level being the main factor that incentivizes consumers to switch from one company to another.[9]

Schinkel and Spiegel, 'Can Collusion Promote Sustainable Consumption and Production?'[10]

[A]ssuming that consumers are willing to pay extra for sustainable products like cleaner energy, sustainable meat, holiday travel, or fair trade clothing, can horizontal agreements among competing firms promote SCP [sustainable consumption and production]? To address this question, we consider a two-stage duopoly in which firms first choose how much to invest in the sustainability of their respective products, and then compete in the product market (in most of the paper, firms compete by choosing quantities, but the results generalize to price competition). A key assumption in our model is that the products of the two firms are differentiated, and the willingness of consumers to pay increases with the product's sustainability level. The two firms internalize sustainability considerations only insofar as they increase the willingness of consumers to pay. We compare four scenarios: competition in both stages; coordination in the choice of sustainability, followed by competition in the product market (sustainability coordination); non-cooperative choices of sustainability, followed by collusion in the product market (production cartel); and collusion in both stages.

Our main finding is that production cartels promote sustainability and may even enhance consumer surplus, while sustainability coordination induces the lowest levels of investment in sustainability and makes consumers worse off than they are absent collusion. Although production cartels may enhance consumer surplus, under a broad range of parameters, they actually harm consumers. A policy which stipulates that exemption from cartel prohibition can be granted only if consumers are fully compensated may remedy this problem. Our analysis shows however that although such a policy ensures that consumers are

[9] This in turn might reduce the incentives of the companies to reach such an output agreement; see Maarten Pieter Schinkel, Yossi Spiegel, and Leonard Treuren, 'Production Agreements, Sustainability Investments, and Consumer Welfare' (2022) 216 *Economics Letters*.

[10] Schinkel and Spiegel (n 8).

> not harmed, firms end up investing in sustainability less than they do absent a cartel, which implies in turn that collusion offers no benefits.[11]
>
> ...
>
> We showed that when consumers are willing to pay extra for sustainable products and firms choose their investment in sustainability before choosing output, allowing firms to coordinate their investment levels (sustainability coordination) leads to lower investments in SCP.
>
> ...
>
> Our analysis should be viewed as a first step toward understanding the trade-offs involved with the use of competition policy to promote SCP. For example, we abstract from the way asymmetric firms choose output levels under a production cartel when they and a lower consumer surplus relative to the no coordination case cannot rely on side payments, we do not explicitly model the actions of the antitrust authority, we implicitly assume that the antitrust authority can perfectly determine if firms collude and if collusion benefits or harms consumers, and we do not consider the possibility that only a subset of firms coordinate their investments in sustainability or production levels. We also abstract from wider policy considerations, such as whether horizontal agreements are actually necessary to promote SCP or whether there are better ways of doing that. We believe that these questions, as well as others, should be further explored in future research to develop a better understanding of whether competition policy should be used to promote SCP, and if so how exactly.[12]

While this model has a duopoly at its core and has also been studied in more detail,[13] Schinkel and Treuren extended the model with similar results looking at corporate social responsibility (CSR) efforts.[14] They modelled markets with more than two firms where all or only some of them had such agreements, and in situations where consumers had a differentiated willingness to pay. Moreover, they introduced a variable on the intrinsic motivation of firms.[15] They found similar

[11] ibid 374–375, references omitted.

[12] ibid 392–393.

[13] Leonard Treuren and Maarten Pieter Schinkel, 'Can Collusion Promote Sustainable Consumption and Production? Not Beneficially Beyond Duopoly' (2018) Amsterdam Law School Research Paper No 2018-02, Amsterdam Center for Law & Economics Working Paper No 2018-01 available at <https://ssrn.com/abstract=3132323> (accessed 10 January 2025).

[14] Maarten Pieter Schinkel and Leonard Treuren, 'Corporate Social Responsibility by Joint Agreement' (June 2023) Tinbergen Institute Discussion Paper 2021-063/VII available at <https://papers.tinbergen.nl/21063.pdf> (accessed 10 January 2025).

[15] For an examination of the different reasons for CSR behaviours by firms, see Roland Bénabou and Jean Tirole, 'Individual and Corporate Social Responsibility' (2010) 77(305) *Economica* 1–19, who distinguish between adopting a more long-term perspective by firms and philanthropy either on behalf of stakeholders, or corporate philanthropy initiated by insiders.

results as long as there is some willingness to pay for improvements in terms of CSR. Overall, the explanation for these findings is that such agreements eliminate competition in terms of CSR so that the firm does not have to invest as much in such efforts. Again, they highlight how only coordination on the output combined with competition over CSR would deliver optimum CSR levels—obviously at the cost of increased prices.

The phenomenon has also been studied by modelling such situations as a combination of private and public good provision. In this case, the public good would stand for improvements in sustainability. Schinkel and Tóth show that a cartel on the level of public benefits will lead to minimal public benefits, while charging the maximum price for the private good.[16] Bagnoli and Watts[17] also modelled such a situation. In their model, the companies can decide between producing only a private good or producing the private good plus a public good, all while taking into account that consumers value the provision of the public good. Firms can either opt to link the private and public good provision (a fixed amount of public good is produced for every private good) or choose to provide the public good unlinked (a lump sum for the provision of public good). In this model, the provision of the public good increases the costs of the private good provision and implicates two consequences. Where the willingness to pay is not high enough, more competition in the context of the private good leads to a lower production of the public good. Overall, the demand for the linked (private) good determines the amount of the public good provided. Under Cournot[18] competition, any reduction in the number of firms providing the unlinked version increases the costs of the unlinked version, which in turn increases the demand for the (relatively cheaper) linked good. Thus, competition is increased with regard to the linked good, reducing its costs and increasing the provision of the public good.

[16] Maarten Pieter Schinkel and Lukás Tóth, 'Compensatory Public Good Provision by a Private Cartel' (January 2020) Tinbergen Institute Discussion Papers 19-086/VII available at <https://www.researchgate.net/profile/Jesper-Fredborg-Huric-Larsen/publication/271521704_Competition_Policy_and_Environmental_Policy/links/5696268908ae425c6898d9b5/Competition-Policy-and-Environmental-Policy.pdf> (accessed 10 January 2025); see also Maarten Pieter Schinkel and Leonard Treuren, 'Green Antitrust: Friendly Fire in the Fight against Climate Change' in Simon Holmes, Dirk Middelschulte, and Martijn Snoep (eds), *Competition Law, Climate Change & Environmental Sustainability* (Concurrences 2021).

[17] Mark Bagnoli and Susan G Watts, 'Selling to Socially Responsible Consumers: Competition and the Private Provision of Public Goods' (2003) 12 *Journal of Economics and Management Strategy* 419–445.

[18] In the Cournot competition model, the competitors decide independently but at the same time on the amount of output.

Bagnoli and Watts, 'Selling to Socially Responsible Consumers: Competition and the Private Provision of Public Goods'[19]

In this paper, we model strategic CSR [corporate social responsibility] as arising from companies seeking a competitive advantage in their product markets. Thus, private provision of a public good (environmentally friendly or socially responsible activities) becomes a by-product of product-market competition between firms. The basic idea behind our model is that consumers may be induced to purchase the product of a firm that engages in these activities rather than the product of a rival that does not. Thus, provision depends on consumers' willingness to pay as well as the structure of competition. This means that to understand the results of private provision as part of companies' marketing or business strategies, we will have to consider alternative representations of product-market competition. To do this, we analyze both Bertrand and Cournot competition in the market for the private good (price-choosing and quantity-choosing games). Further, we examine whether the outcomes are sensitive to the form of private provision of the public good: whether the amount provided is explicitly or implicitly linked to consumer purchases of the private good. To highlight the effects of private provision as part of a marketing or business strategy, we do not allow consumers to adopt separate private-provision mechanisms. Thus, our analysis can be thought of as providing a baseline level of provision, and direct contribution mechanisms can be thought of as being used to supplement the level of provision that results from product-market competition by firms. . . .[20]

We find that when there is an explicit link between the amount of the public good provided and the sales of the private good, less than the efficient amount of the public good is provided in most cases. In particular, too little of the public good is provided when there are a large number of active firms (including the case of free entry) in the market for the private good. Intuitively, the reason is that the firms providing the linked version of the private good are unable to capture enough of the consumers' benefits due to having the public good. What is more surprising is that we identify situations in which, as firms compete for socially responsible consumers, the amount of the public good they provide either equals or exceeds the efficient amount. These situations have one common feature—they have relatively little of the nonlinked version of the private good sold in equilibrium. This is the first of two unexpected trade-offs identified by our analysis: the less competitive market may provide more of the public good. Said differently, there can be a trade-off between more efficient provision of the

[19] Bagnoli (n 17).
[20] ibid 420–421.

> private good and more efficient provision of the public good. ... The second trade-off is related: additional entry into the market for the private good increases the amount of the private good provided but reduces the amount of the public good provided. Thus, when too little of the public good is provided prior to entry, entry results in a more efficient allocation of the private good and a less efficient allocation of the public good. On the other hand, if too much of the public good is provided, entry is unambiguously helpful.
>
> When the public good is implicitly linked to sales of the private good, linkage creates a fixed cost of selling the private good ... we find that under both Bertrand and Cournot competition, less than the efficient amount of the public good is provided in equilibrium, for essentially the same reasons described above. What is more surprising is that more of the public good is provided under the less competitive market structure, Cournot competition. That is, in this case, again, there is a trade-off between more efficient provision of the private good and more efficient provision of the public good.[21]

Similar results have also been suggested with respect to carbon offsets as a public good. In that context, it has been shown that the private provision of this public good in a competitive market leads to a decline in net emissions, but that market power by dirty producers can counteract such effects.[22]

Overall, there are a number of studies that show how the demand side, in the form of consumers valuing the sustainability of goods or services, can drive competition over the sustainability dimension of goods, which in turn leads to more sustainable outcomes.[23]

bb) Supply side

However, not only the demand side might influence the level of sustainability provided under competition. Similarly, supply-side factors can also influence the provision of sustainability. The supply-side factors in terms of sustainability have not been studied extensively, looking in particular at the questions between competition and sustainability. However, it has been suggested[24] that the research on

[21] ibid 339–341, references omitted.

[22] Joshua S Gans and Vivienne Groves, 'Carbon Offset Provision with Guilt-Ridden Consumers' (2012) 21(1) *Journal of Economics & Management Strategy* 243–269.

[23] Crucial in this regard however is the accuracy and observability of information about the sustainability performance of firms; see Aleix Calveras and Juan-José Ganuza, 'The Role of Public Information in Corporate Social Responsibility' (2016) 25(4) *Journal of Economics & Management Strategy* 990–1017.

[24] See Treuren (n 7); Julian Nowag, 'Sustainability and Competition' (2020) OECD Competition Committee Discussion Paper available at <https://www.oecd.org/content/dam/oecd/en/publications/reports/2021/10/sustainability-and-competition_27b106e0/18e2061c-en.pdf> (accessed 10 January 2025) 18.

R&D and competition[25] can provide valuable insights, which are further explored below.[26]

Sustainability efforts improve the production process. For example, such efforts have been shown to increase agricultural yields.[27] Moreover, input costs may also be reduced in other ways. In this regard, de Bettignies, Liu, and Robinson show how purpose-driven firms emerge as an optimal organizational form, as they profit from employees' willingness to accept lower wages, which in turn allows them to invest more in CSR efforts.[28] There are other studies that provide further evidence of reduced costs of labour.[29] However, not only labour but also capital costs can be lowered for companies that score higher on sustainability or CSR measures.[30]

Overall, the literature examining supply and demand suggests that competition can increase sustainability. In fact, Dewatripont and Tirole highlight that the level of ethical concern of consumers and suppliers in these cases is generally more important, and hence more intense competition does not lead companies to behave less ethically as such.[31] Others have suggested that while competition fosters sustainability, in particular where economies of scale are relevant, their relationship might not be linear. In other words, too much competition in the form of so-called 'cut-throat competition', can lead to a plateau where any further intensification of

[25] This questions was studied extensively in the 1990s. See, eg, Michael L Katz, 'An Analysis of Cooperative Research and Development' (1986) 17 *RAND Journal of Economics* 527–543; Claude D'Aspremont and Alexis Jacquemin, 'Cooperative and Noncooperative R&D in Duopoly with Spillovers' (1988) 78 *American Economic Review* 1133–1137; Morton I Kamien, Eitan Muller, and Israel Zang, 'Research Joint Ventures and R&D Cartels' (1992) 82 *American Economic Review* 1293; Kotaro Suzumura, 'Cooperative and Noncooperative R&D in an Oligopoly with Spillovers' (1992) 82 *American Economic Review* 1307–1320.

[26] See section II.1.d).

[27] Adi Ignatius, 'Captain Planet' (2012) 90 *Harvard Business Review* 112–119.

[28] Jean-Etienne de Bettignies, Hua Fang Liu, and David T Robinson, 'Corporate Social Responsibility and Imperfect Regulatory Oversight: Theory and Evidence from Greenhouse Gas Emissions Disclosures' (2020) National Bureau of Economic Research Working Paper 28159 available at < https://www.nber.org/papers/w28159> (accessed 10 January 2025).

[29] See eg Nathan Barrymore and Rachelle Sampson, 'ESG Performance and Labor Productivity: Exploring Whether and When ESG Affects Firm Performance' [2021] *Proceedings—Academy of Management* 13997; Donald F Vitaliano, 'Corporate Social Responsibility and Labor Turnover' (2010) 10(5) *Corporate Governance* 563–573.

[30] See eg Mark P Sharfman and Chitru S Fernando, 'Environmental Risk Management and the Cost of Capital' (2008) 29 *Strategic Management Journal* 569–592; Sadok El Ghoul and others, 'Does Corporate Social Responsibility Affect the Cost of Capital?' (2011) 39(9) *Journal of Banking & Finance* 2388–2406; Beiting Cheng, Ioannis Ioannou, and George Serafeim, 'Corporate Social Responsibility and Access to Finance' (2014) 35(1) *Strategic Management Journal* 1–23.

[31] Mathias Dewatripont and Jean Tirole, 'The Morality of Markets' (2022) ECARES Working Paper 2022-35 available at <https://econpapers.repec.org/scripts/redir.pf?u=https%3A%2F%2Fdipot.ulb.ac.be%2Fdspace%2Fbitstream%2F2013%2F351283%2F3%2F2022-35-DEWATRIPONT_TIROLE-the-morality.pdf;h=repec:eca:wpaper:2013/351283> (accessed 10 January 2025). In a similar direction Francisco Gomez Martinez, Sander Onderstal, and Maarten Pieter Schinkel, 'Can Collusion Promote Corporate Social Responsibility? Evidence from the Lab' (2019) Tinbergen Institute Discussion Paper 2019-034/VII available at <https://www.econstor.eu/bitstream/10419/205324/1/19034.pdf> (accessed 10 January 2025), which shows that social preferences are more important for 'fair' market outcomes than the possibility to coordinate between companies, eg by means of exemptions from competition law.

competition does not increase sustainability.[32] This leads us to now turn to situations where a reduction might improve sustainability.

b) Monopoly/cooperation producing better sustainability outcomes in static analysis

While we have explored numerous studies that show how competition can lead to improvements in terms of sustainability, we will now turn to the opposite: situations where reductions in competition lead to improvements in terms of sustainability. In economic models, reduced levels of competition are typically represented by monopoly, but they can equally be achieved through, for example, cooperation between firms or in duopoly situations.

The economic consulting company, Oxera, in its submission to consultation to the EU draft horizontal guidelines,[33] points out the so-called 'first-mover disadvantage'.[34] In other words, the fact that competition might prevent companies from producing more sustainably, as this increases costs and reduces their competitiveness.[35] They point out that such situations occur in particular in cases where the overall consumer willingness to pay is not high enough, and that cooperation in such situations can increase sustainability. In their submission, they use a game-theoretical approach of competition between two companies with the option of producing a non-green or a more expensive green product. They highlight two things. First, often even where firms cooperate, the payoff might be lower so there is no incentive to jointly adopt the production of the green product. Second, the situation might be different where positive spillover effects/externalities[36] exist; in other words, where a benefit for one firm[37] is created by the production of the green product by the other firm. It should nonetheless be noted that the spillover effect must be sufficiently large.

While this is the submission of an economic consultancy, there are also a number of academic papers that show that, in certain situations, less competition may lead to increases in terms of sustainability. In a static situation, that is to say, leaving innovation aside,[38] reductions in competition can lead to improvements

[32] Christopher Dirzka, 'The Economics of Sustainability Cooperation' in Julian Nowag (ed), *Research Handbook on Sustainability and Competition Law* (Edward Elgar 2024) 104–120.

[33] See Oxera, 'Comments on the Draft Revised Rules on Horizontal Agreements: Prepared in Response to the Public Consultation by the European Commission' (26 April 2022), available at <https://competition-policy.ec.europa.eu/document/download/1964d6cd-fa58-42be-b1d8-3856d5bbd1ea_en?filename=contributions_consultation_2022_hbers.zip> (accessed 10 January 2025).

[34] ibid 9–11.

[35] Oxera points to Lidl's 2018 trial of selling only fairtrade bananas in Germany and Switzerland; in this regard see also see BananaLink, 'Lidl backs away from Fairtrade Bananas' (20 May 2019) available at <https://www.bananalink.org.uk/news/lidl-backs-away-from-fairtrade-bananas/> (accessed 10 January 2025).

[36] The report mentions reputation of the industry and the reduction of an existential threat as such benefits.

[37] As in all cases of externalities, this benefit is enjoyed without having to pay for it.

[38] In this regard see below section II. 1. c).

in terms of sustainability, for example in terms of reduced pollution, thereby increasing overall welfare.

Mergers can also become relevant in terms of sustainability. Choi, Espínola-Arredondo, and Munoz-García[39] examine the effects of mergers on total welfare in a situation of imperfect competition, looking at the environmental and consumer surplus costs and benefits of mergers. They scrutinize the effects of mergers between green and brown firms in situations both with and without an emission fee.[40] The paper shows that where no emission fee is set, reducing competition, thereby reducing output, overall welfare can increase due to reduced pollution. However, this gain would be small compared to a situation where an environmental protection agency plus the competition agency aim to address the same negative externalities.

Choi, Espínola-Arredondo, and Munoz-García, 'Environmental Policy Helping Antitrust Decisions: Socially Excessive and Insufficient Merger Approval'[41]

Our results indicate that, while mergers of symmetric firms under no environmental regulation can lead to a welfare loss, ... mergers can improve welfare when firms are relatively asymmetric in costs and pollution intensities. In these settings, mergers should be promoted. Furthermore, if the [Environmental Protection Agency] can charge emission fees, then first-best outcomes can be achieved whether firms are allowed to merge or not. Our paper then sheds light on the Horizontal Merger Guidelines ..., suggesting that the [antitrust authorities] can approve mergers of differentiated firms if they can save costs and reduce pollution. These criteria may offset the anticompetitive effects of mergers, going beyond the conventional thinking of consumer surplus and efficiency gains in merger evaluation, as in the merger between Boeing Company and McDonnell Douglas Corporation....

Our results further describe that, when the [antitrust authority] does not consider the environmental effects of the mergers, socially excessive mergers can arise when output shifts to firms which environmental damages more than compensate the associated efficiency gains. These occur when firms producing relatively homogeneous goods are relatively asymmetric in their pollution intensities but are relatively cost symmetric. In contrast, socially insufficient mergers that were originally blocked may be reconsidered in light of their reduction

[39] Pak-Sing Choi, Ana Espínola-Arredondo, and Félix Munoz-García, 'Environmental Policy Helping Antitrust Decisions: Socially Excessive and Insufficient Merger Approval' (2022) 67 *Resource and Energy Economics* 101267.

[40] Which represents the costs of complying with environmental regulation.

[41] Choi, Espínola-Arredondo, and Munoz-García (n 39).

of environmental externalities, which happen when firms produce relatively differentiated goods, are relatively asymmetric in costs, and environmental damages are strong.

Our model can be extended in several directions. First, one could assume that the [Environmental Protection Agency] does not set emission fees to maximize social welfare but, instead, Pigouvian taxes that coincide with the marginal environmental damage from each firm's emissions. Second, we could consider that the [Environmental Protection Agency] cannot set firm-specific emission fees, but instead, firm-uniform emission fees. This second-best environmental policy would yield lower welfare levels than those in the first-best scenario we consider in this paper… (In this setting, the [antitrust authority]'s role at the beginning of the game may become more relevant, since the [antitrust authority] no longer anticipates that the EPA will induce socially optimal outcomes in the third stage following its merger approval decisions.). Finally, our model can be extended to allow for the [antitrust authority], the [Environmental Protection Agency], or both agencies, not to observe firms' production costs or pollution intensities, and how merger decisions are affected, when emission fees are used to induce socially optimal output levels….

Benchekroun, Breton, and Chaudhuri report similar findings when examining horizontal mergers in situations of non-renewable resources, which cover situations such as fossil fuel extraction or mining. They show that in situations where environmental rules impose costs or otherwise reduce the profitability of firms, a competitive market incentivizes an increase in the speed of extraction leading to earlier exhaustion and the occurrence of associated emissions.[42]

These findings might not be surprising: if the production of a good is associated with negative effects on sustainability, reduced competition and therefore higher prices and lower output will reduce overall pollution. In the same way, where OPEC, as the 'cartel' of oil-producing states, decides to cut output and thereby raise prices, this can be seen as leading to (unintentionally) lowering the CO2 emissions from oil. As this example succinctly demonstrates, in such cases, there is a direct trade-off between consumer surplus and sustainability. Such an example of a trade-off has also been examined by Huric Larsen and Münch.[43] Their paper examines the trade-off between competition and reduction in an externality that results from production. They show that a monopoly implies lower levels of pollution as compared to perfect competition and suggest that it is superior to the use of

[42] Hassan Benchekroun, Michèle Breton, and Amrita Ray Chaudhuri, 'Mergers in Nonrenewable Resource Oligopolies and Environmental Policies' (2019) 111 *European Economic Review* 35–52.

[43] Jesper Huric Larsen and Angela Münch, 'Competition and Environmental Policy in the EU: Old Foes, New Friends?' (2016) 16(2) *Journal of Industry, Competition and Trade*, 137–153.

environmental taxes or support for sustainable innovation. Overall, they suggest that the optimal market structure from an emission perspective depends on the size of the emission, the damage that the emission causes, and the market size.

This insight already suggests that the trade-off may vary significantly across different situations. We can highlight the following different situations: common pool resources, other resource-sharing situations, cooperation in markets where more and less sustainable products compete, and the provision of public and private goods by firms.

Possibly the most famous case where more competition is detrimental to sustainability is common-pool renewable resources that are limited, for example a fish stock. Uchida and Manning examine how competition affects such renewable resources.[44] They show that in these situations a monopoly/less competition provides beneficial outcomes from a sustainability perspective. Overall, reduced competition lowers the incentive—one might say moral hazard—to extract as much as possible for the individual firm. In the long run, this incentive leads to a depletion of the stock, so all firms and consumers will suffer higher prices due to the collapse of the stock.

Uchida and Manning, 'Are Two Rents Better than None? When Monopolies Correct Ill-Defined Property Rights'[45]

The case of a monopolist resource owner was analyzed extensively in the context of nonrenewable resources ... which led to the notion that a 'monopolist' is the conservationist's friend. In fisheries, the management implications of imperfect competition in both the harvest and processing sectors were explored. A monopolist fishery manager internalizes the impact of harvest on output price and sets marginal revenue equal to the marginal cost of harvest. A seminal book by Clark investigated the dynamic implications of monopoly power on fish harvests. While these studies focused on analyzing the monopolist's behavior in contrast to the first-best outcome, an important question remains unanswered: is having a sole owner with market power preferred to a fishery with ill-defined property rights and prevailing 'race to fish' behavior?

In this article, we extend the fishery monopoly model of Clark to explicitly examine the distributional implications of monopoly management of renewable resources over time. We theoretically distinguish resource and monopoly

[44] See eg Hirotsugu Uchida and Dale Manning, 'Fishery Management: A Monopolist to the Rescue?' in Julian Nowag (eds), *Research Handbook on Sustainability and Competition Law* (Edward Elgar Publishing, 2023) which builds on their work in Hirotsugu Uchida and Dale Manning, 'Are Two Rents Better than None? When Monopolies Correct Ill-Defined Property Rights' (2016) 31(2) *Marine Resource Economics* 141–164; for a similar discussion see Jonathan Adler, 'Conservation Cartels: Competition Policy Can Conflict with Environmental Protection' (2004) 27 *Regulation* 38–45.

[45] Uchida and Manning 'Are Two Rents Better than None?', ibid.

rents and ask how their net effect impacts welfare and its distribution in the fishery sector. Even though a monopolistic regulator restricts harvest in the short run, as fish stocks recover the monopoly harvest can exceed the rent-dissipated harvest, meaning that consumer surplus can increase as a result of the monopolist....[46]

The theoretical results presented herein demonstrate that local resource managers with monopoly power can represent a social gain relative to unmanaged fisheries. The resource steady-state stock level under a monopolist is unambiguously higher than when the resource is unmanaged. Therefore, the monopolist is a conservationist, and we have shown that a monopolist over-conserves even relative to the social optimum. Under some circumstances, a monopoly managed fishery can also have higher sustained harvest levels than the rent-dissipated levels. In this case, consumers gain as a result of the monopoly, although not always compared to the optimal harvest levels. Even if the monopolist's steady-state harvest is less than the rent dissipated harvest, overall surplus can be greater if harvest costs decrease significantly due to higher resource stocks and the internalization of resource user cost. Also, if a resource sector faces an infinitely elastic demand curve, management necessarily represents an improvement over open access because the monopolist's objective to maximize rent only maximizes resource rent. Even in the absence of monopoly power, a manager would produce where price exceeds the marginal cost of harvest, but all the rent is resource rent. Because the generation of resource rent can increase overall welfare relative to open access, the value of local monopoly fishery management should be considered on a case-by-case basis and not deemed illegal without further investigation ...[47]

Overall, we demonstrate the importance of accounting for the net change in welfare when moving from an open-access institution to a local resource manager with monopoly power if a first-best management solution cannot be achieved. Despite the creation of monopoly rent, a monopoly resource manager improves resource stocks and lowers harvest costs and can even result in higher output over time. Therefore, a locally managed fishery with some market power may be preferred to a rent-dissipating fishery.[48]

In a similar direction, Colombo and Labrecciosa show that this outcome of conservation cartels is also beneficial when examining consumer surplus. They demonstrate that while there are short-term reductions in consumer surplus due to reduced competition, the coordination of output decisions can lead to an overall

[46] ibid 142, refences omitted.
[47] ibid 159–160.
[48] ibid 162.

increase in consumer surplus over time.[49] These situations are often addressed by the government imposing fishing quotas, but can equally be tackled by a private body setting these quotas.[50] This also links to Elinor Ostrom's famous work which showed how cooperative solutions to environmental resources—and in particular open access and common pool resources—are possible, as the members' interests are aligned.[51]

Another area where reductions in competition can lead to an increase in terms of sustainability is resource-sharing situations. For example, based on theoretical work and a case study, Christ, Burritt, and Varsei show how cooperation by means of resource-sharing between competitors can improve sustainability outcomes. They exemplify this finding by means of a case study concerning wine logistics, where cooperation leads to the use of spare capacities and better environmental outcomes.[52]

Reduced competition can also be beneficial in another situation of resource-sharing, as examined by Van Moer.[53] He studies the effects of reducing competition on one element of input, namely a natural resource, using a Cournot model of duopolistic competition. Here, the output of the competitors depends on the input of the natural resources and a basket of resources. In these situations, he compares the competitive scenario and two options of reduced competition. Van Moer shows that if the firms jointly set an absolute target for the extraction of the natural resource, the usage of the resource is reduced when compared to the competitive situation or a situation where they set a relative[54] target. The result shows how in such a situation of reduced competition, the competitive pressure shifts and induces greater sustainability. While the agreed reduction in the use of the natural resource leads to a reduction in production quantities and increases profits, there is a competitive incentive to increase efficiency regarding the use of the natural resource per unit of production.

There are also circumstances where reduced competition can have positive impacts. Addressing the relevant incentives of companies, Ahmed and Segerson explore voluntary environmental standards and show that in a market where firms can decide to produce either a high-quality or a low-quality good, it can be profitable for firms to set up agreements to agree on higher-quality standards.[55]

49 Luca Colombo and Paola Labrecciosa, 'Consumer Surplus-Enhancing Cooperation in a Natural Resource Oligopoly' (2018) 92 *Journal of Environmental Economics and Management* 185–193.

50 For a case from the US involving such fishing associations, see also Chapter 3, section IV. 2. b).

51 Elinor Ostrom, *Governing the Commons—The Evolution of Institutions for Collective Action* (CUP 1990); Eleanor Ostrom (ed), *The Future of the Commons—Beyond Market Failure and Government Regulation* (Institute for Economic Affairs 2012).

52 Katherine L Christ, Roger L Burritt, and Mohsen Varsei, 'Coopetition as a Potential Strategy for Corporate Sustainability'(2017) 26 *Business Strategy and the Environment* 1029–1040.

53 Geert van Moer, 'Horizontal Agreements to Limit the Use of a Natural Resource' (10 May 2022) available at <https://ssrn.com/abstract=3952424> (accessed 10 January 2025).

54 Such a target instead sets the usage intensity per unit of production.

55 Rasha Ahmed and Kathleen Segerson, 'Collective Voluntary Agreements to Eliminate Polluting Products' (2011) 33(3) *Resource and Energy Economics* 572–588.

Yet, for such agreements to work they will have to prevent free-riding, which requires enforcement mechanisms. Calveras and Ganuza[56] show that more competition in markets where sustainable and unsustainable products are traded leads to a lower likelihood of entry. In their model, the sustainability level is only imperfectly observable, and firms can either enter the clean market for a fixed fee[57] or simply produce the dirty good without such a fee. Calveras and Ganuza then compare the effects of a collusive price, a competitive (Bertrand equilibrium) price, and an intermediate state. In this setting, they show how less competition leads to greater entry, and thus, a larger number of clean goods being produced.

A final area where reductions in competition and positive effects on sustainability have been studied is the provision of public and private goods by firms. Schinkel and Tóth[58] examine a situation where less competition might provide better outcomes in terms of sustainability. In their model, firms are allowed to cartelize the provision of a private good, in other words increase its price, if they provide a contribution to a public good, such as sustainability. They show how this can increase the provision of the public good, yet they highlight three important caveats. First, this situation leads to a crowding-out of consumers' voluntary contributions to providing the public good. Second, the incentive for the companies is to raise the price for the private good as much as possible while providing the least possible amount of the public good. Third, where consumers have different valuations of the public good, the average consumer of the private good will be worse off. This result stems from the fact that they are not fully compensated for the price increase in the private good through the provision of the public good.

c) Consequences and limitations

This brief overview shows that some important work has been done in these areas. Yet, it seems early in the economic, and in particular, micro-economic examination of such cases. However, a number of trends can be identified. But most importantly, one needs to examine the situations in detail and survey the potential consequences of restrictions on competition, while being mindful of the limitations of the theoretical studies.

aa) Consequences

Overall, we can certainly say that where firms compete over sustainability because consumers value it, competition is an important driver for sustainability.[59] The situation may be different where consumers do not value sustainability and

[56] Aleix Calveras and Juan Jose Ganuza, 'The Role of Public Information in Corporate Social Responsibility' (2016) 25 *Journal of Economics and Management Strategy* 990–1017.

[57] Which in their model represents an investment.

[58] Schinkel and Tóth (n 16).

[59] With a clear exception of free-riding: in other words, a firm's investment in sustainability brings about substantial advantages for its competitors.

where the product itself creates negative impacts on sustainability. However, where consumers value sustainability, competition laws have an important task as they would usually protect competition over this parameter. In fact, where competition on other parameters such as output—and thereby price—is limited, competition over sustainability becomes an even more important factor for product differentiation. In other words, in such cases, sustainability might be the main way companies offer better value to consumers.

In such a situation where consumers value sustainability, the literature suggests that restricting competition rarely provides benefits, with some exceptions, notably competition over different forms of resources. These findings are often a result of the profit motive of firms. It seems only rational to limit competition to the greatest extent possible while providing as little as possible of (costly) sustainability benefits. This strategy raises profit. Thus, it seems sensible to be sceptical of traditional firms that claim that their actions will advance sustainability by restricting competition.

However, this insight is related to the rationale of maximizing profit. It thus provides a first insight into the limitations of these studies. They are—not surprisingly—resulting from the assumptions made. The studies cannot be faulted as such as they use classic economic models and thereby classic assumptions.

bb) Limitations

There are generally four limitations that need to be taken into account when looking at this literature. First, the vast majority of these papers are set in a static setting focusing[60] focusing on the demand side. The second set of limitations relates to the classical assumption of profit maximization, and the third to biases and rational behaviour. The final limitation stems from the more specific set-up of the studies and what these results could imply for other contexts.

Demand focus and innovation With regard to the first limitation, the majority of the papers focus on the demand side and thus on consumer-driven incentives to act more sustainably. Hardly any paper looks at the supply side and incentivizes sustainability from that perspective, for example, demands from employees. It would be even more interesting to see how the combined incentives of supply and demand would play out. Moreover, as highlighted, most of the papers explored above do not consider a dynamic perspective and in particular restrictions of competition that may lead to sustainability innovation.[61] We know that, from an

[60] For this see also the next section, II.1.d).

[61] In general, on the benefits of sustainability innovation for firms, see Fanny Hermundsdottir and Arild Aspelund, 'Sustainability Innovations and Firm Competitiveness: A Review' (2021) 280(1) *Journal of Cleaner Production* 124715.

innovation perspective, restrictions of competition may sometimes be necessary.[62] Similarly, the papers, therefore, often work under the assumption that we need to explore whether current consumers are better off or not, thereby excluding gains for future or potential consumers, who are different from current consumers and have their own preferences.[63]

Profit maximization and rational behaviour At the core of the current economic literature in this area are two axioms—profit maximization and rational behaviour. The former might be questionable in a number of situations. Here, the first important distinction is between traditional limited liability companies traded on public markets with a diluted shareholding and other situations.

Albeit for such publicly traded companies with diluted shareholdings the rational profit maximizer axiom might still be the most appropriate, some questions have arisen. First, numerous business schools around the world now teach future CEOs about sustainable business and environmental, social, and governance matters relating to the running of companies. This move towards sustainability and ESG seems to imply a certain willingness to sacrifice (at least some) profits as reduced profitability maybe seen as inherent in any corporate social responsibility concept.[64] Second, even such companies face internal and external pressure to be more sustainable, not only consumer demand. Internally, there might be demands from employees and investors for more sustainable action.[65] Thus, companies have to make trade-offs between on the one hand sustainability, which involves profit sacrifice, and on the other, profit maximization.[66] A profit sacrifice can often avoid costly conflicts with investors and employees.

Moreover, closely held companies where the owners are often in management positions might equally act differently and may not always be profit maximizing. They may act in such a way not because of specific trade-offs but because of their aspiration. The effect of competition can thereby be rather different where the profit-maximizing motive is absent. The situation of firms motivated not only by

[62] For example, the special rules on R&D cooperation between firms.

[63] See in this regard, eg, Roman Inderst and Stefan Thomas, 'Prospective Welfare Analysis—Extending Willingness-To-Pay Assessment to Embrace Sustainability' (2022) 18(3) *Journal of Competition Law & Economics* 551–583, which is also further explored below, text to n 162ff.

[64] See Einer Elhauge, 'Corporate Profits in the Public Interest' (2005) 80(3) *New York University Law Review* 733–869; more generally Forest L Reinhardt, Robert N Stavins, and Richard HK Vietor, 'Corporate Social Responsibility Through an Economic Lens' (2008) 2 *Review of Environmental Economics and Policy* 219–239.

[65] See for example the letter by BlackRock chief Larry Fink, 'A Fundamental Reshaping of Finance' (2018) available at <https://www.blackrock.com/corporate/investor-relations/larry-fink-ceo-letter> (accessed 10 January 2025).

[66] See Sarah E Light, 'The Law of the Corporation as Environmental Law' (2019) 79 *Stanford Law Review* 185–190 for more details on so-called 'benefit corporations' in the US, their incentive structure, and the explicit legal acknowledgement that the directors can prioritize sustainability over profit-making and allow firm managers to take environmental interests into account.

profits is examined by Inderst in a working paper.[67] The study examines a two-stage model where firms make strategic sustainability investments and then compete in the product market. Typically, sustainability is viewed as a quality attribute that influences consumer willingness to pay and affects costs. However, in this study, the focus is on firms that have an intrinsic preference for sustainability.[68] These intrinsic preferences change the profit maximization axiom and might for example be derived from the preferences of shareholders, employees, or management. The analysis considers various specifications of these preferences. When sustainability leads to lower emissions, firms may have preferences that are either narrow (focusing on their own emissions) or broader (considering total industry emissions). Overall, the study finds that cooperation can lead to higher levels of sustainability if at least one firm has such intrinsic preferences. The paper compares competition and cooperation scenarios and shows that where sustainability efforts only increase marginal costs, cooperation leads to increased sustainability compared to the competitive scenario. For increases in fixed costs, the picture is more nuanced. The results depend on consumers' willingness to pay vs the size of the fixed cost increase. The overall situation is different where the firms do not only have preferences for internal sustainability improvements but also value the overall industrywide sustainability levels. If such broader preferences exist, the likelihood of increases in sustainability levels increases.

Finally, profit maximization incentives will always be tempered by legal requirements that are related to sustainability. For example, the proposed Articles 5 and 7 of the EU Corporate Sustainability Due Diligence Directive[69] impose obligations on the company with regard to environmental damage and human rights violations. Moreover, companies may incur liability under laws such as Modern Slavery Acts in different jurisdictions[70] or general tort law for environmental harm and human rights violations they or their suppliers may have committed.[71] Such legal requirements in turn will involve a similar trade-off between scarifying profit and reducing exposure under such rules.

[67] Roman Inderst, 'Firm Objectives and the Scope for Sustainable (Green) Agreements in Antitrust' (February 2024) available at SSRN <https://ssrn.com/abstract=4381098> (accessed 10 January 2025).

[68] See also Dewatripont and Tirole (n 31).

[69] Directive (EU) 2024/1760 of the European Parliament and of the Council of 13 June 2024 on corporate sustainability due diligence and amending Directive (EU) 2019/1937 and Regulation (EU) 2023/2859 [2024] OJ L 2024/1760.

[70] See, eg, Kadriye Bakirci and Graham Ritchi, 'Corporate Liability for Modern Slavery' (2022) 29(2) *Journal of Financial Crime* 576–588.

[71] On developments in this regard see Cees van Dam, 'Breakthrough in Parent Company Liability: Three Shell Defeats, the End of an Era and New Paradigms' (2021) 18 *European Company and Financial Law Review* 714; for an overview of the case law see also eg Malin Maud Hasselblatt, 'Unravelling Corporate Civil Liability in the Proposal for a Corporate Sustainability Due Diligence Directive through Value Chain Governance and the Concept of Sustainability Due Diligence' available at <http://lup.lub.lu.se/student-papers/record/9135042> (accessed 10 January 2025) 31ff.

Beyond publicly traded companies, where the rational profit maximizer axiom might be closer to reality, other actors on the market may operate under rather different premises. For example, individual traders, non-profit companies, and even charities may also offer goods and services to the market and are then subject to competition law. In this regard, Poret considered a double duopoly model of vertical product differentiation with two NGOs and two firms, in which the NGOs compete to offer firms labels for sustainability quality, and the firms compete to sell the products.[72] It is found that competition between the two NGOs leads to a decrease in the stringency of standards, ie competition decreases overall weighted sustainability quality. In light of this effect, a model that makes policy recommendations based on the assumption of rational profit maximizer may seem far off the mark for cases where restrictions of competition involve such entities.

Overall, these limitations seem to suggest that an important factor in considering policy implications is the governance arrangements of the actors and the agreements involved in the specific case. Crucial here is the extent to which such arrangements moderate the profit maximization motive of the parties involved and channelling gains to sustainability.

Biases As often with microeconomic models, they also assume rational behaviour by companies and consumers. However, in particular with regard to consumers and their purchase choices, such biases may affect the outcome because consumers' purchase choices might not reflect their actual willingness to pay for more sustainable products.[73] This in turn might reduce the incentive of companies to invest in sustainability improvements, as long as the supply side is unable to cater for a more limited number of consumers that are better informed or less affected by the biases.[74] The biases at play here are hyperbolic discounting,[75] the use of heuristics,[76] coordination failures,[77] and a status quo bias/endowment

[72] Sylvaine Poret, 'Label Wars: Competition among NGOs as Sustainability Standard Setters' (2019) 160 *Journal of Economic Behavior & Organization* 1–18.

[73] See Cristina A Volpin, 'Sustainability as a Quality Dimension of Competition: Protecting Our Future (Selves)' (July 2020) CPI *Antitrust Chronicle* 9–18; see also Jordan Ellison, 'A Fair Share: Time for the Carbon Defence?' (2020) available at <https://ssrn.com/abstract=3542186> (accessed 10 January 2025); Maurits Dolmans, 'Sustainable Competition Policy' (2020) 5-6 *Competition Law and Policy Debate* 8.

[74] Volpin, ibid.

[75] See Shane Frederick, George Loewenstein, and Ted O'Donoghue, 'Time Discounting and Time Preference: A Critical Review' (2002) 40 *Journal of Economic Literature* 351–401.

[76] For a good overview see, eg, Lucia Reisch and Min Zhao, 'Behavioural Economics, Consumer Behaviour and Consumer Policy: State of the Art' (2017) 1 *Behavioural Public Policy* 190–206.

[77] On coordination failures see, eg, John B Van Huyck, Joseph P Cook, and Raymond C Battalio, 'Adaptive Behavior and Coordination Failure' (1997) 32(4) *Journal of Economic Behavior & Organization*, 483–503, or with regard to green investments specifically, Jahel Mielke and Gesine A Steudle, 'Green Investment and Coordination Failure: An Investors' Perspective' (PhD thesis 2018) available at <https://publishup.uni-potsdam.de/opus4-ubp/frontdoor/deliver/index/docId/42745/file/mielke_diss.pdf> (accessed 10 January 2025) 78-93.

effect[78]. Hyperbolic discounting relates to the fact that consumers will often prefer cost savings now and ignore even more significant future costs. Consumers often use heuristics to reduce complexity and thus decide based on one or two easily observable parameters such as price, thereby ending up with suboptimal decisions. This heuristics problem is often further intensified by limited information about a good's sustainability footprint[79] as compared to others. But even well-informed consumers might not follow through because of coordination failures. In other words, they will opt for the cheaper product with low sustainability levels because they believe that buying more sustainable products will not make a difference, as the majority of consumers do not buy more sustainable products. Finally, consumers, because of their status quo bias, may stick with the less sustainable product even when more sustainable options are available.

Other limitations The final set of limitations stems from the setup of these papers. The first relates to how consumer benefits are measured, the second to the way sustainability is assumed to exist, and the third one from the type of restriction that is assumed.

First, perhaps not surprisingly for econometric studies, the majority are built on the assumption that the welfare of consumers is only increased by an increase in consumption. While possibly more difficult to model, a more realistic approach would take a different view. For example, a consumer might derive utility from the presence of a forest next to their house, even if they never go into the forest.[80] Moreover, consumers are not one-dimensional, that is to say, they do not only have a financial interest in one specific market but are active in different markets and other spheres with possibly conflicting interests.[81] Thus, we might wonder whether the results would be the same if another approach to measuring the welfare of consumers were taken, for example, taking into account concepts like 'passive use value'.[82]

[78] See especially with regard to environmental matters, eg, Simon Dietz and Frank Venmans, 'The Endowment Effect, Discounting and the Environment' (2019) 97 *Journal of Environmental Economics and Management* 67–91.

[79] On the importance of the observability of sustainability information see Aleix Calveras and Juan-José Ganuza, 'Corporate Social Responsibility and Product Quality' (2018) 27(4) *Journal of Economics & Management Strategy* 804–829.

[80] In environmental economics, we see a distinction between use value (going to the forest) and non-use value. The non-use value can for example be the existence value (the value derived from just having the forest there), the option value (the value derived from having the option to go into the forest tomorrow), and a bequest value (the value derived from the fact that future generation can enjoy the forest). See in this regard, eg, Nadine Watson, 'Measuring Environmental Benefits in Competition Cases' (2021) OECD DAF/COMP(2021)14 available at <https://one.oecd.org/document/DAF/COMP(2021)14/en/pdf> (accessed 10 January 2025).

[81] See Ioannis Lianos, 'Polycentric Competition Law' (2018) *Current Legal Problems* 161–213; Hellenic Competition Commission, 'Staff Discussion Paper—Sustainability Issues and Competition Law (2020), available at <https://www.epant.gr/files/2020/Staff_Discussion_paper.pdf> (accessed 10 January 2025) para 71.

[82] See eg Richard T Carson, 'Contingent Valuation: A Practical Alternative When Prices Aren't Available' (2012) 26(4) *Journal of Economic Perspectives* 27–42.

Second, the vast majority of the papers apply the concept of sustainability or public benefit as one that is linear or at least non-binary, meaning that it can take higher and lower values. However, many[83] sustainability matters will be binary questions[84] that cannot be further optimized by further competition. Take, for example, a commitment not to use forced labour. A scale that measures the level of forced labour, in, for example, percentages does not exist. Either forced labour is used or it is not used. In such a situation, it is more difficult to say that competition would further improve this sustainability parameter.

Finally, even in situations where the sustainability parameter is not binary but can be measured, many of the papers adopt a different kind of binary choice. The papers compare full competition with no competition on the sustainability parameter. The conclusions under this binary model may provide little insight for real life examples, where agreements around sustainability do not fully harmonize sustainability but rather set a floor or minimum level of sustainability. Thus, companies might very well continue to compete over sustainability, but only in the direction that is valued by the consumer. In this sense, such agreements might be compared to maximum retail price maintenance schemes. In these situations, companies can compete on price only in one direction, similar to agreements that set minimum standards for levels of sustainability. However, it should be noted that in the context of maximum retail price maintenance schemes, risks exist,[85] such as schemes de facto becoming cartel prices.[86] In other words, the risk is that competition disappears and that only one price (the maximum price) or one level of sustainability (the one set out in the sustainability agreement) exists. In fact, the papers assume that the sustainability level is set at equilibrium level. In other words, firms are assumed to have no incentive to choose a different, and higher, level of sustainability, at least under these costs and demand levels. However, in reality companies might well have an incentive to 'cheat' and steal business by setting higher levels of sustainability once these variables change, for example in the future. The problem for the jointly set sustainable level is the same as in cartel cases. The stability of the cartel depends on the extent to which punishment is possible where firms cheat on the agreed level. However, where only a minimum standard is agreed upon, punishment is only legally possible when a company offers services below the

[83] Yet, there are indeed other sustainability matters that are non-binary, such as the level of CO2 emissions.

[84] Beyond forced labour, one might think of questions of whether a product is produced with or without child labour, or is deforestation-free.

[85] On the risks of maximum resale price maintenance schemes see, eg, OECD, Roundtable on Resale Price Maintenance (2008) DAF/COMP (2008)37; Andres Font Galarza, Frank P Maier-Rigaud, and Pablo Figueroa, 'PRM under EU Competition Law: Some Considerations from a Business and Economic Perspective' (November 2013) (1) *CPI Antitrust Chronicle*.

[86] The upstream setter of the maximum retail price acting as a hub in a hub-and-spoke type cartel with the different retailers all charging the same price.

standard. It would, thus, be incumbent on the agency to show punishment where a firm offers products of a higher sustainability standard.

d) Sustainability innovation

The above-discussed studies seem to mainly concern static analysis, yet we can also look at sustainability from an innovation perspective. Such an approach is particularly useful as new more sustainable methods and technologies will be crucial in achieving sustainability aims such as climate targets. This section, thus, looks at the economics of identifying new pathways to more sustainable products and production, rather than the pure implantation of well-known ways to increase sustainability. Sustainability is a non-price quality element[87] which also suggests that innovation should also be crucial, as quality improvements will primarily be achieved by innovation.

Simeng, Cheng, Zhang, and Zhu[88] studied green investments in a vertical supply chain. They compared who is better placed to initiate such investments in a game theoretical model, the producer or the retailer. They found that the retailer is better placed, as it is closer to the consumer. Where the retailer takes the initiative, it increases profitability for producers and retailers by reducing double marginalization while similarly leading to higher environmental performance.

Yet overall, there are not many studies that examine sustainability innovation, but general innovation papers should be able to inform a view. In innovation and competition, two areas can be identified. The first relates generally to the relationship between competition/monopoly and innovation, and the other to questions of cooperation to address spillover effects, sometimes also associated with a first-mover disadvantage.

Models from innovation seem to suggest that one size might not fit all practices and situations. The answer to the Schumpeter-Arrow debate[89] over whether competition or monopoly leads to more innovation can be better answered in a

[87] See eg Volpin (n 73).

[88] Wan Simeng and others, 'The Implications of Vertical Strategic Interaction on Green Technology Investment in a Supply Chain' (2020) 12(18) *Sustainability* 7441.

[89] See Joseph A Schumpeter, *Capitalism, Socialism and Democracy* (Harper & Row 1962) ch VIII; Kenneth J Arrow, 'Economic Welfare and the Allocation of Resources for Invention' in National Bureau Committee for Economic Research (ed), *The Rate and Direction of Inventive Activity: Economic and Social Factors* (Princeton University Press 1962) 619ff; for an overview see also Jonathan B Baker, 'Beyond Schumpeter vs. Arrow: How Antitrust Fosters Innovation' (2007) 74(3) *Antitrust Law Journal* 575. Shapiro aimed to combine the insights of Schumpeter and Arrow, see Carl Shapiro, 'Competition and Innovation: Did Arrow Hit the Bull's Eye?' in Josh Lerner and Scott Stern (eds) *The Rate and Direction of Inventive Activity Revisited* (University of Chicago Press 2010) 361–404. Shapiro suggests that innovation is driven by three effects that antitrust authorities need to take into account. First, if their sales are contestable, competition drives innovation. Second, the ability to appropriate (at least parts of) the benefits of the invention (ie to prevent free-riding) drives innovation. Third, cooperation can improve the ability to innovate for example by combining complementary R&D capabilities.

concrete situation.[90] A seminal paper by Aghion, Bloom, Blundell, Griffith, and Howitt, which combined theory and empirics, suggested that the relationship between competition and innovation is complex, in the form of an 'inverted-U' relation.[91] They suggested that the difference between pre- and post-innovation rents is crucial for investment in innovation. Where too little competition exists, there is little incentive for innovation as the firm may cannibalize its own existing product.[92] Yet, where too much competition exists, there may also be little incentive for innovation, as the firm will be unable to recoup the investments.[93] Thus, their paper suggests that in situations of few oligopolists competing, or neck-to-neck competition, innovation incentives should be highest. These insights can also be used in the context of sustainability innovation. In other words:

> the difference between post-innovation and pre-innovation rents is a crucial determinant of investments. Whenever competition increases post-innovation rents relative to pre-innovation rents, it increases [sustainability] innovation. Competition and [sustainability] innovation are negatively related when competition decreases post-innovation rents relative to pre-innovation rents.[94]

One of the few papers that looks more closely at innovation and sustainability is by Aghion, Bénabou, Martin, and Roulet.[95] The paper combines theory and empirical findings and explores R&D spending by automobile industry and the drive to more sustainable products. In their model, increased competition leads to greater output, thereby creating a higher level of pollution. Yet, this competition also creates incentives for R&D investments that in turn reduce these production-linked externalities. Their model assumes that consumers value the price (determined by the output quantity) and the sustainability level. They confirm the idea of an inverted-U shape and suggest that the relationship between competition and pollution is 'hump-shaped'. This result is dependent on the non-negligible preference of consumers for cleaner cars. Where initially sufficient competition exists, it erodes rents prior to innovation, so that increased competition will drive escape

[90] For a good overview of the Schumpter–Arrow debate and questions regarding specific market conditions in Pharma, see Michael A Carrier, 'Two Puzzles Resolved: Of the Schumpeter–Arrow Stalemate and Pharmaceutical Innovation Markets' (2008) *Iowa Law Review* 393.

[91] Philippe Aghion, Nick Bloom, Richard Blundell, Rachel Griffith, and Peter Howitt, 'Competition and Innovation: An Inverted-U Relationship' (2005) 120 *Quarterly Journal of Economics* 120. See however, Mitsuru Igami and Kosuke Uetake, 'Mergers, Innovation, and Entry-Exit Dynamics: Consolidation of the Hard Disk Drive Industry, 1996–2016' (2020) 87(6) *Review of Economic Studies* 2672, who seem to suggest that increased competition increases the rate of innovation until a point where it then plateaus, rather than drops as the U-shaper would suggest.

[92] A central insight proposed by Arrow.

[93] A central insight proposed by Schumpeter. For the reasons why incentives maybe low, see further below where R&D and cooperation are discussed.

[94] Treuren (n 7) 54.

[95] Philippe Aghion and others, 'Environmental Preferences and Technological Choices: Is Market Competition Clean or Dirty?' (2020) 5 *American Economic Review: Insights* 1.

behaviour. This escape behaviour leads to significant investments in R&D which in turn should drive down the externality. The finding seems to suggest that consumer preferences (for sustainability) will be more important where competition is more rigorous, and the importance will increase further as consumer awareness of sustainability levels and benefits increases.[96]

Another area related to sustainability innovation is the literature on R&D cooperation.[97] In this literature, spillover effects, in other words, questions of free-riding, are often crucial for determining whether competition increases or decreases innovation. Where companies engage in innovation by creating new products or establishing new markets, the extent to which competitors that did not make such investments can free-ride[98] is important.[99] In this context, it has been established that the main factor influencing investment in R&D is whether spillovers exist. Where the risk of spillover effects is low, ie companies are able to appropriate the benefits of innovation,[100] cooperation can reduce the incentives to innovate.[101] In such situations, innovation allows firms to compete more aggressively by offering an improved product/cheaper price. If firms cooperate in such situations, they are able to stop the danger of one of their competitors achieving such an innovation advantage. In other words, cooperation softens competition. In the opposite case, where firms face substantial spillover risks, the results are different. In these cases, competitors can free-ride on the benefits of the firm's investment. Thus, the incentives for the individual firm to invest are low.[102] Under these conditions, cooperation can increase the incentives to innovate by breaking a deadlock. The idea of breaking the deadlock is also a reason why competition law often allows R&D cooperation under certain conditions.

In the sustainability context, a similar point with regard to spillover/free-rider points[103] can be made, although in that debate the term 'first-mover disadvantage' is used. The free-riding/first-mover disadvantage element in these situations can result from higher initial investments as compared to late adopters, regulatory uncertainty,[104] a lack of awareness of consumers of the relevant sustainability, and

[96] Treuren (n 7) 55–56.

[97] See eg Michael L Katz and Janusz A Ordover, 'R&D Cooperation and Competition' (1990) Brookings Papers on Economic Activity: Microeconomics 137–203 available at <https://www.brookings.edu/wp-content/uploads/1990/01/1990_bpeamicro_katz.pdf> (accessed 10 January 2025).

[98] For example, employees that move to the competition can take with them the know-how or the actual innovation is being copied once on the market.

[99] Volpin (n 73).

[100] Eg by means of patents.

[101] Massimo Motta and Emanuele Tarantino, 'The Effect of Horizontal Mergers, When Firms Compete in Prices and Investments' (2021) 78 *International Journal of Industrial Organization* 102774.

[102] In other words, any costly investments by one firm cannot be appropriated and thus the other firms benefit without having to incur the cost.

[103] In particular, there is some evidence to suggest free-riding problems in the sustainability context; see, eg, Magali Delmas and Arturo Keller, 'Free Riding in Voluntary Environmental Programs: the Case of the US EPA WasteWise program' (2005) 38 *Policy Sciences* 91–106.

[104] Where future changes in the regulations could either benefit or disadvantage them compared to late adopters.

relatedly a relatively small market at the beginning, or learning effects that late adopters can benefit from.[105] In this area two important contributions are those by Inderst, Sartzetakis, and Xepapadeas[106] and by Paha.[107]

Inderst, Sartzetakis, and Xepapadeas examine the incentives of companies to become more sustainable when a first-mover disadvantage exists. Their analysis explores the difference between sustainability situations and the already well-known incentives such as sharing of fixed cost/infrastructure in, for example, R&D. In their study, a demand-side effect is crucial for their outcome. This effect is that social norms shape consumer preferences. It rests on the observation of a significantly decreased willingness to pay for the unsustainable variant of a product when consumers expect that very few other consumers will select the unsustainable option. In their paper, they identify a first-mover disadvantage and show how coordination in terms of sustainability improves overall sustainability outcomes. This improvement occurs when joint action leads to sufficient expansion in the market. Yet, they also show that coordination amongst the firms will decrease sustainability where an expansion of the market is not to be expected. Overall, their policy suggestion is a cautious approach for cases where the sustainability cooperation covers a great part of the market and the market for the sustainable product is not going to increase substantially because of the cooperation. In these situations, first-mover disadvantages are absent, and the individual adoption of more sustainable production should drive other firms to equally improve the sustainability elements of their products.

Paha[108] approaches the first-mover disadvantage from a game theoretic perspective on the prisoners' dilemma. From this point of view, the individual adoption of a sustainability improvement is unprofitable but becomes profitable if both companies adopt it. In such situations, cooperation leads to the pareto efficient adoption of the higher level of sustainability if the following conditions are fulfilled: ie the firms are involved in a repeated game, transparency regarding the sustainability level exists, sanctioning for non-compliance is possible, and the firms' discount factors[109] are sufficiently high. Note that these conditions mirror those that are needed for the establishment and success of price hardcore price cartels.

[105] Examples etc can also be found in Roman Inderst, Eftichios S Sartzetakis, and Anastasios Xepapadeas, 'Firm Competition and Cooperation with Norm-Based Preferences for Sustainability' (2023) 71 *Journal of Industrial Economics* 1038–1071; Johannes Paha, 'Sustainability Agreements and First Mover Disadvantages; (2023) 19(3) *Journal of Competition Law & Economics* 357–366; see also Helen Jenkins, Timo Klein, and Nicole Rosenboom, 'When to Give the Green Light to Green Agreements' *Oxera Agenda* (13 September 2021) available at <https://ssrn.com/abstract=3959762> (accessed 10 January 2025), who point out that such spillover effects might result for example from a better reputation of the entire industry.

[106] Inderst et al, ibid.

[107] Paha (n 105).

[108] ibid.

[109] The level at which the firm values the future.

Overall, in all these cases the extent[110] of the spillover effects is crucial to determining whether coordination increases investment in (sustainability) R&D as compared to R&D investment under competition. In other words, whether coordination or competition encourages (sustainability) R&D more. The overall conclusion is that spillover effects[111] need to be larger than the business-stealing effects that R&D efforts provide in terms of offering the firm a lower marginal cost or a better quality or brand image.

e) Standardization and coopetition

Another area that is highly relevant in the context of sustainability and competition is sustainability standards. As the EU Commission highlights, '[s]ustainability standardisation agreements often have positive effects on competition'.[112] Standard-setting situations are characterized by firms competing and cooperating at the same time, thus they are in a 'coopetitive'[113] relationship. The literature, particularly in the area of business and management studies, has already examined the effects of such standards in greater detail.

Usually, one would expect that the focal firm—the firm with the highest profit margin and market share—will benefit proportionally from any standardization. In other words, this firm will capture a proportional part of any overall increases in total economic benefits whenever a standard is adopted.[114] The firm can however increase its share of the pie by influencing the direction of the standard. Such an increase is to be expected where the firm is able to influence the standard to be adopted in line with its R&D capabilities and technological trajectory.[115] This allows the firm to achieve a comparative cost advantage, or earlier access to the market that is created by the standard.[116] Such an effect can, for example, be observed where a minimum quality standard is adopted and competitors need to

[110] We might also think about combining the demand- (see classical R&D literature) and supply-side (see Iderst et al) effects in this regard.

[111] In other words, the incentive to jointly increase investments in R&D.

[112] European Commission, 'Guidelines on the Applicability of Article 101 of the Treaty on the Functioning of the European Union to Horizontal Co-operation Agreements' [2023] OJ C 259/1 available at <https://eur-lex.europa.eu/legal-content/EN/TXT/PDF/?uri=CELEX:52023XC0721(01)> (accessed 10 January 2025) para 568.

[113] On the concept of a basic idea of a coopetitive relationship and interaction between cooperation and competition, see Maria Bengtsson and Sören Kock, 'Coopetition in Business Networks: To cooperate and Compete Simultaneously' (2000) 29 *Industrial Marketing Management* 411–426; Augustine A Lado, Nancy G Boyd and Susan C Hanlon, 'Competition, Cooperation, and the Search for Economic Rents: A Syncretic Model' (1997) 22(1) *The Academy of Management Review* 110–141.

[114] See eg the foundational work by Melissa Schilling, 'Winning the Standards Race: Building Installed Base and the Availability of Complementary Goods' (1999) 17(3) *European Management Journal* 265–274.

[115] ibid. On the institutional design of such standards and the effects on producers, see Matteo Fiorini and others, 'Institutional Design of Voluntary Sustainability Standards Systems: Evidence from a New Database' (2019) 37(S2) *Development Policy Review* 193–212.

[116] See also Gina Dokko and Lori Rosenkopf, 'Social Capital for Hire? Mobility of Technical Professionals and Firm Influence in Wireless Standards Committees' (2010) 21(3) *Organization Science* 677–695.

increase investment to meet the standard, but the focal firm does not.[117] Such situations typically exist where the standard-setting and innovation are closely intertwined and where the standardization process is designed in ways that allow the focal player to substantially shape the standard's direction.[118]

Thus, the extent to which these findings will equally apply in the sustainability context depends on the way in which the standard-setting process is structured and the extent to which the standard and innovation are intertwined. From a sustainability perspective, sustainability standards have been shown to have a positive effect[119] and a coopetitive relationship with another firm has a positive spillover effect on the focal firm which increases its environmental performance.[120]

f) Summary: economic theory

Overall, the economic theory on the interaction between competition and sustainability reveals a complex picture. On the one hand, the research shows that competition on the sustainability parameter is an important driver for more sustainable market outcomes, in particular where consumers care about the environment. In these situations, the profit-making motive of firms will ensure competition on the level of sustainability. Thus, abolishing competition on sustainability and replacing it with one specific sustainability level, for example, agreed by the different firms, leads to worse outcomes: it replaces the incentive to be better on the sustainability parameter to steal the rival business with one (lower) level of sustainability.

[117] In this way a standard can raise rivals' cost; see Knut Blind, *The Economics of Standards: Theory, Evidence, Policy* (Edward Elgar Publishing 2004); Steven C Salop and David T Scheffman, 'Raising Rivals' Costs' (1983) 73(2) *American Economic Review* 267–271.

[118] See Magnus Johansson and Niklas L Hallberg, 'Standardization as an Organizational Capability: Examples From a Global Player in the Information and Communication Technology Industry' in Kai Jakobs (ed), *Corporate Standardization Management and Innovation* (IGI Global 2019) 47–67.

[119] See in general Magnus Johansson, 'Consensus Based Sustainability Standards and Competitive Advantage – Coopetition on multiple levels' in Julian Nowag (ed), *Research Handbook on Sustainability and Competition Law* (Edward Elgar 2024) 87–103; similarly Francesco Testa and others, 'EMAS and ISO 14001: the Differences in Effectively Improving Environmental Performance' (2014) 68 *Journal of Cleaner Production* 165–173, who studied the effects of the EMAS and ISO 14001 standards on emissions from energy-intensive industry in Italy; Lucila MS Campos and others, 'Environmental Performance Indicators: A Study on ISO 14001 Certified Companies' (2015) 99 *Journal of Cleaner Production* 286–296, who explore the environmental performance of firms adopting ISO 14001 in Brazil; or the literature review by Olivier Boiral and others, 'Adoption and Outcomes of ISO 14001: A Systematic Review' (2018) 20(2) *International Journal of Management Reviews* 411–432. See also Siarhei Manzhynski and Frank Figge, 'Coopetition for Sustainability: Between Organizational Benefit and Societal Good' (2022) 29(3) *Business Strategy and the Environment* 827–837, who examine the different interactions between the use of economic and environmental resources of two coopeting firms and identify combinations of the two and possible trade-offs which can be both intra-firm and inter-firm, as well as intra-resource and inter-resource trade-offs.

[120] Sachin B Modi and David E Cantor, 'How Coopetition Influences Environmental Performance: Role of Financial Slack, Leverage, and Leanness' (2021) 30(7) *Production and Operations Management* 2046–2068. With regard to the potential of coopetition and supply chains, see also Vahid Mirzabeiki, Qile He, and David Sarpong, 'Sustainability-driven Co-opetition in Supply Chains as Strategic Capabilities: Drivers, Facilitators, and Barriers' (2023) 61(14) *International Journal of Production Research* 4826–4852.

On the other hand, we can also identify situations where this logic does not hold. First, there are a few situations where reduced competition can lead to improved sustainability (and consumer welfare): these cases are often related to inputs such as natural resources. Second, the findings that competition increases sustainability are mainly based on a static assessment focusing on the demand side and do not address innovation where free-riding/spillover effects mean that reductions in competition can lead to greater sustainability and innovation. Third, and partly related, the specific interaction between competition and cooperation in a standard-setting context can follow a different logic. Fourth, the findings are based on a number of assumptions, in particular profit-maximization motive and rational behaviour of consumers and firms, which may not be applicable to the same extent in certain sustainability situations. For example, the involvement of individual traders, non-profit companies, charities, and consumer biases may change the outcome. Similarly, the studies are based on the assumption of a linear increase or at least a non-binary nature of sustainability which is often, but not always, the case. Fifth, the studies usually use a model in which competition on sustainability is replaced completely. The majority of studies do not model situations where a joint sustainability level only provides a minimum standard.

2. Economics: practice

While the previous section focused on the theoretical underpinnings of the relationship between competition and sustainability, we shall now turn to more practical questions such as empirical studies on the relationship between competition and sustainability and questions of measuring sustainability benefits in competition law.

a) Empirical studies on sustainability and competition

Elinor Ostrom lays the foundation with her work on sustainable management of common pool resources,[121] for which she received the Nobel Prize in economics in 1993. In a number of case studies, she examined open-access resources such as finishing grounds. She showed how profit maximization in competition leads to disastrous outcomes in such situations.[122] Yet, in the real world, cooperation to achieve sustainable management of that resource can be expected where the competitors form a cohesive group with joint interests.

[121] See Elinor Ostrom, *Governing the Commons: The Evolution of Institutions for Collective Action* (CUP 1990).

[122] On this theme and with a number of cases studies where competition leads to suboptimal outcomes, see Maurice Stucke and Ariel Ezrachi, *Competition Overdose* (Harper Business 2020).

Beyond this, there are a number of empirical studies aimed at exploring the relationship between sustainability and competition. In many cases these look not specifically at sustainability but, for example, at CSR measures. However, before we explore these, it is important to note a caveat. There are a number of different tools that aim to measure competition or competition intensity; the same goes for sustainability. Moreover, correlations between these two should not lead us to quick suggestions of causation. This is so because the 'sustainability level and the concentration in an industry are equilibrium outcomes that are determined by the choices of firms regarding pricing, investments, entry, and exit so that they are correlated but not directly causally related'.[123]

In any case, there are a number of studies that suggest a positive relationship between increases in competition and sustainability outcomes. One study[124] looked at the level of industry concentration and engagement in CSR, and showed that publicly listed companies in less concentrated industries scored higher on the KLD index[125] of CSR and emitted less.[126] A similar study by Flammer showed how industries with foreign competition are associated with higher CSR scores.[127] Other studies seem to have confirmed this result, in particular for the US, and have suggested that CSR is used strategically to differentiate a product where product market competition is high.[128] Looking at forty-eight different countries, Ding, Levine, Lin, and Xie[129] rely on an index that measures the strength of competition[130] and show that more intense competition leads firms to invest more in CSR activities.[131] Moreover, the above-discussed study by Aghion, Bénabou, Martin, and Roulet[132]

[123] See Treuren (n 7) who also points out that similar points are made more generally in the industrial organization literature: see, eg, Nathan Miller and others, 'On The Misuse of Regressions of Price on the HHI in Merger Review' (2022) 10(2) *Journal of Antitrust Enforcement* 248–259.

[124] Daniel Fernández-Kranz and Juan Santálo, 'When Necessity Becomes a Virtue: The Effect of Product Market Competition' (2010) 19 *Journal of Economics and Management Strategy* 453–487.

[125] This independently constructed index by Kinder, Lyndenberg, and Domini measures environmental and social factors to help with investment decisions.

[126] Simon and Price followed up and showed a nearly 2 per cent reduction in pollutants emitted for every percent reduction in an industry's HHI (Herfindahl–Hirschman index), see Daniel Simon and Jeffrey Prince, 'The Effect of Competition on Toxic Pollution Releases (2016) 79 *Journal of Environmental Economics and Management* 40–54.

[127] Caroline Flammer, 'Does Product Market Competition Foster Corporate Social Responsibility? Evidence From Trade Liberalization' (2015) 36 *Strategic Management Journal* 1469–1485.

[128] Daniel Fernández-Kranz and Juan Santaló, 'When Necessity Becomes a Virtue: The Effect of Product Market Competition on Corporate Social Responsibility' (2010) 19 *Journal of Economics & Management Strategy* 453–487. Strategic CSR seems also to influence financial performance: see Pushpika Vishwanathan, Hans van Oosterhout, Pursey Heugens, Patricio Duran, and Marc van Essen, 'Strategic CSR: A Concept Building Meta-Analysis' (2019) 57 *Journal of Management Studies* 314–350.

[129] Wenzhi Ding, Ross Levine, Chen Lin, and Wensi Xie, 'Competition Laws, Norms and Corporate Social Responsibility' Working Paper 27493 (National Bureau of Economic Research, 2020) available at <http://www.nber.org/papers/w27493> (accessed 10 January 2025).

[130] The index they use focuses on competition law in terms of the 'average stringency' of competition law and the strength of associated legal institutions.

[131] They measure the CSR level by relying on the Thomson Reuters ASSET4 ESG database.

[132] Aghion, Bénabou, Martin, and Roulet (n 95).

used the Lerner index,[133] or openness to trade, as a measure to reveal a positive relationship between competition, sustainable innovation, and consumers' state preferences for sustainability. Beyond CSR, Ennis, Gonzaga and Pike show, that market power may be a substantial contributor to wealth inequality in societies, and that pro-competitive policies can reduce inequality.[134]

However, there are also other studies that suggest a more nuanced picture. For example, Hawn and Kang provide possibly contradictory findings for the US. They show, on the one hand, how increased rivalry increases CSR levels of individual firms, where competitors are also engaged in CSR. On the other hand, at an industry level, a higher number of competitors can lead to a reduction in CSR levels. They explain this apparently contradictory result with equilibrium effects. Once competition is overcome and an equilibrium is achieved, CSR levels might be reduced and regress to the status quo.[135] For China, Duanmu, Bu, and Pittman[136] show that in the period between 2000 and 2005, increased competition did not lead companies to use environmental aspects as a factor for differentiation, thereby escaping competition. Instead, the increase in competition had a negative impact on environmental performance, in particular for firms that adopted a cost leadership strategy.

The topic of the environmental performance of firms and its effects on others has also been studied with regard to the size of the firms. Asgharian, Dzieliński, Hashemzadeh, and Liu[137] highlight the importance of focal firms in terms of environmental performance in networks in particular where the industry is consumer-facing and/or highly concentrated. They examined firm networks (supply chains, consumers, partnerships, competitors) of 2,842 firms in fifty one countries over the period 2004–2019 and showed that large firms' environmental performance has strong effects on their networks. Yet in turn they are less affected by the environmental performance of others. The effect was stronger when the market share was larger, the industry was concentrated, or the large company was consumer-facing.

It has also been shown that the early adoption or joining of standards such as the palm oil standard is associated with increased returns.[138]

[133] A measure of the market power of a firm.

[134] Sean Ennis, Pedro Gonzaga, and Chris Pike, 'Inequality: A Hidden Cost of Market Power' (2019) 35 *Oxford Review of Economic Policy* 518–549.

[135] Olga Hawn and Hyoung-Goo Kang, 'The Effect of Market and Nonmarket Competition on Firm and Industry Corporate Social Responsibility' (2018) 38 *Advances in Strategic Management: Sustainability, Stakeholder Governance, and Corporate Social Responsibility* 313–337.

[136] Jing-Lin Duanmu, Maoliang Bu, and Russell Pittman, 'Does Market Competition Dampen Environmental Performance? Evidence from China' 2018 (39) *Strategic Management Journal* 3006–3030.

[137] Hossein Asgharian and others, 'Green Links: Corporate Networks and Environmental Performance' (2021) Working Paper available at <https://ssrn.com/abstract=3999970> (accessed 10 January 2025).

[138] Yeong Sheng Tey , and others, 'Early Mover Advantage in Roundtable on Sustainable Palm Oil Certification: A Panel Evidence of Plantation Companies' (2020) 252 *Journal of Cleaner Production* 119775.

Thus, empirically there is some evidence that seems to suggest that an increase in competition can improve sustainability efforts by firms, although this relationship is not unambiguous. And we can see that larger firms' environmental performance has broader effects on their network.

However, there is also strong evidence that reduced competition increases overall welfare with regard to products that can be compared to some sustainability situations. The effects of competition on alcohol consumption, a product that also produces negative externalities, has been studied extensively. For example, Conlon and Rao[139] examined the effectiveness of different tools in addressing alcohol consumption. They compared restricting competition in the alcohol market by means of post and hold policy[140] to a taxation measure based on the alcohol volume. They find that the reduction in competition would be less effective as companies could adjust by differentiating, eg, between premium and lower-priced drinks. In contrast to these finding, there is a considerable body of literature that suggests a positive effect of alcohol monopolies on public health. It has, for example, been estimated that abandoning the Swedish alcohol monopoly could increase alcohol-related deaths by 35–92 per cent.[141] Other studies of abandoning the alcohol monopoly in Sweden have found similar results.[142] At US state level, the abolition of state monopolies in the 1980s and 1990s has substantially increased the sale of alcohol.[143] Her and others equally highlight in their review paper examining studies on the effects of the abolition of such monopolies that per capital consumption has increased in both the short and long term.[144] Another systematic review of the literature also found strong evidence that privatization increased excessive alcohol consumption.[145]

Overall, the empirical work on sustainability and other products producing negative externalities does not provide us with a consistent picture as to whether more or less competition is beneficial.

[139] Christopher T Conlon and Nirupama Rao, 'The Cost of Curbing Externalities with Market Power: Alcohol Regulations and Tax Alternatives' (January 2023). NBER Working Paper No w30896, available at SSRN: <https://ssrn.com/abstract=4342395> (accessed 10 January 2025).

[140] Such policies are mandated in a number of states and require wholesalers to 'post' a price with the relevant regulator. For the next thirty-day 'hold' period that price is the price at which any retailer can buy from the distributor.

[141] Tim Stockwell and others, 'Estimating the Public Health Impact of Disbanding a Government Alcohol Monopoly: Application of New Methods to the Case of Sweden' (2018) 18(1) *BMC Public Health* 1400.

[142] Thor Norström and others, 'Potential Consequences of Replacing a Retail Alcohol Monopoly with a Private Licence System: Results from Sweden' (2010) 105 *Addiction* 2113–2119.

[143] Alexander C Wagenaar and Harold D Holder, 'Changes in Alcohol Consumption Resulting from the Elimination of Retail Wine Monopolies: Results from Five U.S. States' (1995) 56(5) *Journal of Studies on Alcohol* 566–572.

[144] Minghao Her and others, 'Privatizing Alcohol Sales and Alcohol Consumption: Evidence and Implications' (1999) 94 *Addiction* 1125–1139.

[145] Robert A Hahn and others, 'Effects of Alcohol Retail Privatization on Excessive Alcohol Consumption and Related Harms' (2012) 42(4) *American Journal of Preventive Medicine* 418–427.

b) Measuring sustainability in the context of competition law

The second, more practical, question relates to the measurement of sustainability benefits within the context of competition law. Two things need to be kept in mind before we delve into this question. First, measurement questions are not purely practical questions. They also relate to some theoretical issues in competition economics, as they may change the overall results of the econometric models.[146] For example, results can change depending on how consumer welfare gains and losses are measured. If only the consumer surplus resulting from the direct consumption of the good is measured, the result can be different to measurements that also take into account indirect welfare gains, or even collective gains accrued to the consumer of the product.[147] Moreover, with regard to measurement and its relationship to theory, we should note frequent mismatches between what theory would suggest and what, for example, surveys reveal.[148] Second, competition law and competition economics typically focus on consumer welfare, measured as consumer surplus. Consumer welfare in this regard is typically the welfare of the consumers of the product concerned, not of all consumers or society more generally.

In the following, we will examine first the most common starting point regarding measurement, ie consumers' willingness to pay, and then we will turn to more measurement questions beyond traditional measurements of consumers' willingness to pay.

Consumers have been shown to be willing to pay a higher price for goods such as T-shirts made from organic cotton, even though the use of such cotton does not provide benefits in terms of appearance or touch.[149] Similar results were found with regard to the sale of fair trade coffee in a coffee shop,[150] supermarkets,[151] and more generally eco-labelling.[152] Green labels also seem to increase office rents, although this can possibly be explained at least partly by anticipated potential energy savings by the users.[153] A number of reasons have been suggested for the higher willingness to pay in such situations. They range from intrinsic altruism, social and

[146] Such as those examined under section II. 1.

[147] See in particular further below in this chapter, text to nn 161–177.

[148] Richard T Carson and Theodore Groves, 'Incentive and Informational Properties of Preference Questions' (2007) 37 *Environmental and Resource Economics* 181–210.

[149] Ramon Casadesus-Masanell and others, 'Households' Willingness to Pay for "Green" Goods: Evidence from Patagonia's Introduction of Organic Cotton Sportswear'(2009) 18 *Journal of Economics and Management Strategy* 203–233.

[150] Chris Arnot, Peter C Boxall, and Sean B Cash, 'Do Ethical Consumers Care About Price? A Revealed Preference Analysis of Fair Trade Coffee Purchases' (2006) 54 *Canadian Journal of Agricultural Economics* 555–565.

[151] Jens Hainmueller, Michael J Hiscox, and Sandra Sequeira; 'Consumer Demand for Fair Trade: Evidence from a Multistore Field Experiment' (2015) 97(2) *The Review of Economics and Statistics* 242–256.

[152] Magali Delmas and David Colgan, *The Green Bundle* (Stanford University Press 2018).

[153] Piet Eichholtz, Nils Kok, and John M Quigley, 'Doing Well by Doing Good? Green Office Buildings' (2010) 100 *American Economic Review* 2492–2509.

self-esteem, and material incentives such as tax-benefits,[154] to the general reputation of the firms.[155]

Orthodox[156] competition assessment relies on revealed preferences,[157] in other word, prices to assess the willingness to pay.[158] While there might be questions about the concept of willingness to pay,[159] there are also questions with regard to measuring the willingness to pay by means of prices as revealed preferences. A focus on revealed preferences by means of prices may reflect rather behavioural biases[160] and current social norms which may change as consumers adjust their behaviour in light of their awareness of sustainability implications.[161] These limitations are particularly acute in the context of competition between sustainable and non-sustainable products. This is so because the willingness to pay can be influenced by other consumers' willingness to pay.[162] Moreover, revealed preferences in terms of prices are more difficult to use for evaluating future benefits such as those of innovation.[163] In such cases, stated preferences in the form of surveys might be better suited.[164] In general, environmental economics has developed tools for

154 Roland Bénabou and Jean Tirole, 'Individual and Corporate Social Responsibility' (2010) 77 *Economica* 1–19.

155 See eg Henri Servaes and Ane Tamayo, 'The Impact of Corporate Social Responsibility on Firm Value: The Role of Customer Awareness' (2013) 59(5) *Management Science* 1045–1061; Tom J Brown and Peter A Dacin, 'The Company and the Product: Corporate Associations and Consumer Product Responses' (1997) 61 *Journal of Marketing* 68–84.

156 For alternative approaches see eg Rutger Claassen and Anna Gerbrandy, 'Rethinking European Competition Law: From a Consumer Welfare to a Capability Approach' (2016) 12(1) *Utrecht Law Review* 1–15; Eva van der Zee, 'European Competition Law: Measuring Sustainability Benefits under Article 101 (3) TFEU' in Julian Nowag (ed) *Research Handbook on Sustainability and Competition Law* (Edward Elgar 2024).

157 With regard to using the theory of revealed preferences see also Lianos (n 81) and the foundational work of Paul A Samuelson, 'A Note on the Pure Theory of Consumers' Behaviour' (1938) 5(17) *Economica* 61–71; Paul A Samuelson, 'Consumption Theory in Terms of Revealed Preference' (1950) 15(60) *Economica* 243–253.

158 The advantage here is you can possibly look at historical data on price.

159 The willingness to pay framework seems to assume a consistent (rational) behaviour of the consumer. However, not only is this assumption problematic with regard to behaviour biases but it also seems to neglect conflicting 'preference maps' that humans have, as they act not only as consumers but also as citizens of a society; see Lianos (n 81) 173. In essence, we might identify a mismatch between what consumers do and what the same people (believe) they ought to do from a societal perspective. On this problem see Mark Sagoff, 'Aggregation and Deliberation in Valuing Environmental Public Goods: a Look Beyond Contingent Pricing' (1998) 24(2–3) *Ecological Economics* 213–230. Further details also in section 1.d) on sustainability innovation.

160 See also above text to n 73ff.

161 See also Roman Inderst and Stefan Thomas, 'Reflective Willingness to Pay: Preferences for Sustainable Consumption in a Consumer Welfare Analysis' (2021) 17(4) *Journal of Competition Law & Economics* 848–876.

162 Thus, we might observe a first-mover disadvantage here, as an individual producer is unable to affect a change in behaviour and willingness to pay of the whole consumer cohort, for a detailed assessment of these questions see Roman Inderst, Felix Rhiel, and Stefan Thomas, 'Sustainability Agreements and Social Norms' (2022) 20(3) *Zeitschrift für Wettbewerbsrecht* 225–242.

163 However, there might be options to consider these by for example experiments: see Watson (n 80). She also explores other ways of measurement, such as field experiments, the travel cost method, hedonic pricing.

164 ibid 21ff. In addition, estimated and observed market behaviour differ substantially; see, eg Andy Bartels, Roman Inderst, and Christoph Wentzien, 'Estimation of (Consumer) Sustainability Benefits

valuation. These are designed to be used to value avoided damage or other future benefits. Tools such as contingent valuation[165] and passive use value have been important and were first seen in the famous US *Exxon Valdez* case.[166] The damages case aimed to obtain damages for the oil spill from the sinking of the *Exxon Valdez* tanker at a remote uninhabited area in Alaska. These methods often involve a high level of uncertainty, for example about the extent of the future damage from climate change.[167] Thus, a discount rate will be applied in all competition cases where future benefits will be taken into account. However, in the case of environmental benefits, it is suggested that the discount rate[168] should be lower, to better reflect the effects that are long-term and to account for the possibility of the worst-case scenario materializing.[169]

However, many competition law regimes have not yet endorsed a broad measurement of welfare, but have focused instead on consumer welfare and often on the welfare of the consumers of the product market affected. Scholars have made suggestions[170] on how the sustainability benefits within that framework can be measured. A practical example, although not directly from the sustainability area,[171] is the Dutch *Chicken of Tomorrow*[172] case concerning animal welfare. The agency

from Horizontal Agreements: A Quasi Ex Post Analysis' (2024) 20(3) *Journal of Competition Law & Economics* 228–245, who compare the later observed market prices with the willingness to pay market prices in the Dutch *Chicken of Tomorrow* case.

165 See eg Richard T Carson, 'Contingent Valuation: A Practical Alternative When Prices Aren't Available' (2012) 26(4) *Journal of Economic Perspectives* 27–42.

166 See Richard T Carson and others, 'Contingent Valuation and Lost Passive Use: Damages from the Exxon Valdez Oil Spill' (2003) 25 *Environmental and Resource Economics* 257–286.

167 Geoffrey Heal and Antony Millner, 'Uncertainty and Decision Making in Climate Change Economics' (2014) 8(1) *Review of Environmental Economics and Policy* 120–137.

168 On the debate about the appropriate discount rate in the context of climate change see eg William Nordhaus, 'Critical Assumptions in the Stern Review on Climate Change' (2007) 317 *Science* 201–202; Nicholas Stern and Chris Taylor, 'Climate Change: Risk, Ethics, and the Stern Review' (2007) 317 *Science* 203–204; Martin L Weitzman, 'On Modeling and Interpreting the Economics of Climate Change', (2009) 91 *Review of Economics and Statistics* 1–19.

169 See Stefano Giglio and others, 'Climate Change and Long-Run Discount Rates: Evidence from Real Estate' (2015) National Bureau of Economic Research Working Paper 21767 available at <http://www.nber.org/papers/w21767> (accessed 10 January 2025). For a detailed consideration of different options of discount rates for competition law see Roman Inderst, Eftichios Sartzetakis, and Anastasios Xepapadeas, *Technical Report on Sustainability and Competition* (Netherlands Authority for Consumers and Markets (ACM) and the Hellenic Competition Commission (HCC) 2021) available at <https://www.acm.nl/sites/default/files/documents/technical-report-sustainability-and-competition_0.pdf> (accessed 10 January 2025).

170 For an overview of the different possibilities to account for broader social benefits and taking into account future generations, see Inderst, Sartzetakis, and Xepapadeas (n 169).

171 Sustainability focuses on environmental protection, social and economic development so that animal welfare is only tangentially related.

172 See ACM, 'ACM's Analysis of the Sustainability Arrangements Concerning the "*Chicken of Tomorrow*"' (2014) ACM/DM/2014/206028, available at <https://www.acm.nl/sites/default/files/old_publication/publicaties/13789_analysis-chicken-of-tomorrow-acm-2015-01-26.pdf.pdf> (accessed 10 January 2025); see also the discussion of the case in Chapter 4, section IV, 2.a).

used a cost-benefit analysis[173] based on consumer surveys and a willingness to pay analysis, where the aim was to compare the price increase with the increase in animal welfare as valued by the consumers.[174] Suggestions have been made to adjust the measurement of consumers' willingness to pay to account for non-use value by applying conjoint analysis and contingent valuation, thereby adding to the measurement of consumer welfare.[175] However, in any such survey, the design and context provided are crucial, in particular with regard to the non-use value of goods.[176] Moreover, some changes with regard to the prospective welfare analysis, which aims to estimate the future benefits, have been suggested, which should ensure the assessment accounts for future changes in consumers' willingness to pay and the broader awareness of sustainability implications.[177] Overall, in practice, it is also worth exploring trade-offs between accuracy and the cost of implementing the methods to quantify sustainability benefits.[178]

c) Summary: economics—practice

The empirical studies and the questions of measurement provide important practical insights into the relationship between competition and economics. In general, the empirical studies seem to support the view that *if* consumers value sustainability, competition can be an important driver for more sustainable market outcomes. We might speculate that the more informed and aware consumers are about the sustainability impacts of their choices, the more competition will drive the market in more sustainable directions. However, whether more or less competition is helpful when products produce negative externalities is less clear. For measuring the sustainability benefits incurred by the consumer, some more advanced measurement tools would need to be employed. These go beyond revealed preferences expressed in the prices of the goods and include state preferences on the willingness to pay to capture not only the use value but also the non-use value that consumers derive.

173 For a description in Dutch see Machiel Mulder and others, 'Economische Effecten van "*Kip van Morgen*"' (2014) available at <https://www.acm.nl/nl/publicaties/publicatie/13759/Onderzoek-ACM-naar-de-economische-effecten-van-de-Kip-van-Morgen> (accessed 10 January 2025). For a summary in English, see Jan Peter van der Veer, *Blogpost* (18 February 2015) available at <http://competitionlawblog.kluwercompetitionlaw.com/2015/02/18/valuing-sustainability-the-acms-analysis-of-chicken-for-tomorrow-under-art-1013/> (accessed 10 January 2025).

174 For a critique of this methodology see, eg, Giorgio Monti and Jotte Mulder, 'Escaping the Clutches of EU Competition Law: Pathways to Assess Private Sustainability Initiatives' (2017) 42(5) *European Law Review* 635–656.

175 Roman Inderst and Stefan Thomas, 'Integrating Benefits from Sustainability into the Competitive Assessment—How Can We Measure Them?' (2021) 12(9) *Journal of European Competition Law & Practice* 705–709.

176 Watson (n 80) 17–20; See also Inderst and Thomas (n 161).

177 Inderst and Thomas (n 161).

178 See Adina Claici and Jasper Lutz, 'Beyond the Policy Debate: How to Quantify Sustainability Benefits in Competition Cases: Lessons Learned from Environmental Economics' (2021) 5(3) *European Competition & Regulatory Law Review* 200–209.

3. Summary: economics in theory and in practice

Having explored the interaction between competition and sustainability from a theoretical and practical standpoint, we can summarize the findings as follows. The models on the interaction between competition and sustainability expose a complex picture where competition often has a positive impact on sustainability outcomes. Yet, in some situations less competition achieves superior outcomes. But these theoretical insights gained from models are based on a number of assumptions that might not hold in the real world, so a closer examination of the realities in individual cases is advisable. From the practical side, we may deduce that where consumers care about sustainability—which they increasingly do—the empirical studies support the view that competition on this parameter leads to better sustainability outcomes. However, to measure the full benefits for consumers we need to update our tools. This update will mean that we will have to rely more often upon questionnaires rather than observations of the prices in the market.

III. Delivering sustainability: states vs markets

In the previous section, we explored how competition can foster sustainability and how, on occasion, restrictions of competition seem to provide superior outcomes in terms of sustainability. In this section, we will briefly look at the role of the state versus markets and companies in achieving a more sustainable world. The first part will look briefly at ways in which the state might foster competition that in turn leads to improvements of sustainability. The second part will question whether and to what extent the state, with its array of tools, is better placed to achieve sustainability as compared to firms.

1. States fostering sustainability outcomes by improving competition: competition policy and other legal tools

The state can be active at different levels to achieve more sustainable market outcomes. It can do so for example by means of subsidies, tax law, or competition law.[179]

A primary way the state might foster sustainability by improving or altering competition is through the provision of finance and other forms of subsidies and aid that should encourage firms to act in more sustainable manners.[180] For

[179] On the use of competition law to foster sustainability see in particular Chapter 2.

[180] See for example the EU's rule on state aid: EU Commission, 'Guidelines on State Aid for Climate, Environmental Protection and Energy 2022' [2022] OJ C 80/1.

example, Lenox and Chatterji[181] explore the crucial importance of collaboration between different levels of government and the private sector in achieving green innovation.

At the same time, rules and regulations in certain parts of the economy might also be set up in ways that prevent, for instance, subsistence farmers and other small and microbusinesses from entering markets or that prevent consumers from making more sustainable choices. This is where competition advocacy might come into play.[182] While there are a handful of studies that aim to evaluate competition advocacy in general,[183] competition advocacy and its interaction with sustainable development have not been studied. However, some competition agencies have aligned their advocacy focus with national development goals.[184]

Another tool that is often thought of as a primary tool well suited to foster sustainability is tax law. Tax law can be used to address matters such as poverty reduction and social equality, environmental pollution,[185] or more generally distributional concerns.[186] A different form to implement such a tax on pollution is a cap-and-trade system, such as an emissions trading system.[187] However, with regard to climate change, it is clear that from a practical point of view, tax law alone can hardly solve the problem. Given the amount of time that has passed, the reduction in CO2 emissions through taxes alone will not be enough to address climate change; instead, the focus has to be on 'eliminat[ing] CO2 emissions entirely,

[181] Aaron Chatterji and Michael Lenox, *Can Business Save The Earth? Innovating Our Way To Sustainability* (Stanford University Press 2018).

[182] On advocacy see, eg, Irina Knyazeva, 'Competition Advocacy: Soft Power in Competitive Policy' (2013) 6 *Procedia Economics and Finance* 280–287; or the OECD's Competition Assessment Toolkit that helps states to assess their laws and regulations, available at <https://www.oecd.org/daf/competition/assessment-toolkit.htm> (accessed 10 January 2025).

[183] For one of the few attempts see Carmen Suarez, 'Evaluation of Competition Advocacy to Government: Assessing the Impact of Influencing Policy-Makers' (2011) 7(1) *Competition Law International* 56–61.

[184] See Leni Papa and Raya Teston, 'Competition Policy, Poverty, Inequality: The Philippine Experience' in Julian Nowag (ed), *Research Handbook on Sustainability and Competition Law* (Edward Elgar 2024) 500–517.

[185] With regard to the limits of tax law in terms achieving environmental sustainability see Mariya Senyk, 'What Tax Law Can and Cannot do for Sustainability with a Focus on Environmental Sustainability in the EU Context' in Julian Nowag (ed), *Research Handbook on Sustainability and Competition Law* (Edward Elgar 2024) 265–283.

[186] Steven Shavell, 'A Note of Efficiency vs. Distributional Equity in Legal Rulemaking: Should Distributional Equity Matter given Optimal Income Taxation?' (1981) 71(2) *The American Economic Review* 414–418; Louis Kaplow and Steven Shavell 'Why the Legal System Is Less Efficient than the Income Tax in Redistributing Income' (1994) 23(2) *The Journal of Legal Studies* 667–681; Louis Kaplow, 'On the Choice of Welfare Standards in Competition Law', Harvard Law and Economics Discussion Paper 693 (2011) available at <http://www.law.harvard.edu/programs/olin_center/papers/pdf/Kaplow_693.pdf> (accessed 10 January 2025); this is sometimes broadened further to cover, eg, corporate governance, employment law, education policies, and in general, public spending; see Carl Shapiro, 'Antitrust in a Time of Populism' (2018) 61 *International Journal of Industrial Organization* 714–748.

[187] On the effectiveness of emissions trading in reducing carbon emissions, see eg Hail Jung and Chang-Keun Song, 'Effects of Emission Trading Scheme (ETS) on Change Rate of Carbon Emission' (2023) 13 *Scientific Reports* 912.

[... and there] the greatest barriers are associated with infrastructure and institutions'.[188] In other words, it seems simply 'too late to rely solely on' traditional regulation and taxes to address the climate change issue.[189]

Nonetheless, the economic argument in this regard is that tax law is better at achieving these objectives than competition law. Or in other words, the transfer of wealth between different members of a society is not the task of competition law but of tax law.

However, as Zac shows, there is a fundamental difference between competition law and other policies—such as tax law—that makes competition law sometimes better suited.[190] He posits that the thesis of the superior efficiency of tax and other policies over competition is based on two assumptions.[191] The first one is that the (tax) system will be used in an efficient way to address the distributional concern.[192] Yet, the empirical evidence[193] seems to suggest that greater inequality leads to less redistribution. Moreover, regulatory competition might prevent redistribution[194] or even lead to a race to the bottom.[195] The second one is embedded in the tax substitution argument.[196] This argument assumes that taxation leads to work–leisure distortions but that other forms of regulation not only lead to work–leisure distortions but also lead to further distortions, such as care-level distortions[197] in the case of torts. Thus, the combined distortion will always be higher than pure work–leisure distortions of taxation. Yet, the tax substitution argument seems to

[188] Anthony Patt and Johan Lilliestam, 'The Case Against Carbon Price' [2018] *Joule* 2, 2487–2510.

[189] Maurits Dolmans, 'The "Polluter Pays" Principle as a Basis for Sustainable Competition Policy' in Simon, Martijn Snoep, and Dirk Middelschulte (eds), *Competition Law & Environmental Sustainability* (Concurrences 2020) 21.

[190] Amit Zac, 'Competition Law and Economic Inequality' (PhD thesis, University of Oxford 2022).

[191] ibid 49–59.

[192] He points to the median voter hypothesis by Joel Slemrod and Jon Bakija, 'Does Growing Inequality Reduce Tax Progressivity? Should It?' (2000) National Bureau of Economic Research Working Paper Series—Working Paper 7576 available at <http://www.nber.org/papers/w7576> (accessed 10 January 2025); Lars-Erik Borge and Jørn Rattsø, 'Income Distribution and Tax Structure: Empirical Test of the Meltzer–Richard Hypothesis' (2004) 48(4) *European Economic Review* 805–826 which suggests that the middles classes would benefit at the expense of the richest and poorest.

[193] See Filipe R Campante, 'Redistribution in a Model of Voting and Campaign Contributions' (2011) 95(7–8) *Journal of Public Economics* 646–656; Konstantinos Matakos and Dimitrios Xefteris, 'Divide and Rule: Redistribution in a Model with Differentiated Candidates' (2017) 63(4) *Economic Theory* 867–902; Brian Kelleher Richter, Krislert Samphantharak, and Jeffrey F Timmons, 'Lobbying and Taxes' (2009) 53(4) *American Journal of Political Science* 893–909; Martin Ardanaz and Carlos Scartascini, 'Inequality and Personal Income Taxation: The Origins and Effects of Legislative Malapportionment' (2013) 46(12) *Comparative Political Studies* 1636–1663.

[194] John Douglas Wilson, 'Theories of Tax Competition' [1999] *National Tax Journal* 269–304; see also with regard to environmental law and sustainability Hans Vedder, 'To Take to Sea in a Sieve: Environmental Law and Competition' in Julian Nowag (ed), *Research Handbook on Sustainability and Competition Law* (Edward Elgar 2024) 284–301.

[195] George R Zodrow and Peter Mieszkowsk, 'Pigou, Tiebout, Property Taxation, and the Underprovision of Local Public Goods' (1986) 19(3) *Journal of Urban Economics* 356–370.

[196] See literature in n 186.

[197] For the care level distortion see eg Hans-Bernd Schäfer and Claus Ott, *The Economic Analysis of Civil Law* (Edward Elgar 2022).

make a questionable assumption that a regulatory regime only creates costs.[198] This assumption readily explains why the tax system is seen as more efficient. However, it has been shown that where market participants react heterogeneously[199] to the new regulatory regime, the core results of the tax substitution argument seem to fall apart. The question is thus not one of comparing the overall efficiency of a tax measure versus other regulatory tools. Instead, it is an optimization problem based on relative effectiveness. People will decide based on the combination of the incentives created by taxation and those created by other regulatory tools. This combination determines the overall efficiency.[200] Based on these insights, Zac develops a theory that foresees a different role for competition law than taxation. He suggests the competition law and its enforcement have a specific role to play at the pre-distribution stage that is the allocation of resources before taxation. Taxation, then, has a role to play in redistribution once the gains from economic transactions have been realized.[201]

Overall, we can say that competition policy can contribute to sustainability. This result can be achieved by focusing on certain areas where barriers to competition prevent more sustainable outcomes or more generally by enforcing competition law as a pre-distributive tool. However, the way this is achieved in practice is very much dependent on how an agency uses the tools explored in Chapters 3 and 4, and more generally how it uses the enforcement toolbox as explored in Chapter 5.

2. States vs firms reducing competition to achieve sustainable outcomes

Previously, we have examined how firms might restrict competition which in turn may, or may not, improve sustainability outcomes. However, not only firms can restrict competition. States more commonly restrict certain forms of competition to ensure public benefits. In this section, we will explore the comparative effectiveness of states and firms in achieving sustainability where they restrict competition. We will examine this question as there is a very valid argument to be made that states are better placed to achieve sustainability aims compared to firms in particular in light of their regulatory and enforcement powers, as compared to restrictions of

[198] For a detailed discussion see Chris William Sanchirico, 'Taxes versus Legal Rules as Instruments for Equity: A More Equitable View' (2000) 29(2) *The Journal of Legal Studies* 797–820.

[199] Because some people might outsource their duty of care and thus create income possibilities for others.

[200] Sanchirico (n 198) 804–805.

[201] See Zac (n 190); see also Amit Zac, 'Pre-Distribution vs Re-Distribution: Why Competition Law Is much more than a Tool to Alleviate Poverty' in Julian Nowag (ed), *Research Handbook on Sustainability and Competition Law* (Edward Elgar 2024) 121–138; Amit Zac, 'Competition Law and Economic Inequality: A Comparative Analysis of the US Model of Law' (2022) 25(3) *Journal of International Economic Law* 484–500.

competition by firms 'regulating' the market.[202] The core of this argument is that state regulation is the answer to problems with regard to sustainability issues. Some have linked this idea back to Ronald Coase's work on externalities[203] and how the state needs to step in with property rights to allow private parties to interact based on these rights.[204] We can also see the argument mirrored in the famous Friedman argument that firms should only be concerned with maximizing their profit.[205] This maximization would ensure that the pie becomes bigger, and the government would then decide how to allocate the pie.

This claim is certainly well-founded in economic theory. Where we assume that government is perfect, we could expect the following:[206] if prices go up, demand will be reduced. It does not matter whether this increase in price results from a tax or regulation, or whether the price increase is the result of a cartel. The major difference is that in the cartel case, the profit margins of the firms will also increase. Thus, it makes producing the harmful goods, although produced in reduced numbers, more profitable. A result that seems rather counterproductive. It is, hence, not surprising that taxes on unsustainable products have been shown to drive demand for more sustainable products.[207] This theoretical insight is also backed up by some empirical work. Conlon and Rao show that taxes are more effective in curbing alcohol consumption.[208] The opposite conclusion is reached by the already discussed paper by Huric Larsen and Münch[209] who suggest a cartel would be more effective in curbing pollution than taxes or state support for green innovation.

In the theoretical ideal world, states are omnipotent. They impose laws and enforce them at will. However, the real world often provides a different picture. In competition economics and law, the assumption is often that regulation by the state would be superior to private action. However, this is not necessarily the case. We need to consider whether, for example, traditional command and control tools of environmental law are efficient.[210] Thus, we need to assess the effectiveness and

[202] Instead of many see eg Cento Veljanovski, 'Why the Case for a Sustainable Competition Law is Exaggerated' in Julian Nowag (ed), *Research Handbook on Sustainability and Competition Law* (Edward Elgar 2024) 211–234 or Treuren (n 7).

[203] Ronald H Coase, 'The Problem of Social Costs' (1960) 3 *The Journal of Law & Economics* 1.

[204] Veljanovski (n 202).

[205] Milton Friedman, 'The Social Responsibility of Business is to Increase its Profits' *The New York Times Magazine* (13 Sept 1970) available at <https://www.nytimes.com/1970/09/13/archives/a-friedman-doctrine-the-social-responsibility-of-business-is-to.html> (accessed 10 January 2025).

[206] Treuren (n 7).

[207] See Daron Acemoglu and others, 'The Environment and Directed Technical Change' (2012) 102(1) *American Economic Review* 131–166; Philippe Aghion and others, 'Carbon Taxes, Path Dependency, and Directed Technical Change: Evidence from the Auto Industry' (2016) 124(1) *Journal of Political Economy* 1–51.

[208] Christopher Conlon and Nirupama Rao, 'The Cost of Curbing Externalities with Market Power: Alcohol Regulations and Tax Alternatives' National Bureau of Economic Research Working Paper 30896 (2023) available at <https://www.nber.org/papers/w30896> (accessed 10 January 2025).

[209] See above text to n 43.

[210] For an overview see Daniel H Cole and Peter Z Grossman, 'When is Command-and-Control Efficient? Institutions, Technology, and the Comparative Efficiency of Alternative Regulatory Regimes for Environmental Protection' [1999] *Wisconsin Law Review* 887–938.

efficiency of government action in comparison to private action in the form of self-regulation while considering questions of government failure. Beyond legislation specifically foreseeing self-regulation,[211] we can imagine numerous failures. In any state, the lawmakers might feel they possess too little understanding of an issue to regulate, they might not have the relevant time to regulate each and every matter, or they are prevented from regulating by special interest lobbying[212] or by concerns about how competition might be affected.[213] Moreover, in particular in developing countries, capacity is a major issue.[214] So even where a developing country has a law on the books, it might not be enforced in reality. This difference between law and reality in developing countries can be attributed to a number of reasons ranging from expertise, funding of enforcement agencies, and corruption,[215] to cases where some parts of the state territory are not under the effective control of law enforcement—for example, under the control by guerrillas. Finally, in the context of transnational environmental problems, it has long been accepted that the state alone is hardly able to deliver effective regulation.[216]

Where we face 'imperfect' or weak government(s), for example, because of enforcement issues, private parties and thus private standards might be seen as replacing state regulation.[217] However, there is limited economic research that compares the effectiveness and efficiency of states with private actors generally or firms more specifically in cases of imperfect/weak government. Yet, some insights from the studies of industry codes of conduct suggest that states can be effective in addressing sustainability challenges.[218] Further complications are observed in the competition between voluntary sustainability standards and domestic public policies. Van and Barnes' case study on soybean farming in Brazil, palm oil production in Indonesia, and pangasius aquaculture in Vietnam shows that public and private governance went through competition before ending in a state of reluctant

[211] For an example of such a regulatory approach, see the European Commission, 'A European Strategy for Plastics in a Circular Economy' (2018) COM(2018)28 Final, which suggests that beyond regulation, private collaboration by industry should play a major role.

[212] See Giorgio Monti, 'Four Options for a Greener Competition Law' (2020) 11(3–4) *Journal of European Competition Law & Practice* 124.

[213] See Vedder (n 194).

[214] See eg Michael G Faure, 'Enforcement Issues for Environmental Legislation in Developing Countries' UNU/INTECH Working Paper No 19 (1995) available at <https://archive.unu.edu/hq/library/Collection/PDF_files/INTECH/INTECHwp19.pdf> (accessed 10 January 2025).

[215] Eg with regard to the value chain of palm oil and the related issues of overlapping jurisdictions, enforcement, and private standard-setting, see Pablo Pacheco and others, 'Governing Sustainable Palm Oil Supply: Disconnects, Complementarities, and Antagonisms Between State Regulations and Private Standards' (2020) 14 *Regulation & Governance* 568–598.

[216] See eg Veerle Heyvaert, *Transnational Environmental Regulation and Governance* (CUP 2018).

[217] With regard to the effect of different sustainability standards on poverty alleviation for coffee producers in Ethiopia, see for example Fikadu Mitiku and others, 'Do Private Sustainability Standards Contribute to Income Growth and Poverty Alleviation? A Comparison of Different Coffee Certification Schemes in Ethiopia' (2017) 9 *Sustainability* 246

[218] For an overview and case studies see, eg, Virginia Haufler, *A Public Role for the Private Sector: Industry Self-Regulation in a Global Economy* (Brookings Institution Press 2013).

complementarity.[219] They argue that the tension is caused by governments' needs to maintain export markets for their goods, instead of goal alignment. Moreover, there are suggestions that too much competition in sustainability standards hampers access for producers in developing countries. Montiel, Christmann, and Zink identify that diversity and dynamism of customer requirements, together with the unpredictability of standards, have deterred firms from following any sustainability standards.[220] However, even taking account of these complications, still little is known in terms of comparing imperfect government action to self-regulation or competition.

Thus, a model that compares the effectiveness and efficiency of state regulation versus self-regulation[221] in a situation where the government is close to perfect will most likely come to different outcome than a model that accounts for an imperfect government. Overall, we might suggest that the further away the state is from the ideal, the more difficult and context-specific the comparison between the effectiveness and efficiency of state regulation versus self-regulation becomes.

3. Summary—states vs markets

In this section, we have explored the interaction between the state and firms in fostering sustainability. We have seen that states have numerous tools in their policy toolbox to foster competition, which in turn improves sustainability outcomes. This can range from classical forms of regulation, taxation, or financial support, competition advocacy concerning entry barriers, to the enforcement of competition law as a pre-distributive tool. Moreover, we have examined the limitations of state action where restrictions of competition might produce more sustainable outcomes and asked whether in such situations firms' self-regulation might be more effective and efficient. Where the government is assumed to be perfect, restrictions of competition by the state seem to be superior to firms restricting competition.

[219] Ven Hamish and David Barmes, 'The Uneasy Marriage of Private Standards and Public Policies for Sustainable Commodity Governance' (2023) 32(8) *Business Strategy and the Environment* 5161–5173.

[220] Montiel Iva, Petra Christmann, and Trevor Zink. 'The Effect of Sustainability Standard Uncertainty on Certification Decisions of Firms in Emerging Economies' (2019) 154(3) *Journal of Business Ethics* 667–681.

[221] We know that companies might be incentivized to adopt self-regulation where government regulation may be forthcoming, see eg Stefan Lutz, Thomas Lyon, and John Maxwell, 'Quality Leadership when Regulatory Standards are Forthcoming' (2000) 48 *Journal of Industrial Economics* 331–348; Na Li Dawson and Kathleen Segerson, 'Voluntary Agreements with Industries: Participation Incentives with Industry-wide Targets' (2008) 84 *Land Economics* 97–114. However, it should be noted that self-regulation can also be used strategically to prevent more stringent state rules: see Neil Gunningham and Joseph Reece 'Industry Self-Regulation: An Institutional Perspective' (1997) 19(4) *Law & Policy*, 363–414.

IV. Conclusion

In this chapter, we explored the relationship between sustainability and competition. In the first part, we gathered insights from economic theory and those related to the more practical aspects of competition and sustainability. From a theoretical perspective, competition and sustainability often have a positive relationship, in other words an increase in competition leads to sustainability improvements. This in particular is the case when consumers value sustainability sufficiently highly. However, there are also instances where less competition fosters sustainability. For example, in cases where agreements concern inputs such as natural resources. Moreover, the majority of studies do not model situations where a joint sustainability level only provides a minimum standard, which may impact their findings. Hence the overall picture is in fact a complex one. The complexity is further increased by the assumptions used in the theoretical works which may not apply in real-world scenarios. Assumptions of profit-maximization and rational behaviour of consumers and firms are some examples that complicate the real-world application of the relevant models.

Nonetheless, to a certain extent, the theoretical finding of improved sustainability levels through competition are supported by insights from practice. There are a number of empirical studies that support the view that, where consumers value sustainability, competition leads to better sustainability outcomes, as it becomes one parameter of competition. However, studies on competition and alcohol consumption-related public health suggest that less competition is beneficial. Notwithstanding, the measurement of sustainability benefits in the competition law and economics worlds can be updated. This update will involve a greater reliance on questionnaires.

In the second part of the chapter, we compared the role of the state to that of firms in promoting sustainability. In particular, we compared state action with actions taken by private parties. First, we explored state tools such as taxation, financial support, regulation, competition advocacy, and the enforcement of competition law as a pre-distributive tool. The tools provide states with important levers to promote sustainability outcomes. Then, we turned our attention to comparing state action that restricts competition to firms restricting competition. In that area, we saw that in models where the government is assumed to be perfect, restrictions imposed by the state are superior to those imposed by firms. Unfortunately, there are virtually no studies that compare the effectiveness in scenarios where government effectiveness is less than perfect.

Overall, when studying the economics of sustainability and competition, three interrelated variables emerge: state regulation, competition, and cooperation/market power, or more broadly speaking, monopoly. The optional solution to any sustainability and competition problem lies in the interplay between these variables. The challenge is to strike the right balance between these three spheres to provide optimal outcomes. In any case, thorough case-by-case assessment is needed where the questions need to be: what is the best path to delivering the sustainability improvement? In other words, individual assessment of the relationship between state tools and market forces, and cooperation versus competition, is needed. Any such case-based assessment needs to take account of the limitations of the current models in terms of their assumptions.[222]

Felipe and the world of sustainability

When Felipe's focus group reports back to the board, it highlights how sustainability has become a parameter of competition between companies and thus might provide opportunities for the firm's development.

They also note how sustainability and resource efficiency overlap with productive and dynamic efficiency while at the same time providing possible advantages in terms of financing and staff employment.

In particular, sustainability innovation has been identified as one area where there should be an increased focus. Questions about whether these matters should be pursued individually by the firm or whether it would make sense and be cheaper to cooperate with other firms and competitors should be decided on an ad hoc basis.

Crucial here will be an investigation of the customer base. Where customers are willing to pay sufficiently more for sustainability, the company could develop a competitive advantage. Where customers are not willing to pay sufficiently for sustainability, cooperation might be a better way forward. A similar investigation can be made with regard to potential employees. Where they value sustainability, sustainability efforts might pay off in terms of recruitment and wages. Yet, Felipe's in-house lawyer raises questions regarding cooperation with competitors, as the firm would need to ensure compliance with antitrust laws.

[222] Such as the discussed assumption of rational profit maximization, consumers' valuation of sustainability, consumer biases, or limitations of government actions.

3
Competition authorities as guardians of sustainability

Amahle and Junior and the price of bread

Amahle and Junior had been through a lot, but they had each other, and now their newborn son, as they lived in a small makeshift settlement on the outskirts of a mid-sized city in South Africa.

While Amahle had a small job in a supermarket in a richer part of the city, Junior helped out as a day labourer, working on farms whenever he could to make ends meet. He was not always lucky to get a job. But his skills enabled him to plant some vegetables behind their hut that provided some welcome variety and additional nutrients to their daily meals which relied heavily on the bread that Amahle bought on her way home from work.

In recent months, they realized that their household budget was not adding up. Consequently, towards the end of every month, they had to borrow some money from their neighbour Melokuhle. They realized that they had to do something to improve their finances, as bread had become quite a bit more expensive. They pondered different options; inter alia, they considered:

(1) They could either continue to borrow money in the hope things would get better. They could replace their gas-stove with a wood-fired one, with Junior going to the nearby woods to source firewood they could use. He would do so on the days that he did not find paid work as a day labourer on the farms around them. Any excess wood would be sold to their neighbours; or

(2) they could get rid of their vegetable plantings and replace them with maize. In this way, they could replace much of their bread with mieliepap (maize porridge), which Amahle could prepare for the week on her day off.

Amahle and Junior's predicament has its source in the increase in the price of one of their staple foods: bread. In their case, this increase leads to financial problems which they try to counter with different rational strategies.

However, these rational strategies in turn lead to some substantial knock-on effects in other parts of their lives and for society.

Global Antitrust and Sustainability. Julian Nowag, Oxford University Press. © Julian Nowag 2025.
DOI: 10.1093/9780191955013.003.0003

For example, Junior's collection of firewood may exacerbate deforestation. At the same time, the family will most likely be exposed to more pollutants from the woodfire. Similarly, replacing vegetables with maize leads to a less varied diet and associated negative health effects. It might also lead to more 'housework' for women in preparing the food, as mieliepap is often prepared by women. Overall, the family will have fewer opportunities to spend time on more meaningful endeavours, as they now face spending time collecting wood and preparing mieliepap and, in general, one might expect less well-being for all involved.

All this, in the end, results from the price increase in bread, which in turn might be due to reduced competition.

I. Introduction

Can competition law help in the strive towards a more sustainable world for Amahle and Junior? A world without poverty, deforestation, malnutrition, and bad health. How can the enforcement of competition law foster sustainability? Or in other words, to what extent can competition law act as a sword in the fight for sustainability so that competition authorities also become guardians of sustainability?

In this chapter, we explore cases where competition agencies can act as guardians of sustainability by enforcing competition law. This applies particularly in situations where competition is good for sustainability and highlights the importance of parameters of competition in attaining sustainability. Put differently, we explore the role that competition law and authorities can play in ensuring that competition delivers the best results for sustainability. This builds on the previous chapter, in which we explored the interaction between competition and sustainability from an economic perspective and highlighted cases where competition is good for sustainability. This chapter provides us with cases from around the world where sustainability is best achieved by competition enforcement because competitive markets are able to deliver the best in terms of sustainability, be that in the environmental or social dimension of sustainability. In this regard, the chapter shows the overlap between sustainability and competition and provides a number of options that competition enforcers can pick and choose from. These can then be adjusted to their own legal requirements and allow the enforcer to act as guardians of sustainability by protecting competition.

We will explore this interaction between competition and sustainability in eight different parts. After this short introduction, we will briefly highlight the main takeaways from Chapter 2, explaining the situations in which competition is good for sustainability. The subsequent sections are organized in an expanding fashion. We will see in section III how orthodox competition law enforcement might still create positive, but coincidental, sustainability improvements. Moving on, we will uncover less and less orthodox approaches to the subject and reveal how they push the boundaries of competition law.

In section IV, we will encounter the first expansion of orthodox competition enforcement. We will explore targeted enforcement actions that have intended positive spillover effects on sustainability. While this section might still be explained by means of orthodox competition enforcement, section V starts to push the boundaries of orthodoxy. In this fifth section, we will focus in particular on cases where sustainability has become part of the competition parameters. In other words, situations where sustainability interacts with traditional parameters of competition such as quality, choice, or price. Section VI shows us how the boundaries of the competition analysis might be pushed even further, so far as to pursue sustainability directly by means of antitrust enforcement.

Before concluding this chapter, we will have a final look at the risks and associated limits of expanding competition law to pursue sustainability, helping us appreciate why different aspects of the interaction between competition law enforcement and sustainability are more or less controversial.

II. When is competition good for sustainability?

As we have already discussed in Chapter 2, there is an overlap between sustainability and traditional parameters of competition such as productive and dynamic efficiency, and thereby the orthodox notion of consumer welfare. In other words, productive efficiency and dynamic efficiency are essential features for achieving sustainability. Moreover, as consumers value sustainability,[1] companies will also compete with regard to the sustainability of their products. The intensity of competition might depend on consumers' valuation of sustainability and their willingness to pay for it. And while these two factors might differ between consumers,[2] it seems a fair hypothesis that a consumer would prefer the more sustainable product in the case of two otherwise identical ones where they are offered at the same price.

We can therefore deduce that competition can foster sustainability. Competition authorities can foster sustainability by ensuring that competition can deliver a more sustainable outcome. Thus, antitrust provisions are enforced against restrictive practices that hamper competition which would lead to more sustainability. As we explore below, this can take the form of protecting the traditional parameters of competition—choice, quality, and innovation. In such situations the effects on sustainability can be coincidental or the result of deliberate enforcement

[1] See, eg, Sungchul Choi and Alex Ng, 'Environmental and Economic Dimensions of Sustainability and Price Effects on Consumer Responses' (2011) 104 *Journal of Business Ethics* 269–282.

[2] On the level of consumers' willingness to pay for sustainability see, eg, the studies by GFK available at <https://www.marketingcharts.com/industries/cpg-and-fmcg-76738> (accessed 17 January 2025) and McKinsey available at <https://www.mckinsey.com/business-functions/sustainability/our-insights/how-much-will-consumers-pay-to-go-green> (accessed 17 January 2025).

targeted at practices that restrict competition over sustainability parameters. In particular, in the latter cases, we will explore how far theories of harm can be pushed to protect competition and sustainability. In the final section, we will explore the more controversial situations that go beyond the traditional theories and target unsustainable business practices more directly.

III. Competition enforcement and coincidental sustainability improvements

Where competition authorities focus on the traditional parameters of choice, quality, and innovation and enforce antitrust rules, we can observe that antitrust intervention which increases competition can coincidentally promote sustainability, as a by-product or spillover of day-to-day enforcement activity. Yet, the coincidental effects on sustainability can also be the result of deliberate choices made by the competition authorities. For example, they might choose to focus enforcement efforts[3] on an area of the economy that is crucial from the perspective of sustainability. In this sub-section, we will focus on both situations. First, we will explore the coincidental effect in merger cases, often an area where competition authorities do not set properties but rather deal with cases that land on their desk. Second, we will look at cases where coincidental effects may have been intended or where competition authorities specifically target areas that have an effect on sustainability.

Coincidental spillover effects on sustainability can occur in cases that seem rather decided along orthodox lines and where the reasoning may not even suggest a relation to sustainability.[4] An obvious example might be intervention in the renewable energy area.[5] In the case of such interventions, the increased or maintained competition after the antitrust intervention coincidentally leads to increased sustainability.[6] Merger cases like *Panasonic/Sanyo* might be an example of an intervention with coincidental spillover effects on sustainability.[7]

[3] The issues of focus and enforcement priorities are discussed in Chapter 5.

[4] For example, in Kenya the introduction of competition in the mobile telecommunications markets lead to a reduction of prices by about 50 per cent. Mobile telecommunications might not be directly related to sustainability, but they enable mobile phone-based payments systems (such as the very successful M-PESA system, an SMS-based, low-cost system that allows person-to-person transfers of money where neither senders nor recipients need to have a bank account) and can provide access to banking service for the poor, to whom such services were previously not available.

[5] With regard to competition law interventions in the clean tech area, see, eg, Craig Waldman and Margaret Ward, 'Antitrust Issues in Clean Technology' [2010] *Antitrust Source* 2–3.

[6] For other examples from the EU, see Annalies Outhuijse, 'Environment and Competition Policy: Trend in Europe and National Cases' (31 January 2019) *e-Competitions Environment and competition policy*, Art N° 88830, 1–2.

[7] FTC, 'FTC Order Sets Conditions for Panasonic's Acquisition of Sanyo', 2009 press release available at <https://www.ftc.gov/news-events/news/press-releases/2009/11/ftc-order-sets-conditions-panasonics-acquisition-sanyo> (accessed 17 January 2025). For a more detailed analysis see, eg, Michael A Carrier, 'An Antitrust Framework for Climate Change' (2011) 9 *Northwestern Journal of Technology and Intellectual Property* 513–532.

Panasonic/Sanyo (US)[8]

The US Federal Trade Commission (FTC) intervened and imposed conditions on Panasonic's acquisition of Sanyo, as it combined the world's two largest manufacturers and sellers of NiMH batteries, rechargeable batteries for consumer electronics.[9] The FTC required divestiture and, amongst other remedies, a transfer of Sanyo's NiMH battery business and related assets (such as the main manufacturing plant, employees, licences, and IP rights) to Fujitsu's subsidiary, FDK.[10]

The FTC's reasoning was based on the fact that although there were two other types of rechargeable batteries that could be used to power portable electronic devices, these were not substitutable for NiMH batteries. Numerous products are designed specifically to accommodate portable NiMH batteries.[11] But even where products can accommodate other batteries (substitutable for NiMH batteries), there was a strong customer preference for NiMH batteries for their performance and cost.[12]

Substantially, Panasonic and Sanyo were producing the highest-quality NiMH batteries, were close competitors, and controlled the overwhelming majority of the market.[13] Post-merger, they would have a worldwide market share for NiMH batteries in excess of 65 per cent.[14]

The FTC highlighted:

> The market for portable NiMH batteries offers very limited prospects for growth ... Existing fringe competitors would have to significantly improve their portable NiMH production facilities, improve the quality of their portable NiMH batteries, and overcome customers' unwillingness to rely on a portable NiMH battery supplier that lacks the track record for producing reliable, high-quality products.[15]

Thus, the goal of the divestment of Sanyo's NiMH business, including its key manufacturing plant and employees, which produced approximately

[8] See Decision and Order of FTC, *Analysis of Agreement Containing Consent Orders to Aid Public Comment—In the Matter of Panasonic Corporation and Sanyo Electric Co, Ltd* (091-050) available at <https://www.ftc.gov/sites/default/files/documents/cases/2009/11/091124panasanyodo.pdf> (accessed 17 January 2025).

[9] This was the product market considered (the geographic market was worldwide); see FTC (n 8).

[10] FTC (n 8).

[11] ibid 2.

[12] ibid (the consumers would not switch to another battery in response to a 5 to 10 per cent price increase in NiMH batteries).

[13] ibid.

[14] FTC, Complaint Docket No C-4274 available at <https://www.ftc.gov/sites/default/files/documents/cases/2009/11/091124panasanyocmpt.pdf> (accessed 17 January 2025) 8.

[15] ibid Complaint 9.

30 per cent of these batteries worldwide, was to ensure that FDK was immediately able to compete with the merged entity so that competition was not diminished.[16] This prevented Panasonic from exercising market power resulting in higher prices, reduced innovation, and decreased quality.[17]

This case does not seem to concern sustainability directly, but instead focuses on the traditional parameters of competition. But the case is relevant for three reasons.

First, rechargeable batteries and battery technology are crucial in the energy transition as they allow for the storage of intermittent renewable energy.[18] Similarly, rechargeable batteries are superior to disposable batteries from other environmental perspectives.[19] Thus, ensuring competition in the battery area makes an important contribution that will indirectly benefit sustainability and reduce CO2 emissions.

Second, the case underscores that the use of products is relevant to the analysis. The FTC highlighted the use of these batteries not as mere batteries but as 'critical batteries', since they were vital for the two-way radios used by police and fire departments. Essentially, the FTC took account of the fact that these batteries had a small but important function for society. Hence, where a product has critical importance from a sustainability perspective, for example, as an input, particular vigilance is required.

Third, the case underlines future improvements to the product and innovation resulting from maintaining competition. Such considerations can also be relevant in the sustainability context where product improvement and innovation might bring about important sustainability improvements.

Crucial in the context of the orthodox application of competition law in a sustainability context is also the market definition. Sustainability effects can certainly inform and delineate markets. The demand side and in particular consumer preferences will shape such an analysis. Such demand-side questions can be of particular importance for consumer-facing products such as regular coffee,[20] bananas,[21] or cocoa[22] vs organic/fair trade coffee, bananas, or cocoa.

[16] ibid Analysis of agreement 3.

[17] ibid Analysis of agreement 2.

[18] See, eg, John P Barton and David G Infield, 'Energy Storage and its Use with Intermittent Renewable Energy' (2004) 19(2) *IEEE Transactions on Energy Conversion* 441–448; AB Gallo and others, 'Energy Storage in the Energy Transition Context: A Technology Review' (2016) 65 *Renewable and Sustainable Energy Reviews* 800–822.

[19] David Parsons, 'The Environmental Impact of Disposable Versus Re-chargeable Batteries for Consumer Use' (2007) 12 *International Journal of Life Cycle Assessment* 197–203; Giovanni Dolci and others, 'Life Cycle Assessment of Consumption Choices: A Comparison Between Disposable and Rechargeable Household Batteries' (2016) 21 *International Journal of Life Cycle Assessment* 1691–1705.

[20] EU Commission, Case M.7292 *DEMB/Mondelez/Charger Opco* paras 57–59.

[21] See eg cases: EU Commission, Case M.8829 *Total Produce/Dole Food Company* paras 34–37; EU Commission, Case M.7220 *Chiquita Brands International/Fyffes* paras 66–73.

[22] EU Commission, Case M.7510 *Olam/ADM Cocoa Business* paras 15–19.

However, similar questions can be considered in more upstream B2B situations.[23] Consequently, the EU Commission's Notice on the Definition of the Relevant Market highlights that:

> [w]hen defining the relevant market, the Commission takes into account the various parameters of competition that customers consider relevant in the area and period assessed. Those parameters may include the product's price, but also its degree of innovation and its quality in various aspects – such as its sustainability, resource efficiency, durability, the value and variety of uses offered by the product ... as well as its availability, including in terms of lead-time, resilience of supply chains, reliability of supply and transport costs. The relative importance of these parameters for customers may change over time.[24]

Moreover, the Notice references sustainability again in the context of the geographic market and 'distance-related factors, transport costs and catchment areas',[25] highlighting that 'factors, such as security of supply considerations, sustainability considerations'[26] can affect the market definition in this regard. Examples in this regard can be found in numerous cases, for instance in the EU Commission's decision in *DEMB/Mondelez/Charger Opco*,[27] and it has equally been highlighted by the French competition authority in a paper that provides an overview of some of its merger decisions.[28]

IV. Targeted enforcement with spillover effects

Having discussed how orthodox enforcement action can create coincidental spillover effects for sustainability, we will now turn to more targeted enforcement. Applying orthodox competition principles might still have substantial sustainability effects, as restrictions of competition can directly impact sustainability. Thus, competition enforcement can be targeted and create positive spillover effects on sustainability where enforcement is aimed at such practices. We

[23] In M.9076 *Novelis/Aleris* paras 112–255 the EU Commission for example distinguished steel and aluminum for the production for cars due to their different weight that effects the CO2 emission of the subsequently produced cars. Similarly, in M.10047 *Schwarz Group/Suez Waste Management Companies* paras 44, 56–58, the Commission used the CO2 emissions resulting from the transport of light plastics to the recycling plant to define the geographical market.

[24] Commission Notice on the Definition of the Relevant Market for the Purposes of Union Competition Law [2024] OJ C/1645 para 15.

[25] ibid para 72.

[26] ibid.

[27] EU Commission, Case M.7292 *DEMB/Mondelez/Charger Opco* C(2015) 3000 final, paras 57–59.

[28] Autorité de la concurrence, 'Merger Control: New "Green" Considerations' (3 June 2024) <https://www.autoritedelaconcurrence.fr/en/merger-control-new-green-considerations> (accessed 22 January 2025).

can observe different forms of such targeted enforcement. Enforcement might be aimed at important input markets for industries that are crucial for sustainability, or target practices that occur in areas that are liable to directly harm the poor. In other words, such (orthodox) competition enforcement protects the poor.

1. Price competition and important input markets

While *Panasonic/Sanyo* might be seen as a more orthodox case with potential spillover effects on sustainability parameters, it shows how agencies can target their enforcement efforts on 'critical' products. Such target enforcement in 'critical' product markets can have intended spillover effects on sustainability. One example might be protecting price competition in the area of recycling, as in the context of the *Aurubis/Metallo* case,[29] a merger of purchasers of copper scrap. The European Commission was concerned about the decrease in the price for the recycled product, caused by the post-merger enhancements in purchasing power, which could potentially disincentivize waste collection and encourage the use of primary copper.[30] Commissioner Vestager highlighted that:

> Copper is an important input needed for electric mobility and digitisation. A well-functioning circular economy in copper is important to ensure a sustainable usage of resources in the context of the European Green Deal. This is why we carried out an in-depth investigation of the merger between Aurubis and Metallo. We initially raised concerns about the transaction and looked into it carefully. Our investigation brought sufficient elements to conclude competition in the copper recycling sector will not be negatively affected by the merger of Aurubis and Metallo.[31]

After an in-depth investigation, the Commission approved the merger. It investigated a price-based theory that linked it to incentives for the collection and recycling of copper scrap on the input side. Another example in the area of using orthodox enforcement tools is the recent predatory pricing case against the Greek Public Power Corporation. This case centred on the energy market, a crucial market for sustainability. The Commission in its statement of objection was concerned that the below-cost pricing would in particular crowd out investment

[29] EU Commission, Case M.9409 *Aurubis/Metallo Group Holding* C(2020) 2752 final.

[30] For an overview, see also Nicole Rosenboom, 'The Role of Sustainability in Merger Control' *Oxera* (16 April 2021) available at <https://www.oxera.com/insights/agenda/articles/the-role-of-sustainability-in-merger-control/#_ftn5> (accessed 17 January 2025).

[31] EU Commission, Press Release IP-20-801, 'Mergers: Commission clears Aurubis' acquisition of Metallo' (Brussels, 4 May 2020) available at <https://ec.europa.eu/commission/presscorner/detail/en/ip_20_801> (accessed 17 January 2025).

into more environmentally friendly energy sources, and over a longer period lead to higher costs for Greek energy consumers and high levels of local emission pollution.[32]

2. Protecting price competition and the fight against poverty

Another archetype of target enforcement with spillover effects is competition enforcement to alleviate poverty.[33] When discussing the alleviation of poverty,[34] we need to keep in mind that while poverty and inequality have some overlap, they are not the same thing.[35] In this area, competition enforcement can focus on the demand side, in particular the prices of essential goods, or on the supply side. The engagement with the supply side would support people living in poverty in their 'capacity as small entrepreneurs, wage earners and job seekers'.[36]

There are numerous examples of such enforcement action around the world, but we will examine the bread cartel case from South Africa on the demand side, and enforcement action against non-poach and non-compete clauses in the United States on the supply side.

Bread Cartel (South Africa)[37]

In South Africa, the extractive model of the economy during the history of colonialism and apartheid can be identified as the origin of poverty.[38] While being an upper-middle income country, poverty is still a substantive problem.

[32] EU Commission, Press Release IP-24-672, 'Commission sends Statement of Objections to PPC over predatory pricing in the Greek wholesale electricity market' (7 February 2024) available at <https://ec.europa.eu/commission/presscorner/detail/en/ip_24_672> (accessed 17 January 2025).

[33] On poverty and competition law see OECD, 'OECD Roundtable Competition and Poverty Reduction' (2013) OECD DAF/COMP/GF(2013)12 available at <http://www.oecd.org/daf/competition/competition-and-poverty-reduction2013.pdf> (accessed 17 January 2025). Thulasoni Kaira, 'The Role of Competition Law and Policy in Alleviating Poverty – The Case of Zambia' in Hassan Qaqaya and George Lipimile (eds), *The Effect of Anti-Competitive Business Practices on Developing Countries and their Development Prospects* (United Nations 2008) 133–177.

[34] See Amartya Sen, *Development as Freedom* (OUP 1999) who argues that economic poverty prevents people from exercising the freedom to satisfy hunger, obtain sufficient nutrition, remedy treatable illnesses, dress with dignity, live in acceptable housing, or have access to clean water and sanitation. See also Amartya Sen, *Commodities and Capabilities* (OUP 1999).

[35] The difference is also discussed in Amit Zac, 'Pre-Distribution vs Re-Distribution: Why Competition Law is Much More Than a Tool to Alleviate Poverty' in Julian Nowag (ed), *Research Handbook on Sustainability and Competition Law* (Edward Elgar 2024).

[36] OECD (n 33) 41.

[37] *Competition Commission v Pioneer Foods (Pty) Ltd* (15/CR/Feb07, 50/CR/May08) [2010] ZACT 9 (3 February 2010).

[38] As the South African contribution to OECD (n 33) points out, 'In South Africa, poverty is located within a history of colonialism, which gave way to an apartheid state that systematically "under-developed" the majority black population. In their recent book, "Why nations fail," scholars Acemoglu

A study[39] showed that in 2008 a large number of people lived in poverty (78 per cent of households lived in poverty, applying the 223 USD per month standard), and 54 per cent lived below the poverty line (using 121 USD per month as the poverty line). Even under the 1.25 dollars per day metric,[40] 14 per cent of households would be counted as falling into this category. To address poverty, the South African Competition Commission has adopted a prioritization framework[41] that includes poverty reduction and an emphasis on food and agro-processing infrastructure, amongst others.

Facts

In 2006, the South African Competition Commission started a preliminary investigation against Tiger Brands, Premier Foods, and Pioneer Foods after receiving information regarding an alleged bread cartel. Premier Food applied for leniency and cooperated with the agency, disclosing the existence of the bread cartel which fixed the selling price of bread, market-sharing, and other trading conditions. In the run-up to the cartel, several attempts to increase prices had been unsuccessful because of discounting or because rivals did not follow the increases. Pioneer's bakery managers were the ring leaders in determining the actual bread price for consumers, while allowing for a discount of up to 15 per cent.

Finding of the court

Unsurprisingly, the proceedings found that Pioneer, Tiger Brands, Premier, and Foodcorp had created a cartel, the most serious form of competition law violation.

When exploring the '[n]ature, gravity and duration' of the infringement, the Tribunal highlighted further that:

> We have already stated our views on the nature and gravity of the offences under consideration. Section 4(1)(b) violations are the most serious violations of competition law and are condemned across the world. Naked cartel behaviour is not justifiable under our legislation and is presumptively harmful. In this particular case, the offences are more so repugnant because

and Robinson characterize the institutions that governed South Africa's economy and society for centuries during colonial and apartheid times as "extractive"' (they make reference to Daron Acemoglu and James A Robinson, *Why Nations Fail* (Random House 2012)).

[39] See Murray Leibbrand and others, 'Trends in South African Income Distribution and Poverty since the Fall of Apartheid' (2010), OECD Social, Employment and Migration Working Papers No 101 available at <https://doi.org/10.1787/5kmms0t7p1ms-en> (accessed 17 January 2025).

[40] World Bank PovCalNet database is available at <https://pip.worldbank.org/#> (accessed 18 January 2025).

[41] Available at <http://www.compcom.co.za/our-strategic-goals/> (accessed 17 January 2025).

> they have affected the poorest of the poor, for whom standard bread is a staple. [Para 158]
>
> And in a similar vein, the tribunal highlighted in the 'Loss or damage as a result of the contravention' section of the judgment that:
>
> Furthermore one must have regard to the fact that the product market pertains to a staple food for millions of South Africans, especially the poorest of the poor and any increases in prices would have a disproportionate impact on this sector. While we cannot determine the total or quantify the extent of the damage accurately, the result of this was that the poorest of all South Africans paid more for their bread than any other person. [Para 160]

The cartel had an obvious and disproportionate effect on the poorest, as the percentage of total household income spent on staple foods is higher than amongst the richer part of society. The increase in price meant that they would need to spend more money on bread. This money would be absorbed by the cartel and these households would have to cut spending elsewhere or reduce consumption of bread, which in the case of the poorest, can have catastrophic consequences in terms of nutrition and their ability to escape poverty.

While this case highlights how targeted enforcement of orthodox competition law can bring about substantial sustainability benefits, three points are worth noting. First, after the enforcement action, the prices went down. However, they increased again after some time.[42] Such findings can equally be expected in other areas of enforcement against cartels. And while this gives us reason to question the effectiveness of cartel enforcement as such and suggests a closer look at this area,[43] we might still conclude that competition enforcement is an important tool to prevent harm from cartels like these. Second, the case was part of a broader scheme by the South African competition authority. The agency investigated the value chain (flour milling, bakeries, etc) and then also took enforcement action with regard to vertical restrictions.[44] Third, the case stimulated interest beyond the usual competition circles and led to the engagement of NGOs[45] fighting against poverty who became aware of the potential of competition law and involved in obtaining compensation for the consumers.[46]

[42] See OECD (n 33) 246–247.
[43] For example, how do these results measure up taking into account different levels of inflation?
[44] OECD (n 33) 245–247.
[45] An example of an important Indian NGO engaged in work on competition and development is the Consumer Unity & Trust Society (CUTS).
[46] ibid.

3. Restrictions in the labour market and poverty

Another example where orthodox antitrust measures can help with poverty reduction[47] is restrictions in the labour market. While there was some activity in this area in the 1950s,[48] the active application of competition law to restrictions in the labour markets has recently received renewed interest.[49] In those cases, competition law is used against non-poach and non-compete agreements by employers that prevent competition in the labour market. In recent years, such enforcement action in the US[50] made headlines, as agencies prosecuted non-poaching agreements as *per se* cartel violations in the high-tech industry. Yet, there were also notable examples where the fast-food industry used non-poach agreements with regard to low-paid restaurant workers.[51] Such cases might well be prosecuted in situations involving poverty, where sustainable development issues are at play. In particular, we could see such investigations where an employer uses such agreements to keep down the wages of the poorest.

US v Knorr-Bremse AG and Westinghouse Air Brake Technologies Corp (US)[52]

In the market for rail equipment, Knorr-Bremse AG (Knorr) and Wabtec Air Brake (Wabtec) were not only the world's largest suppliers but also each other's main competitors, both in the product and in the labour markets. While recruitment takes place internally and externally, the number of skilled workers is limited.

[47] For further insights see Eleanor Fox, 'Economic Development, Poverty and Antitrust: The Other Path' (2007) 13 *Southwestern Journal of Law and Trade in the Americas* 211, and more generally on development and antitrust, Thomas K Cheng, *Competition Law in Developing Countries* (OUP 2020).

[48] See for example in the US, *Union Circulation Co v Fed Trade Commission*, 241 F 2d 652, 658 (2d Cir 1957) or in the UK, *Kores Manufacturing Co Ltd v Kolok Manufacturing Co Ltd* [1959] Ch 108, [1958] 2 WLR. 858, [1958] 2 All ER 65, [1958] RPC 200, [1958] 102 SJ 362.

[49] See in particular Herbert Hovenkamp, 'Competition Policy for Labour Markets – Note by Herbert Hovenkamp – Roundtable on Competition Issues in Labour Markets' (2019) DAF/COMP/WD(2019)67 available at <https://one.oecd.org/document/DAF/COMP/WD(2019)67/en/pdf> (accessed 17 January 2025).

[50] For a comparative view see Valentin Depenne, 'One Size Does Not Fit All: A Comparative Approach to Antitrust Enforcement Against No-Poaching Agreements' (2019) 2(1) *Sorbonne Student Law Review* 242.

[51] 'Fast Food Chains Settle on No-Poach Agreements' *The Telegraph* (15 March 2019) available at <https://www.thetelegraph.com/news/article/Fast-food-chains-settle-on-no-poach-agreements-13692194.php> (accessed 17 January 2025).

[52] *US v Knorr- Bremse AG and Westinghouse Air Brake Technologies Corporation (Wabtec), Case 1:18-cv- 00747, (2018)* available at <https://www.just ice.gov/atr/case-document/file/1084651/download> (accessed 17 January 2025).

Facts

Against this background, Knorr and Wabtec started entering into non-poach agreements which included promises and commitments not to solicit or hire certain groups of workers from each other. At times, these agreements meant that employees could not be hired without the prior approval of the other company.

Before it was acquired by Wabtec, Faiveley, the world's third largest rail equipment supplier, had also entered into a non-poach agreement with Knorr that stipulated that they would contact each other before pursuing an employee from the other company. Later, Faiveley also entered into such agreements with Wabtec.

In 2018, the Department of Justice (DoJ) brought a civil antitrust lawsuit against Knorr and Wabtec for breaching section 1 of the Sherman Act.[53]

While the defendants did not dispute the existence of these agreements, the question was what kind of standard should be applied. Based on precedent from the 1970s[54] the DoJ argued that these agreements would be *per se* illegal and should not be assessed under the rule of reason.[55] The DoJ's argument was that the non-poach agreements were naked restrictions in the labour market and could not be treated differently from traditional customer or market allocation[56] which are similarly not subject to the rule of reason.[57]

Finding of the court

In the end, the case was settled with a consent decree. In the judgment affirming the settlement regarding the violation of section 1, the court noted that 'each defendant is enjoined from attempting to enter into, entering into, maintaining, or enforcing any no-poach agreement or no-poach provisions.'[58]

The decree only allows for a narrow set of agreements 'not to solicit, recruit, or hire employees that is ancillary to a legitimate business collaboration' under strict conditions.[59]

[53] *US v Knorr-Bremse AG and Westinghouse Air Brake Technologies Corporation (Wabtec)*, Case 1:18-cv-00747, complaint document (2018) available at <https://www.justice.gov/atr/case-document/file/1048866/download> (accessed 17 January 2025).

[54] *Broadcast Music, Inc v Columbia Broadcasting Sys*, 441 US 1, 19-20 (1979).

[55] *US v Knorr-Bremse AG and Westinghouse Air Brake Technologies Corporation (Wabtec)*, Case 1:18-cv-00747, Competitive Impact Statement document (2018) available at <https://www.justice.gov/atr/case-document/file/1048891/download> (accessed 17 January 2025), Part C.

[56] ibid Part C. See also *United States v Socony-Vacuum Oil Co*, 310 US 150, 218 (1940); *Palmer v BRG of Georgia, Inc*, 498 US 46, 48–50 (1990) (*per curiam*).

[57] ibid Part C. See also *US v Cooperative Theaters of Ohio, Inc*, 845 F.2d 1367 (6th Cir 1988) where the court held that an agreement among competitors not to solicit each other's customers was a *per se* violation of the antitrust law.

[58] (n 52) see especially Part IV.

[59] ibid Part V.

The case confirms such non-poach agreements as *per se* illegal, falling into the category of worst offences under US antitrust law. Although the case does not directly concern the poorest in society, it could easily be applied in such a way, especially in light of the DoJ's continued efforts to prosecute similar cases[60] and the ongoing case involving low-paid workers in the fast-food sector.[61]

Up until now, the cases have been brought as civil cases. However, with the entry into force of the US criminal sentencing guidelines[62] even harsher punishment for *per se* violations such as these might be expected. The positive effects that competition in the labour market might bring to low-paid workers can be seen in the context of the related issue of firms unilaterally imposing non-compete clauses in labour contracts.[63] For example, in Oregon, a ban on non-compete clauses in labour contracts for low-paid/low-skilled workers has led to an increase in mobility, average occupational status, and a wage increase of 2.2 per cent to 3.1 per cent.[64]

However, while such positive effects for the poor might be observed in developed countries, whether the same effect would materialize in the context of low-paid workers in developing countries is a different question. So far, we have seen little enforcement against non-poaching agreements in developing countries. The sad reality is that we might not find such agreements. Agreements to keep down the wages of the poor might not be needed in a situation where the supply of workers is so large that there is no need to restrict competition. Yet, if such restrictions exist, tough enforcement action is certainly warranted.[65]

Apart from non-poach and non-compete clauses-related enforcement, competition law has been further expanded to ensure workers' positions and benefits in relation to their right to carry out collective industrial actions and their effectiveness. In the US, in *Kroger Company and Albertsons Companies*, the Federal Trade Commission sued to block a merger which it argued would not only harm consumer welfare but also union grocery workers for the two companies, as they would no longer be able to bargain for better terms of employment based on the

[60] For example, with regard to staff in the medical sector, see Duke & North Carolina University (2019) (1:15 -cv-00462).

[61] *Deslandes v McDonald's USA, LLC*, 2018 WL 3105955 (N.D.Il. 25 June 2018).

[62] See the US Federal Sentencing Guidelines, United States Sentencing Commission '2023 Guidelines Manual Annotated' §2R1.1 (2023) available at <https://www.ussc.gov/guidelines/2023-guidelines-manual-annotated> (accessed 17 January 2025).

[63] Evan Starr, JJ Prescott, and Norman Bishar, 'Non-compete Agreements in the U.S. Labor Force' (2021) 64 *Journal of Law and Economics* 53–84. See also Jared Bennet, 'Money and Greed: How Non-compete Clauses Force Workers to Fight for Rights' (October 2018) available at <https://www.theguardian.com/us-news/2018/oct/24/non-compete-clause-low-wage-workers-lawsuits-rights> (accessed 17 January 2025).

[64] For an overview see Michael Lipsitz and Evan Starr, 'Low-Wage Workers and the Enforceability of Non-Compete Agreements' (2021) 68(1) Management Science 143–170.

[65] See eg, Isaure Langlois d'Estaintot, 'Antitrust Policy and EU Labour Markets—Lessons from the US and Comparative Prospects' (PhD thesis, EUI 2024) available at <https://cadmus.eui.eu/handle/1814/76781> (accessed 17 January 2025).

companies' competition post-merger.[66] Based on the complaint, the court[67] granted a preliminary injunction and the merger was abandoned.

4. Summary

We have seen how (orthodox) competition enforcement that focuses on price competition can be targeted at important input markets where a functioning downstream market is crucial from a sustainability perspective. While specific sectors that are important from a sustainability perspective might differ depending on the relevant local conditions, waste collection and renewable energy seem like obvious examples. The other area where enforcement action protecting price competition can be targeted to produce important spillover effects for sustainability is poverty. In particular, where cartels and exclusionary behaviour reduce competition in the area of basic goods, such as basic food, enforcement action has substantial effects on the fight against poverty. The fight against poverty as a sustainable development goal might also come into play when we see enforcement action against restrictions in the labour market. In other words, competition benefits in the form of better wages and employment terms can be protected by means of competition law. The effects of preventing wage competition on the poorest in society might be substantial. While from a theoretical perspective, it might seem less likely that competition in these markets would be restricted due to the substantial supply of cheap labour, we have seen patterns of restrictions. For example, there are issues around non-compete clauses in the fast food and cleaning industries, industries where theoretically the supply of labour at low cost would not be a problem. In this way, competition authorities can act as guardians of sustainability even when applying orthodox ideas of competition enforcement: protecting competition to ensure that markets function effectively, which in turn contributes to sustainability.

V. Competition enforcement and sustainability as competition parameters

We have seen that orthodox competition enforcement can bring about coincidental sustainability benefits that might be intended or unintended by the

[66] See the complaint by Federal Trade Commission in *The Kroger Company and Albertsons Companies, Inc*, available at <https://www.ftc.gov/system/files/ftc_gov/pdf/d9428_2310004krogeralbertsonsp3complaintpublic.pdf> (accessed 17 January 2025) para 62.

[67] *Federal Trade Commission et al v Kroger Company et al*, No 3:2024cv00347—Document 521 available at <https://storage.courtlistener.com/recap/gov.uscourts.ord.178374/gov.uscourts.ord.178374.521.0_1.pdf> (accessed 17 January 2025). While the court accepted that the labour implications were cognizable harm under antitrust, it held that not enough evidence in that regard had been provided.

enforcement action. Yet, there are also areas where sustainability is a parameter of competition. In these cases, more targeted antitrust action with foreseeable effects on sustainability is also possible. Such cases would use more orthodox theories of harm to address anti-competitive conduct that is harmful in sustainability terms. Examples include, on the one hand, cartels that hinder competition on the sustainability parameter as a quality parameter and more general arrangements that restrict the availability of choice so that consumers are prevented from choosing the more sustainable product. On the other hand, as R&D and eco-innovation are important factors for sustainable development, innovation harms can be targeted by competition agencies. Such practices could for example include exclusionary behaviour regarding access to technology[68] or more general cartels or mergers that restrict innovation competition that leads to more sustainability. It is in these innovation-related theories of harm where we can debate how far these can and should be pushed to protect sustainability.

1. Suppressing competition on the sustainability component—quality, choice, and price

Where sustainability is a parameter of competition, anti-competitive activities might aim to suppress such competition. Such a reduction in competition has foreseeable effects on sustainability and enforcement action can make a difference even where rather orthodox theories of harm are employed to establish whether the activity is anti-competitive. Situations like this might be presented in the context, for example, in cartels and merger cases.

a) Cartels effecting choice

The French competition authority has pursued several cartel cases. In this line of cases, sustainability factors have been treated as one of the parameters of competition affecting consumer choices. For example, it investigated companies in the PVC and linoleum floor covering industry and fined them for cartel behaviour as they had agreed not to compete on the environmental dimension of their product.[69]

[68] For example with regard to patents concerning climate change technology, see Carrier (n 7). For further examples see Susanne Kingston, *Greening EU Competition Law and Policy* (CUP 2012) 312–326.

[69] Autorite de la Concurrence, Décision 17-D-20 relative à des pratiques mises en œuvre dans le secteur des revêtements de sols résilients (18 October 2017) available at <https://www.autoritedelaconcurrence.fr/fr/decision/relative-des-pratiques-mises-en-oeuvre-dans-le-secteur-des-revetements-de-sols-resilients> (accessed 17 January 2025).

Hard floor covering case (France)[70]

The case concerned an agreement in the PVC and linoleum floor covering industry and the withholding of environmental performance information in advertising.

The companies Forbo, Gerflor, and Tarkett had arranged a cartel via their trade association (SFEC) and the French competition authority in 2017, therefore imposing a €302 million fine for their cartel activities between 1990 and 2013.[71] The fine imposed was the highest to that day, even after taking into account leniency and settlement procedures.

Findings of the competition agency

The French competition authority established three anti-competitive practices: price-fixing, sharing commercially sensitive information, and signing a non-compete agreement.

Amongst the more established cartel-behaviours, the companies coordinated their pricing policies in secret meetings and discussed, among others, minimum prices and price increases for their products, and exchanged confidential information such as trading volumes, revenues, and sales forecasts with the help of SFEC.[72]

Furthermore, the companies adopted a non-compete agreement. This agreement prevented them from advertising the environmental performance of their products and any such communication on environmental performance was allowed only via the SFEC.

The agency highlighted that:

> the effect of this agreement was to eliminate 'competitive marketing practices based on environmental characteristics' and 'avoid unnecessary controversy relating to particular products and adopt a consistent marketing approach' in order to prevent 'reckless green marketing.' ... Tradesmen, retailers and

[70] Décision n° 17-D-20 du 18 octobre 2017 relative à des pratiques mises en œuvre dans le secteur des revêtements de sols résilients available at <https://www.autoritedelaconcurrence.fr/sites/default/files/commitments//17d20.pdf> (accessed 17 January 2025). For an English summary of the decision see <https://www.autoritedelaconcurrence.fr/en/communiques-de-presse/19-october-2017-cartel-floor-coverings-sector> (accessed 17 January 2025).

[71] For an overview of the case see also Richard Burton, 'The French Competition Authority Fines Three Undertakings and a Trade Association €302 Million in a Cartel Case in the Pvc and Linoleum Floor Sector (Forbo/Gerflor/Tarkett/Sfec)' (2017, Concurrences) e-Competitions October 2017, Art N° 85300 available at <https://www.concurrences.com/en/bulletin/news-issues/october-2017/the-french-competition-authority-fines-three-undertakings-and-a-trade> (accessed 17 January 2025).

[72] Elena Chutrova and McDermott Will & Emery, 'Significant Fine Imposed by the French Competition Authority in Floor Coverings Cartel' *Antitrust Alert* (2017) available at <https://www.antitrustalert.com/2017/10/significant-fine-imposed-by-the-french-competition-authority-in-the-floor-coverings-cartel/> (accessed 17 January 2025).

consumers, increasingly sensitive to the debate surrounding the impact of air quality on human health, specifically as a result of releases from PVC floor coverings, could not receive the standard of information that might have prevailed in the absence of this agreement, and might have enlightened their purchasing decisions. Furthermore, this agreement may have acted as a disincentive to manufacturers to innovate in order to offer their customers products characterised by better environmental performances, thereby impacting a product differentiation factor.[73]

This case shows how traditional elements of cartels might also be related to sustainability where sustainability has become a parameter of competition.[74] In the same vein, the French competition authority has also fined companies for boycotting digitally innovative intermediation platforms in the road freight transport sector.[75] Specifically, the authority highlighted the boycott's consequential limitation on the economic, logistical, and environmental gains—ie reduction in the return of empty containers (or 'empty returns' by carriers), hence reduction in greenhouse gases.[76] More recently, the agency has been concluded with regard to an agreement not to compete with Bisphenol A in food containers.[77] Bisphenol A is a substance that is authorized for use in food containers, but concerns regarding its effects on human health exist.[78] In this case, the companies agreed 'not to communicate on the presence (of Bisphenol A) or the composition' of material used in food containers,[79] thus leaving consumers without information about whether Bisphenol A was present or not.

[73] ibid.

[74] See also Chapter 2 on the economics of competition around sustainability.

[75] See press release, 'The Autorité de la concurrence fines several players in the road freight transport sector for boycotting digital intermediation platforms' (9 September 2021) available at <https://www.autoritedelaconcurrence.fr/en/communiques-de-presse/autorite-de-la-concurrence-fines-several-players-road-freight-transport> (accessed 18 January 2025).

[76] The authority stated that a 1 per cent reduction in empty returns would result in a 0.7 per cent reduction in greenhouse gas emissions. See opinions and decisions 'Enforcement action: a gradually expanding decision-making practice' available at <https://www.autoritedelaconcurrence.fr/en/enforcement-action-gradually-expanding-decision-making-practice> (accessed 18 January 2025).

[77] See press release, 'Bisphenol A in food containers: almost €20 million in fines' (11 January 2024) available at <https://www.autoritedelaconcurrence.fr/en/press-release/bisphenol-food-containers-almost-eu20-million-fines> (accessed 18 January 2025).

[78] See eg Susana Almeida and others, 'Bisphenol A: Food Exposure and Impact on Human Health' (2018) 17 *Comprehensive Reviews in Food Science and Food Safety* 1503–1517; Johanna R Rochester, 'Bisphenol A and Human Health: A Review of the Literature' (2013) 42 *Reproductive Toxicology* 132–155.

[79] See press release, 'Bisphénol A dans les contenants alimentaires: le rapporteur général indique avoir notifié des griefs à 101 entreprises et 14 organisations professionnelles' (12 October 2021) available at <https://www.autoritedelaconcurrence.fr/en/press-release/bisphenol-food-containers-general-rapporteur-indicates-having-stated-objections-101> (accessed 18 January 2025).

b) Mergers and closeness of competition

While vertical mergers might raise questions about foreclosure,[80] competition authorities in horizontal cases most frequently examine the closeness of competition to determine whether the merger would result in an important player vanishing from the market.

The UK competition authority in its revised merger assessment guidelines, highlights that competition takes place not only in the form of price competition but equally in the form of non-price competition:

> [t]he range of possible non-price aspects of competition that firms may use to win customers is wide, and terms such as 'quality' should be interpreted broadly. Examples might include, for example, staffing levels in store; speed and responsiveness to customer queries; the level of privacy offered to users of digital services; the benefits to users of a platform being able to interact with a large base of other users actively using the same platform; the reassurance afforded to customers by a well-known brand or good reputation; *the sustainability of a product or service*; and the ability to enjoy content without being served with advertisements.[81] (Emphasis added.)

Thus, the UK competition authority may intervene against a merger where it substantially lessens competition in terms of sustainability.[82]

More generally, possible merger-specific negative externalities can also be taken into account to a considerable extent, namely by indirectly linking, eg, climate protection concerns to potential restrictions of competition.[83] The EU has had a number of cases where CO_2 emissions played an important part in the closeness of competition analysis. For example, in *GE/Alstom* the Commission identified the parties as close competitors for certain heavy-duty gas turbines with similar emissions, thus targeting the same customers.[84] In *Norsk Hydro/Alumetal*[85] the closeness of competition analysis became more sophisticated, focusing also on the

80 For such vertical mergers concerning foreclosure in the sustainability context see eg the EU Commission decision in *KPS Capital Partners/Real Alloy Europe* (see press release 19 October 2022 available at <https://ec.europa.eu/commission/presscorner/detail/en/IP_22_6274> (accessed 18 January 2025)). The Commission was concerned about the ability to foreclose access to recycled aluminium and certain recycling services related to aluminium cans.

81 UK Competition and Markets Authority, 'Merger Assessment Guidelines' (2021) CMA129 available at <https://www.gov.uk/government/publications/merger-assessment-guidelines> (accessed 18 January 2025) para 2.5.

82 See Nicole Kar and Emma Cochrane, 'Sustainability and Competition in the UK after Brexit' in Julian Nowag (ed), *Research Handbook on Sustainability and Competition Law* (Edward Elgar 2024) section 4.1.

83 Jens-Uwe Franck, 'EU Merger Control and Climate Action: The Struggle for the Proper Framework', Discussion Paper Series – CRC TR 224 (2024) available at <https://www.wiwi.uni-bonn.de/bgsepapers/boncrc/CRCTR224_2024_576.pdf> (accessed 21 January 2025).

84 EU Commission, Case M.7278 *GE/Alstom* para 511ff.

85 EU Commission, Case M.10658 *Norsk Hydro/Alumetal*.

extent to which the products are competing in terms of emissions. This case concerned a merger between two companies producing aluminium used mainly in the automotive industry. One company produced this aluminium from recycled material and the other used non-recycled material but produced it using renewable energy. To examine the closeness of competition the Commission examined what producers of low-carbon suppliers would remain after the merger. As there was no industry definition of low-carbon suppliers, the Commission established who were competing low-carbon suppliers by examining the CO_2 emissions per tonne, the tonnes produced and the individual total CO_2 emissions[86] of the aluminium foundries involved. Based on this assessment the Commission found that the companies were not close competitors in a (hypothetical) low-carbon segment. There were other primary aluminium producers that used or could use renewable energy and recycled aluminium, in any case, and who had an even lower footprint.

2. Suppressing competition on the sustainability component: sustainability innovation

When we look at innovation, we can see how orthodox theories of harm start to widen to address future (innovation) harm. Innovation, R&D and eco-innovation are all crucial to achieving overall sustainability. Thus, innovation is an important area where antitrust enforcement can make a difference in sustainability, whether this is enforcement in relation to the exclusionary behaviour of patents and technology vital for sustainable development[87] or other behaviour that might hamper sustainability. While such cases may be brought under the orthodox theories of (innovation) harm, examining innovation effects where sustainability innovation is concerned seems rather uncontroversial,[88] in particular when we can find concerns about innovation effects in general both in the US as well as EU merger guidelines.[89]

In fact, already in the 1960s a cartel case in the US was brought. In that case, the four largest automobile manufacturers and their association were charged under

[86] The Commission linked the tonnes produced and the CO_2 emitted in this regard.

[87] For example with regard to patents concerning climate change technology, see Carrier (n 7). For further examples see Susanne Kingston, *Greening EU Competition Law and Policy* (CUP 2012) 312–326.

[88] See also Ioannis Lianos, 'Polycentric Competition Law' Centre for Law, Economics and Society Research Paper Series (April 2018) available at <https://www.ucl.ac.uk/cles/sites/cles/files/cles_4-2018_final.pdf> (accessed 18 January 2025).

[89] See US Department of Justice and Federal Trade Commission, *Horizontal Merger Guidelines* (2010) available at https://www.justice.gov/atr/horizontal-merger-guidelines-08192010 (accessed 18 January 2025) 2; Commission, 'Guidelines on the Assessment of Horizontal Mergers Under the Council Regulation on the Control of Concentrations Between Undertakings' [2004] OJ C31/5, paras 8, 20, 38, and 81; Commission, 'Guidelines on the Assessment of Non-Horizontal Mergers Under the Council Regulation on the Control of Concentrations Between Undertakings' [2008] OJ C265/7, paras 10 and 26.

section 1 of the Sherman Act. The charge was that their agreement had hindered the development of pollution control technology, resulting in millions of vehicles being driven without effective emission control devices and thus causing air pollution.[90] The case was concluded by a consent judgment to the effect that the defendants would terminate their collaborative hindrance but made no admission to their contravention of the law.[91]

More recently, the European Commission pursued a similar case which brought sustainability-related innovation harms to the fore. The Commission's decisional practice shows us how sustainability concerns can be addressed by more orthodox means but equally by a broadening of theories of innovation harm. In *BMW, Daimler and VW*,[92] the Commission alleged a cartel that reduced innovation competition, while in *Bayer/Monsanto*[93] it looked at potential innovation harms resulting from the merger.

a) Cartels and innovation

The *BMW, Daimler and VW* decision is a case where an innovation-based theory of harm in the context of a cartel was pursued.

Car Emissions—Bayerische Motoren Werke Aktiengesellschaft/ Daimler AG/Dr. Ing. h.c. F. Porsche Aktiengesellschaft/ Volkswagen Aktiengesellschaft (EU)[94]

The EU Commission in the Car Emissions case found that BMW, Daimler, and VW (including VW's Audi and Porsche), as the so-called 'circle of five', had infringed EU competition law by colluding to restrict competition with regard to the development of emission cleaning technology between 2006 and 2014.

While the initial investigation also focused on 'Otto' particle filters[95] the final decision concerns competition in selective catalytic reduction (SCR) technology only. This technology is crucial for diesel engines in passenger cars to comply with the relevant emissions standards in the EU. SCR for diesel cars

[90] *United States v Automobile Manufacturers Ass'n*, 307 F Supp 617 (CD Cal 1970).

[91] For more details on the US emission case, see also Sarah E Light, 'The Law of the Corporation as Environmental Law' (2019) 79 *Stanford Law Review* 171–175 who portrays it as an important development in the control of vehicle emissions.

[92] See Case AT.40178 *Car Emissions*; Commission Press Release, 'Antitrust: Commission sends Statement of Objections to BMW, Daimler and VW for restricting competition on emission cleaning technology' (Brussels, 5 April 2019) IP/19/2008 available at <https://ec.europa.eu/commission/presscorner/api/files/document/print/en/ip_19_2008/IP_19_2008_EN.pdf> (accessed 13 July 2025).

[93] Case M.8084 *Bayer/Monsanto* C/2018/1709 [2018] OJ C 459/10.

[94] Case AT.40178 *Car Emissions* (COMP.G.4/GM (8 July 2021, Brussels)) available at <https://ec.europa.eu/competition/antitrust/cases1/202146/AT_40178_8022302_3050_5.pdf> (accessed 18 January 2025).

[95] The investigation into 'Otto' particle filters was dropped due to insufficient evidence.

works by injecting urea (also called 'AdBlue') which eliminates harmful nitrogen oxides (NOx) by turning them into harmless water and nitrogen. AdBlue is constantly injected from a special tank, and larger tanks allow cars to travel greater distances without refilling. While larger tanks might be more convenient for users, they are more difficult to integrate into the construction space of passenger cars, and make the cars heavier.

Between 2009 and 2014 the parties had regular technical meetings to discuss the development of the SCR technology. As part of these meetings, the parties exchanged information and agreed on matters for the development of SCR systems, including their effectiveness (average AdBlue consumption not exceeding 0.8–1.01 litre per 1000 kilometres), the size of AdBlue tanks (small tanks, holding about 8–10 litres of AdBlue), and as a result agreed on the AdBlue range (up to 10,000 kilometres). The parties were aware that the injection of more AdBlue would provide more effective NOx-cleaning and thereby reduce emissions, and that such reductions would go beyond regulatory requirements ('over-fulfilment'). But they signalled to each other that they would not strive for over-fulfilment.

The Commission found that the agreement amounted to a restriction of competition *by object*:

> By its very nature, the conduct with regard to SCR systems was liable to restrict competition on product characteristics and thus in terms of technical development in the field of NOx cleaning for new diesel passenger cars for the EEA and to limit choice for customers. That conduct served to reduce uncertainty as to their future conduct on the market in relation to certain aspects of the SCR systems to be installed in new diesel passenger cars. [para 125]
>
> **Aim of the agreements and/or concerted practices**
> With regard to NOx cleaning beyond regulatory requirements, the exchange of information on average AdBlue consumption served to reduce uncertainty about future conduct of the manufacturers on the market. It served also to prevent the risk that any of them would be worse off for failing to have gone along with more effective NOx cleaning. [para 126]
>
> … DAIMLER, VW and BMW agreed on AdBlue refill ranges of approximately 10 000 km to ensure that there would be no competing offers with significantly longer refill ranges. [para 127]
>
> By reducing uncertainty about NOx cleaning beyond regulatory requirements and the customer-friendliness of AdBlue refills, DAIMLER, VW and BMW wanted to avoid competition on how best to achieve their (sometimes contradictory) objectives. The coordination served to eliminate the competitive risks arising from the divergent solutions 'small tank or large tank' and

> 'cleaning solution with the sole aim of meeting or exceeding regulatory requirements'. [para 128][96]
>
> The Commission also highlighted the nature of the cars sold, some of which were 'premium' cars, so that the companies involved:
>
> ... in view of their market position, technical capabilities and self-image, ... were in a position to compete on over-fulfilment.... [para 129]
>
> [Moreover], diesel engines had been promoted as environment-friendly technology for several years, risks for their public image existed in connection with NOx cleaning.... [para 131]
>
> The Commission therefore concludes that DAIMLER, VW and BMW entered into agreements and/or engaged in concerted practices which, by their nature, were liable to restrict competition regarding product characteristics of their new diesel passenger cars as concerns AdBlue tank sizes, refill ranges and NOx cleaning beyond regulatory requirements; and, thus, to restrict technical development in the area of NOx cleaning with SCR systems for new diesel passenger cars in the EEA and to limit customer choice. [para 139]

The case was the first time the Commission had pursued a restriction of competition on (sustainability) innovation[97] as a cartel, classifying the agreement as an object restriction. However, it was also the first time that the Commission had pursued such a theory of harm when the cartel emerged from legitimate R&D cooperation. The Commission also took the unusual step of publishing a comfort letter.[98] The letter contained guidance to the parties (and others) on what cooperation in terms of emission cleaning technology would be legal.[99]

The parties had also argued that the restriction of competition served a legitimate purpose (to encourage the mineral oil industry to offer more AdBlue refill infrastructure) or was exempt under Article 101(3) TFEU as standardization reducing the costs of the SCR system. The Commission rejected these claims as a fixing of the tank sizes, refill ranges, and the exchange of information on average AdBlue consumption were not necessary, either for encouraging more refill infrastructure or for cost savings of standardization.

[96] Citations omitted.

[97] Or 'technical development', as the Commission called it.

[98] The Commission highlighted the standardization (eg quality standards), joint development efforts, and the build-up of relevant infrastructure, see Comfort Letter Case AT.40178 *Car Emissions* (n 93).

[99] It mentions standardization of AdBlue filler necks, AdBlue quality standards, or cooperation on the development of a joint AdBlue dosing software platform.

Overall, the case received some attention from the Commission. Commissioner Margrethe Vestager's press release explained:

> The five car manufacturers—Daimler, BMW, Volkswagen, Audi and Porsche possessed the technology to reduce harmful emissions beyond what was legally required under EU emission standards. But they avoided to compete on using this technology's full potential to clean better than what is required by law. So today's decision is about how legitimate technical cooperation went wrong. And we do not tolerate it when companies collude. It is illegal under EU Antitrust rules. Competition and innovation on managing car pollution are essential for Europe to meet our ambitious Green Deal objectives. And this decision shows that we will not hesitate to take action against all forms of cartel conduct putting in jeopardy this goal.[100]

The Commissioner also highlighted the environmental effect:

> In today's world, polluting less is an important characteristic of any car. And this cartel aimed at restricting competition on this key competition parameter.[101]

While the Commissioner's statement highlights the negative environmental effect resulting from the collusion, it is important to note that it was not this negative environmental effect that brought about the substantial fine for the car makers. Instead, the focus of the case was the restriction of (sustainability) innovation which in turn leads to less polluting cars. The sustainability benefit is a spillover effect. However, this spillover effect seems to have motivated the Commission to pursue the case. Moreover, the Commission also linked the environmental harm back to consumers, highlighting that environmental performance is nowadays an important parameter of competition in the context of car purchases.

Another case that might be mentioned in this context is the *Nespresso* case[102] by the French competition authority. This case started after a complaint by a smaller competitor, the Ethical Coffee Company. It concerned an abuse of dominance by the maker of *Nespresso* coffee machines and the 'aftermarket' of coffee capsules that could be used in these machines. The authority's action and the subsequent commitment decision allowed consumers to buy and use other, eg, bio-degradable capsules from other suppliers in their Nespresso coffee machines. With this opening up we can equally imagine that coffee produced with higher levels of social sustainability might now become available to consumers.

[100] See <https://ec.europa.eu/commission/presscorner/detail/en/ip_21_3581> (accessed 18 January 2025).

[101] See <https://ec.europa.eu/commission/presscorner/detail/en/statement_21_3583> (accessed 18 January 2025).

[102] Decision 14-D-09 of 04 September 2014.

b) Innovation in the merger and abuse context

The *BMW, Daimler and VW* case concerned an agreement, or one might say cartel, not to compete on innovation that would increase the sustainability of cars. However, negative effects on innovation that are relevant to sustainability can also be examined in the context of mergers or abuse cases. For example, it has been suggested that the *Bayer/Monsanto*[103] merger would not only increase industry concentration, entrench market power leading to higher prices for farmers and locking them in, but also affect the availability of seed diversity. Overall, the mergers could lead to increased use of fossil fuel-based herbicides and pesticides, thereby negatively affects sustainability.[104] In this case, the Commission went further than a more orthodox approach might have suggested. It not only looked at potential price increases, which result from reduced innovation competition, but also looked at the effects on innovation as such by examining post-transaction incentives for new or more environmentally friendly products. Hence, the Commission was able to address some of these concerns[105] in the context of its examination of possible innovation harms, in particular innovation efforts.

Bayer/Monsanto (EU)[106]

Bayer/Monsanto concerned the merger of two giants, the German Bayer and US-based Monsanto, both active in seeds, pesticides/herbicides, fertilizers, and digital agriculture product markets around the globe.

Background of the case

The *Bayer/Monsanto* merger, following the *Dow/DuPont* and *ChemChina/Syngenta* mergers, created the largest corporation globally in seeds, traits, and crop protection through digital agriculture, which is crucial for agribusiness and food production. This raised concerns about environmental impact and increased chemicals-based farming, prompting over 50,000 petitions to the EU Commission.[107] After settling the case with the US

[103] (n 93).

[104] In particular with regard to biodiversity, climate, and health. See in this regard Ioannis Lianos and Dmitry Katalevsky, 'Merger Activity in the Factors of Production Segments of the Food Value Chain: A Critical Assessment of the Bayer/Monsanto Merger' (2017) Centre for Law, Economics and Society Policy Paper Series 2017/1 available at <https://www.ucl.ac.uk/cles/sites/cles/files/cles-policy-paper-1-2017.pdf> (accessed 18 January 2025); also critical with regard to the decision, see Fair Trade Advocacy Office, 'EU Competition Law and Sustainability in Food Systems: Addressing the Broken Links' (February 2019) available at <http://www.responsibleglobalvaluechains.org/images/PDF/FTAO_-_EU_Competition_Law_and_Sustainability_in_Food_Systems_Addressing_the_Broken_Links_2019.pdf> (accessed 18 January 2025).

[105] (n 93).

[106] ibid.

[107] It received them 'through emails, postcards, letters and tweets expressing concerns about the proposed acquisition'. See European Commission Press Release: Mergers, 'Commission clears Bayer's

DoJ,[108] the EU Commission approved the merger with structural remedies, noting the highly concentrated industry and the potential for reduced competition and innovation.[109]

The Commission's findings

The Commission mainly identified unilateral effects/non-coordinated effects with regard to price and innovation. The innovation effects were examined on their own. And, as with price effects, the Commission examined first- and second-order effects. It used a four-layer competitive assessment to examine present and future effects: 1) product/price competition between actual products of the parties, 2) competition between actual and forthcoming products and among forthcoming ones, and 3) innovation competition, including incentives to discontinue, delay, or reorient ongoing projects, as well as 4) incentives to innovate in the future.[110]

It highlighted that not only current innovation effects and but equally future ones are core of the mergers analysis.[111] The Commission's assessment of current innovation projects centred on overlapping research lines and similar pipeline projects targeting the same markets with a focus on possible discontinuation, delay, or redirection of these projects. This is likely if one party's research competes with the other party's existing or potential products.[112] One concern the Commission had about future effects was that the merger would reduce innovation competition by merging two of the few global R&D organizations in their field. Given the high entry barriers, any discontinuation of one R&D organization could significantly reduce overall innovation in the crop protection and seed industry.[113] Thus the Commission explained that the assessment of innovation competition requires:

> first ... the identification of those companies which, at an industry level, do have the assets and capabilities to discover and develop new products [and bring them to the market]. Secondly, ... to identify and analyse those spaces in which innovation competition occurs in the trait industry. [Since] R&D players do not innovate for all the product markets ... at the same time [and]

acquisition of Monsanto, subject to conditions', Brussels, 21 March 2018, available at <http://europa.eu/rapid/press-release_IP-18-2282_en.htm> (accessed 18 January 2025); see also the Commissioner's reply to the petitioners of 22 July 2017, available at <https://ec.europa.eu/competition/mergers/cases/additional_data/m8084_4719_6.pdf> (accessed 18 January 2025).

108 *US v Bayer AG, Monsanto Company, and BASF SE* Case 1:18-cv-01241 (JEB).
109 *Bayer/Monsanto* (n 93) para 229.
110 ibid, para 49. Pointing to Commission Decision in Case M.7932 *Dow/DuPont* (2017), recitals 272 to 302 regarding incentives for future innovation.
111 *Bayer/Monsanto* (n 93) paras 63–64, 66.
112 ibid para 53.
113 ibid para 55.

> do not innovate randomly without targeting specific spaces within that industry. [The setting up of] innovation capabilities and ... research, ... ha[s] specific discovery targets. [paras 1009–1010]

To assess the broader effects the focus was on innovation capabilities[114] of the players with research assets and capabilities that are developing new products in the 'crop protection and/or seed industry'.[115] In the second part of the analysis, the focus was on effects on 'innovation spaces'.[116] It found that the parties'

> incentives to innovate are driven by the risk that successful innovation by their rivals may lead to a loss of market share (and, consequently, profits) and by the prospect of gaining valuable sales from their rivals.... [T]here is also evidence [of] cannibalisation when introducing new products. That [means taking] into account ... that this new product may subtract sales revenues from another [current or developed] product[s]. [para 79]

Importantly, in this decision, the Commission not only considered effects in (the usual) immediate time frame but also the long-term effects of the new entity's 'reduced incentives to develop ... the same number of new products'[117] compared to the but-for scenario. Overall, these effects would lead to consumer harm

> directly by a loss of innovation and ultimately by a loss of product variety and quality, by a lower rate of introduction of new and improved products, or by a reduced intensity of future product market competition in the overlap markets where the discontinued, deferred or redirected products would have been introduced but for the Transaction. More generally, the loss of an independent innovator brought about by the Transaction would be ultimately associated with a reduction in competition for future innovative products. This harm resulting from the absence of competition between the Parties in those markets could be felt repeatedly year after year for any possible future interaction between the Parties. [para 88]

[114] In this regard see David J Teece, Gary Pisano, and Amy Shuen, 'Dynamic Capabilities and Strategic Management' (1997) 18(7) *Strategic Management Journal* 509–533.

[115] *Bayer/Monsanto* (n 93) para 54.

[116] Footnote 23 of the decision provides a short explanation which builds upon Case No COMP/M.7932 *Dow/DuPont* C(2017) 1946 final paras 342–361. The term aims to capture the relatively unspecific but targeted nature of innovation; in other words, the innovation will target a specific problem and might do so with a specific approach. The final product will then be a specific pathway within this broader direction. It should be noted that this approach differs from the 'innovation markets' approach found for example in the US, in that it focuses on innovation as an 'input activity for both the upstream technology markets and downstream markets' (Case No COMP/M.7932 *Dow/DuPont* para 348; Case No COMP/M.8084 *Bayer/Monsanto* paras 1008–1023, 1089).

[117] *Bayer/Monsanto* (n 93) para 83.

Using the same approach, the Commission also examined possible effects on innovation with regard to bee health[118] and digitally enabled agriculture.[119]

Interestingly, the Commission felt that it also had to address the issue of 'non-competition concerns'[120] raised by third parties (eg NGOs) which included impacts on biodiversity, food safety, and loss of environmentally friendly innovation. It clarified that it is 'bound to take into consideration a plurality of objectives including human health, environment and consumer protection, in defining and implementing the Union policies and activities.'[121] Therefore it has

> placed its competitive assessment ... within the general framework of the achievement of the fundamental objectives referred to in the EU Treaties. In particular, the Commission is mindful of the potential implications of a possible reduction of competition caused by the Transaction on human health, food safety, consumer protection, environmental protection and climate. [And thus] has carried out a thorough and rigorous assessment of the likely effects of the Transaction not only on current and potential price and product competition, but also on innovation competition, including, in particular, both the incentives to discontinue, delay or reorient ongoing pipeline projects, and the incentives to develop new and better quality products in the future. [paras 3011–3012]

Yet, it also highlighted that it is bound by the principle of conferral. In other words, it has to act within the limits of its powers.[122] It is, thus, limited to assessing the implications of a transaction on the objective of EU merger control, namely

> to protect competition in the internal market and more specifically to permit 'the effective control of all concentrations in terms of their effect on the structure of competition in the Community' .... Therefore, whilst the general framework of the achievement of the other mentioned criteria not related strictly to competition is taken into account in the competitive appraisal, the Commission is nevertheless bound to ... clear a merger when its competition appraisal, taking into account all relevant criteria, concludes that it does not significantly impede effective competition. [paras 3018–3020]

118 More specifically, varroa mite infestations of bee colonies, ibid paras 2409–2441.
119 ibid paras 2442–2872.
120 Which it considered those 'not related to the protection of effective competition', ibid para 3005.
121 ibid para 3010.
122 ibid paras 3014–3016, 3019, 3022.

The *Bayer/Monsanto* decision builds on the decision in *Dow/Dupont*[123] where the Commission carried out an in-depth assessment of innovation competition[124] in the 'form of discontinuation, deferment or redirection of competing lines of research and early pipeline products'[125] which could cause 'long-term harm to consumers in the markets where a reduction of variety would take place'.[126] In that decision, the Commission set out that it would 'consider metrics of innovation taking place at an industry level as well as innovation taking place in [innovation] spaces'[127] and highlighted the environmental benefits of new developments.[128]

Building on these considerations, *Bayer/Monsanto* applied an expanded innovation analysis by focusing on the concept of innovation spaces. It was thereby able to examine some effects that the merger might have on sustainability, both upstream and downstream. Similarly, it is important to note that the Commission also broke ground by examining effects on innovation as a separate element of its analysis. By examining innovation *per se* and not only the price effects of innovation, the Commission also defines the boundary between, on the one hand, what it considers still within the competition analysis and, on the other, 'non-competition concerns'.

These cases show how sustainability might already play a role in the assessment of innovation in a merger context. Yet, it is possible to further expand the Commission's innovation theories of harm, thereby pushing this boundary.[129] There are a number of reasons why the Commission's innovation assessment may be seen as too limited.[130] The most important elements seem to be that the Commission's theory in *Bayer/Monsanto* does not examine the merger's impacts on the variety of innovation paths and innovation targets. This is the result of the Commission's analysis, which is backward-looking and examines previous commercial success of innovation outputs, rather than, for example, whether previous innovations were ground-breaking. The unilateral effects analysis in the decision

123 *Dow/DuPont* (n 116).

124 On the interaction between sustainability innovation in this decision see also Lianos and Katalevsky (n 105) 20–23.

125 Commission Decision (n 116), para 277.

126 ibid para 283.

127 ibid para 352.

128 See eg ibid para 774 (herbicides) and para 1173 (insecticides).

129 For a view that suggests that the Commission's approach with regard to innovation spaces can be extended to efficiencies and failing firms in merger cases, see Emanuela Lecchi, 'Sustainability and EU Merger Control' (2023) 44(2) *European Competition Law Review* 70–80.

130 See eg Elias Deutscher and Stavros Makris, 'Sustainability Concerns in EU Merger Control: From Output-Maximising to Polycentric Innovation Competition' (2023) 11(3) *Journal of Antitrust Enforcement* 350–399, who also suggest ways how these limitations could be rectified based on Hayek's and Polanyi's work; or Ioannis Lianos, 'The Bayer/Monsanto merger: a critical appraisal' (2018) 19(9) *Deutscher Bundestag Ausschussdrucksache* 90 available at <https://www.bundestag.de/resource/blob/561882/f3c2c54c94f77f312e806e7d97615d18/sv-lianos-data.pdf> (accessed 18 January 2025), arguing that the seed and agro-chem mergers affect the future control of food production and innovation substantially, so that one would have to ask whether narrow price, output, and innovation theories are sufficient to capture what is at stake.

ignores crowding-out effects that the merger might have beyond the two parties. Thus, the effects on companies competing via more remote innovation paths are irrelevant in the analysis. As a consequence, the decision does not protect consumers from negative effects on such remote innovation paths which might provide more sustainable solutions, for example by controlling the growth of unwanted plants in other ways than with herbicides and plant seeds or traits that are herbicide-resistant.

In a more recent case, the EU Commission looked at innovation efforts and capabilities to protect innovation with regard to sustainability. *Sika/MBCC*[131] concerned a merger regarding chemicals used in construction, in particular in the concrete/cement industry. The parties were both strong innovators, both also leading green R&D. This green R&D was important to meeting sustainability challenges in the industry and was examined as part of the closeness of competition analysis. Concerns in this regard led to an extensive global divestiture of parts of the business and R&D facilities. Broadly speaking, in such cases the Commission also has an eye out for 'green killer acquisitions'.[132]

While such questions frequently occur in the context of mergers, similar questions about preventing sustainability innovation can also occur in the context of abuse of dominant position. A concrete illustration could be the recent decision by the Italian competition authority in *Corepla*.[133] The case concerned the dominant company's exclusivity clauses and refusal to deal with a competitor regarding recovery of plastic packaging. The agency imposed first interim measures and then a fine. and highlighted how preventing competition in the recycling of plastic would reduce competition and innovation in waste management and harm environmental causes.

3. Summary

We have seen how competition enforcement can address some sustainability concerns with more orthodox tools sometimes applied in more innovative ways where sustainability is seen as a competition parameter.

On the one hand, cases can be explained through the lens of another more orthodox theory, the protection of (consumer) choice[134] or closeness of competition.

[131] EU Commission, Case M.10560 *Sika/MBCC*.

[132] See Catherine Ellwanger and others, 'EU Green Mergers & Acquisitions Deals – How Merger Control Contributes to a Sustainable Future' (2023) 2 *Competition Merger Brief* available at <https://competition-policy.ec.europa.eu/system/files/2023-09/kdal23002enn_mergers_brief_2023_2.pdf> (accessed 18 January 2025).

[133] ICA Decision (October 2020) No 28430, Case A351 *Riciclo Imballaggi Primari/Condotte Abusive COREPLA*.

[134] On choice as a standard for competition enforcement see eg, Robert H Lande, 'Consumer Choice as the Ultimate Goal of Antitrust' (2001) 62(3) *University of Pittsburgh Law Review* 503–525; Paul Nihoul, '"Freedom of Choice": The Emergence of a Powerful Concept in European Competition Law'

While the closeness of competition examined in merger reviews is rather orthodox,[135] a choice can equally be seen in this way. Where the competition law in a country is specifically designed or enforced to protect choice, sustainability can be protected as an aspect of such choice. In the EU, choice is an important factor,[136] but even in countries like the US, choice helps to explain numerous cases.[137] As such, it is not surprising that sustainability can be part of a choice-based assessment, as focusing on behaviour that artificially restricts choice helps in protecting 'innovation, variety, quality, safety and other aspects of non-price competition'.[138] Overall, in such cases, competition law enforcers can step in and protect competition that fosters sustainability, acting as guardians of sustainability by safeguarding competition.[139]

On the other hand, competition enforcers can also act as guardians of sustainability by means of a more targeted intervention, as in the case of sustainability innovation. In this area, rather than coincidentally affecting sustainability, the cases by the European Commission show a clear focus on sustainability innovation. The Commission aims to protect innovation that leads to sustainability, which is very much in line with the UN's sustainable development goals and their emphasis on innovation to assist in their achievements. The foundation was set in *Dow/Dupont* where the Commission set out its framework for assessing innovation competition. *Bayer/Monsanto* then built upon this framework and applied it to sustainability innovation with a focus on innovation spaces, clearly establishing innovation effects as a separate category beyond price effects. These innovation-based cases provided the Commission with a springboard to then pursue their first cartel case concerning a restriction of (sustainability) innovation. The case was given the telling name *Car Emissions*, and the Commissioner's statement highlights the negative environmental effect resulting from the collusion as well as linking the environmental harm back to consumers, for whom environmental performance has become an important factor of competition when purchasing cars. While the Commission has started to explore previously unknown territory, the boundaries of the innovation analysis could be pushed further. In particular, exploring the effects of the variety of innovation (paths and targets) might allow the enforcer to

(2012) 3 *Concurrences* 55–70; see however with regard to the dangers Renato Nazzini, *The Foundations of European Union Competition Law—The Objective and Principles of Article 102* (OUP 2011) 30–32; see also ibid 31 where he notes 'when consumer choice is seen as an objective in its own right, it may become a disguised form of competitor protection: a competitor deserves to be protected solely on the basis that it offers a differentiated product'.

[135] Although some methods to determine the closeness of competition may be innovative, such as the EU Commission's.

[136] Nihoul (n 134).

[137] Lande (n 134) 508–510.

[138] ibid 505.

[139] See also Chapter 2 on competition as a means to enhance sustainability.

protect consumers from harm to more remote innovation paths, especially those that are more beneficial for sustainability.

VI. Competition enforcement and directly fostering sustainability: on the margins of competition law

Having examined how competition enforcement can be used indirectly to foster sustainability, it is time for us to look a bit closer at whether and to what extent competition law can be used in more direct ways to foster sustainability. We will, in particular, look at the related regulation of superior bargaining power and exploitative abuses. Such an approach might push the boundaries of what some people might see as the proper scope of competition law.

1. Exploitative abuses and superior bargaining power

Where companies have substantial market power so that they can be considered to be in a dominant position, we might imagine a focus on exploitative practices to address sustainability concerns, for example with regard to poverty and prices for farmers.[140] The idea of examining exploitative abuses is possibly also supported by the fact that a relationship exists between higher levels of market power and unsustainable business practices.[141] Market power might enable a company to disregard consumers' preferences for sustainability.[142] While the focus in many jurisdictions in competition law has been on exclusionary abuses, a refocusing of enforcement efforts on exploitative abuses could bring unsustainable practices within the scope of competition law's abuse provisions.[143]

[140] See Simon Holmes, 'Climate Change, Sustainability and Competition Law' (2020) 8(2) *Journal Antitrust Enforcement* 384–387; Hellenic Competition Commission, 'Staff Discussion Paper—Sustainability Issues and Competition Law (2020) available at <https://www.epant.gr/files/2020/Staff_Discussion_paper.pdf> (accessed 18 January 2025) para 91. See also Marios Iacovides and Christos Vrettos, 'Radical For Whom? Unsustainable Business Practices as Abuses' in Simon Holmes, Dirk Middelschulte, and Martijn Snoep (eds), *Competition Law, Climate Change & Environmental Sustainability* (Concurrences 2021) 91–103.

[141] Marios Iacovides and Christos Vrettos, 'Falling Through the Cracks No More? Article 102 TFEU and Sustainability: the Relation between Dominance, Environmental Degradation, and Social Injustice' (2022) 10(1) *Journal of Antitrust Enforcement* 32–62, who highlight that the market power either enables or facilitates unsustainable business practices, see ibid 45–52.

[142] ibid section 6.1, pointing also to Ding Wenzhi and others, 'Competition Laws, Norms And Corporate Social Responsibility' (2020) Nber Working Paper Series Working Paper 27493 available at <http://www.nber.org/papers/w27493> (accessed 18 January 2025) who show empirically that higher competition leads to greater CSR activity.

[143] See Simon Holmes and Michelle Meagher, 'A Sustainable Future: How Can Control of Monopoly Play a Part? Part II. Using Competition Law to Tackle Unsustainable Practices as Abuses of Monopoly Power' (2023) 44(2) *European Competition Law Review* 61–69.

Closely related to exploitative abuses are situations of superior bargaining power, in particular in the context of sustainability and poverty. Such questions may arise especially in cases where few buyers source input from a large group of atomized buyers who are living in poverty. The issue of buyer power is treated differently in different jurisdictions. Such situations might in some jurisdictions also be subject to competition law *strictu sensu*, while other jurisdictions deal with such issues under competition law-related regimes. For example, the UK addressed issues of buyer power in the context of supermarkets using the Groceries Supply Code of Practice,[144] by means of an order after a market investigation. And the South African competition authority issued guidelines on the interpretation of sections 9 and 8(4)[145] of the Competition Act, prohibiting the abuse of a dominant position. These provisions prohibit dominant buyers in certain sectors[146] from price discrimination and from imposing unfair prices or trading conditions on small and medium-sized companies and historically disadvantaged persons.

Buying-Power Guidelines[147] (South Africa)

The guidelines first explain the legal framework in general terms and highlight the sectors to which the prohibition applies. These are 'agro-processing, grocery wholesale & retail and the e-commerce & online services sector'.[148] The online services include services using sub-contracts 'to supply the service that forms the basis for an online sale'[149] but also 'e-market places, application stores and "gig economy" services'.[150]

After explaining whether a buyer is dominant in a certain market with a focus on market shares,[151] the guidelines explain that two benchmarks would be applied to determine unfair pricing:

> namely [a)] if the price is lower than the price paid to other suppliers of like products and [b)] the price previously paid to the same supplier for their product. The imposition of costs is a variant on the latter insofar as it reduces the net price received by the supplier.

[144] Which was the result of an order by the Competition Commission after a market investigation, see 'The Groceries (Supply Chain Practices) Market Investigation Order' (2009) available at <https://webarchive.nationalarchives.gov.uk/ukgwa/20111108202701/http://competition-commission.org.uk/inquiries/ref2006/grocery/pdf/revised_gscop_order.pdf> (accessed 18 January 2025).

[145] Which came into effect in January 2020.

[146] Eg Agro-processing, grocery wholesale & retail, e-Commerce and online services.

[147] Competition Commission, Buyer Power Enforcement Guidelines (12 May 2020) available at <https://www.compcom.co.za/wp-content/uploads/2020/05/Buyer-Power-Guidelines.pdf> (accessed 18 January 2025).

[148] ibid para 4.1.1.

[149] ibid.

[150] ibid.

[151] ibid paras 4.2–4.5.

> The Commission further notes that the regulations do not provide an exhaustive list of unfair pricing conditions …[152]

The guidance then sets out the details as to how the Commission will assess '[u]njustified lower price relative to other suppliers of like goods or services'[153] and on '[u]nfair downward adjustment to existing net prices'.[154] It provides an example from the dairy sector, where fresh milk (with the same properties) was purchased from a historically disadvantaged farmer at a 10 per cent discount as compared to prices paid to other non-disadvantaged farmers (at similar volumes and costs).

Regarding '[i]mposing Or Requiring An Unfair Trading Condition', the guidelines note the relevant EU rules[155] and the general buyer power provisions introduced in Kenya. The agency highlights that beyond the factors and benchmarks set out specifically in the act, it will take into account:

> [s]pecific types of practices identified as unfair trading practices in other jurisdictions.
>
> Instances where a trading condition is imposed on an SME or HDP firm but not on other suppliers …. The Commission notes that [even] uniformly imposed [conditions] across all suppliers may … be deemed unfair ….
>
> Instances where a uniform trading condition may have a disproportionate burden on SME or HDP firms. For example, unduly long payment terms, even if uniformly applied, are particularly burdensome to smaller businesses which have limited working capital. Similarly, contractual terms which impose a cost that is fixed irrespective of volumes supplied will be more onerous, on a per unit basis, to SMEs suppling smaller volumes.[156]

The Guidelines are accompanied by a list of trading terms and conditions that are likely to be abusive, and specifically address grocery retail, agro-processing, e-commerce, and online services. These lists contain for example payments later than thirty days after delivery, short-notice cancellations of perishable goods, or restrictions that enforce exclusivity of 'the provider's e-commerce or online service'.

[152] ibid paras 6.2–6.3.

[153] ibid paras 6.4–6.14.

[154] ibid paras 6.15–6.22.

[155] In particular Directive (EU) 2019/633 of the European Parliament and of the Council of 17 April 2019 on unfair trading practices in business-to-business relationships in the agricultural and food supply chain [2019] OJ L 111/59 and Regulation (EU) 2019/1150 of the European Parliament and of the Council of 20 June 2019 on promoting fairness and transparency for business users of online intermediation services [2019] OJ L 186/57.

[156] ibid paras 7.4.1–7.4.3.

These Buying-Power Guidelines[157] highlight a number of exploitative practices that can also be found in similar guidelines around the world and are occasionally reflective of the relevant legal provisions on the abuse of dominance under the relevant competition law. These guidelines and the general abuse of dominance provisions are not specifically designed to address sustainability concerns. But their format allows the South African authorities to use them proactively with regard to the social dimension of sustainability and in particular in the fight against poverty. The EU tried to address such abusive practices by adopting a directive on unfair trading practices in business-to-business relationships in the agricultural and food supply chain.[158]

However, it is important to note that market power/dominance is a requirement, before such practices can be considered abusive. This approach seems to reflect a general idea that is also inherent in the prohibition of exploitative abuses under EU competition law. EU competition law uses the concept of 'special responsibility'[159] of dominant undertakings to explain the imposition of the corresponding duty not to abuse that position. Some countries, such as Belgium[160] and Germany,[161] set a lower relative level of market power, while others, such as France and Kenya, go further and impose a general fair dealing obligation without a requirement of dominance.[162] In other jurisdictions, closely related obligations under rules on unfair competition may exist.

2. Unsustainable business activity as abuse

We might even observe how the boundaries are pushed further in addressing sustainability concerns by means of competition law. Some have noted a link between market power and unsustainable business behaviour.[163] This finding in turn has also led to suggestions that unsustainable business practices, as such, should be

[157] Commission Decision (n 147).

[158] See Directive (EU) 2019/633 (n 155).

[159] On the concept of special responsibility, see eg Giorgio Monti and Ekaterina Rousseva, 'The Special Responsibility of Dominant Undertakings' in Pınar Akman, Or Brook, and Konstantinos Stylianou (eds), *Research Handbook on Abuse of Dominance and Monopolization* (Edward Elgar 2023).

[160] Royal Decree of 31 July 2020 amending books I and IV of the Code of Economic Law as concerns the abuse of economic dependence, BS/MB 12 August 2020. For an overview see Jan Blockx, 'Belgian Prohibition of Abuse of Economic Dependence Enters into Force' (2021) 12 *Journal of European Competition Law & Practice* 321–325.

[161] Section 20 of the German Act against Restraints of Competition.

[162] See for example the Kenyan buyer power provisions, or the French provisions of Article L.420-2, para 2 of the French Commercial Code.

[163] Marios Iacovides and Christos Vrettos, 'Falling Through the Cracks No More? Article 102 TFEU and Sustainability: the Relation between Dominance, Environmental Degradation, and Social' (2022) 10(1) *Journal of Antitrust Enforcement* 32–62.

considered an abuse of dominance in the context of EU competition law. This argument[164] is based on the broad range of goals of EU competition law identified in the case law[165] and the fact that the list of abuses under EU law is non-exhaustive.[166] Such a constitutional reading suggests that the concept of abuse 'must be construed as including unsustainable business'.[167] Such a reading can result from finding that unsustainable business practices either fall within the established categories of abuse or fall under new categories.

One approach is focused on the exclusionary effect of providing firms with an unfair advantage, as unsustainable business practices distort prices, create entry barriers, and reduce innovation.[168] In these, competition is not based on the merits but on for example 'bribery, extortion, human rights violations, destruction of habitats and livelihoods, offering exploitative salaries and working conditions'.[169] The effect of such unfair advantages is the exclusion of competitors and reduced innovation incentives which already seem to protect interests under abuse prohibition.[170] The European Commission in fact seems to have adopted this idea in the Article 102 TFEU case against Zoetis.[171] Zoetis acquired a late-stage pipeline product[172] which would have been able to compete with Zoetis's own biological medicine Librela. It is alleged that Zoetis terminated the development and also refused to transfer the product further.

[164] Marios C Iacovides and Christos Vrettos, 'Radical For Whom? Unsustainable Business Practices as Abuses of Dominance' in Simon Holmes, Dirk Middelschulte, and Martijn Snoep (eds), *Competition Law, Climate Change & Environmental Sustainability* (Concurrences 2021) 97–99; see also Simon Holmes and Michelle Meagher, 'A Sustainable Future: How Can Control of Monopoly Power Play a Part? Part II. Using Competition Law to Tackle Unsustainable Practices as Abuses of Monopoly Power' (2023) 44(24) *ECLR* 61–69; Johannes Persch, 'The Output/Sustainability Paradox – a Pro-Enforcement Perspective on Sustainability in EU Competition Law' (2023) 15(2) *European Competition Law Review* 139–162.

[165] Konstantinos Stylianou and Marios C Iacovides, 'The Goals of EU Competition Law: A Comprehensive Empirical Investigation' (2022) 42(4) *Legal Studies* 620–648.

[166] See eg Case 6/72 *Continental Can* EU:C:1973:22 para 26; Case C-52/09 *TeliaSonera Sverige* EU:C:2011:83, para 26; Case C-280/08 *Deutsche Telekom v Commission* EU:C:2010:603, para 173; Case T-612/17 *Google LLC v Commission* EU:T:2021:763, para 154.

[167] Iacovides and Vrettos (n 141) 99.

[168] Marios C Iacovides and Valentin Mauboussin, 'Unilateral conduct and sustainability under EU competition law' in Julian Nowag (ed), *Research Handbook on Sustainability and Competition Law* (Edward Elgard 2024) section III.

[169] Iacovides and Vrettos (n 141) 101.

[170] ibid 102.

[171] See press release, 'Commission opens investigation into possible anticompetitive conduct by Zoetis over novel pain medicine for dogs' (26 March 2024) accessible at <https://ec.europa.eu/commission/presscorner/api/files/document/print/en/ip_24_1687/IP_24_1687_EN.pdf> (accessed on 18 January 2025).

[172] A medicine for chronic pain in dogs.

3. Summary

The idea of exploring the potential of using exploitative abuses to foster sustainability certainly has some way to go. Exploitative abuses have not been the focus of antitrust enforcement in recent years. However, with the pandemic, and even before, we have seen a renewed interest in this area of the law. Moreover, concerns about fairness and competition also permeate the rules on superior bargaining power, an area that, particularly in the food sector, has been the focus for some time.[173] While these issues are certainly not within what many would consider the core of competition law, they have received increasing attention. Not only because of the number of jurisdictions adopting such rules but also because we are seeing a similar development in the digital world where fairness in the marketplace becomes a concern. A prominent example may be the EU's Digital Market Act. The idea of seeing unsustainable business practices as abusive in themselves is going even further in pushing the boundaries of competition law. As this approach relies heavily on the EU's constitutional setup, we can ask whether a similar approach can be taken elsewhere. To answer this question for another jurisdiction, we would need to have a closer look into its competition law and its more general legal and constitutional setup. However, we can certainly perceive the tools existing in the context of exploitative abuses and superior bargaining power, and the concept of fairness as a way for authorities to act as guardians of sustainability and undoubtedly be able to push the boundaries. However, we should indeed also explore limiting principles in this regard, which we look at in the next section.

VII. Limits of competition enforcement for sustainability

In the previous sections, we have explored how fostering sustainability through the enforcement of competition can occur within more or less orthodox theories of harm. We have also seen areas where the boundaries of competition law are pushed; and sometimes pushed beyond what some people might see as the proper scope of competition law. This pushing of boundaries is not without risk in individual cases, and at some point might indeed transgress the limits of competition law. First, we do not find exploitative abuses to be a prohibited practice in all jurisdictions by means of competition law. For example, federal US antitrust law[174]

[173] For more details on how the human right to food might impact the application of competition law see eg Ioannis Lianos and Amber Darr, 'Hunger Games: Connecting the Right to Food and Competition Law' in Ioannis Lianos, Alexey Ivanov, and Dennis Davis, *Global Food Value Chains and Competition Law* (CUP 2022) 420–477.

[174] However, at state level, unfair and deceptive acts and practices laws might be applicable in some cases of exploitation. Moreover, a number of states, eg Arizona, Delaware, Ohio, have general price gouging laws, while others eg Texas have such laws that apply in cases of emergency situations.

does not foresee such a prohibition. Second, we can observe a certain hesitance by competition authorities, in particular in cases of exploitative abuses in the form of excessive pricing.[175] In these areas, competition authorities are particularly careful not to be conceived as price-setting authorities. Third and relatedly, competition authorities need to be mindful of not being perceived as standard-setting authorities: neither as price-setting authorities nor as setting the relevant sustainability standard. This mindful approach follows from the separation of powers principle and capacity concerns in terms of acting as a regulator, setting the relevant sustainability standard.[176] Yet, it is important to highlight that 'being mindful' does not mean it cannot be done, as the comparison to excessive pricing cases shows. Just because establishing excessive pricing is difficult, it does not follow that it can never be established as an abuse. Mindful of this limitation, the Dutch competition authority in its draft guidelines for sustainability[177] made reference[178] to standards adopted by the competent national authority or by means of international law.[179]

VIII. Conclusion

This chapter examined efforts and possibilities for competition enforcers to act as guardians of sustainability by enforcing the competition provisions. Overall, we can observe that sustainability can be fostered by means of enforcing competition laws. In other words, there is an overlap between sustainability and protecting competition. The extent of this overlap can vary depending on the jurisdiction and their specific priorities. Notably, traditional competition tools can be utilized to promote sustainability, even when applied in the most orthodox way. However, we might also see the use of these tools in more creative ways to broaden the overlap between sustainability and the protection of competition, leading to more sustainable outcomes.

In this regard, quality parameters—and in particular (sustainability) innovation—provide an avenue for achieving more sustainability via competition

[175] See eg OECD, 'Excessive Prices in Pharmaceutical Markets—Background Note by the Secretariat' (2018) DAF/COMP(2018)12; OECD, 'Excessive Prices—Background Paper by the Secretariat' (2011) DAF/COMP(2011)18.

[176] In this regard see Julian Nowag, *Environmental Integration in Competition and Free-Movement Laws* (OUP 2017) 141–142.

[177] ACM, 'Second draft—Guidelines Sustainability Agreements: Opportunities Within Competition Law' (January 2021) available at <https://www.acm.nl/sites/default/files/documents/second-draft-version-guidelines-on-sustainability-agreements-oppurtunities-within-competition-law.pdf> (accessed 18 January 2025).

[178] Although this reference was made in the context of private parties adopting a standard (see the next chapter), rather than in the situation where competition authority acts as guardians of sustainability by enforcing the competition law.

[179] See ACM (n 177), eg paras 27–29, 45, 48. It might also be noted that in the Netherlands, as a monist country, international treaties are directly binding without further implementing acts and therefore also bind the national competition authority.

law. Quality and innovation are concerns that seem to fall naturally within the purview of competition authorities. Thus, it seems not far-fetched for a competition authority to examine whether quality in terms of sustainability parameters of a product or sustainability innovation is impacted by certain practices.

However, some jurisdictions are able to go further. For instance, jurisdictions with provisions relating to exploitative business practices seem to have an additional tool to foster sustainability. The prosecution of exploitative business practices seems particularly apt to be used where business practices harm sustainability. And while there are risks involved in an expansive interpretation of specific competition provisions, an expansive interpretation is not always needed. In some jurisdictions, specific laws are in place to address for example issues of buyer power. These provisions and their use may be seen by some as going beyond the proper role of competition law. Yet, such views are often shaped by the legal setup of a particular jurisdiction. It is difficult to make broad and general statements about the 'proper role' of competition law without considering the specific rules and the legal and institutional context.[180]

Regardless of individual views on the 'proper role' of competition law, we can observe that competition law and policy can play a significant role in the broader sustainability debate.[181] This chapter has thus provided a toolbox of antitrust enforcement measures. Competition enforcers can strategically pick and choose in their pursuit of sustainability from a competition law angle, taking into account their specific competition laws. In this way, competition enforcement can act as a guardian of sustainability.

Amahle and Junior and the price of bread

If the increase in prices for Amahle and Junior's bread was indeed caused by a cartel or other anti-competitive activities, the enforcement action by the South African competition authority in the bread cartel case will help in addressing the price rise for bread. And while it will not solve all the sustainability problems

[180] To take an example more frequently encountered by competition lawyers, see the EU Digital Markets Act (DMA). This act has competition issues at its heart. But, then, it is not antitrust in its traditional sense. Instead it is a new form of regulation. Does this mean that the DMA goes beyond the proper role of competition law? Or do the principles of competition law not apply to this legislation? In the end, it is a (new) form of regulation. More generally, in this and other regulated areas, we would typically see a logic applied that is different from traditional antitrust.

[181] See in particular the OECD report on poverty and competition, OECD (n 33). Moreover, eg in South Africa, competition policy has been seen as an important tool, adopted as part of the reforms after the end of apartheid. Competition policy is used with regard to the legacy of apartheid in fostering the participation of black-owned companies, addressing the historical legacy of a highly concentrated economy. See Simon Roberts, 'The Role for Competition Policy in Economic Development: the South African Experience' (2010) 21 *Development Southern Africa* 227–243.

that South Africa faces, the enforcement action can still make a difference for Amahle and Junior, as they can hope to buy their bread at cheaper prices again.

In this sense, the action by the competition authority might make a contribution to the fight against poverty, but also towards issues related to deforestation and health outcomes. More concretely, the lower price of bread might mean that Amahle and Junior can continue to use the gas stove, and that Junior does not have to spend his time and energy on collecting firewood and chopping down trees for cooking. Moreover, they can continue growing vegetables in their garden, and Amahle will not have to spend her only day off from work preparing food, but can make better use of her time.

4

Competition authorities as public enablers of private sustainability efforts

Ujang and Wati and the clearing of rainforest

Ujang and Wati had been through a lot; they had just moved deeper into the jungle and Wati had carried their little one all the way on her back, as their old habitation was no longer safe. That night, they heard eerie sounds again. While it had been unsettling, they had become used to the sounds of the monstrous beasts and their supporting armies. The next morning, they woke up as trees were falling. As Ujang saw Wati and their child being hit by a tree, he attacked the red beast in rage and desperation, trying to stop it from further destroying the forest. Unfortunately, he failed and was quickly knocked out by the beast.

Ujang woke up in an orang-utan sanctuary after forest workers had tranquillized him as he was 'fighting' with the claws of a red harvester used to clear the rainforest to clear space for a palm oil plantation.

Clearing of forest for palm oil plantations is one of the main drivers of deforestation in Southeast Asian countries such as Indonesia. While small-scale farmers may also deforest land for subsistence farming, large-scale deforestation for palm oil production remains a main driver for the loss of rainforests, with devastating effects not only on habitats for plants and animals like the endangered orang-utans, but also on the climate. Deforestation happens mostly in remote locations. And while deforestation in those areas may be illegal, enforcement of laws protecting the rainforests is minimal.

Palm oil is mainly used as an input for industrial food and cosmetic production. It can be found in a wide range of foods such as chocolates, ice creams, biscuits and cakes, margarine, and even fruit juice. It is also used for soap and shampoo, toothpaste, cosmetics, and detergents. The vast majority is produced in Borneo.

As part of the UN 2014 climate negotiations, the Indonesian Palm Oil Pledge was made by the biggest palm oil companies to achieve zero-deforestation in palm oil production. While welcomed by the smallholders, the government and

Global Antitrust and Sustainability. Julian Nowag, Oxford University Press. © Julian Nowag 2025.
DOI: 10.1093/9780191955013.003.0004

later the competition authority saw this pledge as a threat to competition from smallholders and started a competition law investigation, after which the pledge was abandoned.[1]

I. Introduction

How does competition law treat such initiatives by firms that are aimed at improving the sustainability situation? When are such initiatives seen as restrictions of competition? How do the structural and governance arrangements affect the assessment of whether a restriction exists? What happens if a restriction of competition is established? Can positive sustainability benefits be used to justify such a restriction? How would this be assessed?

While the previous chapter examined the enforcement of competition law provisions against actions that harm sustainability and competition, this chapter turns our attention to efforts by companies that improve sustainability. It covers situations where competition does not foster sustainability and a conflict appears to exist, as exemplified by the Palm Oil Pledge. This area involves the more contentious issues regarding the interaction between business actions in support of sustainability and competition law. The key question here is: what limits does competition law impose on the pursuit of sustainability by market participants? In this chapter, we will investigate the different ways and means by which competition authorities across the globe can ensure that competition law does not unnecessarily prevent or limit the achievement of sustainability goals.[2] The chapter provides a menu of options with which to address perceived conflicts between sustainability and competition. The presented options allow competition enforcers to choose

[1] For an overview and discussion, see Ahmad Dermawan and Otto Hospes (2018) 'When the State Brings Itself Back into GVC: The Case of the Indonesian Palm Oil Pledge' 9 *Global Policy* 21–28. A similar governmental standard was subsequently adopted, but issues of enforcement certainly remain. For two opposing comments on the pledge and its effectiveness in the overall development of the saga, see Scott Poynton, 'Failure of Indonesia's Palm Oil Commitment 'Not Bad News' [Commentary]' (27 July 2016) available at <https://news.mongabay.com/2016/07/failure-of-indonesias-ipop-not-bad-news-commentary> (accessed 22 January 2025) and for the other side of the debate, Dave McLaughlin, 'IPOP's Demise Undercuts Palm Oil Industry Progress [Commentary]' (8 August 2016) available at <https://news.mongabay.com/2016/08/ipops-demise-undercuts-palm-oil-industry-progress-commentary/> (accessed 22 January 2025).

[2] The number of cases where sustainability was considered as a 'defence' in competition proceedings more than doubled in the years 2018–2021 (twenty-two cases) as compared to 2015–2017 (eight cases); see Hungarian Competition Authority, 'Sustainable Development and Competition Law—Survey Report (Special Project for the 2021 ICN Annual Conference)' (30 September 2021) available at <https://www.gvh.hu/pfile/file?path=/en/gvh/Conference/icn-2021-annual-conference/sustainability_survey_REPORT_3rdEd_2021_09_30_final_PUBLIC.pdf1&inline=true> (accessed 22 January 2025) 33.

solutions that are best suited and can be adjusted to the local legal context, making them public enablers of private sustainability efforts.

In the heat of the sustainability and competition debate, nuance is sometimes lost, and too often the focus is placed solely on balancing the restriction of competition against the benefits of sustainability. To introduce more nuance, we will revisit the two conceptually different options[3] highlighted in Chapter 1.[4] The first option, covered in the first half of the chapter, involves situations where sustainability activities are altogether excluded from the scope of competition law. In other words, this option covers scenarios where, prima facie, a conflict appears to exist between the protection of competition and sustainability. However, upon closer examination, this conflict dissolves like a mirage, as the prohibitions of competition law on anti-competitive conduct do not apply to such sustainability actions by market participants.

The second part of the chapter moves us closer to the heated debate—balancing competition and sustainability. It covers such situations and explores how anti-competitive actions are balanced with the resulting benefits, for example in terms of consumer welfare. We will see that even within this balancing exercise, not all issues are hotly debated, and only a small area is subject to intense (and justified) debate. Hence, in the second part, we will explore in more detail the two different forms of balancing between competition and sustainability. In particular, we will delve into 'abstract balancing' and 'competition-specific balancing'.[5] In the case of abstract balancing, sustainability benefits are directly weighed against reductions of competition. In contrast, competition-specific balancing first 'translates' sustainability benefits into the language of competition law and then conducts an 'orthodox' competition assessment. In this assessment, mostly economics concepts, such as consumer welfare, are employed to measure the benefits that result from the restriction of competition. In most cases, sustainability benefits can be translated into the economic language of competition law without complications, but still there are limitations on how far competition lawyers would and could adjust their usual toolbox to incorporate aspects of sustainability claims that do not fit the current standards.[6] We will address these questions of abstract and competition-specific balancing in the final section of this chapter.

[3] See Julian Nowag and Alexandra Teorell, 'Beyond Balancing: Sustainability and Competition Law' (2020) 4 *Concurrences - On-Topic*, paras 6–9; and in more detail, Julian Nowag, *Environmental Integration in Competition and Free-Movement Laws* (OUP 2017) 31–49.

[4] See in this regard also Chapter 1.

[5] For a similar distinction see also Christopher Townley, *Article 81 and Public Policy* (Hart 2009) who in part B of his book distinguishes between 'mere-balancing' and 'market-balancing'.

[6] For an overview see, eg, Nowag and Teorell (n 3); Julian Nowag, 'Competition Law's Sustainability Gap? Tools for an Examination and a Brief Overview' (2022) *Nordic Journal of European Law* 149–165.

II. Of prima facie and actual conflicts

Where competition law prima facie appears to be an obstacle to pursuing business activities that foster sustainability, a closer look is always worth the effort. The perceived problem can be a mirage that dissolves upon closer examination. The crux here is how we define the scope of competition law;[7] taking into account its exceptions and intricacies that exist generally or are available in specific jurisdictions. The exceptions exclude certain sustainability activities from the scope of competition law altogether. This area encompasses situations related to the definition of commercial activity that is subject to competition law, platform arrangements, sectoral exemptions, state action/compulsion matters, agreements to comply with local laws, and platform arrangements, as well as cases where no restrictions of competition in the sense of the competition provisions exist. Standards that comply with certain conditions are prime examples of such activities not restricting competition. Where any of these exceptions apply, the sustainability action is outside the scope of competition law. Where none of them applies, we need to explore what options balancing the law provides to solve such actual conflicts.

III. The mirage of a conflict: matter outside the scope of competition law

This section looks at the mirage of a conflict between competition and sustainability. Upon closer inspection, this apparent conflict disappears, as relevant rules have been designed in a way to exclude the application of competition law. This can be the case because the activity is considered generally outside the scope of competition law, such as not being an economic/commercial activity, or happening within a single commercial unit rather than on the market. However, other arrangements also fall outside the scope of competition law and are examined in turn. These include, for example, certain forms of platform arrangements, situations, where a sector in which the sustainability activity takes place is exempted from the application of competition law, situations where the state has forced the companies to act in such a way, or a part of the state itself adopted the measure. Similarly, in certain jurisdictions, arrangements that mirror applicable legal standards are excluded. Finally, this section looks at sustainability rules, which are set as part of a standard that complies with certain conditions, and situations where the sustainability arrangement does not substantially affect competition.

[7] The terms are used here in a broad-brush way. For more details on this distinction between scope and balancing in the competition law see the literature in (n 1).

1. Arrangements generally outside the scope of competition laws

Across the world, there are numerous activities that are not covered by competition law *per se*. These are situations where the activities are, for example, not of a commercial/economic nature; or the activities occur within rather than between firms, or form part of collective bargaining rather than activities between firms.

a) Commercial/economic activities covered by competition law

Not every activity contributing to sustainability matters is automatically subject to competition law. Numerous jurisdictions define the scope of their competition law by reference to certain criteria by which only corporations[8]/enterprises or business and economic activities are subject to competition law. Such rules can be particularly relevant when non-governmental organizations (NGOs) such as registered charities engage in sustainability activities that may or may not conflict with competition law.

The Scope of Japan's Antimonopoly Act

The Japanese Antimonopoly Act[9] and its provisions on private monopolization and unreasonable restraint of trade are set out in Chapter 2 of the act; those on unfair trade practices, in Chapter 5, apply to 'enterprises'; whereas Chapter 4's rules on mergers and acquisitions are specifically addressed to companies.[10]

The definition of enterprises can be found in Article 2(1):

> The term 'enterprise' as used in this Act means a person who operates a commercial, industrial, financial or other business. Any officer, employee, agent or

[8] See for example the Australian Competition and Consumer Act 2010 which for reasons of the allocation of powers in the federal system, only applies to corporations. However, the relevant competition code extends the application of the rules on anti-competitive conduct to unincorporated entities/individuals engaged in 'business'. And while the act does not define the term 'business', it clarifies that profit-making is not necessary (section 4 CCA) and that certain governmental activities do not amount to business activity (see section 2C(1) CCA).

[9] Act on Prohibition of Private Monopolization and Maintenance of Fair Trade (Act No 54 of 14 April 1947) (Japan).

[10] See, eg, Art 10 AMA: '(1) No company may acquire or hold shares of any other companies if its acquisition or holding of shares substantially restrains competition in any particular field of trade, nor may any company use unfair trade practices to acquire or hold shares in another company.'; Art 15 AMA: '(1) No company may effect a merger if any of the following items applies: (i) if the merger substantially restrains competition in a particular field of trade (ii) if unfair trade practices are employed in the course of the merger.' But see Art 14 AMA: 'A person other than a company may not acquire or hold shares in a company if the person's doing so substantially restrains competition in any particular field of trade, nor may a person that is not a company use unfair trade practices to acquire or hold shares in a company.'

other person who acts for the benefit of any enterprise is deemed to be an enterprise with regard to the application of the provisions of the following paragraph or of Chapter III.

The Supreme Court interprets this to mean that it covers 'any entity that engages in economic activities repeatedly and continuously for which economic interest of any nature is provided and consideration is provided in return', regardless of its legal form.[11] Thus, while it is not a necessary factor to establish the existence of an enterprise, entities that do not receive consideration for their purely charitable activities cannot be regarded as enterprises.[12]

The approach under Japanese competition law and in particular the definition by the Supreme Court closely resemble those of the EU under its functional approach. EU competition law applies to undertakings. Given the various forms of companies regulated under the laws of the member states, the EU's functional approach shifts the focus away from the legal form of the entity. Instead, attention is given to the activity in which the entity is engaged. The EU, thus, defines an undertaking as an 'entity engaged in an economic activity, regardless of the legal status of the entity and the way in which it is financed'.[13] This approach provides for a more in-depth analysis in cases where, for example, environmental charitable NGOs are involved which might otherwise *per se* be outside the scope of competition law because of their legal status.

A case in point is *Germany v Commission*.[14] This case concerned environmental, charitable NGOs which had been tasked with the management of national environment heritage sites. The question was whether these NGOs could be considered undertakings in certain situations (provision of fishing licences and the operation of camping sites) and thus be within the scope of EU competition law.[15]

[11] As translated in Masako Wakui, *Antimonopoly Law: Competition Law and Policy in Japan* (2nd edn, 2018), available at <https://ssrn.com/abstract=3270141> (accessed 22 January 2025) 48, referring to Supreme Court, 14 December 1989, 43 Minshu 2078 (*Tokyo Slaughterhouse*).

[12] ibid.

[13] See for example Case C-41/90 *Höfner and Elser v Macrotron* EU:C:1991:161 para 21; Case C-280/06 *ETI and Others* EU:C:2007:775 para 38; Case C-350/07 *Kattner Stahlbau* EU:C:2009:127 para 34.

[14] Case T-347/09 *Germany v Commission* EU:T:2013:418; for a comment see Iris Hohmann, 'Economic Activities in Natural National Heritage? Annotation on the Judgment of General Court of 12 September 2013 in Case T-347/09, *Federal Republic of Germany v European Commission*' (2015) 14(1) *European State Aid Law Quarterly* 161–165.

[15] In this case the competition provision relating to state aid/subsidies.

Germany v Commission (EU)[16]

Background

In Germany, local governments transferred natural heritage sites to NGOs for free, along with conservation funds. These NGOs, mainly charities, bore the costs and risks of the transfers but could generate income from land exploitation, such as by issuing hunting and fishing licences, selling wood obtained from forestry activities, and tourism. However, excess revenue had to be used for site preservation or returned to the transferring institution. The Court had to decide if these revenue-generating activities constituted 'economic activity' subject to EU state aid law. Germany argued that, as non-profits without economic objectives, these NGOs were not undertakings, and their services were a result of their non-economic activities.[17]

Findings of the Court

The Court found without much hesitation that:

> It was common ground between the parties to the proceedings that the nature conservation activity, which is part of the measures at issue, is exclusively of a social nature and does not constitute an economic activity (para 31).[18]

But that did not apply to all activities without further examination. The question was whether these NGOs could with regard to the other activities (eg selling wood, granting fishing and hunting licences, and tourism) be considered as undertakings and thus be subject to competition law. It held that:

> It cannot be ruled out that the nature conservation organizations, in addition to their tasks of purely social nature, carry out activities … that have a purpose other than a social one, namely that are of an economic nature (para 32).[19]

The Court then examined whether the ancillary activities were economic in nature, and whether they were inextricably connected to the nature conservation activities, which were exclusively social and non-economic in nature, or whether they went beyond such non-economic activities.[20] On the facts of the case, the Court found that the activities were offered under normal market conditions, in competition with private undertakings running for profit. Although

[16] Case T-347/09 *Germany v Commission* (n 14).
[17] As translated by the author.
[18] ibid para 31, as translated by the author.
[19] ibid para 32, as translated by the author.
[20] ibid para 34.

the NGOs had no intention of making a profit, they were competing with economic operators who did have this intention and offered similar goods and services[21] Moreover, the Court found that these ancillary activities could be separated from the main activity, and noted the main non-economic activity did not require the ancillary activities. They were not integral or sufficiently linked to the main non-economic conservation activity.[22]

The Court, therefore, found that the ancillary activities were economic in nature.[23] It also held that while 'environmental protection was one of the essential aims of the Union and would need to be considered'[24] when applying competition rules, it did not require that ancillary activities should be excluded from the scope of competition law.

As EU competition law is not concerned with legal status but solely explores the activities in question, the crucial question is whether the activities carried out are economic in nature. The Court highlighted that the environmental protection of managing the natural heritage sites is non-economic and therefore not subject to competition law. However, instead of looking at each task individually and in separation, the Court highlighted that it was necessary to explore whether the other connected activities (such as the fishing licences) were sufficiently closely connected to the main non-economic activity. For the case in question, the Court found that they were not sufficiently closely connected. However, the Court also highlighted the principle that the EU institutions were under an obligation to integrate environmental protection when applying competition law.[25]

b) Actions within an entity, and collective bargaining

Another area that is linked to whether the actions are subject to competition law in the first place is cases where competition law considers the action as taking place internally within one entity rather than the activities of an entity on the market. We can observe such situations in particular where legally separate companies are, for example, part of the same corporate group and therefore considered one single company for the purpose of competition law. EU competition law applies the so-called doctrine of 'single economic entity'.[26] Thus, where companies within a single economic entity

[21] ibid paras 40 and 48.
[22] ibid para 41.
[23] ibid para 43 and 45.
[24] ibid para 48, as translated by the author.
[25] ibid para 48. See also Case C-594/18 P *Austria v Commission* EU:C:2020:742 para 100; Case C-409/00 *Spain v Commission* EU:C:2003:92 para 46; Case C-487/06 P *British Aggregates v Commission* EU:C:2008:757 para 92.
[26] See Carsten König, 'The Boundaries of the Firm and the Reach of Competition Law: Corporate Group Liability and Sanctioning in the EU and the US' in Marco Corradi and Julian Nowag (eds), *Intersections Between Corporate and Antitrust Law* (CUP 2023) 63–85.

engage in sustainability activities, they are not performing activities on the market and are therefore not subject to competition law.[27] In this category, or closely related, there are also situations where sustainability arrangements take place between principals and agents or main and subcontractors.

Similarly, agreements between an employer and its employees are often not subject to competition law. The employee is part of the employer's economic unit and the employee itself does not constitute an entity that is subject to competition law. For example, EU competition generally excludes employees from the scope of competition law. The Court in *Becu* held that a dockworker would not be subject to competition law as 'for the duration of that relationship, incorporated into the undertakings concerned and thus forming an economic unit with each of them, [they] do not therefore in themselves constitute "undertakings" within the meaning of Community competition law'.[28]

A similar logic would apply where, for example, a collective agreement between employees and employers addresses sustainability questions. We could, for example, think about agreements between employers and employees that address questions related to the social dimension of sustainability such as social equity, health equity, community development, or more specifically human and labour rights. Such agreements between employers and employees can be outside the scope of competition law.

Provisions to similar effect are also found in Hong Kong's Competition Commission's guideline on the First Conduct Rule, paragraph 2.18 of which specifically states that:

> The Commission does not consider an employee to be an undertaking. Discussions or arrangements in relation to salary or other working conditions between one or more employees and their employer take place within the framework of a single economic unit and are outside of the scope of the First Conduct Rule.[29]

And with regard to the more difficult subject of trade unions, it has also been expressly stated that:

[27] See, eg, European Commission, 'Guidelines on the Applicability of Article 101 of the Treaty on the Functioning of the European Union to Horizontal Co-operation Agreements' [2023] OJ C 259/1, available at <https://eur-lex.europa.eu/legal-content/EN/TXT/PDF/?uri=CELEX:52023XC0721(01)> (accessed 22 January 2025) para 529.

[28] Case C-22/98 *Becu and Others* EU:C:1999:419 para 26. On the matter in general see also Jaspers Teun, 'Collective Bargaining and EU Competition Law' in Beryl ter Haar and Attila Kun (eds), *EU Collective Labour Law* (Edward Elgar Publishing 2021) 376–395.

[29] Hong Kong Competition Commission, 'Guideline—The First Conduct Rule' (27 July 2015) available at <https://www.compcomm.hk/en/legislation_guidance/guidance/first_conduct_rule/files/Guideline_The_First_Conduct_Rule_Eng.pdf> (accessed 22 January 2025).

> where a trade union acts on behalf of its members in collective bargaining with an employer on terms and conditions of work, the trade union is not engaged in economic activity and is not an undertaking.[30]

Therefore, any such agreement is not subject to competition law.[31]

In some countries, the question of whether such agreements are outside the scope of competition law can be more difficult to answer. For example, in India, issues around strikes and unions can indeed be subject to competition law. In particular, strikes can also be subject to criminal sanctions and civil claims. Certain protections to unions are offered under sections 17 and 18 of the Trade Unions Act; however, these are only available for unions registered under section 4(1). In *Indian Motion Pictures Producers' Association*,[32] the Commission found that leave and pay negotiated by a registered union 'fall within the realm of legitimate trade union activities when it is duly negotiated by a registered trade union. Thus, the same is not anti-competitive'.[33] Yet this labour exception to antitrust is rather limited, as *Vipul Shah*[34] makes clear.

Vipul Shah (India)[35]

In *Vipul Shah,* which was decided by the Commission before the case of the *Indian Motion Pictures Producers' Association,* the case concerned a registered trade union that attempted to prevent movie producers from hiring non-union members. The Commission stepped in and found that the Trade Union Act would not prevent the Commission's jurisdiction, so that it could examine the union's acts and their compliance with competition law.

It found that:

> There is no dispute between the freedoms enshrined in the Constitution of India and the right of the parties to form associations or unions within the constitutionally circumscribed limits. Undoubtedly, trade unions can undertake activities which protect and secure the rights of their members. However, the activities of any such union(s) should not be intended to restrain competition or harm consumers or be used for the purpose of bringing about or

[30] ibid para 2.19.
[31] ibid.
[32] *Re: Indian Motion Picture Producers' Association and Federation of Western India Cine Employees*, Case No 45 of 2017.
[33] ibid para 6.
[34] *Re: Vipul Shah and All India Film Employee Confederation*, Case No 19 of 2014.
[35] ibid.

attempting to bring about any understanding or agreement ... amongst competitors with regard to practices of limiting or controlling production, supply, markets etc. When these trade unions transgress their legal contours and facilitate collusive or collective decision making with the intention of limiting or controlling the production, distribution, sale or price of or trade in goods or provision of services by its members, it amounts to violation of the provisions of the Act. The Commission, therefore, is of the opinion that if the impugned conduct of trade union falls foul of the Act, the same needs to be examined under the relevant provisions thereof. Competition law is not an impediment to appropriate trade union activities and members of such unions should be fully aware of the types of conduct such law proscribes when carrying out the union's programs and activities.[36]

In other jurisdictions, the exclusion of unions and their agreements and dealings with employers are regulated more clearly under the relevant antitrust laws. Such examples can be found in Canada, the US, and the EU.

Section 4 of the Competition Act (Canada)

Collective bargaining activities

(1) Nothing in this Act applies in respect of
  (a) combinations or activities of workmen or employees for their own reasonable protection as such workmen or employees;
  (b) contracts, agreements or arrangements between or among fishermen or associations of fishermen and persons or associations of persons engaged in the buying or processing of fish relating to the prices, remuneration or other like conditions under which fish will be caught and supplied to those persons by fishermen; or
  (c) contracts, agreements or arrangements between or among two or more employers in a trade, industry or profession, whether effected directly between or among the employers or through the instrumentality of a corporation or association of which the employers are members, pertaining to collective bargaining with their employees in respect of salary or wages and terms or conditions of employment.

(2) Nothing in this section exempts from the application of any provision of this Act a contract, agreement or arrangement entered into by an

[36] ibid para 103.

employer to withhold any product from any person, or to refrain from acquiring from any person any product other than the services of workmen or employees.

The Canadian Act covers traditional collective bargaining situations between workers and their employers, but goes a step further regarding fishermen. In many jurisdictions, fishermen would be considered independent economic actors. However, the Canadian Competition Act excludes cartel-like behaviour from the scope of competition law. Given the importance of the industry for Canada, and that fish is a primary product, the exclusion of fishing from competition law might be compared to the exclusion of the agricultural sector, explored further below.[37]

In the US, a similar exemption for agreements between workers and their employers exists in the Clayton Act.

Clayton Act (USA)[38]

In general, the US antitrust rules apply to businesses and individuals. However, section 6 of Clayton Act provides an exception to antitrust rules for labour:

> The labor of a human being is not a commodity or article of commerce. Nothing contained in the antitrust laws shall be construed to forbid the existence and operation of labor, agricultural, or horticultural organizations, instituted for the purposes of mutual help, and not having capital stock or conducted for profit, or to forbid or restrain individual members of such organizations from lawfully carrying out the legitimate objects thereof; nor shall such organizations, or the members thereof, be held or construed to be illegal combinations or conspiracies in restraint of trade, under the antitrust laws.

Furthermore, the Norris-La Guardia Act[39] contains a number of rules that prevent courts from issuing restraining orders and injunctions with regard to labour disputes, as long as these are non-violent. Hence, sustainability measures that would be negotiated within these relations would not be subject to competition law.

The EU takes a similar approach, and the European Court of Justice in *Albany*[40] decided that collective bargaining between employees and employers is not subject

[37] See under section III. 4.
[38] 15 US Code. §§ 12–27, 29; US Code §§ 52–53.
[39] 29 US Code § 101.
[40] Case C-67/96 *Albany* EU:C:1999:430.

to competition law. Yet, it had also decided that this exclusion did not apply to collective bargaining by those who are self-employed.[41] The question of how to distinguish between those two situations has thus come up in *FNV Kunsten Informatie en Media*,[42] where the Court aimed to draw a distinction between the genuinely self-employed, to whom the exception does not apply, and those who are falsely self-employed,[43] to whom the *Albany* exception applies.

FNV Kunsten Informatie en Media (EU)[44]

This case concerns the scope of competition law and the status of employed and self-employed musicians playing in (the same) orchestra. The relevant law allowed trade unions to conclude collective labour agreements not only for employees but also for independent service providers who were members of those organizations. As a result, the employees' association (FVN) and the employer's association concluded a collective labour agreement that regulated minimum fees for substitute musicians. This agreement covered not only employed substitutes but also self-employed substitutes.

Findings of the Court

The Court first recalled the *Albany* judgment, where it found that collective labour agreements, which improve working conditions, are not subject to EU competition law. Then, it examined the situation of self-employed workers and highlighted that self-employed persons are undertakings for the purposes of Article 101(1) TFEU, as they offer their services for remuneration on a given market. Therefore, when the employees' organization carries out negotiations in the name and on behalf of self-employed workers, it does not act as a trade union but as an association of undertakings and is subject to Article 101(1) TFEU.

However, the Court acknowledged the complexity of defining the scope of self-employed service providers that are undertakings vis-à-vis employees. It highlighted that there might be '"false self-employed", that is to say, service providers in a situation comparable to that of employees'[45] and that 'in today's

[41] Case C-180/98 to C-184/98 *Pavlov and Others* EU:C:2000:428.
[42] Case C-413/13 *FNV Kunsten Informatie en Media v Staat der Nederlanden* EU:C:2014:2411.
[43] On the issue of self-employment in the gig economy and competition law, see also Ioannis Lianos, Nicola Countouris, and Valerio De Stefano, 'Re-Thinking the Competition Law/Labour Law Interaction: Promoting a Fairer Labour Market' (2019) 10(3) *European Labour Law Journal* 291.
[44] *FNV Kunsten* (n 42).
[45] ibid para 31.

economy, it is not always easy to establish the status of some self-employed contractors':[46]

> according to settled case-law, on the one hand, a service provider can lose his status of an independent trader, and hence of an undertaking, if he does not determine independently his own conduct on the market, but is entirely dependent on his principal, because he does not bear any of the financial or commercial risks arising out of the latter's activity and operates as an auxiliary within the principal's undertaking...[47]
>
> ... that the status of 'worker' within the meaning of EU law is not affected by the fact that a person has been hired as a self-employed person under national law, for tax, administrative or organizational reasons, as long as that person acts under the direction of his employer as regards, in particular, his freedom to choose the time, place and content of his work, ... does not share in the employer's commercial risks, ... and, for the duration of that relationship, forms an integral part of that employer's undertaking, so forming an economic unit with that undertaking...[48]

The Court of Justice did not possess the relevant facts. Thus, it tasked the national court to apply these criteria to ascertain whether the formally self-employed musicians were in fact 'false self-employed' and thus employees.

The case clarifies that the scope of EU competition law does not depend on the formal description of a person as self-employed or as an employee. Instead, a functional approach is employed where a number of criteria are used to determine the level of independence which determines the status as employee (not subject to competition law) or self-employed (subject to competition law). However, this distinction can still be difficult to draw, in particular with regard to platform work. In the US, courts have held that platform workers cannot benefit from the exemption from antitrust rules for collective bargaining. Even when in 2015 the city of Seattle adopted an ordinance to allow collective bargaining for on-demand drivers and platforms such as Uber and Lyft, the appeal court struck down the ordinance as a violation of US antitrust laws.[49]

[46] ibid para 32.
[47] ibid para 33.
[48] ibid para 36.
[49] *Chamber of Commerce of the United States of America v Seattle*, No 2:17-cv-00370 (WD Wash); No 17-35640 (9th Cir).

The same area has also spurred questions in the EU. The European Commission has issued guidelines[50] that do not only apply to platform situations but, more generally, to collective bargaining and solo self-employed persons. In these guidelines, the Commission distinguishes between situations outside the scope of competition law per the *FNV Kunsten* case and situations where the Commission will not take enforcement action.

Guidelines on the application of EU competition law to collective agreements regarding the working conditions of solo self-employed persons (EU)[51]

In those guidelines, the EU Commission highlights that competition law would not apply in the following situations:

1) economically dependent solo self-employed persons that earn at least 50 per cent of their income from one counterparty.[52]
2) solo self-employed persons working side by side with workers.[53]
3) solo self-employed persons providing their services via a digital labour platform,[54] where the service is

> (i) it is provided, at least in part, at a distance through electronic means, such as a website or a mobile application; (ii) it is provided at the request of a recipient of the service; and (iii) it involves, as a necessary and essential component, the organization of work performed by individuals, irrespective of whether that work is performed online or in a certain location.[55]

Yet, in other areas the Commission commits not to intervene against such collective agreements; these situations include cases where a group of solo self-employed concludes the collective agreement with a counterparty of certain[56] economic strength[57] or where the collective agreement has a basis in national or EU legislation.[58]

[50] EU Commission, Guidelines on Applying EU Competition Law to Collective Agreements Regarding the Working Conditions of Solo Self-Employed Persons [2022] OJ C-374/2.
[51] ibid.
[52] ibid paras 24–25.
[53] ibid paras 26–27.
[54] ibid para 31.
[55] ibid para 2.
[56] This is the case where the counterparty 'represent[s] the whole sector or industry' or where the counterparty or the group of counterparties together have an aggregated turnover in excess of 2 million euro or where a staff headcount of ten or more, see para 34.
[57] ibid paras 33–35.
[58] ibid paras 36–40.

The EU Commission thus explains the conditions of the *FNV Kunsten* and provides further details on its application. The second element is one of enforcement priorities. The EU Commission makes a commitment not to enforce competition law in these situations. However, this commitment is based on the EU Commission's enforcement priorities and is without prejudice to the decision of the EU or national courts or national competition authorities. An example where the Commission would not enforce competition law in the context of collective bargaining is the EU Copy Rights Directive, foreseeing the possibility of collective bargaining for authors and performers in certain areas.[59]

c) Summary

We have seen that sustainability activities are not subject to competition law where they are non-commercial/non-economic and, similarly, arrangements within the same entity. Different competition laws worldwide may draw the exact boundary differently as to what is 'within' and 'outside' the relevant economic entity. Yet, in many jurisdictions, agreements such as agency agreements or agreements with a subcontractor are not subject to competition law. Likewise, many jurisdictions consider certain forms of collective labour agreements outside the scope of competition law; so that sustainability-promoting clauses within them are not subject to competition law. To what extent these principles apply to situations of service providers on platforms is a difficult question.[60] We have seen that the US and the EU seem to take different approaches, with the EU having a greater tendency to exclude such situations from the scope of competition law.

2. Platforms

We have just explored collective agreements and highlighted how these might fall outside the scope of competition law when made between platform workers and platforms. Now, we turn to other platform arrangements that may be outside the scope of competition law. In general, numerous issues agreed between the platform and those offering their goods or services via the platform might be outside the scope of competition law; this might even be debated regarding prices.[61]

[59] Arts 19(5), 20(1), and 22(5) Directive (EU) 2019/790 Copyright and related rights in the Digital Single Market [2019] OJ L 130/92.

[60] See, for example, Marina Lao, 'Workers in the "Gig" Economy: The Case for Extending the Antitrust Labor Exemption to Them' (2018) 51(4) *UC Davis Law Review* 1543; Giorgio Monti, 'Collective Labour Agreements and EU Competition Law: Five Reconfigurations' (2021) 17(3) *European Competition Journal* 714.

[61] For a discussion regarding prices, see Julian Nowag, 'When Sharing Platforms Fix Sellers' Prices' (2018) 6(3) *Journal of Antitrust Enforcement* 382; see also Mark Anderson and Max Huffman, 'The Sharing Economy Meets the Sherman Act: Is Uber a Firm, a Cartel, or Something in Between?' [2017] *Columbia Business Law Review* 869.

Thus, sustainability arrangements made via a platform may fall outside the scope of competition law.[62]

Brazilian Uber Investigation (Brazil)[63]

In 2016, the Association of Autonomous Drivers (AMA) brought a complaint against Uber that was subsequently transferred to the Brazilian Competition Authority (CADE). In the complaint, the association alleged amongst other things that Uber was organizing a hub-and-spoke cartel amongst the independent drivers.

Findings of CADE

CADE did not find sufficient evidence for the existence of an infringement of competition law, so as a matter of enforcement priorities, it closed the proceedings. As part of its proceedings, CADE explored and highlighted the innovative business model and in general innovation that Uber would bring to the market. It found that Uber is only an intermediary that connects individual passengers and drivers. Uber would not be active in the private transportation market but strictly provides such intermediation services to third-party drivers, and Uber would not compete with the drivers.[64] CADE also explored the possibility that the relationship between Uber and the drivers was a hub-and-spoke cartel.[65] CADE highlighted that the drivers were able to set their own prices and that Uber was only setting maximum prices although these, in reality, were the effective prices charged.[66] Moreover, Uber and its drivers do not operate in the same market.[67] With regard to the possibility of the existence of a hub and spoke cartel, CADE explained that:

[62] Nowag and Teorell (n 3) paras 26–29.

[63] See MJ Conselho Administrativo de Defesa Econômica—CADE, Nota Técnica nº 26/2018/CGAA4/SGA1/SG/CADE. Brasília/DF, 2 October 2018 and the decision that endorses this note as reason for rejecting the complaint, Ministério da Justiça—MJ Conselho Administrativo de Defesa Econômica—CADE, Procedimento preparatório nº 08700.008318/2016-29. Brasília/DF, 24 October 2018 available at <https://sei.cade.gov.br/sei/modulos/pesquisa/md_pesq_processo_exibir.php?0c62g277GvPsZDAxAO1tMiVcL9FcFMR5UuJ6rLqPEJuTUu08mg6wxLt0JzWxCor9mNcMYP8UAjTVP9dxRfPBcSmaZSnn4I7X4mkhqtj_-iWhtS5xu8FqKCeJDiVKLoHF> (accessed 22 January 2025).

[64] Nota Técnica (n 63) paras 26–31.

[65] ibid paras 68–94.

[66] ibid para 88.

[67] ibid para 90.

> Regarding the possible existence of a hub and spoke cartel, it should be noted that:
>
> i. Uber does not act in a way so as to allow its partner-drivers to communicate with each other; if such communication occurs, it takes place through other means.
>
> ii. The fact that the partner-drivers accept the terms established by Uber should not be interpreted as sufficient evidence to establish an agreement between them. In other words, the acceptance of Uber's terms by the partner-drivers establishes a purely contractual relationship between Uber and each of its partner-drivers. Thus, no agreement can be envisaged between the partner-drivers on that account; ... and
>
> iii. There is no centralized collusion objective on part of Uber. The alleged uniformity of conduct, especially related to pricing, is derived from the Uber business model.[68] (para 93)
>
> Therefore, there is no exchange of competitively sensitive information and there is also no agreement established between the partner-drivers as a result of Uber's actions, which would be necessary requirements for the finding of a hub-and-spoke cartel.[69]

In this case, we can see that the CADE was, on the one hand, rather convinced by the benefits that Uber and its platform as an innovative business model brought about, such as reduced information asymmetries and increased service quality.[70] On the other hand, it took a rather strict approach in terms of the evidence. It required direct evidence of communication between the drivers which was enabled by Uber. If this stance was not enough to justify its conclusions, the CADE also argued that entry barriers were low and that there was a lot of competition from other platforms.

This case shows how what may be called a sustainability platform can operate, or how other (normal) platforms enjoy considerable room to manoeuvre to implement sustainability matters.[71] Such platforms would likely escape the scope of competition law, in particular where no action is taken against vast platforms such as Uber that operate in a similar fashion. Where such a platform is, for example, set up by an independent third party, eg an NGO, it can connect buyers and sellers and influence the contractual arrangement in a sustainable way and may even be able to set what is sometimes called sustainable prices.

[68] ibid para 93.
[69] ibid para 94.
[70] By allowing customers to monitor the trip via GPS. Moreover, by the ability to rate the service.
[71] See Nowag and Teorell (n 3), paras 26–29.

3. Sectoral exceptions

In some jurisdictions, we might find that certain sectors are outside the scope of the general competition rules.[72] Often, such sectoral exemptions may apply to regulated industries or agriculture. Where companies take sustainability measures in these sectors, the regular competition rules do not apply.

Agriculture is an area that is particularly important in the context of sustainability, considering the environmental, social, and economic aspects of sustainable development, an important element being food security.[73] In many jurisdictions,[74] agriculture is either exempted or is governed by special provisions.[75] For example, in the US the Clayton Act allows for the setting up of cooperatives with the intention of 'mutual help', and the Capper-Vostead Act ensures that includes collective processing, handling, marketing and preparing products for the market. Yet, these Acts do not provide full antitrust immunity, but only partially exempt such activities as cooperatives are not allowed to engage in anti-competitive conduct.[76]

Agriculture and Antitrust (USA)

The core of the agricultural exemption in the US is contained in section 6 of the Clayton Act and the Capper-Volstead Act.[77]

Section 6 sets out that

> ... Nothing contained in the antitrust laws shall be construed to forbid the existence and operation of labor, agricultural, or horticultural organizations, instituted for the purposes of mutual help, and not having capital stock or conducted for profit, or to forbid or restrain individual members of such organizations from lawfully carrying out the legitimate objects thereof; nor shall

[72] There might however be more sector-specific rules that apply.

[73] See eg Tomaso Fernando and Claudio Lombardi, 'EU Competition Law and Sustainability in Food Systems: Addressing the Broken Links' (Fair Trade Advocacy Office, February 2019).

[74] For an overview of the EU situation, see Kati J Cseres, '"Acceptable" Cartels at the Crossroads of EU Competition Law and the Common Agricultural Policy: A Legal Inquiry into the Political, Economic, and Social Dimensions of (Strengthening Farmers') Bargaining Power' (2020) 65(3) *The Antitrust Bulletin* 401.

[75] For a comparative view of the EU, the US, the UK, and Israel, see Arie Reich, 'The Agricultural Exemption in Antitrust Law: A Comparative Look at the Political Economy of Market Regulation' (2006–2007) 42 *Texas International Law Journal* 843, and for an even broader comparison also covering Canada, Argentina, Brazil, Colombia, and Mexico, see Juan David Gutiérrez Rodríguez, 'Agricultural Exceptions to Competition Law' (2010) 6(6) *Rev Derecho Competencia* 173–287.

[76] Arie Reich, 'The Agricultural Exemption in Antitrust Law: A Comparative Look at the Political Economy of Market Regulation' (2006–2007) 42 *Texas International Law Journal* 848.

[77] Capper-Volstead Act (Pub L 67-146), officially the Co-operative Marketing Associations Act (7 USC 291, 292).

such organizations, or the members thereof, be held or construed to be illegal combinations or conspiracies in restraint of trade, under the antitrust laws.[78]

The Capper-Volstead Act clarifies the conditions and the boundaries of this exception:

Persons engaged in the production of agricultural products as farmers, planters, ranchmen, dairymen, nut or fruit growers may act together in associations, corporate or otherwise, with or without capital stock, in collectively processing, preparing for market, handling, and marketing in interstate and foreign commerce, such products of persons so engaged. Such associations may have marketing agencies in common; and such associations and their members may make the necessary contracts and agreements to effect such purposes: Provided, however, that such associations are operated for the mutual benefit of the members thereof, as such producers, and conform to one or both of the following requirements:

First. That no member of the association is allowed more than one vote because of the amount of stock or membership capital he may own therein, or,

Second. That the association does not pay dividends on stock or membership capital in excess of 8 per centum per annum.

And in any case to the following:

Third. That the association shall not deal in the products of nonmembers to an amount greater in value than such as are handled by it for members.[79]

Hence, the Capper-Volstead Act expands the exception to organizations with capital stock and also allows for the exchange of competitively sensitive information. However, the Court also made clear that members of such organizations must be agricultural producers.[80]

In the context of the US exemption to antitrust, it is important to note that the exemption is not absolute, and under section 292 the Secretary of Agriculture has powers to initiate proceedings for violations of antitrust 'to such an extent that the price of any agricultural product is unduly enhanced'.[81] However, such intervention may not seem likely. Overall, the idea of the antitrust exception of cooperatives

[78] 15 US Code § 17.

[79] 7 US Code § 291.

[80] Even one non-producer will prevent the antitrust immunity: see *Case-Swayne Co v Sunkist Growers Inc*, 389 US 384 (1967), 386.

[81] Although the Secretary of Agriculture has never used this power, this does not prevent courts from ruling on such matters: see *US v Borden Co.* 308 US 188, 204 (1939).

was to allow the build-up of countervailing power against the buying power of middlemen[82] who connected farmers and final consumers.[83] This exception is rather far-reaching as it even allows for price-fixing via the cooperatives.

However, this exception is not the panacea. Its success seems to have created problems that it originally intended[84] to fix.[85] The US agricultural market is highly concentrated, with small and medium-sized farms struggling, in particular in the dairy industry.[86] In other words, what started as small cooperatives became bigger and bigger and are now controlling large parts of the market, with, for example, the Dairy Farmers of America cooperative controlling around one-third of the US raw milk supply.[87] These large cooperatives have substantial market power and there have been antitrust cases against them. For example, in *Allen v Dairy Farmers of America Inc*[88] the claimants alleged price-fixing between different cooperatives, and exclusionary practices relating to vertically integrated milk bottling plants forcing independent farmers to join the cooperative. The court noted that as long as separate agricultural associations fulfil the condition of immunity, they can engage in price-fixing agreements.

> [The Capper-Volstead Act] grants dairy cooperatives antitrust immunity with respect to price-fixing agreements with other dairy cooperatives, '[p]rovided, however, [t]hat such associations are operated for the mutual benefit of the members thereof...' 7 U.S.C. § 291. The Act does not, however, extend immunity for conduct 'outside the "legitimate objects" of a cooperative,' including restraining or monopolizing trade, or suppressing competition.[89]

In the end, the case was settled, which might have to do with the fact that courts have failed to provide clear guidance about the boundaries of cooperatives' powers.[90]

[82] Who held important supply and demand information, technical expertise to process and distribute, etc.

[83] Arie Reich, 'The Agricultural Exemption in Antitrust Law: A Comparative Look at the Political Economy of Market Regulation' (2007) 42(3) *Texas International Law Journal* 843–874.

[84] See Sarah R Phillips, 'The Future of Dairy Cooperatives in the Modern Marketplace: Redeveloping the Capper-Volstead Act' (2019) 124 *Dickinson Law Review* 175–202, who argues that the Capper-Volstead Act is no longer functioning as originally intended.

[85] For further details on the 'weak' enforcement of antitrust principles in US agriculture, see Peter C Carstensen, 'The State of American Competition Law with Respect to the Food Chain' in Ioannis Lianos, Alexey Ivanov, and Dennis Davis, *Global Food Value Chains and Competition Law* (CUP 2022).

[86] In the last decade around 17,000 dairy farms closed down, on this and the developments see Eduardo Castro, '"For the Mutual Benefit of Members Thereof": Attacking Capper-Volstead Immunity and Challenging Diary Cooperative Power' (2020) 38 *Minnesota Journal of Law & Inequality* 145–168.

[87] ibid.

[88] 748 F Supp 2d 323 (D Vt 2010).

[89] At 345, citing *Maryland & Virginia Milk Producers Ass'n, Inc v United States*, 362 US 458, 468, 80 S Ct 847, 4 L Ed 2d 880 (1960); *Fairdale Farms, Inc v Yankee Milk, Inc*, 635 F 2d 1037, 1044 (2d Cir 1980).

[90] Sarah K Phillips, 'The Future of Dairy Cooperatives in the Modern Marketplace: Redeveloping the Capper-Volstead Act' (2019) 124 *Dickinson Law Review* 190.

In the EU there are also specific rules for the agricultural sector,[91] and the new Common Agricultural Policy (CAP) for 2023–2027 introduced a specific exemption for the field of sustainability.[92] These balance the restriction of competition with the sustainability benefits and are explored in more detail in the section below that deals with balancing.[93]

4. State action and state compulsion, the right to petition to the government

Another important reason why measures by companies are not subject to antitrust prohibitions is that the measures are taken because they have been mandated by law or because companies act together with agencies in specific ways to achieve sustainability aims. We can find such rules in a number of jurisdictions, for example, in the US, Canada, the EU, the Netherlands, and Singapore.

The US DoJ, for instance, closed an investigation[94] into an agreement by car manufacturers to comply with more stringent emission standards which were set by the Californian regulator. Such behaviour is excluded from the scope of US antitrust law by the state action defence.[95] While the exact reasons for ending the investigation remain unclear, one crucial element was the involvement of California, which had ultimate control over the standard.[96]

The situation is similar in Canada. When exploring arrangements that involve parts of the state, the Competition Bureau examines the so-called 'regulated conduct doctrine' and explores a range of factors such as the nature of the scheme, the objectives, and the concrete involvement of state authorities.[97]

[91] See eg Cseres (n 74) 401.

[92] Introduced via Regulation (EU) 2021/2117 [2021] OJ L 435/262.

[93] See below under section IV.1.c).

[94] See Office of Governor Gavin Newsom, 'California and Major Automakers Reach Groundbreaking Framework Agreement on Clean Emission Standards' (25 July 2019) available at <https://www.gov.ca.gov/2019/07/25/california-and-major-automakers-reach-groundbreaking-framework-agreement-on-clean-emission-standards/> (accessed 22 January 2025).

[95] See Grant Petrosoyan, 'DoJ's probe into Four Automakers: Impartial Investigation or Politization of Antitrust?' *Competition Policy International* (29 October 2019) available at <https://www.competitionpolicyinternational.com/DoJs-probe-into-four-automakers-impartial-investigation-or-politicization-of-antitrust/#_edn2> (accessed 22 January 2025); Herbert Hovenkamp, 'Are Agreements to Address Climate Change Anticompetitive?' *Regulatory Review* (September 2019) available at <https://www.theregreview.org/2019/09/11/hovenkamp-are-regulatory-agreements-to-address-climate-change-anticompetitive/> (accessed 22 January 2025).

[96] ibid.

[97] See Competition Bureau, 'Technical Bulletin on "Regulated" Conduct' (2010) available at <https://ised-isde.canada.ca/site/competition-bureau-canada/en/how-we-foster-competition/education-and-outreach/publications/regulated-conduct> (accessed 22 January 2025).

The Extended Producer Responsibility and Collusion (Canada)

The Competition Bureau has committed itself to examining cases involving Canada's extended producer responsibility on a case-by-case basis and has provided further guidance in a bulletin.[98]

Background

Canada introduced a so-called extended producer responsibility (EPR) as part of its waste policy. This imposes an obligation for disposal of waste material at the end of a product's life cycle. Responsibility for this is imposed on original producers and (first) importers of products. At the same time, the EPR policy also aims to promote the development of collaborative arrangements between market participants, including competitors.

This collaboration might trigger competition concerns. As a response to the EPR, a non-profit association was set up. The non-profits aim to promote the implementation of EPR among industry participants, stakeholders, and public officials. Its main task is developing efficient and effective programmes for waste disposal, their implementation, and management.

Guidance

The Canadian Competition Bureau issued a bulletin to guide this and other forms of cooperation that might be considered collusive and anti-competitive but are also regulated by other federal or provincial laws such as EPR policy. It highlighted that any such agreement would be examined on a case-by-case basis considering the following aspects:

- the parties involved;
- the conduct of the parties;
- the potentially applicable provisions of the Competition Act and of the other law;
- purpose of the Competition Act and other applicable law which regulate the conduct;
- interests sought to be protected by both laws;
- the principles of statutory interpretation applicable to the case.

Based on these aspects it could be concluded either that the Competition Act does not cover the measure or that it does apply.

[98] ibid.

While this assessment under Canadian competition law considers many factors, EU competition law applies a more dualistic approach. Under the EU's state action doctrine developed in *Ladbroke*,[99] the crucial question is whether the regulative action leading to possibly anti-competitive conduct leaves room for autonomous conduct. Only where the company does not have room for autonomous conduct is it shielded from the application of competition law. In other words, the application of EU competition law is only barred where a government measure requires specific actions to foster sustainability and there is no room for the company to take another course of action to achieve that objective. Singapore takes a similar approach. The Singaporean competition authority in its Environmental Sustainability Collaboration Guidance Note explains that agreements with anti-competitive effects to comply with Singapore national law are excluded from enforcement of competition law.[100]

In the Netherlands, the EU's approach has resulted in an interesting legislative proposal. Under the proposal, a group of companies can submit a request for a binding sustainability standard to the minister. After consulting with stakeholders, the minister can consider making the proposed sustainability arrangement mandatory.

Room for Sustainability Proposal (Netherlands)[101]

In 2019, a Dutch legislative proposal (*Wet ruimte voor duurzaamheidsinitiatieven Kamerstuk 35247)* on competition law and sustainability was submitted to the Netherlands House of Representatives. The aim was to address perceived obstacles presented by competition law, particularly the rules on anti-competitive agreements, to joint sustainability initiatives by companies.

The proposal allowed individuals, companies, and organizations to propose sustainability standards to the relevant minister. The minister could then make them legally binding for five years as a general administrative order *(algemene maatregel van bestuur)*, with the possibility of a single extension However, any further extension would have to be adopted as a regular legislative act by parliament.

[99] Joined Cases C-359/95P and C-379/95P *Commission and France v Ladbroke Racing* EU:C:1997:531. On the EU state action doctrine, see eg Damien Gerard, 'EU Competition Policy after Lisbon: Time to Review the "State Action Doctrine"?' (2010) 1:3 *Journal of European Competition Law & Practice* 202.

[100] Competition & Consumer Commission Singapore, 'Environmental Sustainability Collaboration Guidance Note' (2024) available at <https://www.cccs.gov.sg/legislation/competition-act/environmental-sustainability-collaboration-guidance-note> (accessed 22 January 2025) see also Competition Act 2004 Third Schedule para 2(1).

[101] *Kamerstuk 35247*; the whole legislative process can be accessed at <https://zoek.officielebekendmakingen.nl/dossier/35247> (accessed 22 January 2025).

The proposal required that such an initiative should contain a detailed description of the objectives, the level of support for the initiative by the parties and other stakeholders, and the effects of the initiative in terms of sustainability and effects on the market.

When assessing the initiative, the minister would be obliged to take advice on the competitive effects from the competition authority and consider, amongst others, the practicability as well as the extent to which it could be enforced. The minister would also examine compliance with international obligations, and whether less restrictive alternatives exist. The proposal also foresaw an exemption procedure for alternative arrangements by companies. Exemption from the generally applicable framework could be obtained if it was shown that the proposed measure achieved the same level of sustainability.

The original proposal adopted a wide interpretation of sustainable development as any development towards an economic, social, and environmentally friendly sustainable future for present and future generations. However, Article 2.2 initially limited the requests submitted to the minister to greenhouse gas emissions, sustainable energy production or energy saving, and animal welfare. There were numerous amendments that aimed to take into account, for example, questions of supply chains[102] or bio-diversity.[103]

The proposal was controversial[104] and the government, in January 2022, decided to postpone the legislative proposal.[105]

This Dutch proposal addresses two issues. On the one hand, it addresses EU competition law limits, where a measure would not be legal because it was considered to restrict competition under Article 101(1) TFEU and did not satisfy the exemption criteria under Article 101(3) TFEU. At the same time, it turns the private initiative into a public one, enabling the defence of state action. On the other hand, it also addresses questions about the democratic legitimacy of such private standards, because the decision is made by the government. Yet, as this proposal makes the standard a government measure, compliance with international obligations under for example WTO and EU free-movement rules is crucial. Overall, it will be interesting to see whether this or similar proposals are ever adopted.[106] Notwithstanding, we can see how the interaction between private initiatives and state action leads to the inapplicability of competition law.

[102] Amendement van de leden Futselaar en Alkaya over het toevoegen van internationale ketenverantwoordelijkheid TK, 5.

[103] Amendement van het lid Bromet over duurzaamheidsinitiatieven voor biodiversiteit TK, 9.

[104] See TK 35.718, nr 9.

[105] See TK 35.788, 109.

[106] With the successful engagement of the Dutch competition authority with sustainability, it seems less likely that such an approach will be felt necessary.

5. Activities that reflect the applicable legal framework

In the field of sustainability, we see how some jurisdictions have lately reacted to claims that applicable environmental, human rights, and labour standards are not complied with. Such non-compliance can, for example, result from weak state institutions and law enforcement. Thus, companies might agree to 'voluntarily' comply with a relevant legal standard, as they would face no consequences for not complying with those standards in that jurisdiction, simply for a lack of enforcement. For example, the law on the book may say that it is illegal to cut down rainforests for farming purposes. However, if there is no law enforcement in the jurisdiction to ensure compliance with this obligation, firms could, in practice, violate those rules and thereby obtain a competitive advantage, eg obtain cheaper agricultural products.

To address such a situation, the Dutch competition authority, in its draft guidelines, had specified that agreements between companies that mirror compliance with applicable local laws would not be subject to competition law.[107] The draft guidelines explain that agreements do not restrict competition where the agreement ensures that competitors and their up- or downstream counterparties comply with the relevant laws or international standards[108] in the countries they are operating in, in particular with regard to developing countries.[109] In such countries even where laws and standards exist that prohibit slave and/or child labour or set minimum standards for health and safety, they may not be enforced. There are numerous reasons for non-enforcement. We can think of institutional inability, corruption, or parts of the country that are not under full control of the state as various insurgents or guerrilla groups exercise effective control.

This push has been partly taken over by the European Commission, which now highlights that such agreements are likely to fall outside the scope of competition law if they

> aim solely to ensure compliance with sufficiently precise requirements or prohibitions in legally binding international treaties, agreements or conventions, whether or not they have been implemented in national law (for example, compliance with fundamental social rights or prohibitions on the use of child labour,

[107] ACM, 'Draft Guidelines Sustainability agreements: Opportunities within competition law' (July 2020) available at <https://www.acm.nl/sites/default/files/documents/2020-07/sustainability-agreements%5B1%5D.pdf> (accessed 22 January 2025) para 23.

[108] In particular, rules that ban child labour, set a minimum wage, stipulate the right to unionize or rights of indigenous peoples, or prohibit bribery or the logging of certain types of tropical wood.

[109] ACM, Draft Guidelines 'Sustainability Agreements': Opportunities within competition law (26 January 2021) available at <https://www.acm.nl/en/publications/second-draft-version-guidelines-sustainability-agreements-opportunities-within-competition-law> (accessed 22 January 2025) paras 27–29.

> the logging of certain types of tropical wood or the use of certain pollutants) and which are not fully implemented or enforced by a signatory State, fall outside the scope of Article 101. This exclusion from Article 101 only applies if the agreement provides that the participating undertakings, their suppliers and/or their distributors must comply with such requirements or prohibitions, for example, by preventing, reducing or eliminating the production or importation into the EU of products contrary to such requirements or prohibitions. Such agreements may be an appropriate measure to enable undertakings to implement their sustainability due diligence obligations under national or EU law and can also form part of wider industry cooperation schemes or multi-stakeholder initiatives to identify, mitigate and prevent adverse sustainability impacts in their value chains or their sector.[110]

This suggestion is narrower than the Dutch approach, which was applicable to a wider range of laws. However, in substance, many issues that the Dutch draft guidelines had mentioned, like human rights or child labour, are embedded in binding international law and should thus also be covered by the EU's position. After the adoption of the EU guidelines, the Dutch competition authority, however, adjusted to the EU position. But—beyond the EU's approach—it will deprioritize[111] all agreements that are made to comply with binding national, EU, or international legal rules on sustainability matters.[112]

The Portuguese competition authority followed the EU Commission in its best practices guidance, where it highlights that there would be

> no infringement of competition law [where the agreement] ensure[s] compliance with requirements or prohibitions in legally binding international treaties, agreements or conventions. For example, an agreement to ensure prohibitions on the use of child labour; or to ensure limitations on the exploitation of certain types of tropical wood or limitations on the use of certain pollutants.[113]

In Hong Kong, the Competition Ordinance also provides similar exemptions to avoid conflicts between the Ordinance and an international obligation related to

[110] Guidelines (n 27) para 528.

[111] ACM, 'ACM's Oversight of Sustainability Agreements: Competition and Sustainability' (4 October 2023) available at <https://www.acm.nl/system/files/documents/Beleidsregel%20Toezicht%20ACM%20op%20duurzaamheidsafspraken%20ENG.pdf> (accessed 22 January 2025) paras 7–9, 20–24.

[112] Further examined in Chapter 5, section II. 2.

[113] Portuguese Competition Authority, 'Best Practices Guide on Sustainability Agreements' (2024) available at <https://www.concorrencia.pt/sites/default/files/documentos/guias-promocao-da-concorrencia/Best%20Practices%20Guide%20on%20Sustainability%20Agreements%20-%20Final%20Version.pdf> (accessed 22 January 2025) 7.

Hong Kong.[114] However, the non-application of competition law in this case is contingent upon an exemption decision by the Chief Executive of the Council.

6. Standard-setting and its special treatment

In many jurisdictions, standards that set technical or quality requirements receive more lenient treatment under competition law.[115] In some jurisdictions, standards may even be considered outside of the scope of competition law if they fulfil certain conditions which ensure that the standards are not used for exclusionary practices.[116] Thus, a standard may allow companies to engage in actions promoting sustainability without being subject to competition law prohibitions.[117]

Sustainability standards often involve some form of certification to reduce information asymmetries.[118] One example of such a well-known and widely used sustainability standard is ISO standard 14031.

ISO standard 14031[119]

International Standard Organization (ISO) is a worldwide organization comprising national standard bodies, and has adopted the Environmental Management—Environmental Performance Evaluation Guidelines (ISO 14031:2013). As the name indicates, the standard is not focused on certification but on environmental management. It includes a commitment to compliance with legal and other requirements, to prevent pollution, and to continuous improvement.

[114] See Hong Kong Competition Ordinance (Cap 619) Sec 32.

[115] For a comparison between the EU and US see, eg, Björn Lundqvist, *Standardization under EU Competition Rules and US Antitrust Laws – The Rise and Limits of Self-Regulation* (Edward Elgar 2014).

[116] With regard to such benefits and risks see, eg, the Joined Report from the Nordic Competition Authorities, 'Competition Policy and Green Growth—Interactions and Challenges' (No 1/2010) available at <https://en.samkeppni.is/media/skyrslur-2010/competition_policy_and_green_growth_final_version.pdf> (accessed 22 January 2025) 58–62.

[117] Apart from sustainability implications, the economic benefits of the adoption of standards need to be noted. It has been shown that the early adoption or joining of standards such as the palm oil standard is associated with increased returns; see Yeong Sheng Tey and others, 'Early Mover Advantage in Roundtable on Sustainable Palm Oil Certification: A Panel Evidence of Plantation Companies' (2020) 252 *Journal of Cleaner Production* 119775.

[118] For a detailed look at standards, labels, and certification processes, see Klaas Hendrik Eller, 'Food Chain Certification and the Social Pluralism of Competition Law' in Ioannis Lianos, Alexey Ivanov, and Dennis Davis (eds), *Global Food Value Chains and Competition Law* (CUP 2022) 397–419.

[119] Details available at <https://www.iso.org/obp/ui/#iso:std:iso:14031:ed-2:v1:en> (accessed 22 January 2025).

ISO 14031 standardizes tools to identify, measure, assess, and communicate environmental performance using key performance indicators such as comparing past and present environmental performance.

The central part of the standard is contained in chapter 4, which contains a 'plan-do-check-act' management method. In the first phase (plan), the organization has to choose its indicators amongst the standard's key environmental performance indicators. These key performance indicators allow for measurement. Moreover, they have to set out their target with regard to the chosen indicator. The second phase is the 'do' phase, where they collect and analyse data. These provide the basis for the environmental performance evaluation compared to the organization's goals, providing the roadmap to adjust and improve.

The four-step process must be guided by the principles of relevance, completeness, consistency and accuracy, and transparency. This means that:

1. environmental performance information should be related to the organization's management of environmental factors (relevance);
2. environmental performance information should be complete and should be completed to ensure that all factors are addressed (completeness);
3. environmental performance information should be consistent and accurate in order to effectively compare past, current, and rewarded environmental performance (consistency and accuracy);
4. environmental performance information should be clear and transparent, so that its users can obtain and understand environmental performance data and make decisions with reasonable credibility (transparency).

While the ISO standard 14031 focused on environmental management, ISO has other standards such as ISO 14020:2000 *Environmental Labels and Declarations—General Principles* or ISO 14024:2018 *Environmental Labels and Declarations—Type I environmental labelling—Principles.* The latter is also relevant for sustainability purposes. ISO 14024:2018 addresses the principles of setting requirements for environmental labels using life cycle considerations and how these labels certifying compliance should be awarded. The labels are voluntary and based on a third-party programme with multiple criteria. The standard also addresses the award of the licence to use the label for products. The label certifies compliance with the requirements, which indicate an overall better environmental performance[120] of the product.

120 Based on life cycle considerations.

Professional standard-setting organizations are not the only organizations that set such standards. The UN is also actively supporting voluntary standards with the United Nations Forum on Sustainability Standards,[121] and the UN Conference on Trade and Development has equally adopted an assessment toolkit framework for assessing the impacts of voluntary sustainability standards.[122]

Sustainability standards such as these set technical and quality requirements and are often more leniently assessed when compared to other horizontal agreements since standards are presumed to play an important role in technical innovation.[123] For example, the US Supreme Court in *Allied Tube*[124] held that safety standards such as those set by the National Fire Protection Association are generally pro-competitive.

Allied Tube & Conduit Corp v Indian Head, Inc (USA)[125]

Facts

The case concerned the National Fire Protection Association (NFPA), which is a non-profit standard-setting organization with around 50,000 members and numerous technical committees. It traces its history back to 1895 and the establishment of a standard for the design and installation of automatic fire sprinklers by pipe manufacturers and insurance companies. The standards adopted by the NFPA often form the basis for government regulations, where those regulations stipulate that the NFPA standards as binding.

Allied Tube & Conduit Corp v Indian Head, Inc concerns NFPA's standard on the design and installation of electrical wiring systems. The claimant alleged an orchestrated conspiracy in contravention of section 1 of the Sherman Act to prevent it from being included in the standard. In particular, just before a crucial vote on whether the claimant's product would be included in the standard, new members were signed up and voted against inclusion of the claimant.

The district court rejected the case as the defendant's activities were said to be protected under the *Noerr-Pennington*[126] doctrine as petitioning of the government.

[121] Which is a joint initiative of FAO, ITC, UNCTAD, UN Environment, and UNIDO.

[122] See UNCTAD, *Framework for the Voluntary Sustainability Standards Assessment Toolkit* (2020) UNCTAD/DITC/TAB/INF/2020/5 available at <https://unctad.org/system/files/official-document/ditctabinf2020d5_en.pdf> (accessed 22 January 2025).

[123] See for example EU Commission, 'Guidelines on the Applicability of Article 101' (n 27) paras 257, 263.

[124] *Allied Tube & Conduit Corp v Indian Head, Inc* 108 S Ct 1931, 1934 (1988).

[125] ibid.

[126] *Eastern Railroad Presidents Conference v Noerr Motor Freight, Inc*, 365 US 127 (1961) and *United Mine Workers of America v Pennington*, 381 US 657 (1965).

Decision

On appeal, the case was reversed. Even though the NFPA's standards were often subsequently included in government regulation, the standard-setting organization was not part of the government and had no official authority but was made up of entities pursuing their own economic interests. Thus, NFPA was not a quasi-legislative body, and the *Noerr-Pennington* doctrine did not apply. The normal antitrust principles would apply to the case and the court held that:

> Typically, private standard-setting associations, like the Association in this case, include members having horizontal and vertical business relations. ... There is no doubt that the members of such associations often have economic incentives to restrain competition and that the product standards set by such associations have a serious potential for anticompetitive harm. ... Agreement on a product standard is, after all, implicitly an agreement not to manufacture, distribute, or purchase certain types of products. Accordingly, private standard-setting associations have traditionally been objects of antitrust scrutiny. ...
>
> When, however, private associations promulgate safety standards based on the merits of objective expert judgments and through procedures that prevent the standard-setting process from being biased by members with economic interests in stifling product competition, ... those private standards can have significant procompetitive advantages. It is this potential for procompetitive benefits that has led most lower courts to apply rule-of-reason analysis to product standard-setting by private associations. ...[127]

The case highlights that (sustainability) standards are not immune from scrutiny under US antitrust law. But the pro-competitive benefits usually outweigh the exclusion of certain types of products, as long as the processes and behaviours of the participants within the standard-setting organization do not give rise to anti-competitive conduct. It is also worth keeping in mind that applying the rule of reason as endorsed by the Supreme Court *de facto* means claimants are limited to arguing that the internal processes and behaviours were anti-competitive, this argument is unlikely to succeed, and litigation thereby incurs significant sunk costs.[128]

[127] *Allied Tube* (n 124)(references omitted).

[128] In general, see eg Maurice E Stucke, 'Does the Rule of Reason Violate the Rule of Law?' (2009) 42 *UC Davier Law Review* 1375–1490.

While the US case discussed above relates to standards in general, the Japanese competition authority has dealt with a specific environmental standard by an association that represented the main producers of building materials and found that it did not infringe competition law.[129]

JFTC, Building Materials Standard (Japan)[130]

Facts

Association X is an association of manufacturers of building materials. The members represent around 70 per cent of the suppliers of the specific building material that is sold to construction firms and used in the building of houses. The standard meant that an old product that used a chemical compound with a negative effect on greenhouse gas emissions and other negative environmental effects would be replaced by a new product without such effect.

Finding

The JFTC advised the companies that there was no restriction of competition. The agency found that the new product had almost the same quality and price as the product it replaced, and it was expected that the price would drop even further with more widespread adoption. Moreover, it was not technically difficult to produce the new product and no substantial capital investments were needed to change the production from the old to the new product. In particular, the JFTC found that the standard would not restrict competition within the meaning of Article 8 of the Antimonopoly Act because

- Abandoning the old production of the more harmful product would not unduly harm consumers, due to the commercialization of the new product.
- It [was] not particularly difficult for manufacturers of building materials to switch production, and as no substantial capital investment [was] needed to switch production, members would not be unduly discriminated.
- The reduction of greenhouse gas emissions is a legitimate social and public purpose to [pursue by changing] production.
- The members could decide whether or not to comply with the new standard or continue to produce the old product. This voluntary element would also ensure that competition was not hindered.

[129] Dokusenkinshihō ni kansuru sōdan jireishū (Heisei 24 nendo) Jirei 9 [JFTC, Compilation of case consultations (FY 2012), Case No 9] available at <https://www.jftc.go.jp/dk/soudanjirei/h25/h24nendomokuji/h24nendo09.html> (accessed 22 January 2025).

[130] ibid.

This case shows a standard can be used to replace one material with a more sustainable alternative. The JFTC presents the case on its webpage as a guide explaining its approach. It highlights that when certain conditions are fulfilled, standards for the phase-out of unsustainable products do not restrict competition. The JFTC has followed up with a similar approach in its guidelines,[131] finding that standards-setting does not restrict competition if certain conditions are fulfilled. In particular, the standard cannot foresee 'arrangements for selling prices, etc, [exclude] competing specifications; [contain] unreasonable expansion of the scope of specifications; [exclude] unreasonably other technology proposals, etc.; and [restrain] participation in the standardization activity'.[132]

JFTC, Toward the Realization of a Green Society Under the Antimonopoly Act Guidelines (Japan)[133]

The guidelines address voluntary standards that do not restrict competition, then explain when such standards restrict competition, and finally address situations where no restriction of competition exists if firms are excluded/boycotted for non-compliance.

It explains that voluntary standards such as those on 'types, quality, specifications, etc. of their products or services for the purpose of reducing greenhouse gas emissions' often do not pose problems as they are pro-competitive leading to 'the prompt launch of a market for products adopting the unified specifications or an expansion of demand for such products.'[134]

However, standard-setting might also create anti-competitive effects which, according to the guidelines, will be assessed by first examining

> the presence and degree of any anti-competitive effects ... [while] comprehensively considering ... the rationality of the purpose ... and the adequacy of the means employed. In this comprehensive consideration, the following are taken into account: (i) whether it unjustly harms the interests of users by restraining means of competition; (ii) whether it unjustly discriminates among enterprises; and (iii) whether it is within what is regarded as the reasonably

[131] Japan Fair Trade Commission, 'Guidelines Concerning the Activities of Enterprises, etc. Toward the Realization of a Green Society under the Antimonopoly Act' (31 March 2023, revised on 24 April 2024) available at <https://www.jftc.go.jp/en/pressreleases/yearly-2024/April/240424EN2.pdf> (accessed 22 January 2025).
[132] ibid 18–19.
[133] ibid.
[134] Ibid 14 (footnotes omitted).

> necessary scope in light of legitimate purposes such as social and public purposes.[135]

It, then, highlights a number of examples of standards that do not restrict competition in which

> voluntary standards indicat[e] the desirable manner of conducting business activities ... [for] decarbonization [and] standards do not include any contents concerning matters constituting important means of competition, such as prices. ... and specifications for products/services toward the reduction of greenhouse gas.[136]

The guidelines then continue and highlight situations where restrictions of competition seem possible with a number of examples:

> **Supposed case that does not pose problems under the Antimonopoly Act**
> Supposed case 30: Formulation of the specifications of components, etc. with the aim of facilitating efficient use of resources)—Since the manufacturing processes of Product A generate waste from Component B used for the manufacturing of the product, one of the issues that manufacturers of Product A face are how to achieve the efficient reuse of such waste in order to reduce environmental burdens and greenhouse gas emissions. For that reason, X, Y, and Z, which are manufacturers of Product A, have decided to formulate common specifications for Component B and use Component B based on those specifications as much as possible for the purpose of facilitating the recycling of the component and raising its recycling ratio.[137]

In terms of non-compliance with the relevant standard, the guidelines explain the following under the heading 'Boycotts':

> Supposed case 59: Refusal of certification of products that fail to meet the voluntary standards of a trade association)—Trade Association X, which consists of manufacturers of Product A, established voluntary standards including a standard requiring a 10 per cent reduction in the greenhouse gas emissions generated in the manufacturing processes of Product A compared with conventional products. X approves its constituent enterprises to attach to their Product A meeting the above standards a label assuring general consumers of the product's greenhouse gas reduction effect, and issues the label at the

[135] ibid 15 (footnotes omitted).
[136] ibid 15–16.
[137] ibid 24.

request of each constituent enterprise manufacturing Product A that meets the voluntary standards. However, certain consumers are buying Product A without the said label.

Originally, Enterprise Y, which is a constituent enterprise of X, conducted sales activities with the label issued by X on the grounds that Y's Product A met the voluntary standards. However, it has been revealed that Y did not actually meet the voluntary standards. Since the label issued by X guarantees, as a trade association, Product A's greenhouse gas reduction effect and this information is necessary for general consumers to select products on the basis of correct information, the attachment of the label on Product A that does not meet the voluntary standards may cause general consumers to make errors in their choice of products and thereby cause the credibility of the label to be damaged. For that reason, in order to protect general consumers from being misled and maintain the credibility of the label, X has decided to refuse to issue the label to Y until this enterprise becomes able to sell Product A that meets the voluntary standards.

[Commentary]This act is refusal of issuing the label by Trade Association X assuring the fulfillment of voluntary standards to a constituent enterprise selling Product A which does not fulfill the voluntary standards. With regard to a constituent enterprise's fulfillment of the voluntary standard, the constituent enterprise's freedom must be inherently secured. However, the purpose of the act, which is to prevent disadvantages to consumers caused by the situation where the label is attached to Product A which does not fulfill the voluntary standards, is found to be rational. In addition, the implementation of the act within limited period which is genuinely necessary for solving the problem is found to be adequate as a mean. Therefore, the act can be implemented without posing problems under the Antimonopoly Act.[138]

The situation, as explained in the JFTC's guidelines, is similar in the EU. The European Commission perhaps goes even a step further with its new guidelines on horizontal cooperation, which now contain a specific section on sustainability standards. It first explains how such sustainability standards can be used 'to phase out, withdraw, or, in some cases, replace non-sustainable products (e.g. fossil fuels such as oil and coal, plastics) and processes (for example, coal-fired steel production) with sustainable ones'.[139] The guidelines explain that these standards are often pro-competitive[140] and then set out conditions which such standards must meet to benefit from what the Commission calls a 'soft safe harbour', as

138 ibid 44–45.
139 EU Commission, 'Guidelines on the applicability of Article 101' (n 27) para 538.
140 ibid para 545.

such sustainability standards 'are unlikely to produce appreciable negative effects on competition'[141] and will most likely fall outside Article 101(1) TFEU. A closer examination of the effects on competition will be necessary for standards that do not meet the condition.

European Commission Horizontal Guidelines (EU)[142]

Definition of sustainability standard

The guidelines characterize and define sustainability standards as standards to 'phase out, withdraw, or, in some cases, replace non-sustainable products ... harmonise packaging materials ... or sizes ... [to reduce waste], [or] purchase only sustainable inputs [that are not] agreements between competitors that limit ... output'.[143] These agreements are

> used to specify requirements that producers, processors, distributors, retailers or service providers in a supply chain have to meet ... [and they] provide rules, guidelines or characteristics for products and processes in relation to ... sustainability metrics [and] range from codes of conduct adopted by undertakings, to standards driven by civil society organisations and multi-stakeholder initiatives that involve undertakings across the value chain. These Guidelines only [apply to] standards developed by competitors or in which competitors ... [144]

The guidelines then highlight the pro-competitive effects of such standards, in particular:

> the development of new products or markets, increasing product quality or improving conditions of supply or distribution [and how sustainability labels] empower consumers to make informed purchase decisions [helping in the] development of markets for sustainable products. Lastly, sustainability standards can also level the playing field between producers [subject to] different regulatory requirements.[145]

While setting out instances where sustainability standards might restrict competition because they involve 'price coordination, foreclosure of alternative

[141] ibid para 549.
[142] ibid.
[143] ibid para 538.
[144] ibid para 539 (footnotes omitted).
[145] ibid para 545.

standards, and the exclusion of, or discrimination against certain competitors',[146] the guidelines set out six conditions ensuring that such effects are unlikely to occur and thus the standards fall outside the scope of Article 101(1) TFEU. These conditions are:

> First, the procedure for developing the sustainability standard must be transparent, and all interested competitors must be able to participate in the process leading to the selection of the standard.
>
> Second, the sustainability standard must not impose on undertakings that do not wish to participate in the standard any direct or indirect obligation to comply with the standard[147]
>
> Third, in order to ensure compliance with the standard, binding requirements can be imposed on the participating undertakings, but they must remain free to apply higher sustainability standards.
>
> Fourth, the parties to the sustainability standard must not exchange commercially sensitive information that is not objectively necessary and proportionate for the development, implementation, adoption or modification of the standard.
>
> Fifth, effective and non-discriminatory access to the outcome of the standard-setting process must be ensured. This includes allowing effective and non-discriminatory access to the requirements and conditions for using the agreed label, logo or brand name, and allowing undertakings that have not participated in the process of developing the standard to adopt the standard at a later stage.
>
> Sixth, the sustainability standard must satisfy *at least one* of the following two conditions:
>
> (a) The standard must not lead to a significant increase in the price or a significant reduction in the quality of the products concerned;
> (b) The combined market share of the participating undertakings) must not exceed 20 per cent on any relevant market affected by the standard.[148]

With regard to price increases resulting from the standards, the guidelines highlight that 'where the standard is adopted by undertakings representing a significant part of the market, significant economies of scale may be achieved,

[146] ibid para 546.

[147] Footnote 379 of the guidelines reads: 'See paragraph 464. In other words, undertakings that do not wish to participate in the standard should not be hindered from continuing to supply the market and consumers with products that meet legal requirements but do not meet the additional requirements created by the new sustainability standard.' Fn 324 of the Guidelines.

[148] ibid para 549 (footnotes omitted, emphasis added).

allowing undertakings to preserve the previous price level or to apply only an insignificant price increase'.[149]

And while complying with these conditions indicates that the standard is unlikely to affect competition, a failure to meet all conditions 'does not create a presumption ... [of a restriction of competition, instead] it is necessary to carry out an individual assessment.[150]

Overall, the guidelines adopt a rather broad definition of sustainability standards. Thus, a large number of agreements to phase out or replace non-sustainable products could benefit from this category. For such agreements to fall outside the scope of Article 101(1) TFEU, the EU Commission set out conditions to address the main anti-competitive risks associated with such standards. These risks are price coordination occurring as a result of the interactions between competitors in the standards-setting process, foreclosure of alternatives, in particular alternative standards and discrimination or the exclusion of competitors. To address these concerns, the guidelines set out six conditions that can be summarized as follows: 1) there must be a transparent procedure and open participation in the adoption; 2) non-discriminatory access must be guaranteed, and firms must remain free to decide whether or not to join the standard; 3) the firms must also be able to adopt higher levels than the standard prescribed; 4) it must be ensured that information is not shared for anti-competitive purposes; 5) there must be effective and non-discriminatory access to the outcome of the standard setting process; and 6) the standard should not lead to a substantial price increase or only cover a small part of the market.

Furthermore, it is important to note that the Commission acknowledges and accepts that such standards may lead to a certain extent of price increase for consumers. Accepting such increases offers an alternative to passing on the costs of standards in the supply chain, often on the ultimate producer of the input. For example, the costs for standards in UK groceries (for instance hygiene, food safety, or traceability) have been shown to be passed on to Kenyan producers.[151] This passing on of the costs may, in turn, lead to further consolidation upstream pushing out smallholders in favour of large farms.[152]

[149] ibid para 551.
[150] ibid para 552.
[151] Salomon Asfaw, Dagmar Mithofer, and Hermann Waibel, 'What Impact Are EU Supermarket Standards Having on Developing Countries' Export of High-Value Horticultural Products? Evidence From Kenya' (2010) 22(3/4) *Journal of International Food & Agribusiness Marketing* 252–276.
[152] Olivier De Schutter, 'Addressing Concentration in Food Supply Chains. The Role of Competition Law in Tackling the Abuse of Buyer Power' (December 2010) Briefing note by the Special Rapporteur on the right to food.

The UK Competition Authority, in its guidelines[153] sets out conditions similar to those in the EU. It explains that the environmental sustainability standards are unlikely to restrict competition to an appreciable effect where they fulfil the following conditions:

- the process for developing the standard is transparent, and it is possible for any business in markets affected by the standard to participate in the development of that standard;
- no business is obliged to implement the standard if it does not wish to do so (albeit the standard may require businesses that have committed to implement the standard to comply with the requirements of the standard, and may provide for a mechanism to monitor such compliance);[154]
- any business can implement the standard on reasonable and non-discriminatory terms. This includes allowing effective and non-discriminatory access to the requirements and conditions for using the agreed label (or logo or brand name) for the standard, and permitting businesses that have not participated in the process for developing the standard to implement the standard at a later stage;
- businesses implementing the standard are free to go beyond the minimum environmental sustainability requirements set by the standard, or to develop or implement additional higher standards (or, if applicable, to develop alternative standards for any competing products they sell outside of the standard); and
- the standard is unlikely to result in an appreciable reduction in the availability of suitable products for consumers to purchase. A standard is, in particular, unlikely to result in an appreciable reduction in product choice if at least one of the following applies:
  (i) the participating businesses are free to sell alternative competing products outside of the standard on the relevant market(s) affected by the standard, and remain free to independently determine which of their products the standard will apply to; or
  (ii) the combined market share of the participating businesses is sufficiently small (for example, below 20 per cent on any relevant market affected by the standard) to allow sufficient alternative choices for consumers).[155]

[153] CMA, 'Green Agreements Guidance: Guidance on the application of the Chapter I prohibition in the Competition Act 1998 to environmental sustainability Agreements' (October 2023) CMA 185 available at <https://assets.publishing.service.gov.uk/media/6526b81b244f8e000d8e742c/Green_agreements_guidance_.pdf> (accessed 22 January 2025).
[154] Footnote 37 of the guidelines reads: 'If the standard or code only applies to certain products sold by a business, then the obligation to comply with the standard should only apply to those products.'
[155] ibid para 315 (footnotes omitted).

A practical application of this exception for standards can be found in guidance that the Dutch competition authority provided in *Thuiswinkel*.[156] *Thuiswinkel* concerns a Dutch trade association in the e-commerce sector. It introduced a standard administered by a non-profit. This standard is the first sector-wide standard for businesses that wish to reduce their impact on the environment in six areas: strategy, product selection, packaging, delivery, returns, and circularity. The Dutch competition authority had no objections to the proposed standard and found that the standard would not restrict competition for the following reasons: 1) members of Thuiswinkel can voluntarily choose whether or not to participate in the standard; 2) certification was determined by an independent organization; 3) participants can determine their own vision, objectives, and sustainability choices and are free to take additional sustainability measures; 4) the standard offers room for new sustainable innovations; 5) it was guaranteed that commercially sensitive information would not be exchanged; and 6) participants would only communicate their sustainability efforts in accordance with ACM's guidelines regarding sustainability claims, informing consumers of information about the sustainability benefits of their products and services.

Generally, in many jurisdictions standards are looked upon more favourably by antitrust rules, as compared to other horizontal agreements. The reason is that it is accepted that standards are often pro-competitive. We have also seen that some jurisdictions specifically address standard-setting for sustainability purposes and that if certain conditions are met, sustainability standards are considered unproblematic and thus do not fall within the scope of competition law. The conditions and the reason why sustainability standards are considered unproblematic reflect the specific anti-competitive risk associated with sustainability standards, such as price-fixing as the result of the (regular) interaction between members of the standard-setting organization and foreclosure of competitors and competing standards. If we compare these risks to concerns about anti-competitive behaviour in the context of technical standards for internet or communication technology or other quality standards, it becomes clear that they overlap. Even in jurisdictions that do not specifically address sustainability standards, the standards would be treated more favourably where they do comply with conditions that ensure that such anti-competitive risks are minimized.

[156] Authority for Consumer & Market, 'ACM: Thuiswinkel's Sustainability Initiative Fits with Competition Rules' *ACM.nl* (11 April 2024) available at <https://www.acm.nl/en/publications/acm-thuiswinkels-sustainability-initiative-fits-competition-rules> (accessed 22 January 2025).

7. Other cases

Beyond the already discussed situations, where measures aimed at fostering sustainability can prove exempt from competition law, we can identify a number of other options. Examples of these are intellectual property (IP) pooling, agreements not affecting prices, choice, or innovation, and agreements relating to adherence to the relevant laws and regulations.

a) IP pooling

IP pooling is an area that is closely related to traditional standards, in particular with regard to so-called patent pools. Such pools can, for example, contain patents or other IPs relevant to sustainability. Contributors to the pool grant royalty-free access to their IP contained in this pool, with the aim of fostering innovation and faster implementation of (sustainable) industrial processes. Thus, such patent pools are often not subject to the competition law prohibitions.[157]

Sometimes, such patent pooling can also be related to joint research and development initiatives. For example, in *EUCAR* the EU Commission issued a comfort letter to a research collaboration between Europe's leading car manufacturers, explaining that their technological collaboration fell outside the scope of Article 101(1) TFEU. In its reasoning, the research would take place at what the Commission called the 'pre-competition' stage, as the collaboration involved basic research, so that the outcomes would not be directly usable. Moreover, all intellectual property derived from the project would be freely accessible and usable by all participants.[158] The EU horizontal guidelines similarly explain that R&D agreements typically do not raise competition concerns where the research activity is outsourced to a specialized body such as an undertaking or research institute, and the results are then available to the participating companies.[159] Moreover, restrictions of competition typically do not exist where joint exploitation (eg joint licensing, production, or marketing) does not take place.[160]

Overall, for patent pools, the main concerns are the same as in the case of technical standards. Thus, the Japanese JFTC explains in its Guidelines on Standardization and Patent Pool Arrangements that 'competition among the patented technologies is not restricted when only the essential patents are pooled, and licensing conditions are fixed'.[161]

[157] An example for such a pool could be the Eco-Patent Commons, which was launched by the World Business Council for Sustainable Development with a number of companies such as IBM, Nokia, Pitney Bowes, and Sony in January 2008.

[158] Case No IV/35.742 – F/2 – *EUCAR* OJ [1997] C 185/05.

[159] Guidelines (n 27) paras 138–139.

[160] ibid para 76.

[161] JFTC, Guidelines on Standardization and Patent Pool Arrangements (2005), Part 3. 2(1)a., pp 6–7, available at <https://www.jftc.go.jp/en/legislation_gls/imonopoly_guidelines_files/Patent_Pool.pdf> (accessed 22 January 2025). The situation is different however once non-essential patents are pooled.

JFTC, Guidelines on Standardization and Patent Pool Arrangements (Japan)[162]

In its guidelines, the JFTC recognizes the importance of standards and patent pools for innovation.

The JFTC's main distinction with regard to patent pools relates to non-essential and essential patents. If non-essential patents are pooled, the pooling activity is regarded as likely to raise competition concerns under AMA.[163] In contrast, if only patents essential to the specification are pooled, competition among competitors is not restricted as essential patents are mutually complementary for adopting the functions and utilities for the specifications. The guidelines, therefore, explain that

(1) **Technological characteristics of patents**

a. **If only patents essential to the specifications are pooled.**

The effects on competition of pooling patents for specifications can differ, for example between the case when all patents in the pool are essential for adopting the functions and utilities for specifications (namely, 'essential patents' (Note11)) and other cases.

Because essential patents are mutually complementary for adopting the functions and utilities for the specifications, competition among the patented technologies is not restricted when only the essential patents are pooled and licensing conditions are fixed. To exclude completely the risk of violating the AMA, it is necessary to limit patents in the pool to essential patents only.

It is also necessary to ensure that assessment of whether each patent is essential is not arbitrary and for that purpose the assessment should be made by an independent third party with technical expertise. Even in a case when only essential patents are pooled, the patented technologies should be excluded from the pool as soon as superior technologies providing alternative functions and utilities for specifications are developed.

(Note 11) Here, a patent that is essential for exploiting the functions and effects of the specifications refers to a patent that will be inevitably

[162] ibid.
[163] ibid 7.

infringed upon in adopting the specifications, or a patent that will be inevitably infringed upon in practical terms, even though it is avoidable technically.[164]

The guidelines then continue to explain the problems that can exist when non-essential patents are pooled.[165]

The JFTC's distinction between essential and non-essential patents could equally be applied to patents that are relevant for more sustainable production. Thus, where only essential patents for such a new, more sustainable product are pooled, the JFTC would not consider competition to be restricted.

b) Actions not substantially affecting prices, choice, or innovation

For an agreement to fall under the prohibition of Article 101(1) TFEU, an agreement must either have the object of restricting competition or restrict competition with an appreciable effect. The European Commission, in its draft guidelines, specifically sets out a number of situations where an agreement would be unlikely to raise any competition concerns because the agreement does not seem to restrict competition by object, nor creates appreciable effects on competition. This is the case in two situations.

First, an agreement that does not restrict competition by object might not have an appreciable effect on competition and might thus benefit from the safe harbour provided by the De Minimis Notice.[166] For this to be the case, the aggregate market share of competitors who are parties to the agreement shall not exceed 10 per cent of any of the affected relevant markets.

Second, the guidelines explain that, in particular, agreements that 'do not affect parameters of competition, such as price, quantity, quality, choice or innovation, ... are not capable of raising competition law concerns'.[167] Some examples of such agreements can be found in the EU Commission's guidelines, the EU Commission's case law, as well as in the Dutch guidelines and in the JFTC's and CMA's guidelines.

164 ibid 6–7.
165 ibid.
166 See the Commission Notice on agreements of minor importance which do not appreciably restrict competition under Article 101(1) of the Treaty on the Functioning of the European Union (De Minimis Notice), OJ C 291, 30.08.2014, p 13.
167 EU Commission, 'Guidelines on the applicability of Article 101' (n 27) para 527.

European Commission Horizontal Guidelines (EU)[168]

The guidelines set out three examples of agreements that are unlikely to be caught by Article 101(1). This list is supposed to be 'illustrative and not exhaustive'[169].

> [A]greements that do not concern the economic activity of undertakings, but their internal corporate conduct, will generally fall outside the scope of Article 101. Competing undertakings may seek to increase the reputation of their industry for being environmentally responsible, and for this purpose agree, for example, on measures to eliminate single-use plastics from their business premises; not to exceed a certain ambient temperature in their buildings, or to limit the volume of internal documents that they print.[170]
>
> [A]greements to set up a database containing general information about suppliers that have (un)sustainable value chains (for instance, suppliers that respect labour rights or pay living wages); use (un)sustainable production processes, or supply (un)sustainable inputs, or information about distributors that market products in a(n) (un)sustainable manner, but which do not forbid or oblige the parties to purchase from such suppliers or to sell to such distributors, will in general not restrict competition and fall outside the scope of Article 101 (369). Such limited forms of exchange of information may again help undertakings to fulfil their sustainability due diligence obligations under national or EU law.[171]
>
> [A]greements between competitors relating to the organisation of industry-wide awareness campaigns, or campaigns raising customers' awareness of the environmental impact or other negative externalities of their consumption, provided that they do not amount to joint advertising of specific products, will also generally not restrict competition and fall outside the scope of Article 101.[172]

The Commission moreover explains that even where an in-depth analysis of the effects of an agreement needs to be carried out as the agreement covers a substantial amount of the market, it is still possible that no restrictive effects exist. The guideline sets out:

[168] ibid.
[169] ibid para 527.
[170] ibid para 529.
[171] ibid para 530.
[172] ibid para 531.

> ... Even if the market coverage of the sustainability standardisation agreement is significant, the constraint exerted by potential competition may still be sufficient, in particular in cases where the sustainability standardisation agreement is limited to establishing a label, leaving the participating firms free to also operate outside the label. In that case, consumers have the choice of buying products that bear the label or other products, possibly produced by the same undertakings, that do not comply with the label, and hence competition is unlikely to be restricted. In cases where a sustainability standardisation agreement is likely to lead to a significant increase in price or reduction in output, product variety, quality or innovation, the agreement may nonetheless fulfil the conditions of Article 101(3).[173]

Beyond the guidelines, the EU Commission, in its decisional practice, has treated leniently the so-called 'loose commitments' and agreements that are necessary to create a new market(s). Loose commitments were found not to restrict competition in cases like *ACEA*,[174] *JAMA*, and *KAMA*.[175] These concerned sector-wide reductions of emissions by car manufacturers; the Commission found no appreciable effect on competition. This finding was based on the fact that the agreement left it to the manufacturers how to achieve these reductions, instead of imposing certain technical/technological approaches, leaving it to competition how the emission reduction would be achieved.[176]

Commission Decisions in ACEA, JAMA, and KAMA (EU)[177]

Facts

At the end of the 1990s, the EU Commission set out a new plan to reduce the CO2 emission from new passenger cars, with the aim of achieving an average of 120 g/km by 2005 (2010 at the latest). But instead of legislating—which might

[173] ibid para 555, footnote omitted.

[174] European Commission, *XXVIIIth Report on Competition Policy 1998* (Office for Official Publications of the European Communities 1999) 151; European Commission, Commission Press Release (IP/98/865).

[175] European Commission, *XXIXth Report on Competition Policy 1999* (Office for Official Publications of the European Communities 2000) 160.

[176] European Commission, *XXIXth Report on Competition Policy 1999* (Office for Official Publications of the European Communities 2000) 151.

[177] European Commission, *XXVIIIth Report on Competition Policy 1998* (Office for Official Publications of the European Communities 1999) 151; European Commission, Commission Press Release (IP/98/865); European Commission, *XXIXth Report on Competition Policy 1999* (Office for Official Publications of the European Communities 2000) 160.

have been politically difficult—the Commission signed agreements with associations of car manufacturers. The first agreement was signed with the European Automobile Manufacture Association (ACEA), which represented over 90 per cent of car registrations in the EU in 1999. In the agreement the association's members committed themselves to achieving 140 g/km of CO2 emissions by the end of 2008. As part of this agreement, the ACEA demanded that the Commission would not take action against diesel cars, ensure the availability of improved fuels (low sulphur) by 2005 content, and that the Commission would aim to achieve similar agreements with car importers or major car manufacturing countries to implement similar policies. A year later, in 1999, the Association of Japanese Automobile Manufacturers (JAMA), which accounted for 3.1 per cent of car registrations in the EU in 1999, and the Association of Korean Automobile Manufactures (KAMA) also made the same commitment to reduce CO2 emissions to an average of 140g/km for their new passenger cars sold in the EU by the year 2009.

Decision

The agreements guaranteed that the associations would not impose any obligation on each manufacturer, but only an average target for all the members of the association. Moreover, companies were free to choose any emission technologies to reach the target. This feature ensured that competition would not be distorted among car manufacturers nor between different technologies for the reduction of CO2 emission. The EU Commission highlighted in particular that the agreement ensured that

> new CO2 efficient technologies [would be developed] independently and in competition.[178]

Moreover, the official monitoring reports would not show the individual companies' achievements.

Overall, while the agreements had some success in reducing CO2 emissions, not all associations reached the target.

Along similar lines, the UK competition authority found that a voluntary initiative of packing and yogurt producers for the environmental performance of yogurt pots did not infringe competition law.[179] It is also now contained in the new

[178] European Commission, *XXVIIIth Report on Competition Policy 1998*, ibid.

[179] See OECD, 'Horizontal Agreements in the Environmental Context' (2010) DAF/COMP(2010)39 available at <https://www.oecd.org/daf/competition/49139867.pdf> (accessed 22 January 2025) 100.

guidance.[180] The same goes for 'the setting of non-binding targets or ambitions for the whole industry with regard to environmental sustainability objectives',[181] including cooperation on setting sustainability targets, and developing a common calculation and reporting methodology.[182]

These cases show how loose commitments might be helpful in achieving sustainability aims. Yet, they are no panacea. Depending on the arrangement they might need to be stronger to fully achieve the aim. Moreover, it needs to be ensured that these agreements do not become the platform for competition law violations.[183]

Moreover, the European Commission found that there is no restriction of competition where the agreements are necessary to create a new, otherwise non-existent, market. *DSD*[184] concerned an agreement on collecting plastic waste that has not been previously recycled. Under the newly introduced German rules on packaging waste, this form of plastic had to be collected and recycled. The agreement in question required all contractors that collected and sorted the waste to supply this plastic waste free of charge to a designated recycling company. This zero-interface clause effectively set the price and established exclusivity, yet it was found not to restrict competition. While the German rules on packing waste aimed at establishing a market for this waste, such a market did not yet exist when the agreement was made. In fact, the price of such plastic waste[185] was often negative, so much plastic was disposed of by cheaper means instead of being recycled. For the Commission, there was no restriction of competition as long as a functioning market for such plastic waste had not yet emerged.[186]

The Japanese JFTC guidelines also distinguish between '[a]cts that do not pose problems under the Antimonopoly Act', '[a]cts that pose problems under the Antimonopoly Act', and '[a]cts that require attention in order not to pose problems under the Antimonopoly Act'.[187] It then sets out situations that would not pose problems as they do not affect 'matters that constitute important means of competition including prices, not restraining entry of enterprises, and not excluding incumbents from markets'.[188]

180 See CMA, 'Green Agreements Guidance' (n 153) paras 3.19–3.20.
181 ibid paras 3.21–3.23.
182 ibid.
183 For example, if meetings as part of this agreement are used for price-fixing or market-sharing.
184 *DSD* (COMP/34493) Commission Decision 2001/837/EC [2001] OJ L319/1.
185 Note the difference to markets for glass, paper, etc for which markets existed.
186 *DSD* (n 184) paras 113–114.
187 JFTC, 'Guidelines' (n 131) 3.
188 ibid 6 (footnote omitted).

JFTC, Realization of a Green Society Under the Antimonopoly Act Guidelines (Japan)[189]

In its guidelines, the JFTC explains first the general principle of cases that do not restrict competition. Acts are not anti-competitive where they are 'not affecting matters that constitute important means of competition including prices, not restraining entry of enterprises, and not excluding incumbents from markets'.[190] It then sets out seven example cases where competition is not restricted.

> **Supposed case 1: Industry-wide awareness-raising campaign**
> Trade Association X ... organize[d] an awareness-raising campaign to promote the activities of individual enterprises in the industry toward the realization of a green society. ... X has ensured the following matters: it is to be implemented to an extent that it will not affect any matters constituting important means of competition; entry of new enterprises will not be restrained; incumbents will not be excluded from the market; and it will not restrict the business activities of individual enterprises.[191]
>
> **Supposed case 2: Compliance with statutory obligation**
> ... to ensure the achievement of that [legally mandated] recycling ratio, X [a trade association] ... encourage[d] its members to publish on their websites that they are making efforts to achieve the goals, and ... publish[es] the accomplishment rate of each member enterprise on X's website.[192]
>
> **Supposed case 3: Industry targets and activity guidelines**
> ... for carbon neutrality, Trade Association X ... set an industry-wide non-binding goal of X% reduction. X organized those challenges that needed to be resolved ... to achieve the goal and compiled general activity guidelines [with] specific measures ... [for] each manufacturer ..., including changes to the raw materials and procured parts, revisions to the manufacturing processes, and the introduction of new technologies.[193]
>
> **Supposed case 4: Dispatch of information (i)**
> ... [this case concerns a] website for general consumers and therethrough to release information on each retailer's effort [in switching the packaging to recycled material][194]

[189] ibid.
[190] ibid 68.
[191] ibid 8
[192] ibid 8.
[193] ibid 8.
[194] ibid 8–9.

Supposed case 5: Dispatch of information
... manufacturers of Product A, were each considering changing manufacturing process for Product A.... [C]hanging manufacturing process for Produce A, ... significantly reduce[s] greenhouse gas emissions ... [but comes with significantly increased costs].... [The] enterprises discussed how to address these common concerns, and in order to gain the understanding of the consumers of Product A, they informed business partners and consumers of the significant rise of cost in manufacturing, as well as the purpose and effects of changing manufacturing process [and]. jointly disseminate information [about their] current situation....[195]

Supposed case 6: Recommendation for energy saving at business establishment
... Trade Association X has set out the reference heating and cooling temperature levels [for] member enterprise ... and has recommended the use of LED light bulbs [for] saving electricity. The use of heating and cooling temperature levels and LED light bulbs will not affect competition among the member enterprises of the Trade Association.[196]

Supposed case 7: Information exchange irrelevant to important means of competition
... [Firms] exchanged ... information on their respective activities for reducing greenhouse gas emissions, such as how to calculate the emissions, measures for energy saving, experiences of greenhouse gas emissions reduction leading to new transaction opportunities, and used that information as a reference for their respective activities. The matters constituting their important means of competition, such as their respective prices of Product A, were not subject to the information exchange.[197]

Supposed case 8: Establishment of standards for reducing greenhouse gas emissions and publicizing the fact, necessary for the standards to be complied with
Product A that emits a large amount of greenhouse gases. ... [The relevant] laws established a specific midterm target of reduction ... which each manufacturer of Product A should accomplish. Trade Association Y... set that statutory standard as the one with which each member enterprise should comply and decided to publicize the fact of non-compliance, to the extent necessary for ensuring compliance with the standard.[198]

[195] ibid 9 (Commentary omitted).
[196] ibid 9.
[197] ibid 9.
[198] ibid 9.

These example cases illustrate the fact that many activities in the sustainability field are not restricting competition in the first place.

In a similar vein, the Singapore Competition Commission also distinguishes between agreements that are unlikely, less likely, and likely to raise competition concerns.[199] Agreements that are unlikely to raise competition concerns include those excluded from the enforcement of section 34 Competition Act prohibition (ie agreements preventing, restricting, or distorting competition).[200] Such agreements include agreements to comply with national law, agreements that do not affect how businesses compete with each other, eg do not concern price, quantity, quality, choice, or innovation of goods/services supplies. Specifically, the Commission in its Environmental Sustainability Collaboration Guidance Note[201] stipulated that

> An agreement between businesses to jointly carry out certain activities which, objectively, none of the parties could do independently is similarly unlikely to be problematic. This may be the case where the businesses involved do not have all the necessary technical capabilities or lack the necessary scale, individually, to undertake the activity on their own.[202]

The guidance then goes on to provide the example of the development of a new sustainable fuel, in which neither of the parties would have been able to develop it on their own. The conduct was considered not problematic as there could not be competition from the very start if parties did not collaborate.

Agreements that are less likely to raise competition concerns are those concerning developments of industry standards to facilitate businesses adopting green practices, or those on joint production and commercialization such as sharing common distribution/logistics systems to reduce unnecessary pollution, and lastly, those fostering joint research and development.[203]

The guidelines of the Commerce Commission of New Zealand apply a similar distinction between collaborations that are unlikely to affect competition, those

[199] Guidance Note (n 100).
[200] Competition Act 2004, s 35 and Third Schedule.
[201] Guidance Note (n 100)
[202] ibid 2.6.
[203] The guidance also includes guidance on how businesses can potentially minimize competition concerns for each of the scenarios, such as to include conditions for each type of collaboration, refer to the Guidance Note. However, the Commission also highlighted that any of such collaboration, including the aforesaid, should not contain any other anti-competitive restrictions, eg through exclusivity clauses, which are likely to raise competition concerns.

that may restrict competition,[204] and those that affect competition where parties may seek authorization or clearance.[205]

The UK Competition Authority also specifically highlights that

> any concerns about competition law compliance [are ruled out] if the environmental sustainability agreement in question does not affect or engage with the way those businesses compete. This is likely to be the case when the agreement does not affect the main parameters of competition between those businesses, such as price, quantity, quality, choice, or innovation.[206]

The guidance then sets out examples of agreements such as internal conduct such as eliminating single-use plastic, agreements on pooling of funds for joint awareness campaigns in the industry or consumers, and joint lobbying with regard to legislation or policy questions in terms of the environment.

c) Shareholder agreements

As an important capital market, the UK guidance also contains another area that has gained more attention recently: shareholder agreements. It highlights that shareholder agreements to promote sustainability action by corporations are unlikely to infringe competition law.

CMA, 'Green Agreements Guidance' (UK)[207]

As part of its section on 'environmental sustainability agreements which are unlikely to infringe the Chapter I prohibition', the guidance also addresses 'agreements between shareholders to vote for promoting corporate policies that pursue environmental sustainability':

> In some instances, shareholders in a company will compete among themselves in other markets (for example, asset managers may compete with each other by investing in different commodities for their clients). An agreement between shareholders of a single business to vote in support of corporate policies that pursue climate change or environmental sustainability agreements or against policies that do not, or to lobby jointly for corporate changes that

[204] Commerce Commission New Zealand, Collaboration and Sustainability Guidelines (November 2023) available at <https://comcom.govt.nz/__data/assets/pdf_file/0033/335985/Collaboration-and-Sustainability-Guidelines-30-November-2023.pdf> (accessed 22 January 2025) paras 23–27.

[205] ibid paras 25, 29.

[206] CMA, 'Green Agreements Guidance' (n 153) para 3.6.

[207] ibid.

> pursue environmental sustainability objectives, will be unlikely to infringe competition law.[208]
>
> Equally, one shareholder indicating how it will vote regarding such policies is also unlikely to infringe applicable competition law.[209]
>
> Similarly, where there is an agreement (or network of similar agreements together) covering shareholders' conduct in relation to several businesses that are competitors in a market, there is unlikely to be a negative effect on competition in that market if the corporate policies, or the changes the shareholders are agreeing to, support, encourage or require the adoption of any of the categories of agreement set out in Section 3 [on environmental sustainability agreements which are unlikely to infringe the Chapter I prohibition] of this Guidance.[210]
>
> Where the shareholder activity falls outside of one of the categories set out in paragraphs 3.24 to 3.26, the shareholder activity may nonetheless be permissible but would need to be assessed under other parts of this Guidance (see Sections 4 [on environmental sustainability agreements which could infringe the Chapter I prohibition], 5 [on an exemption for environmental sustainability agreements generally] and 6 [on exemption for climate change agreements]).[211]

8. Specific rules in some countries

Some countries also have specific rules that take sustainability-related arrangements out of the scope of competition law. For example, the Chinese Antimonopoly Law (AML) contains such a clause in Article 15. It sets out that:

> Agreements among undertakings with one of the following objectives shall be exempted from the application of article 13, 14 if:
> (i) agreements made to improve technology, to research and develop new products.
> (ii) agreements made for the purpose of improving product quality, reducing cost, improving efficiency, unifying standards, norms, or specialise;

[208] ibid para 3.24.
[209] ibid para 3.25.
[210] ibid para 3.26.
[211] ibid para 3.27. The guidance in its footnote 45 then explains: 'See also the Guidance on Horizontal Agreements and Guidance on Vertical Agreements. For example, where shareholders exercise decisive influence over a company, the agreement would need to be assessed by reference to the guidance on agreements between parent companies and their joint venture (see paragraphs 3.12–3.14 of the Guidance on Horizontal Agreements).'

(iii) agreements made by small and medium-sized enterprises to improve operational efficiency and to enhance their competitiveness;
(iv) agreements made to cope with economic depression, to mitigate a serious decrease in sales volumes or excessive overstock;
(v) agreements made to achieve public interests, such as saving energy, protecting the environment, relieving the victims of a disaster, and so on.

This provision, particularly, Article 15 subsection (v), seems to take agreements outside of the scope of the general prohibition if they aim to achieve sustainability-related matters. However, how this provision would be applied and whether some form of balancing between the restriction of competition and the sustainability benefit would take place is unclear. In 2016, the National Development and Reform Commission issued draft guidelines[212] for comment, under which the parties would have to prove that competition was not substantially restricted and that society and consumers share the benefits of the agreement. The draft focused on procedural elements but was in any case never formally adopted. Moreover, there has been a very limited number of cases where the provision was applied[213] and the Chinese competition authorities have not yet provided any further official guidance on the application of this provision.[214]

9. Summary

In this section, we explored several situations where actions to promote sustainability are not subject to competition law. While at first sight, a conflict between competition law and sustainability might exist, this perceived conflict dissolves as a mirage upon closer examination.

We explored how many competition regimes apply their prohibitions only to commercial or economic activities so that non-commercial or non-economic

[212] For an overview see Practical Law China, 'NDRC Circulates Draft Guidelines on Monopoly Agreement Exemptions' (2016) available at <https://uk.practicallaw.thomsonreuters.com/3-628-5665?transitionType=Default&contextData=(sc.Default)&firstPage=true> (accessed 22 January 2025).

[213] Since 2013 there have been only eight cases in which environmental protection exemptions have been used as a defence in the application of the Antimonopoly Law, as published by SAMR and the China Judicial Instruments Network, and neither the SAMR nor the courts have upheld this defence. These cases are *Liaoning Industrial and Commercial Bureau* Document [2012] No 2, *Shanxi Market Supervision and Price Monitoring* Document [2019] No 7, Competition Law Enforcement Notice 2015 No 3, Competition Law Enforcement Notice 2017 No. 2, *Henan Industrial and Commercial Bureau* Document [2016] No. 11-15, Chongqing First Intermediate People's Court Administrative Final Case [2020] No. 861, Guangdong Higher People's Court Civil Final Case [2012] No. 155. (辽工商处字[2012]2号、晋市监价监字[2019]7号、竞争执法公告2015年第3号、竞争执法公告2017年2号、豫工商处字[2016]第11-15号、(2020)渝01行终861号、(2012)粤高法民三终字第155号).

[214] See Nicole Kar and Sima Ostrovsky, 'Competition and Sustainability: Quantifying the Environmental Benefits of Cooperation' (7 May 2020) available at <https://www.linklaters.com/en/insights/blogs/linkingcompetition/2020/esg/competition-and-sustainability/quantifying-the-environmental-benefits-of-cooperation>(accessed 22 January 2025).

activities are not subject to competition law. This allows certain sustainability activities to be exempt from competition law. Subsequently, we took a closer look at issues around actions within an entity, collective bargaining, as well as platform arrangements. We examined how sustainability-related activities, when structured accordingly, might escape the scope of antitrust via these routes. Equally, we highlighted how sectorial exemption, state compulsion, or state action might immunize actions from competition law where they are aimed at fostering sustainability. Later, we also showed that certain jurisdictions accept agreements as not restricting competition. These agreements ensure compliance with internationally recognized legal standards in the sustainability field, such as rules on child labour, in particular, where local enforcement is weak or non-existent. We equally examined the more lenient treatment of standards and IP pools that might allow certain arrangements that foster sustainability to avoid the antitrust prohibitions. Finally, we saw how some jurisdictions might exclude sustainability agreements from the scope of their competition law and stressed how agreements that foster sustainability but do not substantially affect prices, choice, or innovation are seen as not restricting competition. This category of agreements can also include agreements that create new markets and shareholder agreements fostering sustainability.

While in these situations, a direct conflict between pursuing sustainability and complying with the competition rules does not exist, the next section explores situations where such a conflict exists. It explores how different competition regimes aim to strike a balance between competition and sustainability via different forms of balancing.

IV. Balancing to resolve conflicts

1. Introduction

In the previous section, we highlighted how many actions fostering sustainability are considered to be outside the scope of competition law. This section focuses on situations that are often more contentious, situations where anti-competitive actions aimed at improving sustainability are within the scope of competition law. We will observe how different jurisdictions deal with such conflicts and how they aim to strike a balance in such situations, either using abstract balancing or balancing within economic frameworks.[215] In the first sub-section, we will explore

[215] See also Christopher Townley, *Article 81 EC and Public Policy* (Hart 2009) who distinguishes between 'mere balancing' and 'market balancing'. The UK's OFT also suggested distinguishing between economic and non-economic concerns, and then further between direct and indirect economic benefits, see OFT contribution to the OECD, 'Horizontal Agreements in the Environmental Context' (n 178) 101–108.

abstract balancing via public interest clauses and their operation in different jurisdictions. In cases of abstract balancing, sustainability benefits specifically or a public interest benefit more generally are balanced in an abstract way outside economic frameworks, using for example a proportionality assessment. In the second part of this section, we look more closely at balancing sustainability benefits against competition harms within economic frameworks such as efficiency and consumer welfare.

2. Abstract balancing via public interest clauses

Abstract balancing takes place within public interest clauses in competition law statutes or is established by case law. Where these rules are applied by competition authorities and courts, such balancing often involves a proportionality assessment. But occasionally, the striking of such a balance is 'outsourced' to political actors such as ministers. Moreover, public interest clauses that may take into account sustainability concerns can be public interest clauses that apply generally to all public interests. Such general clauses may even apply to all restrictions covered by competition laws in that jurisdiction. In other jurisdictions, such clauses might be more restricted. For example, the clauses apply only to mergers or are applied to a number of specified public interests or the public rules might be applicable only to a very specific area like sustainability and competition in the agricultural sector.

a) General public interest clauses

The Swiss competition law contains possibly the clearest example of a general public interest clause.[216] Article 8 of the Swiss Cartel Act is entitled 'Exceptional authorisation for compelling public interest reasons' and sets out that:

> Agreements affecting competition and behaviour by dominant undertakings that have been declared unlawful by the competent authority may be authorised by the Federal Council at the request of the undertakings involved if, in exceptional cases, they are necessary for compelling public interest reasons.

The Chinese competition law's Article 15 could also be seen as a form of abstract public interest balancing. While it is not clear whether a balancing would be carried out, the above-mentioned draft guideline published by the National Development and Reform Commission in 2016[217] seems to suggest some kind of balancing. While the guidelines were never formally adopted, the text of Article 15 AML specifies a number of specific interests that might exempt agreements.

[216] A similar clause exists for mergers in Art 11 of the Cartel Act.
[217] See above, text to (n 212).

Paragraph (v) states that the prohibitions do not apply to 'agreements made to achieve public interests, such as saving energy, protecting the environment, relieving the victims of a disaster and so on'. The 'and so on' suggests that this provision is a general public interest clause that could be applied to sustainability and other public interests.[218]

Similarly, Australia's system applies a general public clause. Part VII, section 90 of the Competition and Consumer Act 2010 foresees the possibility for authorization if the action provides 'a benefit to the public'. This general description of 'benefit to the public' can also be applied in the context of sustainability. For example,[219] in 2020 the Australia Competition Agency (ACCC) granted an authorization to the Battery Stewardship Council (BSC).[220] This scheme set up nationwide collecting and recycling of batteries which charged its members a small levy to finance collection and recycling costs. The ACCC granted an authorization as the scheme provided substantial environmental benefits and increased public awareness and innovation which outweighed the competitive harms.

The Battery Stewardship Scheme (Australia)[221]

Facts

In 2018, the Battery Stewardship Council (BSC) was set up as a not-for-profit company. The overall aim was to increase battery collection and recycling significantly. This was important as, at that time, only about 3 per cent of handheld batteries in Australia were recycled, and the rest would mainly go to landfill. More specifically, the BSC aimed at:

- increasing resource recovery and recycling rates of end-of-life batteries and thereby removing a potentially significant contaminant;
- developing an efficient and innovative domestic battery recycling industry;
- fostering a circular economy where batteries are recovered for recycling and reused to make new batteries or other products.

[218] As Wendy Ng, points out 'China's approach to competition law is motivated by the interests of the state, whatever they may be.' See Wendy Ng, 'State Interest and the State-Centered Approach to Competition Law in China' (2020) 65(2) *The Antitrust Bulletin* 311.

[219] For a good summary of earlier decisions see OECD, 'Horizontal Agreements in the Environmental Context' (n 179) 29–36.

[220] See ACCC, *Determination Application for authorisation AA1000476 lodged by Battery Stewardship Council in respect of the Battery Stewardship Scheme Authorisation number: AA1000476* (4 Sept 2020) available at <https://www.accc.gov.au/public-registers/authorisations-and-notifications-registers/authorisations-register/battery-stewardship-council> (accessed 22 January 2025). For a detailed case assessment see Gaetano Lapenta and Matteo Giangaspero, 'Greening Antitrust: Lessons from the ACCC's Authorisation of a Recycling Co-operation Agreement' (2021) 12:10 *Journal of European Competition Law & Practice* 758–764.

[221] ibid.

To achieve this aim, battery-makers and importers could (voluntarily) join the scheme. A levy of four cents per 24 grams (the weight of an AA battery) would be charged as part of the scheme. This fee would be passed through to consumers and would be transparent. From this income, recyclers would receive payments to help offset the cost of collecting, sorting, and processing expired batteries. Part of the scheme was that members agreed to deal exclusively with other members along the supply chain, although limited exceptions, such as for pre-existing arrangements, existed. The levy and the obligation on scheme members to only deal with other scheme members would risk breaching the Competition and Consumer Act 2010, hence BSC sought authorization.

Findings

The final decision by the ACCC applying the authorization test was made in 2020. Under this test, the ACCC has to examine and compare the likely future with and without the restriction. It then decides whether the conduct would result in or likely result in a benefit to the public and whether that benefit would outweigh the detriment to the public. In its decision, the ACCC recognizes that the disposal of batteries to landfill results in toxic chemicals leaking into soil and water over the long term and accepts that the scheme seeks to reduce this and the need for costly remediation. It also highlights that the environmental harms of disposing of batteries to landfill as well as the costs of recycling batteries are currently not reflected in the prices charged and that there is a lack of commercial incentive, as the responsibility for managing disposal of batteries currently falls to local governments. The levy would therefore better align the price of batteries with the cost of disposal and thereby increase the incentive for recycling.

ACCC highlighted that the obligation of members of the scheme to deal only with other members would likely result in some public detriment. In particular, it held that it would

- prevent non-members from competing in the supply of services to members of the Scheme or themselves obtaining Eligible Batteries; and
- limit the number of recyclers who can service businesses that do not participate in the Scheme.[222]

However, these detriments are likely to be largely mitigated by the exceptions to the obligation on members of the Scheme to only deal with other Scheme

[222] ibid para 4.74.

members, the ability for businesses to join the Scheme without charge, and the likely increase in collection, sorting and recycling service availability over time.[223]

The Scheme is also likely to result in some public detriment through the administrative burden on participating businesses.[224]

In terms of public benefits, the ACCC held that the Scheme would create significant environmental benefits, increase public awareness of battery disposal and re-use, and support innovation, research, and development.[225]

Overall, the ACCC found that the Scheme, subject to conditions relating to developing a so-called 'Button Battery Safety Strategy' and establishing an advisory committee in this regard, would likely result in a benefit to the public and such benefit would outweigh the detriment to the public. Hence, an authorization was granted until 26 September 2025.

Similarly, the ACCC had already in 2000 authorized the so-called Homeworkers Code of Practice on application by the Textile, Clothing, and Footwear Union of Australia and the Council of Textile and Fashion Industries.[226] The code had, amongst others, the benefit of reducing the exploitation of disadvantaged groups which in this case were mainly migrant women with a poor level of English. It has been reauthorized after renewed examination a number of times, lastly in 2018.[227] The numerous cases show the operation of the broad public interest test in Australia which contrasts with the narrower consumer welfare-focused test in parts of Europe and North America. The experience of the ACCC with the public interest test highlights that situations where sustainability matters are at stake do not create particular legal problems for the ACCC. Where questions arise those are rather of an evidential/factual nature.[228] Notably, the Australian

[223] ibid para 4.75.

[224] ibid para 4.76.

[225] ibid para 4.24.

[226] ACCC, 'Application for Authorisation by The Textile, Clothing and Footwear Union of Australia and the Council of Textile and Fashion Industries in respect of the Homeworkers Code of Practice' (July 2000) A90722, available at <https://www.accc.gov.au/system/files/public-registers/documents/D05%2B12089.pdf> (accessed 22 January 2025).

[227] ACCC, *Application for revocation of A91354-A91357 and the substitution of authorisation AA1000418 lodged by Homeworker Code Committee Incorporated in respect of the Homeworkers Code of Practice (to be renamed 'Ethical Clothing Australia's Code of Practice incorporating Homeworkers')* (August 2018) available at <https://www.accc.gov.au/system/files/public-registers/documents/AA1000418%20-%20Homeworkers%20Code%20Committee%20Incorporated%20-%20Final%20Determination%20-%2030.08.18%20-%20PR.pdf> (accessed 22 January 2025).

[228] See also, including a detailed examination of the cases, Georgina Foster, 'Australia: Sustainability as a Public Benefit to be Weighed Against the Anti-Competitive Detriments of Competitor Collaborations' in Julian Nowag (ed), *Research Handbook on Sustainability and Competition Law* (Edward Elgar 2024) 488–499.

Competition Tribunal addressed specifically the tension between qualitative and quantitative measures of sustainability effects,[229] and the likelihood that quantitative measures may be less informative, in *Re Qantas Airways Ltd*. The Australian Competition Tribunal suggested that, while the balancing exercise (or benefit analysis) should be 'robust and commercially realistic, in the sense of being both significant and tangible',[230] the advantages to pursuing a quantitative analysis are not without limits:

> All other things being equal, detailed quantification is the best option. However, quantification at all costs is not required by the Act, and has never been sought by the Tribunal. There are diminishing returns to the quantification exercise. Benefits should be quantified only to the extent that the exercise enlightens the Tribunal more than the alternative of qualitative explanation.[231]

Kenya and South Africa are other jurisdictions with broad public interest clauses. Section 46(2)(c) of Kenya's Competition Act also sets out an abstract balancing between competition and the public interest. The competition authority can assess 'the extent to which the proposed merger would be likely to result in a benefit to the public which would outweigh any detriment which would be likely to result from any undertaking, including an undertaking not involved as a party in the proposed merger'. Following the 2018 amendments, the South African Competition Act now also aims 'to promote a greater spread of ownership, in particular to increase the ownership stakes of historically disadvantaged persons' (Sec 2(1)(f)). It thus foresees exemptions with regard to historically disadvantaged persons in Sec 10. In particular, Sec 10(1) sets out that:

> A firm may apply to the Competition Commission to exempt from the application of this Chapter
> ... if
> (b) the agreement or practice concerned, or category of agreements or practices concerned, contributes to any of the following objectives:
> ...
> (ii) promotion of the effective entry into, participation in or expansion within a market by small and medium businesses or firms controlled or owned by historically disadvantaged persons;

[229] See Section IV Part 2.
[230] (2005) APR 42-065 [206]. Referred to in Gaetano Lapenta and Mattero Giangaspero, 'Greening Antitrust: Lessons from the ACCC's Authorisation of a Recycling Co-operation Agreement' (2021) 12(10) *Journal of European Competition Law & Practice* 758, 763.
[231] ibid para 208.

A similar ground can be found regarding mergers in Sec 12A, which explains that:

> (3) When determining whether a merger can or cannot be justified on public interest grounds, the Competition Commission or the Competition Tribunal must consider the effect that the merger will have on
>
> ...
>
> (c) the ability of small and medium businesses, or firms controlled or owned by historically disadvantaged persons, to effectively enter into, participate in or expand within the market;
>
> (e) the promotion of a greater spread of ownership, in particular to increase the levels of ownership by historically disadvantaged persons and workers in firms in the market.

There has been some experience with the application of these provisions by the Commission and subsequently by the courts.[232] And while these provisions do not specifically address the broader sustainability issue, the provisions may well be employed with regard to social elements of sustainability in South Africa with regard to poverty of historically disadvantaged persons.

Hong Kong's competition law equally contains a specifically designed pathway for the executive branch to exempt an agreement or a class of agreement[233] or even merger[234] from the application of competition law through an executive order if an exemption is warranted by 'exceptional and compelling reasons of public policy'. Notably, the government in this regard enjoys extensive power in issuing such exemptions, as such power could be exercised even in the absence of any application or proceeding.

b) Public interest clauses in mergers and with regard to anti-competitive agreements

As just described, the South African competition rules provide for a specific public interest exemption for all areas of competition law, including mergers. In other jurisdictions, public interest justification might be more limited and apply only to certain areas of competition, such as mergers.

[232] For a good overview with the relevant cases, see Liberty Mncube and Hardin Ratshisusu, 'Competition Policy and Black Empowerment: South Africa's Path to Inclusion' (2022) 11(1) *Journal of Antitrust Enforcement* 74–90. See also Simbarashe Tavuyanago, 'Public Interest Considerations and their Impact on Merger Regulation in South Africa' (2015) 15(7) *Global Journal of Human-Social Science* 23–43; Ziyanda Buthelezi and Yongama Njisane, 'The Incorporation of Public Interest Considerations During the Assessment of Prohibited Conduct: A Juggling Act' in Frederic Jenny and Yannis Katsoulacos (eds), *Competition Law Enforcement in the BRICS and in Developing Countries* (Springer 2016) 289–307.

[233] Hong Kong Competition Ordinance (Cap 619) Sec 31

[234] ibid Sch 7 para 9.

Spain, for example, has a general public interest provision in its rules on mergers that specifically addresses environmental issues. Where a merger is about to be prohibited in a phase II decision by the competition authority, the Minister of Economy and Finance can refer the matter to the Council of Ministers for assessment according to Article 60 of the Spanish Competition Act 15/2007. The Council of Ministers can either confirm the prohibition decision or conditions by the competition authority or decide differently. Article 10(4) clarifies that the assessment of economic concentrations could consider not only competition but also general public interests, including environmental protection.

General public interest clauses are relatively common in merger regulations.[235] For example, Article 24/A of the Hungarian Competition Act, or section 42 of the German Competition Act, contain such clauses. In Germany, the Minister overruled a prohibition decision in the *Miba/Zollern* case[236] on public interest grounds, which in part referred to reasons such as CO2 emissions, environmental protection, and sustainability.[237]

Miba/Zollern (Germany)[238]

Facts

The case concerns the joint venture between two medium-sized companies. These companies wanted to integrate their engine-bearing segments.

In 2019, the German competition authority prohibited the merger as it was concerned about competition regarding the engine-bearing sector and, in particular, with regard to markets for so-called hydrodynamic plain bearings for large engines used in locomotives and ships and power generators.

The companies applied for ministerial approval of an exemption under Sec 42 of the Competition Act and argued innovation concerns, international competitiveness, job preservation, the creation of a European Champion, and the relevance of these bearings for the defence industry. According to Sec 42(1), '[t]he Federal Minister for Economic Affairs will' authorize the individual merger if the harm to competition is 'outweighed by advantages to the economy as a whole resulting from the concentration or if the concentration is justified by

235 For a good overview see OECD, 'Public Interest Considerations in Merger Control— Background Paper by the Secretariat (2016) DAF/COMP/WP3(2016)3.

236 I B 2 - 20302/14-02 (19 August 2019) available at <https://www.bmwi.de/Redaktion/DE/Downloads/V/verfuegung-verwaltungsverfahren-miba-zollern.pdf?__blob=publicationFile&v=4> (accessed 22 January 2025). For a discussion in English see Maximilian Konrad, 'Ministerial Approval Miba/Zollern: A Green Industrial Policy For Medium-Sized Companies' (20 August 2019) D'Kart Antitrust Blog available at <https://www.d-kart.de/en/blog/2019/08/20/ministererlaubnis-miba-zollern-gruene-industriepolitik-fuer-den-mittelstand/> (accessed 22 January 2025).

237 ibid para 169ff.

238 ibid.

an overriding public interest' and the minister will take account of 'the competitiveness of the undertakings concerned in markets outside the area of application of this Act' and ensure that 'the restraint of competition does not jeopardize the market economy system'.

Finding

The minister authorized the merger. While the majority of public interest considerations were rejected, sustainability and CO2 reductions featured prominently. The decision highlighted that

> [a]chieving environmental policy goals for climate and environmental protection represents an overriding public interest [recognized previously in *E.ON/Ruhrgas*]. When interpreting the indeterminate legal concept of 'overriding public interest' within the meaning of Section 42 GWB, Article 20a of the German Constitution (Protection of the natural foundations of life and animals) must be taken into account. Climate protection - and the associated promotion of the energy transition - are covered by Article 20a's protection objective. The Federal Constitutional Court and the Federal Administrative Court qualify the climate as a protected object of Art. 20a. [239]

Moreover, the minister highlighted the promotion of sustainable development as a 'fundamental goal and benchmark of government action' and that the stated 'aim is for the economic policy measures of the Ministry for Economic Affairs to be in line with the sustainability and climate protection goal' to which the government has committed itself under the UN's 2030 Agenda with its '17 global goals for sustainable development'.[240] The minister then highlighted SDG 7, for which the ministry would be responsible. It would thus aim to provide 'everyone with access to affordable, reliable, sustainable, and modern energy' and is implemented nationally 'by means of the energy transition which sets the framework for a sustainable energy policy with long-term goals [and] is also an important part of German climate protection policy (SDG 13)'.[241] After this broader context, the minister then focused on the transaction and explained:

> With their joint venture, the parties ... can make a contribution to achieving the environmental policy goals for climate and environmental protection outlined above. On the one hand, this contribution consists in the faster opening

[239] ibid para 172 (references omitted). As translated by the author.
[240] ibid para 173.
[241] ibid para 174.

of new future applications for plain bearings, which are important in the context of the energy transition. On the other hand, through its R&D the joint venture can contribute to the reduction of fuel consumption by engines and to the development of new (more environmentally friendly) materials and thus implement the guiding principle of sustainability.[242]

This is only possible through the cooperation by the parties ... via the joint venture, in which both contribute their know-how (patents, etc.) and their do-how (manufacturing knowledge). The R&D is based on these and further develops and combines both technologies. For this reason, the innovation potential through the joint venture is considerably greater than the parties ... would conduct R&D separately. Only through cooperation along the entire value chain of plain bearings (from development to application maturity) can the innovation potential be raised, which is why the public interest of 'know-how and innovation potential for energy transition and sustainability' could not be realized with mere R&D cooperation.[243]

...

As a result, the intended creation of the joint venture by the parties [...] fulfils the public interest ground of 'know-how and innovation potential for energy transition and sustainability' ...[244]

The authorization by the minister was granted subject to conditions: operating the joint venture for at least five years and a condition for investment.

The decision is one of the rare situations where an application has been made to the minister. Part of the ministerial authorization process under Sec 42 is an opinion by the independent *Monopolkommission* (an expert commission). The ministry, however, came to a conclusion different from the commission. It found that only a joint venture would ensure substantial R&D progress with regard to the engine bearings and that these bearings were crucial for the energy transition and, in particular, turbines used for wind and other energy production.

In EU competition law, the legal text does not foresee the opportunity for EU institutions to raise public interests and, thereby, possibly sustainability to justify an otherwise prohibited restriction of competition. Yet, they still play a role in two ways. First, the European Merger Regulation allows EU Member States

242 ibid para 180.
243 ibid para 181.
244 ibid para 201.

to raise certain public interests to block a merger.[245] Second, case law allowing restrictions of competition to be justified by public interests exists and can therefore be considered by the EU institutions when applying the competition rules. In particular, where companies pursue a legitimate objective, and the measures are proportional to their aim, restrictions of competition under Article 101 TFEU can be justified by means of the *Wouters*[246] line of case law or as objective justifications[247] under Article 102 TFEU. Thus, where applicable, sustainability would be balanced against the restriction of competition using a proportionality assessment.[248]

Wouters and Others (EU)[249]

Facts

The case concerned the Dutch bar, which adopted a regulation that prohibited lawyers who were members of the bar from forming partnerships with other professions, eg accountants. This rule was challenged as it would restrict competition and prevent innovative new forms of services for clients from being developed.

[245] Art 21(4) Council Regulation (EC) No 139/2004 of 20 January 2004 on the control of concentrations between undertakings (the EC Merger Regulation) OJ L 24/1 sets out: 'Notwithstanding paragraphs 2 and 3, Member States may take appropriate measures to protect legitimate interests other than those taken into consideration by this Regulation and compatible with the general principles and other provisions of Community law; Public security, plurality of the media and prudential rules shall be regarded as legitimate interests within the meaning of the first subparagraph. Any other public interest must be communicated to the Commission by the Member State concerned and shall be recognised by the Commission after an assessment of its compatibility with the general principles and other provisions of Community law before the measures referred to above may be taken.' So while the EU Commission cannot raise public interests in a merger, it scrutinizes those that are raised by Member States when attempting to block a merger. Those could theoretically be related to sustainability. For an overview of how EU merger control could be adjusted to allow more justification for environmental sustainability, see also Tristan Lécuyer and Annabelle Leclercq, 'Is Green Becoming a Grey Area? A Discussion on Sustainability and Merger Control' (2023) 8(2) *Competition Policy Debate* 81–91; Emanuela Lecchi, 'Sustainability and EU Merger Control' (2023) 44(2) *European Competition Law Review* 70–80.

[246] Case C-309/99 *Wouters and Others* EU:C:2002:98.

[247] See Guidance on the Commission's enforcement priorities in applying Article 82 of the EC Treaty [now Article 102 of the TFEU] to abusive exclusionary conduct by dominant undertakings [2009] OJ C 45/7 paras 28–29; see also Case T-30/89 *Hilti v Commission* EU:T:1991:70; Case T-83/91 *Tetra Pak International v Commission (Tetra Pak II)* EU:T:1994:246.

[248] See also Giorgio Monti and Jotte Mulder, 'Escaping the Clutches of EU Competition Law Pathways to Assess Private Sustainability Initiatives' (2017) 42(5) *European Law Review* 645; Gianni De Stefano, 'EU Competition Law & The Green Deal: The Consistency Road' *CPI Antitrust Chronicle* (July 2020) 47; Anna Gerbrandy, 'The Difficulty of Conversations About Sustainability and European Competition Law' *CPI Antitrust Chronicle* (July 2020) 65; Hellenic Competition Commission, 'Staff Discussion Paper—Sustainability Issues and Competition Law' (2020), available at: <https://www.epant.gr/files/2020/Staff_Discussion_paper.pdf> (accessed 22 January 2025) paras 56–58.

[249] *Wouters* (n 246).

Findings

The European Court of Justice ruled that while one might see this as a form of restricting competition, as limiting production and technical development,[250] it would not constitute a restriction of competition within the meaning of Article 101(1) TFEU.

However, it held that in the 'overall context' of the rule, no restriction of competition could be established, because the bar pursued a legitimate aim in a proportional way. The Court held that:

> However, not every agreement between undertakings or every decision of an association of undertakings which restricts the freedom of action of the parties or of one of them necessarily falls within the prohibition laid down in Article [101(1)] of the Treaty. For the purposes of application of that provision to a particular case, account must first of all be taken of the overall context in which the decision of the association of undertakings was taken or produces its effects. More particularly, account must be taken of its objectives, which are here connected with the need to make rules relating to organisation, qualifications, professional ethics, supervision and liability, in order to ensure that the ultimate consumers of legal services and the sound administration of justice are provided with the necessary guarantees in relation to integrity and experience (see, to that effect, Case C-3/95 *Reisebüro Broede* [1996] ECR I-6511, paragraph 38). It has then to be considered whether the consequential effects restrictive of competition are inherent in the pursuit of those objectives.[251]

After exploring the specific situation of the legal profession in the Netherlands and the bar's regulation, the Court found that the regulation did not go beyond what is necessary in order to ensure the proper practice of the legal profession.[252]

While this line of case law was criticized and explained as the result of the peculiar procedural situation of the case,[253] the European Court of Justice has reaffirmed it in a line of cases.[254] In this regard, the Court in *OTOC* explained that any

[250] The bar's rule was said to hinder the offering of a wider and new range of services and might even prevent lower fees as a result of economies of scale, ibid 86–90.
[251] ibid para 97.
[252] ibid 109.
[253] The case was decided at a time when a notification and exemption system applied. Those arrangements that were not notified and did not receive an exemption were considered void according to Art 101(2) TFEU.
[254] For an overview see Julian Nowag, '*Wouters*, When the Condemned *Live Longer*: A Comment on *OTOC* and *CNG*' (2015) 36(1) *European Competition Law Review* 39–44.

examination of conduct or 'its effects ... account must be taken of its objectives'.[255] Yet, it is unclear whether this line of cases only applies to certain areas or whether certain further conditions must be met to be applicable[256] but it may well apply to cases concerning sustainability.[257]

Thus, a number of jurisdictions either have general public interest clause rules that can be used in the sustainability context or have such clauses that address elements of sustainability specifically—most often environmental sustainability. While such clauses are most common in rules mergers, they may also apply to other situations, such as anti-competitive agreements.

c) Public interest tests for certain areas of the economy

Particularly in jurisdictions that do not foresee general public interest clauses that are applicable to all areas of competition law (concerted action/agreements, unilateral conduct, mergers), more specific rules of certain areas may apply. The EU, for example, applies different rules for so-called services of general (economic) interests and in the areas of agriculture where sustainability is at play.

Article 106(2) TFEU exempts 'undertakings entrusted with the operation of services of general economic interest' from the competition rules if the application of such rules would 'obstruct the performance, in law or in fact, of the particular tasks assigned to them'. With regard to sustainability, the European Court of Justice held in *Sydhavnens Sten & Grus*[258] that waste management as an environmental protection matter is a service of general interest. Thus, if this task is assigned formally to a company, the competition rules are only applicable to the extent that they do not hinder the performance of this task. To assess whether the application of the competition rules can be excluded, the Court uses a proportionality test.[259] In other words, the Court balances the other objective against the restriction of competition.

In the EU there are also specific rules for the agricultural sector,[260] the so-called Common Agricultural Policy (CAP). The CAP partly exempts farmers and their associations but, more specifically, the new CAP for 2023–2027[261] foresees a

[255] Case C-1/12 *Ordem dos Técnicos Oficiais de Contas v Autoridade da Concorrência* EU:C:2013:127 para 93.

[256] For example, many cases concerned organizations of professionals.

[257] See Nowag (n 1) 215–221.

[258] Case C- 209/98 *Sydhavnens Sten & Grus* EU:C:2000:279; see also, eg, aid measures implemented by the Netherlands for AVR for dealing with hazardous waste, Commission Decision 2006/237/EC [2006] OJ L84/37.

[259] ibid.

[260] See eg Cseres (n 74) 401.

[261] See the new Common Agricultural Policy (CAP) for the period 2023–2027 and in particular Regulation (EU) No 1308/2013 of the European Parliament and of the Council of 17 December 2013 establishing a common organization of the markets in agricultural products and repealing Council Regulations (EEC) No 922/72, (EEC) No 234/79, (EC) No 1037/2001 and (EC) No 1234/2007 OJ [2013] L 347/671 as amended by Regulation (EU) 2021/2117 of the European Parliament and of the Council of 2 December 2021 OJ [2021] L 435/262.

specific exemption for sustainability reasons.[262] These provisions can be crucial in fostering different elements of sustainability in the context of agriculture. While the exemption for farmers might make a difference with regard to poverty, the associated risk discussed in the context of the US exclusion of agriculture from antitrust needs to be borne in mind.[263]

According to Article 42 TFEU, the competition rules apply to the production of and trade in agricultural products only to the extent determined by the European Parliament and the Council, while taking into account the following objectives of common agricultural policy provided for in Article 39 TFEU: increasing agricultural productivity, achieving a fair living standard of the agricultural community, market stabilization, assuring availability of supplies, and ensuring reasonable consumer prices.[264] Thus, the Treaty on the Function of the European Union and in particular '... Article 42 TFEU recognises that the common agricultural policy takes precedence over the objectives of the Treaty in the field of competition and also recognises the EU legislature's power to decide to what extent the rules on competition are to be applied in the agricultural sector'.[265] The CAP does not operate a system of blanket exclusions but provides for a certain form of balancing. The Court of Justice of the European Union confirmed this balancing approach in *APVE and Others*.[266] The case concerned the exchange of commercially sensitive information, coordination of volume, and fixing of minimum sale prices. The Court held that it is also one of the CAP's objectives to maintain effective competition,[267] so that a proportionality test is applied to determine whether the practices are strictly necessary to achieve the objectives.[268]

This proportionality test to balance the CAP objectives with competition is also visible in the relevant rules of the CAP. The main rules addressing matters of relevance in terms of competition can be found in Regulation No 1308/2013[269] on the common organization of the markets in agricultural products ('CMO'). The regulation provides for the general application of the competition rules except where provided for specifically by the regulation. The regulation has a number of special

[262] For an overview see, eg, Report from the Commission to the European Parliament and the Council, *The Application of the Union Competition Rules to the Agricultural Sector* (COM(2018) 706) ('Report') 8 available at <https://ec.europa.eu/competition/sectors/agriculture/report_on_competition_rules_application.pdf> (accessed 22 January 2025); Commission Staff Working Document, *Accompanying the Document Report from the Commission to the European Parliament and the Council: The Application of the Union Competition Rules to the Agricultural Sector* (SWD(2018) 450 final) available at <https://ec.europa.eu/competition/sectors/agriculture/staff_working_paper.pdf> (accessed 22 January 2025).

[263] See above text to (nn 62–76).

[264] Arts 42 and 39 TFEU.

[265] Case C-671/15 *APVE and Others* EU: C:2017:860 ('Endives case') para 37.

[266] ibid.

[267] ibid paras 47–48.

[268] ibid paras 49 and 67.

[269] Regulation (EU) No 1308/2013 of the European Parliament and of the Council of 17 December 2013 establishing a common organisation of the markets in agricultural products and repealing Council Regulations (EEC) No 922/72, (EEC) No 234/79, (EC) No 1037/2001 and (EC) No 1234/2007 OJ L 347/671.

derogations for specific agricultural sectors[270] and contains, since 2018, a derogation for so-called producer organizations (horizontal cooperations)[271] that have been recognized by the state in Articles 152–156 CMO. Such organizations need to have a specific aim, and an objective specified in the regulation such as 'contributing to a sustainable use of natural resources and climate change mitigation' (Article 152(1)(c)(viii)). The regulation also contains more specific exceptions. Article 209 CMO reads:

> 1. Article 101(1) TFEU shall not apply to the agreements, decisions and practices referred to in Article 206 of this Regulation necessary for the attainment of the objectives set out in Article 39 TFEU.
>
> Article 101(1) TFEU shall not apply to agreements, decisions and concerted practices of farmers, farmers' associations, or associations of such associations, or producer organisations recognised under Article 152 of this Regulation, or associations of producer organisations recognised under Article 156 of this Regulation, which concern the production or sale of agricultural products or the use of joint facilities for the storage, treatment or processing of agricultural products, unless the objectives of Article 39 TFEU are jeopardised.
>
> This paragraph shall not apply to agreements, decisions and concerted practices which entail an obligation to charge an identical price or by which competition is excluded.
>
> 2. Agreements, decisions and concerted practices which fulfil the conditions referred to in paragraph 1 of this Article shall not be prohibited, no prior decision to that effect being required.
>
> In any national or Union proceedings for the application of Article 101 TFEU, the burden of proving an infringement of Article 101(1) TFEU shall rest on the party or the authority alleging the infringement. The party claiming the benefit of the exemptions provided in paragraph 1 of this Article shall bear the burden of proving that the conditions of that paragraph are fulfilled.

Thus, the article allows for a balancing of the restriction of competition and the achievement and pursuit of the objectives of the EU's agricultural policy objectives contained in Article 39 TFEU. The new rules for agriculture in the EU now also contain an Article 210a, which specifically addresses sustainability. It reads:

> 1. Article 101(1) TFEU shall not apply to agreements, decisions and concerted practices of producers of agricultural products that relate to the production

[270] These are: raw milk (Ars 149–150 CMO); olive oil, beef and veal, arable crops (Arts 169–171 CMO); ham (Art 172 CMO); fruit and vegetables (Art 33 CMO); sugar (Art 125 CMO); wine (Art 167 CMO).

[271] The Regulation also foresees the option for non-horizontal organizations, so called interbranch organizations, see Arts 157–158 and the specific rules on competition in Art 210 CMO.

of or trade in agricultural products and that aim to apply a sustainability standard higher than mandated by Union or national law, provided that those agreements, decisions and concerted practices only impose restrictions of competition that are indispensable to the attainment of that standard.

2. Paragraph 1 applies to agreements, decisions and concerted practices of producers of agricultural products to which several producers are party or to which one or more producers and one or more operators at different levels of the production, processing, and trade in the food supply chain, including distribution, are party.
3. For the purposes of paragraph 1, 'sustainability standard' means a standard which aims to contribute to one or more of the following objectives:
   (a) environmental objectives, including climate change mitigation and adaptation, the sustainable use and protection of landscapes, water and soil, the transition to a circular economy, including the reduction of food waste, pollution prevention and control, and the protection and restoration of biodiversity and ecosystems;
   (b) the production of agricultural products in ways that reduce the use of pesticides and manage risks resulting from such use, or that reduce the danger of antimicrobial resistance in agricultural production; and
   (c) animal health and animal welfare.
4. Agreements, decisions and concerted practices that fulfil the conditions referred to in this Article shall not be prohibited, no prior decision to that effect being required.

The article then also addresses more procedural questions such as the requirement for the Commission to issue guidelines or the rules on the powers of the Commission and national competition authorities. The aim of the Article 210a exemption is specifically to balance the restriction of competition with the benefits in terms of sustainability.[272] In particular, agreements between producers horizontally but also vertically, within the value chains usually covered by the general competition rules (Article 101 TFEU), can be justified with regard to environmental protection aims, climate change, and animal health/welfare. To benefit from the rule contained in Article 210a, such agreements need to be aimed at ensuring higher standards than those required by law, and the restrictions of competition need to be proportional to the benefits. The Commission has also adopted its guidelines with regard to Article 210a.[273] These make clear that an abstract

[272] For a good overview see eg Cseres (n 74) 401.

[273] Commission guidelines on the exclusion from Article 101 of the Treaty on the Functioning of the European Union for sustainability agreements of agricultural producers pursuant to Article 210a of Regulation (EU) No 1308/2013 (C/2023/8306 final) available at <https://eur-lex.europa.eu/legal-content/EN/ALL/?uri=PI_COM:C(2023)8306> (accessed 22 January 2025).

balancing exercise[274] is carried out between sustainability and competition principles. The guidelines itself further define the permissible sustainability objectives, provide more details on the parties that can benefit from the exception, and that the proportionality test applied, is one of the least restrictive measures.

Commission guidelines on the exclusion for sustainability agreements of agricultural producers pursuant to Article 210a[275]

In 2023, the Commission adopted the guidelines in this regard which interpret Article 210a narrowly while taking into account the objectives pursued by the exclusion.[276]

Content

The general test applied is one where the scope of the exception is limited to certain actors and to certain objectives and must go beyond what is already legally required. However, as long as such actors are involved and pursue such objectives, the Commission will only ensure that the measures chosen are the least restrictive, rather than examining whether consumers are compensated. Regarding the scope, it is important to note that Article 210 applies only when at least one party is an agricultural producer, and it is a vertical or horizontal agreement. The agreement must relate to the 'production of, or trade in … agricultural products listed in Annex I to the TFEU'. Moreover, Article 210a(3) sets out a specific list of environmental sustainability objectives.

The Commission in it guidance explains that a 'sustainability agreement must aim to attain a sustainability standard that contributes to' these sustainability objectives and should identify it specifically.[277] Moreover, the results of the agreement 'need to be tangible and measurable [or at least] observable and describable'.[278] The standard must go beyond what is already directly mandatory for these producers in the EU, or first introduce such a standard where no standard exists.[279] The relevant standards in the EU are also the reference point for cases where a producer from a third country is involved.[280]

The last condition is that the agreement is indispensable. In this regard, the guidelines set out that the standards for Article 210a indispensability assessment are broadly similar to Article 101(3) TFEU, although 'there are certain

[274] On other cases of balancing see also section IV.
[275] Guidelines on Article 210a (n 272).
[276] ibid para 14.
[277] ibid paras 43–46.
[278] ibid para 56.
[279] ibid paras 57–66.
[280] ibid para 59.

key differences between the two articles, as a result of which the standard for indispensability necessarily differs'.[281] In particular, 'serious restrictions [such as] price fixing or reducing output, may be considered as indispensable'[282] and a market coverage analysis is not needed.[283] The Commission thus applies a two-stage test:

> (i) whether it is necessary for them to cooperate in order to achieve the sustainability standard instead of doing so individually; and (ii) analyse whether the sustainability standard could be achieved by means of another less restrictive type of provision. To conduct the assessment under step 2, operators must consider the nature and intensity of the restriction and determine whether such restriction is the least restrictive means available to achieve the sustainability standard.[284]

The first step thus involves an assessment whether the parties could individually 'attain the sustainability standard ... rather than through cooperation ... [or] could attain it more quickly and with less costs and effort through cooperation'.[285] While the first test examines the suitability of the agreement and the restriction, the second focuses on the necessity of the relevant restrictions.[286] This depends on the nature and the intensity of the restriction,[287] which also includes the duration of the restriction.[288]

The benefits of Article 210a are only available for effective agreements. Thus, absent force majeure, parties cannot continue to rely on exclusion if the agreement fails to deliver.[289] Moreover, 'the parties [have to] continuously review ... the agreement's implementation'[290] and an emergency brake exists in Article 210a(7) for competition authorities 'to modify, discontinue or prevent it from being implemented'.[291]

As the guidelines make clear, the scope of Article 210a is substantial in terms of environmental sustainability. Numerous environmental sustainability issues will

[281] ibid para 87.
[282] ibid para 89.
[283] ibid para 132.
[284] ibid para 90.
[285] ibid para 97.
[286] ibid paras 114–115.
[287] ibid para 115.
[288] ibid para 129.
[289] ibid paras 139–141.
[290] ibid para 143.
[291] ibid paras 175–183.

involve agricultural production either in or outside of the EU and can potentially benefit from this exemption. The exemption takes a remarkably different approach to Article 101(3) TFEU. The Article 210a exemption does not require the parties to show that affected consumers will be compensated and only imposes a least restrictive measure requirement. It thus allows sustainability measures that would not be able to benefit from the traditional test of Article 101(3) TFEU. Yet, certain limitations exist: Article 210a applies only to certain aspects of sustainability and animal welfare that go beyond already binding standards and it is only available to actors in that space. However, the broad scope and flexibility of Article 210a are balanced with broad supervisory powers by the Commission. The procedural options contained in Article 210a allow the Commission not only to step in if concerns exist but equally to amend its assessment if the conditions change. This option provides not only the opportunity to address concerns about changing conditions, it also allows the Commission to address concerns about greenwashing. More importantly, it merely needs to communicate its new assessment to the companies concerned, and it applies *ex nunc*.

d) Summary abstract balancing via public interest clauses

In this section, we examined abstract balancing via public interest clauses and their operation in different jurisdictions around the world. In these jurisdictions, a balance between the public benefit in terms of sustainability and the restriction of competition takes place, often in the form of a proportionality assessment. In some jurisdictions, such public interest clauses specifically mention sustainability aspects, while in others, the general public interest clauses encompass sustainability matters. The clauses sometimes apply to all areas of competition law or only to mergers, anti-competitive agreements, or even in certain areas of the economy such as agriculture. Overall, there is some experience in applying these clauses to sustainability matters, but the area seems still to be developing.[292] We need to distinguish this form of public interest balancing with regard to sustainability from questions about how an economics—often consumer welfare—focused approach addresses these matters.[293] This will be explored in the subsequent section.

3. Balancing within economic frameworks of competition law

In the previous section, we have seen how sustainability can feature as part of a public interest test applied in some competition laws. Many other jurisdictions only have public interest clauses for specific areas, or none at all. In such jurisdictions,

[292] See Hungarian Competition Authority (n 2) 42.
[293] For an overview with regard to the EU's abstract balancing under *Wouters* as compared to Art 101(3) TFEU, see Nowag (n 1) 248–252.

the competition rules contain exceptions focused on economic frameworks of efficiency and consumer welfare to determine whether an allegedly anti-competitive act is legal because of its economic benefits. As we will see in this section, the approaches to sustainability adopted around the world build in part on the insights of Chapter 2 that deal with the economics of sustainability and competition. This section explores an area where the debate about sustainability and competition is most fierce. However, as we will see, even in applying the established frameworks of efficiency and consumer welfare in competition law, less and more contentious areas can be identified. Distinguishing them in spectral dimensions helps focus our minds on the debates where actual disagreement exists. It is important to note that this debate is relevant to only a few potentially extreme cases.[294]

Also note that when we approach this area, previous work has occasionally drawn a distinction between 'non-economic' and 'economic' benefits of agreements,[295] or between 'competition' and 'public policy' or 'non-competition' concerns.[296] While this distinction is often used[297] and has some attractiveness at an abstract level, the distinction is often not straightforward in concrete cases. In practice, public policy or non-economic concerns can often be 'translated' into the traditional language of efficiencies used in competition law and economics.[298] For example, reductions in CO2 can be measured and expressed in monetary terms. Similarly, consumers of a product might value improvements in the product's sustainability as quality improvements. We will explore these kinds of translation exercises in this section, starting with less controversial ones and slowly moving to more and more controversial ones. The extent to which such translation is needed depends on the national legal framework governing competition law.

294 These are cases where the outcome in an individual cases hinges on whether there is a more restrictive or more encompassing approach to matters of efficiency and consumer welfare. There are cases where orthodox theories would mean that the sustainability activity is prohibited, while a more encompassing—and contentious—interpretation would find that the activity is perfectly legal.

295 It has been further distinguished between direct (cost and qualitative efficiencies enjoyed by the users of the product in question) and indirect economic benefits (cost and qualitative efficiencies in other markets), see Office of Fair Trading, 'Article 101(3)—A Discussion of Narrow versus Broad Definition of Benefits' (2010) available at: <https://webarchive.nationalarchives.gov.uk/20140402172423/http://oft.gov.uk/shared_oft/events/Article101(3)-summary.pdf> (accessed 22 January 2025).

296 See eg Townley (n 214); Assimakis P Komninos, 'Non-competition Concerns: Resolution of Conflicts in the Integrated Article 81 EC' (2008) University of Oxford Centre for Competition Law and Policy Working Paper (L) 08/05 available at <https://www.law.ox.ac.uk/sites/default/files/migrated/cclp_l_08-05.pdf> (accessed 22 January 2025).

297 See for example also Or Brook, 'Struggling with Article 101(3) TFEU: Diverging Approaches of the Commission, EU Courts and Five Competition Authorities' (2019) *Common Market Law Review* 121; Giancarlo Piscitelli and Anna Gerbrandy, 'The Sustainability Dilemma in Competition Law' (2018/19) 8(1) *ECDPM Great Insights* 19, 22. available at <https://ecdpm.org/work/civil-society-business-pulling-in-the-same-direction-volume-8-issue-1-winter-2018-2019/the-sustainability-dilemma-in-competition-law> (accessed 22 January 2025).

298 Critical of this distinction, see also Simon Holms, 'Climate Change, Sustainability, and Competition Law' (2020) 8(2) *Journal of Antitrust Enforcement* 371–372.

Within the economic frameworks, sustainability can feature as a quality parameter, or it can be part of the assessment of choice. This assessment of sustainability is fairly uncontentious. Matters become more contentious when sustainability concerns appear in the context of innovation and future benefits. It becomes even more contentious where future benefits occur in other markets, or outside national markets. We will then look at another possibly more contentious option, adopting broader efficiency measurements. Finally, we will address situations where the debate has been directly addressed by the legislator.

a) Quality

As such, quality improvements seem a rather uncontentious option[299] of incorporating sustainability into the competition analysis.[300] For example, the UK Competition Authority's 2021 merger guidelines explain that

> benefits in the form of environmental sustainability and supporting the transition to a low carbon economy are relevant customer benefits in some circumstances. A merger may lead to lower energy costs and some benefits that customers may value (such as a lower carbon footprint of the firm's products).[301]

This quote shows how sustainability might be considered as a quality dimension in competition proceedings. However, while we might debate how to measure quality exactly,[302] we can observe an approach of measuring quality in the Dutch animal welfare case—*Chicken of Tomorrow*.[303] While animal welfare does not fall under classical sustainability matters,[304] such an approach could equally be applied in a sustainability context as suggested by the EU Commission's horizontal guidelines. It was highlighted that 'sustainability benefits can be taken into account

[299] Note that 'uncontentious' refers to the fact that quality improvements are part of an orthodox competition law analysis, not to the fact that the outcome of that analysis or its methodology are uncontentious; see for example Monti and Mulder (n 248) for a critique of the methodology with regard to the Dutch ACM's quality assessment in the *Chicken of Tomorrow* case.

[300] See for example Christina Volpin, 'Sustainability as a Quality Dimension of Competition: Protecting our Future (Selves)' *CPI Antitrust Chronicle* (2020) available at <https://www.competitionpolicyinternational.com/wp-content/uploads/2020/07/02-Sustainability-as-a-Quality-Dimension-Cristina-A.-Volpin.pdf> (accessed 22 January 2025).

[301] CMA, 'Merger Assessment Guidelines' (March 2021) (CMA129) available at <https://assets.publishing.service.gov.uk/government/uploads/system/uploads/attachment_data/file/1011836/MAGs_for_publication_2021_--.pdf> (accessed 22 January 2025) para. 8.21.

[302] See OECD, 'The Role and Measurement of Quality in Competition Analysis' (2013) DAF/COMP(2013)17 available at <https://www.oecd.org/competition/Quality-in-competition-analysis-2013.pdf> (accessed 22 January 2025).

[303] ACM, 'ACM's analysis of the sustainability arrangements concerning the "Chicken of Tomorrow"', ACM/DM/2014/206028, case number 13.0195.66 (26 Jan 2015) available at <https://www.acm.nl/en/publications/publication/13789/ACMs-analysis-of-the-sustainability-arrangements-concerning-the-Chicken-of-Tomorrow> (accessed 22 January 2025).

[304] Under the most commonly accepted definition of sustainability animal welfare would not be part of the sustainability, although environmental effects that might follow from, eg, reduced mass production of animals, might well be.

as qualitative or quantitative efficiency gains in the assessment under Article 101(3)'.[305] The final version takes up this idea and now examines individual use and non-use benefits.

Chicken of Tomorrow (Netherlands)[306]

The 'Chicken of Tomorrow' initiative, agreed upon by suppliers and supermarkets, aimed to improve the welfare of chickens sold in supermarkets. It set a new minimum standard for chicken welfare that went beyond the statutory minimum requirements, but was not applicable to meat for export or meat sold outside the supermarkets involved. The initiative aimed, for example, to reduce the injuries and stress of chickens, by increasing the number of dark hours to at least six hours, usage of straw and materials such as bales of straw and roosting poles, the use of slower-growing chicken breeds (with increases in the lifetime of chicken by about 10 per cent—forty-five rather than forty days). Moreover, the standard reduced the number of chickens per square metre from twenty-one to nineteen, restricted the use of antibiotics to cases of symptoms of illness, and required the use of sustainably grown soy.

Overall, the participating supermarkets agreed to replace all regular chicken with 'Chicken of Tomorrow', with these supermarkets accounting for 95 per cent of chicken meat sold to Dutch consumers.

The agency assessed the agreement under the exception of Article 101(3) TFEU (and the Dutch equivalent) and identified a resulting price increase of around 1.46 euro per kilo of chicken filet.

When examining the quality improvements and how the consumers valued these improvements, the authority relied on data collected 'from the participating organizations, and on opinions of animal welfare experts, among others'[307] and conducted a willingness to pay analysis.[308] It used a so-called conjoint analysis which measures consumers' willingness to pay for product attributes by providing consumers with choices alternatives. It would, for example, ask consumers which option they would choose between a 'chicken of tomorrow' for 10 euros per kilo, or a chicken with the lower standards at 8.54 euros per kilo. By using different alternatives and by asking a sufficiently large

[305] Guidelines (n 27) para 549.
[306] See (n 302).
[307] ibid 5.
[308] For the full analysis, see ACM Office of the Chief Economist, 'Economische effecten van de Kip van Morgen' (October 2014) available at <https://www.acm.nl/sites/default/files/old_publication/publicaties/13759_onderzoek-acm-naar-de-economische-effecten-van-de-kip-van-morgen.pdf> (accessed 22 January 2025).

number of people (in this case, more than 1600 consumers), the authority's analysis can estimate the willingness to pay off all consumers for improved quality.
Overall, the authority noted:

> In such studies, the value that consumers attach to animal welfare measures is converted into a degree of willingness of consumers to pay for these measures (hence the name 'willingness-to-pay').
>
> First of all, the study reveals that consumers are only willing to pay a small amount for the animal welfare measures as agreed upon in the 'Chicken of Tomorrow' arrangements, which is 68 euro cent per kilo of chicken filet. In addition, it turns out that the environmental effects have a positive effect, which is 14 eurocent per kilo of chicken filet. Finally, public health has no positive effect, which is 0 eurocent per kilo of chicken filet. The latter is because the objective of reduced use of antibiotics will already be achieved irrespective of the sustainability arrangements concerning the 'Chicken of Tomorrow.' Therefore, the total benefits of the 'Chicken of Tomorrow' are: 82 eurocent per kilo of chicken filet....
>
> The above shows that the additional costs per kilo of chicken filet for implementing the measures for the 'Chicken of Tomorrow' exceed the benefits with regard to animal welfare, the environment, and public health. The 'Chicken of Tomorrow' does not generate any net benefits for consumers....

If we try to summarize the case in layperson's terms, we could say that consumers did not think that the price increase was justified for a bit of straw, extended dark time, and an increase of space per chicken of about the size of a mobile phone (10 x 5cm). Beyond the outcome and the debate about the price application of the method used,[309] the case shows how the Dutch competition authority translated animal welfare concerns into the language of competition law.

A slightly different situation concerning quality can be found in a French case.[310] That case concerned a small, tranquil island, Saint Honorat Island, which was owned by monks and only had small-scale day tourists visiting, a hotel business, and a pontoon for a boat service run exclusively by the monks. The monks were found to be justified in rejecting the application of a commercial operator to offer a boat service, so as to maintain the tranquil quality of the island. An alternative

[309] Whether the right methodology was used for this translation has been debated; see Monti and Mulder (n 248).

[310] Décision n° 05-D-60 du 8 novembre 2005 relative à des pratiques mises en œuvre par la congrégation cistercienne de l'Immaculée Conception, la société Planaria, l'État et la commune de Cannes, available at <https://www.autoritedelaconcurrence.fr/sites/default/files/commitments//05d60.pdf> (accessed 22 January 2025).

passenger quota system could not guarantee this in a practical manner. While not directly a sustainability case, one could easily imagine islands where, for environmental reasons, the number of visitors would need to be limited.

b) Choice

Choice can be an important parameter when pursuing sustainability through the enforcement of competition law. In other words, how preventing the choice[311] of a more sustainable alternative can be prohibited by competition law. A similar point can be made with regard to sustainability choices and the balancing with apparent restrictions of competition. Where, for example, a sustainable product alternative can only be created by cooperation, the negative effects may be outweighed by greater (sustainable) choice on offer for consumers.

Another example in this context might be the treatment of R&D in competition law. Here, there is an overlap with the discussion we just explored in the previous section, considering sustainability as a quality improvement. This is in particular, the case where a product differentiation in terms of sustainability is the result. At the same time, we can also observe an overlap with innovation which is covered in the next section, where an alternative of a whole new sustainable product is the result.

c) Future benefits and innovation

Sustainability benefits are often benefits that accrue in the future. Such benefits might be more or sustained benefits in the future, eg a stock of animals is not going extinct. They might also be more generally sustainability innovations of products. Where sustainability is part of quality or new sustainable products, the debate about the interaction between competition, cooperation, and innovation[312] is relevant. In other words, sustainability innovation might be a reason why, for example, cooperation between competitors provides benefits for consumers. Using the tools commonly known from innovation considerations provides a helpful pathway to consider sustainability within an economics-based competition policy.

In both situations, questions[313] arise that are slightly more contentious but that only need to be answered where a case does not pass the more orthodox quality

[311] On choice in EU competition law, see eg Paul Nihoul, Nicolas Charbit, and Elisa Ramundo, *Choice: a New Standard for Competition Law Analysis?* (Concurrences Review 2016); Inge Graef, 'Consumer Sovereignty and Competition Law: From Personalisation to Diversity' (2021) 58(2) *Common Market Law Review* 471–504.

[312] See eg Carl Shapiro, 'Competition Policy and Innovation' (2002) OECD Science, Technology and Industry Working Paper, No 2002/11 DSTI/DOC(2002)11; Paul Nihoul and Pieter Van Cleynenbreugel (eds), *The Roles of Innovation in Competition Law Analysis* (Edward Elgar 2018); Bundeskartellamt, 'Innovations—Challenges for Competition Law Practice' (2017) available at <https://www.bundeskartellamt.de/SharedDocs/Publikation/EN/Schriftenreihe_Digitales_II.pdf?__blob=publicationFile&v=3>(accessed 22 January 2025).

[313] Just as in other innovation cases.

framework. These are questions regarding future benefits. In traditional innovation cases, just as in sustainability (innovation) cases, we may wonder how to deal with benefits that occur only in the future. In other words, how do we treat benefits that do not benefit the current but only future consumers? What seems clear is that in cases of future benefits, competition authorities often apply discount rates.[314] An example of future benefits in the sustainability context can for example be the prevention of over-fishing. For the long-term conservation of fish stocks, a joint reduction of fishing today might be needed. In 2000, the US DoJ issued a positive business review letter to the Akutan Catcher Vessel Association:[315]

Akutan Catcher Vessel Association[316]

This case from 2000 concerned an agreement by a fishing association. A fishing quota of certain Alaskan pollock was allocated to members of the association. Under the old 'Olympic' system, every vessel would try to catch as much fish as possible and as fast as possible until the total quota for the association was fulfilled. The Akutan Catcher Vessel Association aimed at replacing this 'Olympic' system with a more fixed system where each vessel would be sub-allocated parts of the overall quota. It claimed that it 'would ensure an increased value of the caught pollock while reducing the amount of incidental by-catch'.[317] The DoJ cleared the agreement as it found that:

> The proposed Agreement affects only harvesting activity; it allocates the fixed annual catcher vessel quota among all the members of that group. The proposed collective activity does not extend to processing, marketing or sales of any of the Members' production.
>
> … From a consumer perspective, the harvesting agreement does not reduce the output of processed Alaskan Pollock or the end products into which it is incorporated—e.g., surimi. On the contrary, if the Applicant's assertion that 'haste makes waste' is true, then eliminating the race will increase processing efficiency and concomitantly the output of Alaskan Pollock products. Since the prices paid for Alaskan Pollock products by consumers will be determined

[314] See, eg, European Commission 'Guidelines on the Application of Article 81(3) of the Treaty' [2004] OJ C 101/97 para 87; ACM (Netherlands Authority for Consumer & Markets), 'ACM Position Paper Competition & Sustainability' (July 2013), 15 available at <https://www.acm.nl/sites/default/files/old_publication/publicaties/11733_acm-position-paper-competition-and-sustainability.pdf> (accessed 22 January 2025).

[315] DoJ, Business Review Letter by Joel I Klein, Assistant Attorney General (29 February 2000) available at <https://www.justice.gov/atr/response-akutan-catcher-vessel-associations-request-business-review-letter> (accessed 22 January 2025).

[316] ibid.

[317] ibid 2.

> by the intersection of supply and demand for those products, elimination of the race to gather an input whose output is fixed by regulation seems unlikely to reduce output or increase price under any likely scenario.
>
> To the extent that the proposed agreement allows for more efficient processing that increases the usable yield (output) of the processed Alaskan Pollock and/or reduces the inadvertent catching of other fish species whose preservation is also a matter of regulatory concern, it could have procompetitive effects.[318]

Fishing is a good example of future benefits, and a similar decision in the fishing area was handed down in the Netherlands. The Dutch competition authority in *MSC Shrimp Fishery*[319] provided informal guidance on a system established to limit overfishing. It highlighted that such a system could be justified where it is necessary to meet sustainability concerns identified by scientific studies. More recently, in its Draft Guidelines on 'Sustainability Agreements',[320] the agency suggested that it would use the standard social-cost-benefit tool used by the Dutch government authorities to evaluate future benefits. Within this analysis, sustainability benefits in terms of avoided environmental damage are monetized by means of so-called environmental or 'shadow' prices.[321] However, these references were omitted in the final guidelines in light of the adopted EU guidelines that did not directly mention such an approach. The EU guidelines merely stated that '[e]vidence for collective benefits contained in public authorities' reports or in reports prepared by recognized academic organisations may be of particular value for this assessment'.[322]

On a practical level, we need to consider the time frame needed for such benefits to materialize. This question is well known from the more orthodox assessment of innovation benefits in competition law.[323] As such, the question seems rather a matter of proof rather than one of policy[324] and the parties should be able to

[318] ibid 2–3.
[319] *Informele zienswijze Managementplan MSC Garnalenvisserij* [2011] 7011/23.B27 (MSC Shrimp fisheries).
[320] See ACM, Draft Guidelines (n 109).
[321] ibid para 50.
[322] EU Commission, 'Guidelines on the Applicability of Article 101' (n 27), para 588.
[323] For an overview, see Nihoul and Van Cleynenbreugel (n 311), in particular Pieter Van Cleynenbreugel, 'Innovation in Competition Law Analysis: Making Sense of On-Going Academic and Policy Debates' in ibid 2–12.
[324] Kevin Coates and Dirk Middelschulte, 'Getting Consumer Welfare Right: the Competition Law Implications of Market-Driven Sustainability Initiatives' (2019) 15(2–3) *European Competition Journal* 321.

furnish the relevant evidence if innovation is paramount to their transaction.[325] However, if any form of discounting that will need to be applied to future sustainability benefits it needs to be ensured that these are not simply 'discounted away' because as climate change shows, future costs are often grossly underappreciated.[326] Finally, we might ask whether competition authorities should be 'agnostic about the direction of innovation'.[327]

d) Benefits in other markets

Having explored elements of sustainability innovation, we now move on to more contentious situations where future benefits are occurring not only in the product market but in other markets. A situation that we see frequently in the sustainability context. For example, the development of a more sustainable production method in the agricultural sector might mean that it will be possible to use these not only with regard to one product but also for other agricultural products, or it might even open new markets. We can think of, for example, a technology that results in the production of a crop without the use of herbicides. The same technology may be used for other crops. Moreover, after some time, the abandonment of herbicides allows the producers to switch production to organic food. For the production of organic foods, it is often a prerequisite that herbicides and pesticides have not been used on the field for some years.

Thinking about sustainability with a focus on innovation is again helpful. In particular, concepts such as innovation markets and innovation spaces are helpful as they allow us to think about sustainability markets that create tomorrow's sustainability products for future consumers.[328] Fundamentally, innovation cases take for granted the willingness of current consumers to pay higher prices for future benefits. Future consumers will benefit either from an improved product in the relevant market where the restriction takes place or because completely new products will be created that will give rise to or compete in different markets.[329] In this way, an innovation assessment entails an aggregation across generations and markets.[330]

[325] See also Emanuela Lecchi, 'Sustainability and EU Merger Control' (2023) 44(2) *European Competition Law* 70–80.

[326] Hellenic Competition Commission (n 248) para 111.

[327] See in this regard Ruben Maximiano and Cristina Volpin, 'Merger Control for Green Innovation' in Julian Nowag (ed), *Research Handbook on Sustainability and Competition Law* (Edward Elgar 2024) 176–193 or Maurice Stucke and Ariel Ezrachi, *Competition Overdose: How Free Market Mythology Transformed Us from Citizen Kings to Market Servants* (Harper Business 2020).

[328] In this direction also Ioannis Lianos, 'Polycentric Competition Law' (2018) 71 *Current Legal Problems* 161–213, Hellenic Competition Commission (n 248) para 75.

[329] ibid 22

[330] See in this regard, Christopher Townley, 'Inter-generational Impacts in Competition Analysis: Remembering Those Not Yet Born' (2011) 11 *European Competition Law Review* 580–589.

The translation of sustainability into the language of innovation by means of eco/sustainability innovation is one route to consider benefits to future consumers or consumers in other markets. The question in this context is often whether harm to one group can be balanced against benefits that occur elsewhere. Where different markets are involved, it is often required that the markets where the harm occurs and those where the benefits occur are closely related.[331] In the case law, the issue has come to the forefront with regard to credit cards, both in the US and the EU. The US Supreme Court majority considered the two-sided markets found in *American Express*, where the cost on one side can be compensated by benefits on the other side of the market by defining the two sides as part of the same market.[332]

Ohio et al v American Express Co et al[333]

American Express is a case about competition between credit card companies. Credit card companies make their money through fees charged to cardholders and, more importantly, by fees charged to the merchants for payments that the consumer makes with their card. Merchants are charged typically a percentage of the payment for the transaction by the credit card company.

The contracts between American Express and merchants accepting American Express cards contained so-called 'anti-steering provisions'. These provisions prevented merchants from encouraging consumers to use other cards with lower transaction fees by, for example, sharing the savings the merchants would make or by offering discounts for the use of other cards. In effect, the 'anti-steering provisions' meant that American Express could maintain its higher fees, which were in part used to provide benefits for cardholders.

While a similar case involving MasterCard and Visa was settled in 2010, American Express took the case to court, arguing that its policies benefited its cardholders, as the higher fees would help in maintaining benefits for cardholders.

The majority noted that in determining the anti-competitive effect of the said provisions:

> ... We must first define the relevant market. Once defined, it becomes clear that the plaintiffs' evidence is insufficient to carry their burden.[334]
>
> ...

[331] More details on the EU case law in this regard see, eg, Nowag, *Environmental Integration* (n 1) 234–236.

[332] *Ohio v American Express Co* 138 S Ct 2274; 201 L Ed 2d 678.

[333] ibid.

[334] ibid 10.

As explained, credit-card networks are two-sided platforms. Due to indirect network effects, two-sided platforms cannot raise prices on one side without risking a feedback loop of declining demand. And the fact that two-sided platforms charge one side a price that is below or above cost reflects differences in the two sides' demand elasticity, not market power or anticompetitive pricing. Price increases on one side of the platform likewise do not suggest anticompetitive effects without some evidence that they have increased the overall cost of the platform's services. Thus, courts must include both sides of the platform—merchants and cardholders—when defining the credit-card market.[335]

...

Evaluating both sides of a two-sided transaction platform is also necessary to accurately assess competition.[336]

...

On the other side of the market, Amex uses its higher merchant fees to offer its cardholders a more robust rewards program, which is necessary to maintain cardholder loyalty and encourage the level of spending that makes Amex valuable to merchants.[337]

Lastly, there is nothing inherently anticompetitive about Amex's antisteering provisions. These agreements actually stem negative externalities in the credit-card market and promote interbrand competition. When merchants steer cardholders away from Amex at the point of sale, it undermines the cardholder's expectation of 'welcome acceptance'—the promise of a frictionless transaction. A lack of welcome acceptance at one merchant makes a cardholder less likely to use Amex at all other merchants. This externality endangers the viability of the entire Amex network. And it undermines the investments that Amex has made to encourage increased cardholder spending, which discourages investments in rewards and ultimately harms both cardholders and merchants. Perhaps most importantly, antisteering provisions do not prevent Visa, MasterCard, or Discover from competing against Amex by offering lower merchant fees or promoting their broader...

In sum, the plaintiffs have not satisfied the first step of the rule of reason. They have not carried their burden of proving that Amex's antisteering provisions have anticompetitive effects. Amex's business model has spurred robust interbrand competition and has increased the quality and quantity of credit-card transactions. And it is '[t]he promotion of interbrand competition,' after all, that 'is... "the primary purpose of the antitrust laws.' "[338]

[335] ibid 12 (references omitted).
[336] ibid 14.
[337] ibid 16.
[338] ibid 20 (reference omitted).

Two things stand out. First, the majority sees the anti-steering provisions as justified by addressing a negative externality. Sustainability and environmental issues are often the consequence of such negative externalities. Second, the case seems to require a balance between the harms and the benefits of the anti-steering provision. This balancing could be seen as a balance between harms in one market versus benefits in another directly related market. Yet, the majority defines the two sides as one market. However, it should be noted that this ruling that allows for the balancing of harms and benefits seems to apply only to a small subset of platforms, so-called 'translation platforms'.[339]

In the EU, the issue has also come up in the context of credit cards. While the case concerned Master Card, which has a different setup from American Express, the EU also seems to have taken a slightly different approach. In *Master Card*,[340] the court accepted that there are two connected markets. In the case of two such connected markets, there are limits to balancing harms in one market that produce benefits in another.

Master Card and Others v Commission[341]

Master Card concerned the setting of so-called multilateral interchange fees (MIF) for cross-border payments. The setting of this fee restricted price competition between the banks and increased merchant charges. Master Card had argued that the fees would need to be balanced against the benefits for the cardholders parties and after the General Court rejected that argument it was appealed to the Court of Justice. The Court found:

> As regards the arguments that the General Court wrongly ignored the two-sided nature of the system and the advantages flowing from the MIF for cardholders, first of all, it is settled case-law that the improvement, within the meaning of the first condition laid down in Article [101](3) [TFEU], cannot be identified with all the advantages which the parties obtain from the agreement in their production or distribution activities. The improvement must in particular display appreciable objective advantages of such a character as to compensate for the disadvantages which that agreement entails for competition.[342]

[339] Tim Wu, 'The American Express Opinion, the Rule of Reason, and Tech Platforms' [2019] *Journal of Antitrust Enforcement* 118. Wu also highlights the difficulties and 'arbitrariness' of the market definitions.

[340] Case C-382/12 P *MasterCard and Others v Commission* EU:C:2014:2201 para 240.

[341] ibid.

[342] ibid para 234 (references omitted).

> ... Furthermore, under Article [101](3) [TFEU], it is the beneficial nature of the effect on all consumers in the relevant markets that must be taken into consideration.[343]
>
> It follows from this that, in the case of a two-sided system [when assessing] whether a measure ...— in so far as it creates restrictive effects in regard to one of the two groups of consumers associated with that system — can fulfil the first condition laid down in Article [101](3) [TFEU], it is necessary to take into account the system of which that measure forms part, including, where appropriate, all the objective advantages flowing from that measure not only on the market in respect of which the restriction has been established, but also on the market which includes the other group of consumers associated with that system, in particular where, as in this instance, it is undisputed that there is interaction between the two sides of the system in question. To that end, it is necessary to assess, where appropriate, whether such advantages are of such a character as to compensate for the disadvantages which that measure entails for competition.[344]
>
> ...
>
> [T]he General Court was, in principle, required, when examining the first condition laid down in Article [101](3) [TFEU], to take into account all the objective advantages flowing from the MIF, not only on the relevant market, namely the acquiring market, but also on the separate but connected issuing market.[345]
>
> It follows from this that, should the General Court have found that there were appreciable objective advantages flowing from the MIF for merchants, ... all the advantages on both consumer market*s* in the MasterCard scheme, ... could, if necessary, have justified the MIF if, taken together, those advantages were of such a character as to compensate for the restrictive effects of those fees.[346]
>
> However, ... examination of the first condition laid down in Article [101](3) [TFEU] raises the question whether the advantages derived from the measure at issue are of such a character as to compensate for the disadvantages resulting therefrom. Thus, where, as in the present case, restrictive effects have been found on only one market of a two-sided system, the advantages flowing from the restrictive measure on a separate but connected market ... cannot, in themselves, be of such a character as to compensate for the disadvantages resulting from that measure in the absence of any proof of the existence of

[343] ibid para 236 (references omitted).
[344] ibid para 237.
[345] ibid para 240.
[346] ibid para 241(emphasis added).

> appreciable objective advantages attributable to that measure in the relevant market, in particular, ... where the consumers on those markets are not substantially the same.[347]
>
> In the present case, ... there was no proof of the existence of objective advantages flowing from the MIF and enjoyed by merchants. In those circumstances, it was not necessary to examine the advantages flowing from the MIF for cardholders, since they cannot, by themselves, be of such a character as to compensate for the disadvantages resulting from those fees ...[348]

The Court highlighted that it is possible to take into account the benefits in another connected market.[349] These benefits can be used to establish whether the benefits of the agreement outweigh its harm. However, the court made clear that the customer in a market where the harm occurs must at least have some benefits before benefits in other markets can be taken into account. In other words, the harmed customers must obtain some benefit, and only if this condition is met can we continue the analysis.[350] But if those customers obtain some benefit, the benefits in other markets can be added to determine whether the overall balance is positive.[351]

The judgment clarifies the standard for private benefits that occur in another market. It also is in line with previous case law.[352] In *Compagnie Générale Maritime*[353] the Court had found that:

> regard should naturally be had to the advantages arising from the agreement in question, not only for the relevant market, namely that for inland transport services provided as part of intermodal transport, but also, in appropriate cases, for every other market on which the agreement in question might have beneficial

[347] ibid para 242.

[348] ibid para 243.

[349] Viktoria HSE Robertson, *Competition Law's Innovation Factor: The Relevant Market in Dynamic Contexts in the EU and the US* (Hart Bloomsbury 2020) 43.

[350] For interpretations that are critical of this approach or at least try to limit the effects of the judgment see, eg, see Luc Peeperkorn, 'Competition and Sustainability: What Can Competition Policy Do?' (2020) 4 *Concurrences*, para 35; Edith Loozen, 'EU Antitrust in Support of the Green Deal. Why Better is not Good Enough' (2024) 12(1) *Journal of Antitrust Enforcement* 75–97.

[351] See also Frederic Pradelles and Andreas Scordamaglia-Tousis, 'The Two Sides of the *Cartes Bancaires* Ruling: Assessment of the Two-Sided Nature of Card Payment Systems under Article 101(1) TFEU and Full Judicial Scrutiny of Underlying Economic Analysis' (2014) 10 *Competition Policy International* 147f.

[352] See also the General Court in Case T-168/01 *GlaxoSmithKline Services and Others v Commission* EU:T:2006:265, which held in paras 248 and 251 that: 'It is therefore for the Commission, in the first place, to examine whether the factual arguments and the evidence submitted to it show, in a convincing manner, that the agreement in question must enable appreciable objective advantages to be obtained ..., it being understood that these advantages may arise not only on the relevant market but also on other markets' (references omitted).

[353] Case T- 86/95 *Compagnie Générale Maritime* EU:T:2002:50 para 343.

> effects, and even, in a more general sense, for any service the quality or efficiency of which might be improved by the existence of that agreement. . . . Article 101(3) TFEU [envisage] exemption in favour of, amongst others, agreements which contribute to promoting technical or economic progress, without requiring a specific link with the relevant market.

Similarly in *ASNEF-EQUIFAX* it was held that 'under Article [101(3) TFEU] . . . the beneficial nature of the effect on *all consumers* in the relevant *markets* [are] taken into consideration, not the effect on each member of that category of consumers'.[354] This approach to the benefits under Article 101(3) TFEU also seems sensible as defining markets is not without difficulties.[355] And it shows that a consideration of benefits in other markets is certainly possible.

However, with *Master Card*, we can see the imposition of a further requirement. The requirement that customers in the affected markets need to be 'substantially the same' as those in the other market, if the benefit only accrues in the other markets. Otherwise, the consumers in the affected market also need to obtain benefits in order for Article 101(3) TFEU to apply. Yet, it is important to note that the limitation established in *Master Card* was decided in a context concerning private benefits only. But private and public benefits are not the same. We cannot be sure whether the court would have also imposed this additional requirement if a public benefit had been at stake. In particular, in cases where the customers in the affected market automatically/directly incurred a benefit, the need for this additional requirement is questionable. We might imagine CO2 reductions as a public benefit that is automatically/directly incurred by the customers as the reduction of CO2 emissions benefits everyone. Moreover, the Court imposed this requirement for situations where the group harmed and those benefitted 'are not substantially the same'. In cases concerning CO2 reductions, it is not immediately clear that the two groups 'are not substantially the same' as everyone benefits.

The competition authorities like New Zealand and Singapore adopt a broader efficiency-focused assessments, which is to some extent similar to the EU and US approach but diverge substantially when public benefits are at stake. New Zealand in its new guidelines explains that it would balance the loss of competition versus the public benefit in terms of efficiency and highlights that sustainability is such a public benefit.[356] In the assessment, the focus is not only on the benefits to one

[354] Case C-238/05 *ASNEF- EQUIFAX* EU:C:2006:734 para 70, emphasis added.

[355] See Christopher Townley, 'The Relevant Market: An Acceptable Limit to the Competition Analysis' (2011) 32(10) ECLR 491–492. See also Okeoghene Odudu, 'Interpreting Article 81(1): Demonstrating Restrictive Effect' (2001) 26(3) *European Law Review* 273–274.

[356] Commerce Commission New Zealand, Collaboration and Sustainability Guidelines (November 2023) available at <https://comcom.govt.nz/__data/assets/pdf_file/0033/335985/Collaboration-and-Sustainability-Guidelines-30-November-2023.pdf> (accessed 22 January 2025) para 48.

specific group, such as the affected consumers,[357] but instead on benefits to New Zealand as a whole.[358] Similarly, the Singapore Guidance[359] applies not a consumer welfare but a net economic benefit test. The test in Schedule 3, Sec 9 of Singapore's Competition Act 2004 looks similar to the one applied by the EU.[360] However, it does not contain a fair share for the consumers' criterion. Thus, the net economic benefit test is fulfilled if the agreement is 'improving production or distribution; or [is] promoting technical or economic progress', while not imposing restrictions that are 'indispensable to the attainment of those objectives' and/or eliminating competition 'in respect of a substantial part of the goods or services in question'. For this test to be fulfilled the authority examines whether the agreement 'i) leads to economic benefits that outweigh the negative competition effects; ii) these economic benefits cannot be achieved without the agreement and any restrictions in it; and iii) competition is not eliminated in a substantial market part of the market'.[361] In light of Singapore's whole-of-nation effort[362] to tackle climate change,[363] the authority considers environmental sustainability objectives such as reducing pollution and greenhouse gas emissions to provide benefits under the net economic benefit test. Thus, the benefits will be considered to the extent that they accrue to Singapore as a whole and not only to the extent that they accrue to the affected consumers.[364]

e) Broader efficiency measurements

We have already considered numerous examples of how sustainability benefits might feature within competition law and the consumer welfare framework. However, the standard efficiency and consumer welfare approaches that we have seen applied in this context might be more contentious.[365] The benefits considered

[357] ibid para 52.
[358] ibid para 48.
[359] Competition and Consumer Commission of Singapore, Guidance Note on Business Collaborations Pursuing Environmental Sustainability Objectives (Guidance Note) (1 March 2024) available at <https://www.cccs.gov.sg/-/media/custom/ccs/files/media-and-publications/media-releases/environment-sustainability-guidance-note-1-mar-24/cccs-environmental-sustainability-collaboration-guidance-note_full.ashx> (accessed 22 January 2025).
[360] Comparing the different standards in the EU, the UK, Singapore, and New Zealand with regard to the net benefit gain, see Sini Sofia Bono, 'Assessment of Green Horizontal Agreements Between Competitors under Article 101(3) TFEU: An Unfair Share for the Environment under the European Competition Regime?' (Masters thesis, Lund University 2024) available at <http://lup.lub.lu.se/student-papers/record/9163049> (accessed on 22 January 2025).
[361] ibid para 2.14.
[362] See ibid para 1.4, for the difference between the whole-of-government approach and the even broader whole-of-nation approach (which is understood as encompassing not only the government but also private parties); see 'Public Service to go from "whole-of-government" to "whole-of-nation"', *The Straits Times* (10 May 2018) 254, available at <https://www.straitstimes.com/politics/public-service-to-go-from-whole-of-government-to-whole-of-nation> (accessed 22 January 2025).
[363] Available at <https://www.greenplan.gov.sg> (accessed 22 January 2025).
[364] Guidance Note, para 2.17.
[365] This standard might be different even though the same legal framework is applied, eg with regard to the application of Art 101 (3) TFEU by national competition authorities in the EU; see Or Brook,

within the consumer welfare framework encompass, in particular, quality improvements and sustainability innovation. Especially, quality improvements are often measured via willingness to pay.[366] This assessment is traditionally focused on the user experience directly resulting from the product.

This efficiency measurement can, however, be broadened. The European Commission, in its Guidelines on Horizontal Cooperation, suggests the use of three different measures for its economic assessment: 'individual use value benefits', 'individual non-use value benefits', and 'collective benefits'. Within the standard measure, we would see an assessment of the 'individual use benefit', that is to say, the benefit that the consumer experiences from the direct use of the improved good. The other two measures go beyond what would often be measured. The 'individual non-use value benefits' is a quality improvement that measures the readiness of the consumer to pay for more sustainable products because they produce societal benefits.[367] The collective benefits, in turn, are objective benefits that the consumer incurs irrespective of the individual appreciation.[368] For example, an increase in life expectancy can be measured irrespective of whether or not an individual values their increased life expectancy. However, the Commission limits the expansion to collective benefits to some extent.[369] It will only take them into account to the extent that they accrued to the consumer of the affected market.[370]

European Commission, 'Horizontal Cooperation Guidelines' (EU)[371]

In the guidelines, the EU Commission first sets out its definition of sustainability and then explains how it would balance sustainability benefits in general. After this explanation, it further elaborates with examples.

The Commission defines a sustainability agreement 'as any horizontal cooperation agreement that pursues a sustainability objective'[372] and that they are not a distinct category of agreements so that the sustainability agreements

'Struggling with Article 101(3) TFEU: Diverging Approaches of the Commission, EU Courts and Five Competition Authorities' (2019) 56 *Common Market Law Review* 121.

[366] On quality assessment in competition law, see, eg, OECD (n 235).
[367] EU Commission, 'Guidelines on the applicability of Article 101' (n 27) para 575. In other words, 'voluntary (altruistic) choices of individual consumers', para 582.
[368] ibid para 582.
[369] eg paras 583–585.
[370] See also above, text following (n 326ff).
[371] EU Commission, Guidelines (n 27).
[372] ibid para 521.

chapter of the guidelines applies together with the other sections of the guidelines if they apply to an agreement.[373]

When explaining the assessment of the consumer benefits, it highlights that the 'overall effect on consumers in the relevant market [must be] at least neutral. Therefore, the sustainability benefits that result from an agreement must accrue to the consumers of the products covered by that agreement.'[374] The guidelines explain that a detailed assessment of the benefits may not always be needed. In particular, such an assessment is not needed where the 'competitive harm is clearly insignificant compared to the potential benefits for the consumers in the relevant market' or where the opposite is true so that it is 'obvious ... that the claimed sustainability benefits do not accrue to the consumers in the relevant market or [are not] significant enough to compensate for the harm suffered by those consumers.[375]

After setting out that the consumer needs to be compensated, the Commission explains the different measurements it will use. these are not only 'individual use benefits' but also 'individual non-use value' and 'collective benefits'. As for the individual non-use value, the EU Commission explains that these stem 'form consumers' appreciation of the impact from of their sustainable consumption on others', as 'some consumers may value their consumption of a sustainable product more highly than the consumption of a non-sustainable product because the sustainable product has less negative impact on others'.[376] Thus,

> ... consumers may opt for a particular washing liquid not because it cleans better but because it contaminates the water less. Similarly, consumers may be willing to pay a higher price for furniture made from wood that is grown sustainably, not because of the better quality of the furniture but because they want to stop de-forestation and the loss of natural habitats. Likewise, drivers may opt to use more expensive fuel not because it is of higher quality and better for their vehicles, but because it pollutes less.[377]
>
> In these cases, the consumer's experience of the product is not directly improved. Nevertheless, consumers may be willing to pay a higher price for a sustainable product or to limit their choice of products (by not buying non-sustainable variants) in order to benefit society or future generations. Hence, indirect, non-use value benefits accrue to consumers within the relevant

[373] ibid para 523. The parties can rely on the more favourable chapter of the guidelines, however, for sustainability standardization agreements only the sustainability chapter applies, see ibid para 525.
[374] ibid para 569.
[375] ibid para 570.
[376] ibid para 575.
[377] ibid para 576.

market via their individual valuation of the effect on others, including on non-users outside the relevant market.[378]

… such indirect qualitative benefits are no different from the quality-enhancing benefits that increase the direct use value of a product, as discussed in Section 9.4.3.1. Such indirect, non-use value benefits can in some cases be measured by investigating consumers' willingness to pay, for instance, through customer surveys.[379]

There may be a difference between what consumers declare to be their preferences and what their purchasing behaviour shows to be their actual preferences. This may indicate that consumers' declared preferences either over-estimate or under-estimate their true preferences. To mitigate such biases, which often result from hypothetical questions in consumer surveys, such surveys should provide appropriate context. In addition, the questions posed should take into account societal norms, consumer knowledge and habits, and expectations about the behaviour of others.[380]

Finally, with regard to collective benefits, the Commission explains:

individual non-use value benefits … are limited to voluntary (altruistic) choices by individual consumers. However, not all negative externalities can be cured through voluntary, individual consumer actions. As the sustainability impact from individual consumption accrues not necessarily to the consuming individual but to a larger group, a joint initiative, such as a cooperation agreement, may be needed to internalise negative externalities and bring about sustainability benefits for a wider section of society. … These benefits are referred to as 'collective benefits', as they occur irrespective of the consumers' individual appreciation of the product and accrue to a wider section of society than just consumers in the relevant market.[381]

… [W]here consumers in the relevant market substantially overlap with, or form part of the group of beneficiaries outside the relevant market, the collective benefits to the consumers in the relevant market that occur outside that market can be taken into account if they are significant enough to compensate the consumers in the relevant market for the harm that they suffer.[382]

… To the extent that a substantial overlap of consumers (the drivers in this example) and the wider beneficiaries (citizens) can be established, the

[378] ibid para 577.
[379] ibid para 578 (footnote omitted).
[380] ibid para 579.
[381] ibid para 582 (footnotes omitted).
[382] ibid para 584 (footnotes omitted).

sustainability benefits of cleaner air can be taken into account, provided that they compensate the consumers in the relevant market for the harm suffered. Conversely, consumers may buy clothing made of sustainable cotton that reduces the use of fertilisers and water on the land where the cotton is cultivated. Such environmental benefits could in principle be taken into account as collective benefits. However, in this case there is unlikely to be any substantial overlap between the consumers of the clothing and the beneficiaries of the environmental benefits, as these occur only in the area where the cotton is grown. Therefore, it is unlikely that these collective benefits would accrue to the consumers in the relevant market. They could therefore only be taken into account if and to the extent that consumers of the clothing are willing to pay more for clothing that is made of sustainably grown cotton (individual non-value benefit, see Section 9.4.3.2).[383]

Most importantly, the Commission then sets out the conditions under which collective benefits can be taken into account. The parties must:

(a) describe clearly the claimed benefits and provide evidence that they have already occurred or are likely to occur;
(b) define clearly the beneficiaries;
(c) demonstrate that the consumers in the relevant market substantially overlap with the beneficiaries or form part of them; and
(d) demonstrate that the share of the collective benefits that accrues to the consumers in the relevant market, possibly together with individual use and non-use value benefits accruing to those consumers, outweighs the harm suffered by those consumers as a result of the restriction.[384]

The EU Commission also explains that any of the different benefits or any combination of them can be presented to satisfy the fair share condition[385] and that future benefits will be taken into account, but that a discount rate will be applied.[386]

In the guidelines, the EU Commission tries to square the circle. On the one hand, it aims to stay within its established position of ensuring that only benefits accrued to the consumers affected by the restriction of competition are taken into account. On the other hand, it broadens the choice of tools with which benefits to these consumers are measured.

383 ibid para 585.
384 ibid para 587 (footnotes omitted).
385 ibid para 590.
386 ibid para 591.

Crucially, we can see the Commission highlighting that all benefits count in their assessment, and would be added up in the overall assessment.

The question of how to measure or what counts as economic benefit or consumer welfare is particularly important in jurisdictions that do not offer an abstract balancing[387] within their legal framework or in specific cases. The expansion of measurements adopted for efficiency and consumer welfare narrows the difference in outcomes to jurisdictions and cases where an abstract balancing is applicable.

One concrete example of measuring such objective collective benefits can be found in the case of Dutch coal-fired power plants. In that case, the agency used an avoided cost measurement and examined the price increase by comparing it with the health benefits and increased life expectancy expressed in monetary terms.[388]

SER Energieakkoord (Netherlands)[389]

The case concerned an agreement between energy companies for the early closure of five coal-fired power plants. The Dutch competition authority examined the remaining benefits of the agreement while highlighting that the agreement would not produce any CO2 emissions savings as the emission rights obtained by the companies under the emissions trading scheme would simply be transferred to other activities.

Yet, the agency examined the other environmental benefits and compared them to the increase in energy cost resulting from the agreement.[390] Beyond the CO2 emissions, the agency examines the effects of the reduction on other harmful substances for which it relied upon calculations for which it had contracted the ECN (an independent public research institute) and found that:

> Closing down the plants in question will lead to emission reductions ... sulfur dioxide (SO2), nitrogen oxide (NOx) and particles. ECN's calculations revealed that closing down the plants will result in an average annual emission reduction of ... 1.5 kton NOx, 2.0 kton SO2 and 0.1 kton particles ....
>
> The emission reduction of SO2, NOx and particles can help improve air quality in the Netherlands, or savings can be achieved in relation to the

387 See above section IV. 1.

388 This approach can also be found in the Dutch draft guidelines; see ACM, Draft Guidelines (n 109) para 50ff.

389 ACM, 'Notitie ACM over sluiting 5 kolencentrales in SER Energieakkoord' (26 September 2013) available at <https://www.acm.nl/nl/publicaties/publicatie/12033/Notitie-ACM-over-sluiting-5-kolencentrales-in-SER-Energieakkoord> (accessed 22 January 2025).

390 The agency has published a note that explains its calculation, available at ACM, 'Analysis by the Netherlands Authority for Consumers and Markets (ACM) of the Planned Agreement on Closing Down Coal Power Plants from the 1980s as part of the Social and Economic Council of the Netherlands' SER Energieakkoord' (26 September 2013) available at <https://www.acm.nl/sites/default/files/old_publication/publicaties/12082_acm-analysis-of-closing-down-5-coal-power-plants-as-part-of-ser-energieakkoord.pdf> (accessed 22 January 2025).

measures that should be taken otherwise in order to realize the same improvement. [The agency] is of the opinion that, in principle, this can be taken into consideration when assessing the question of whether Section 6 (3) and Article 101 (3) TFEU respectively apply. (p. 4).

To evaluate the effect of this reduction, the agency used ... shadow prices, which is common practice when valuing the costs of polluting emissions or of the benefits of measures to prevent such emissions. For the valuation of the emissions reductions of NOx and SO2, it is important to note that these emissions are capped at a national level (National Emissions Ceilings). With the emissions reductions, fewer other measures need to be taken in the Netherlands in order to prevent these ceilings from being exceeded. This results in a benefit for Dutch society, which can be quantified by using the prevention costs method. This means that the value of the agreement's environmental benefits is determined using the costs of other (efficient) measures that, as a consequence, do not have to be taken (avoided costs). Using this method, the reductions of NOx and SO2 emissions can be valued at EUR 9.40 per kilo NOx and EUR 5.40 per kilo SO2.6

No emissions ceiling is currently in place for particles. Therefore, the right approach for determining the value of emissions reductions is the damage costs approach. In this approach, it is assumed that the agreement actually leads to reduced emissions, and it is estimated what that reduction's value is for Dutch citizens (particularly in terms of health and life expectancy). The emissions reductions as a result of the agreement are thus projected at EUR 44.30 per kilo. The value of the aforementioned average emissions reductions of 1.5 kton NOx, 2.0 kton SO2 and 0.1 kton particles is thus estimated at EUR 30 million in total per year over the period of 2016-2021 (that is EUR 180 million for the entire period).[391]

The agency then compared these benefits with the expected costs to the Dutch consumers which amounted to for the period and found that:

When comparing the estimated price increase with the environmental benefits using the shadow prices, it is revealed that the agreement's expected drawbacks to the electricity consumers in terms of prices may be substantially higher than the estimated value of the positive environmental effects. This suggests that the positive conditions of Section 6 (3) Mw [the Dutch Competition Act] and Article 101 (3) TFEU respectively are not met.

[391] ibid 4–5 (reference omitted).

While the agency rejected the agreement at issue,[392] the decision shows how sustainability benefits, in particular those related to environmental benefits, can be measured and translated into the language of competition. In this case, we should note that the agency did not apportion the benefits only to those consumers affected by the restriction. On the one hand, this approach may contradict the Commission's suggestion in its guidelines. On the other hand, the benefits were already too little to outweigh the costs. Moreover, the nature of electricity means that the category of Dutch electricity consumers is so broad that it will nearly fully overlap with Dutch citizens. Finally, it is noteworthy that the case is special in that the benefits were limited. Benefits in terms of CO2 reductions, possibly the main benefit associated with the closure of coal-powered power plants, did not exist. The companies were part of the EU emission trading scheme and had been allocated emission rights for those power plants; those certificates would not be destroyed. Thus, the emission rights could be sold on, and the same amount of CO2 would then be emitted by others.

f) Benefits in markets abroad

The most controversial question is related to the issue of benefits that occur in other markets and how these can be balanced against restrictions of competition. The debate exists specifically in situations where a restriction of competition produces sustainability benefits in markets abroad. The question in this regard is whether these benefits can be taken into account or whether they should not be considered. This issue may become relevant in the environmental protection context but is particularly important when looking at sustainability and its focus on economic development and poverty in developing countries. In these situations, the benefits are often localized and do not produce direct benefits in other jurisdictions as, for example, CO2 reductions. This question has only recently been discussed. We can see some who suggest that the extra-territorial application of competition law would justify the inclusion of such benefits.[393] Above, we have seen that the European Commission on the one hand rejects taking into account such benefits as far as they occur abroad. Yet, on the other hand, it takes them into account as collective benefits as far as the affected consumers accrue them or as far as those consumers value these benefits (as non-use benefits).[394] In its draft guidelines, the Dutch competition authority had suggested that for 'environmental-damage

[392] The European Commission had included a similar example in its Draft Guidelines as covering a 'green tree' label for furniture which is made from sustainably grown wood (para 620) which however disappeared in the final version of the document.

[393] Ioannis Lianos and Amber Darr, 'Hunger Games: Connecting the Right to Food and Competition Law' (2019) CLES Research Paper Series 2/2019 available at <https://www.ucl.ac.uk/cles/sites/cles/files/cles_2-2019.pdf> (accessed 22 January 2025) 27-47.

[394] EU Commission, 'Guidelines on the Applicability of Article 101' (n 27) para 585.

agreements',[395] all benefits shall be taken into account, not only those accrued to the affected consumers.

Dutch Draft Guidelines on Sustainability Agreements[396]

The draft guidelines first explained that a basic principle of EU and, therefore, Dutch competition law is that:

> users should be compensated at least for the harm caused by the restriction of competition to them. In that context, users should, for each relevant market, be seen as a group. [Yet the] ACM believes there is good reason to deviate from this basic principle if two criteria are met: (i) the agreement aims to prevent or limit any obvious environmental damage, and (ii) the agreement helps, in an efficient manner, comply with an international or national standard to prevent environmental damage to which the government is bound. These criteria are cumulative.[397]
>
> Therefore, ACM makes in these Guidelines a distinction between environmental-damage agreements and other sustainability agreements. Environmental damage agreements are agreements that aim to improve production processes that cause harm to humans, the environment, and nature. In that context, think of agreements aimed at reducing emissions of pollutants, and at preventing the use of pollutive raw materials in products. Undertakings also make sustainability agreements that concern social sustainability or other forms of sustainability. One example of such 'other' sustainability agreements are agreements where undertakings set requirements for labor conditions or animal welfare.[398] Such an agreement could concern paying a fair wage in developing countries that do not have a minimum wage. Other examples are minimum requirements for animal welfare in the production of meat or changing the recipes of food products for public-health reasons.[399]
>
> *Environmental-damage agreements*
>
> ACM believes that, with regard to environmental-damage agreements, it should be possible to take into account benefits for others than merely the users. For example, if undertakings in a certain sector jointly decide to use carbon-neutral energy only, greenhouse gas emissions will decrease as a result

395 ACM, Draft Guidelines (n 109) paras 39–44.
396 ibid.
397 ibid para 38.
398 Note that under the usual definition of sustainability animal welfare as such is not part of sustainability and can only come into play where it affects the environmental, social, or economic dimension of sustainability.
399 ibid para 39.

thereof. This is a benefit that both customers of the producers involved as well as the rest of Dutch society can reap. As a consequence, the agreement will also help realize the government's policy objective of reducing CO2 emissions.[400]

In such situations, it can be fair not to compensate users fully for the harm that the agreement causes because their demand for the products in question essentially creates the problem for which society needs to find solutions. However, in that context, the agreement must contribute to a policy objective that has been laid down in an international or national standard to which the Dutch government is bound. Moreover, that contribution must be efficient. In such cases, users will, as a rule, reap the benefits in the same way as the rest of society does.[401]

In other cases, where the two abovementioned criteria are not met, users still need to be fully compensated for the harm they suffer caused by the restriction of competition. Think of product standards or environmental standards that are more ambitious than the existing, binding standard for the government.[402]

Other sustainability agreements

With regard to other sustainability agreements, too, ACM follows the basic principle that users must be fully compensated by the benefits of the sustainability agreements for the harm that they suffer caused by a restriction of competition.[403]

This means that, for example, if a sustainability agreement leads to a quality improvement in production, but also leads to a price increase, the users (as a group) will have to attach sufficient value to those quality improvements to offset the price increase.[404]

The Dutch competition authority here made a clear distinction between environmental protection and other situations. Due to the diffuse and cross-boundary nature of environmental damage, the distinction seems to make sense, particularly with regard to CO2 emission reductions where everyone incurs benefits. However, even for environmental benefits, it might occasionally be problematic to see such benefits as occurring to national consumers, producers, or citizens, as the Dutch competition authority put it—for example, the agreement by fashion manufacturers to reduce or phase out the use of pollutants in the washing and colouring

[400] ibid para 40.
[401] ibid para 41 (reference omitted).
[402] ibid para 42.
[403] ibid para 43.
[404] ibid para 44.

processes of the apparel. Where the production sites are located in East Asia, and the pollutant is washed into local rivers and only produces negative effects on people and the environment there, the benefits to Dutch consumers, producers, or citizens seem rather questionable. However, the Dutch have now abandoned this approach and adopted the Commission's stance, but added a non-enforcement approach.[405]

The UK Competition Authority is one authority that specifically takes account of some of the benefits that occur abroad.[406] However, it does so only for 'climate change agreements'[407] and then considers all the climate benefits for UK citizens.

CMA, Green Agreements Guidance (UK)[408]

Specifically with regard to climate change agreements, the guidelines explain that

> there is a concern that having regard only to the climate change benefits accruing to the consumers in the relevant market would have perverse and harmful effects. If, for example, an individual business is minded to switch to energy use that will reduce carbon emissions, such as abandoning fossil fuels, which would be more costly in the short term (giving an immediate competitive disadvantage), it might be reluctant to do so unless its competitors in the same market do so too. Its fear of the 'first mover disadvantage' might therefore constrain it from switching to energy sources that would combat or mitigate climate change (and thereby benefit all UK consumers). It is only if that business can coordinate such a switch of energy use with its competitors, that this constraining factor is removed and the business (and indeed its competitors) is willing to make the (beneficial) switch. The same may be true in respect of businesses agreeing to supply lower-emitting but more costly or less profitable goods or services. Such coordination between competitors is to be encouraged.[409]

[405] See the discussion under Chapter 5 section II. 2.

[406] For a detailed analysis see Nicole Kar and Emma Cochrane, 'Sustainability and Competition in the UK after Brexit' in Julian Nowag (ed), *Research Handbook on Sustainability and Competition Law* (Edward Elgar 2024) 426–456.

[407] They defined them in the following way: 'For the purpose of this Guidance, the term covers agreements which contribute to combating climate change. Such agreements will typically reduce the negative externalities arising from greenhouse gases, such as carbon dioxide and methane, emitted from the production, distribution or consumption of goods and services. These negative effects (and so the benefits of reducing them) are typically global in nature and are realized over long time periods (with uncertainty about their scale).' CMA, 'Green Agreements Guidance' (n 153) para 2.4, footnotes omitted.

[408] ibid.

[409] ibid para 6.3.

For climate change agreements the CMA thus adopts a different approach to the 'fair share to consumers' condition and

> taking into account the totality of the climate change benefits to all UK consumers arising from the agreement, rather than apportioning those climate change benefits between consumers within the market affected by the agreement and those in other markets.[410]

It justifies this different approach by the exceptional nature of climate change harms, which pose a

> special category of threat, … [the] sheer magnitude of the risk that climate change represents (including the need for urgent action), the degree of public concern about it, and the binding national and international commitments that successive UK governments have entered. [As well as the] devastating effects inside the UK and outside of the UK and immeasurable long-term effects on the whole planet once certain tipping points are reached.[411]

To benefit from this special treatment, climate change benefits need to be demonstrated that exceed the 'existing legally-binding requirements' both at the national and international level including the Paris Agreement, and show that 'UK consumers benefit from the agreement and that the benefits offset the harm'.[412]

> In taking account of these benefits, both the direct and indirect benefits to the consumers in the relevant market and the benefits to UK consumers in general are potentially relevant. Such an assessment will therefore require an appraisal of both climate change benefits and negative effects. Businesses should carefully describe the climate change benefits (and harm caused by climate change, if applicable) and any effect on the consumers of the relevant products. … [W]e would expect businesses to apply the same considerations as to whether there is a need to quantify and, in cases where there is a need to quantify, for them to apply appropriate quantification techniques in a way commensurate with the relative size of the agreement's effects and to follow best practice recognised in the industry in which they operate and appropriate for

[410] ibid para 6.4.
[411] ibid para 6.4.
[412] ibid para 6.6.

the nature of environmental benefits and effects on competition at hand. As with any other agreement that restricts competition appreciably, the parties to a climate change agreement will also have to demonstrate that the other conditions of exemption are met.[413]

In this sense, the UK competition authority might set itself apart as a climate leader amongst the competition agencies. Yet, this approach would still not consider certain local benefits (no matter the size) that occur abroad as far as affected consumers do not value them.[414] Thus, in the example above where river pollution is reduced in the country of production, this would only be considered as far as the affected consumer values these.

An alternative possible way to address this problem is by exploring different, broader measurements of such benefits. For jurisdictions that aim to move beyond the economic frameworks, suggestions have been made on how insights from the social sciences might provide alternatives.[415]

4. Summary

After exploring how certain arrangements by economic actors to promote sustainability might be outside of the scope of competition law, in this section, we turned to situations where a restriction of competition is balanced against sustainability benefits. We first explored different areas where jurisdictions use a form of abstract balancing. This form of balancing between sustainability benefits and the restriction of competition can either be foreseen only for certain areas, often mergers rules, or it can take the form of a general clause. In both cases, we have seen that the clauses allowing for such balancing might either address public interests overall or focus on specific sustainability matters. In jurisdictions or areas of competition law where such abstract balancing does not exist, we have observed different pathways to how sustainability might play a role in traditional economics-focused competition law frameworks. This can take place either as part of the assessment of quality or the choice of consumers. While this approach is rather straightforward to implement. The more difficult questions arise where the harm affects certain

[413] ibid para 6.6 (footnotes omitted).
[414] As use on non-use benefits.
[415] See, eg, Rutger Claassen and Anna Gerbrandy, 'Rethinking European Competition Law: From a Consumer Welfare to a Capability Approach' (2016) 12(1) *Utrecht Law Review* 1–15; Eva van der Zee, 'European Competition Law: Measuring Sustainability Benefits under Article 101 (3) TFEU' in Julian Nowag (ed) *Research Handbook on Sustainability and Competition Law* (Edward Elgar 2024) 412–425.

consumers only directly while sustainability benefits appear only in the future or on different markets. We also noted how some competition agencies adjust their tools and apply broader efficiency measurements. The matter can get even more difficult when the benefits appear to be outside of the jurisdiction where restrictive effects are felt. In many of these cases, it is important *who* makes the decision as to whether the sustainability benefits justify the restriction of competition. It might be the competition authority or special institutions such as a minister, a situation we often see in merger cases.[416] The questions about who and on what basis the decision is made, reflect concerns about accountability and democracy. As we will see in the next section, some jurisdictions have decided to address this issue directly in their competition laws.

V. The economic frameworks and legislative choices

The debate about how to balance restrictions of competition where they lead to improvements in terms of sustainability is often related to the debate about legislative choices or democratic accountability.[417] The argument is that competition authorities would lack the democratic mandate to take into account sustainability matters as non-competition or public policy considerations and balance these against restrictions of competition. Beyond the options to address these concerns explored in section IV, in some jurisdictions, the legislature has decided to step in. In these cases, the law addresses specific aspects of sustainability and their relationship to other areas of law and their enforcement. In some cases, the legislature adopted general legal provisions. On other occasions, it has specifically tackled the interaction between sustainability aspects and competition law.

Germany adopted a climate protection law to achieve the German emission reduction goals under the Paris Agreement and the EU rules. Section 13 of this climate protection law contains a 'consideration requirement' in paragraph 1, which states that

> Bodies discharging public duties shall give due consideration to the purpose of this Act and to the targets set for its implementation. The foregoing shall be without prejudice to the powers of the Länder, municipalities and municipal associations to determine the manner of their compliance within their respective areas of responsibility. . . .[418]

[416] On the different institutional setup options see OECD, Background Paper by the Secretariat, 'Public Interest Considerations in Merger Control' (2016) DAF/COMP/WP3(2016)3 available at <https://one.oecd.org/document/DAF/COMP/WP3(2016)3/En/pdf> (accessed 22 January 2025).

[417] See in detail on this debate Nowag, *Environmental Integration* (n 1) 38–48.

[418] Federal Climate Action Act of 12 December 2019 (Federal Law Gazette I, p. 2513), as last amended by Article 1 of the Act of 15 July 2024 (Federal Law Gazette I No. 235).

It would thus appear that the German competition authority has to take into account the aim of the act and its reduction targets when making competition decisions.

Other countries have specifically addressed sustainability and climate change in their competition laws. For example, Ecuador's competition law[419] explains in Article 1 that

> [t]he purpose of this Law is to avoid, prevent, correct, eliminate and punish the abuse of economic operators with market power; the prevention, prohibition and sanction of collusive agreements and other restrictive practices; control and regulation of economic concentration operations; and the prevention, prohibition and punishment of unfair practices, seeking efficiency in the markets, fair trade and the general well-being of consumers and users, for the establishment of a *social, supportive and sustainable economic system.*[420]

Moreover, Austria recently amended its competition act to include a provision on climate change matters and sustainability. This amendment took shape against the background of the debate about the powers and mandate of competition authorities to take into account sustainability matters when deciding competition cases. The 2021 amendment to the Competition Act clarified that environmental sustainability and climate benefits are considered reasons that can justify an exception. In particular, the Austrian Cartel Act in section 2 subsection 1 now includes a clarification; the full exception reads:

> Cartels which contribute to improving the production or distribution of goods or to promoting technical or economic progress, while allowing consumers a fair share of the resulting benefits and which do not
>
> a) impose on the undertakings concerned restrictions which are not indispensable to the attainment of these objectives, or
> b) afford such undertakings the possibility of eliminating competition in respect of a substantial part of the products in question shall be exempt from the prohibition pursuant to § 1.
>
> *Consumers shall also be deemed to enjoy a fair share of the benefits which result from improvements to the production or distribution of goods or the promotion of technical or economic progress if those benefits contribute substantially to an ecologically sustainable or climate-neutral economy.*[421]

[419] Ley Orgánica de Regulación y Control del Poder de Mercado, 2 Suplemento del Registro Oficial No 555, 13 de Octubre 2011 Normativa: Vigente Última Reforma: (Suplemento del Registro Oficial 899, 09-XII-2016).

[420] Translation by the author; emphasis added.

[421] Emphasis added.

The Austrian competition authority was also tasked by the legislature with drafting guidelines on the matter.[422]

Bundeswettbewerbsbehörde, Guidelines on Sustainability Agreements (Austria)[423]

The Austrian guidelines are mindful of the fact that they should not conflict with EU competition law, and thus explain that the principles set out in the guidelines only apply as far as EU competition law does not apply.[424]

For the climate-related exception to apply, the cooperation would have first to lead to an 'efficiency gain' which consists also of 'an improvement in the use of scarce resources so that the welfare of society as a whole is enhanced'[425] such an improvement exists

> in particular [where] when the same output ... is delivered using fewer resources or ... greater output [with] same amount of resources. [The] efficiency gain may be realised in monetary form, as a cost saving for example, or in non-monetary form, as an innovation or reduction of harm to the environment for example.[426]

For such an improvement to be shown the undertakings have to specify the timeframe for the benefits and it includes benefits for 'later generations ... [which] may be appropriate [in cases] of irreversible harm to the environment. However, the time horizon ... should usually be certain or at least foreseeable'[427] and needs to be demonstrated.[428]

With regard to the indispensability of the restriction, the following parameters would be assessed: (1) that the cooperation is needed as otherwise the effect could not be achieved (so-called deadweight effects), (2) the duration,

[422] This drafting process was a particularly delicate matter, as Austrian competition law is subject to the requirement of not contradicting EU competition law where cross-border effects exist. Previously the text of the Austrian competition act was exactly the same as that of the EU prohibitions, but with the amendment the text now diverges.

[423] Bundeswettbewerbsbehörde, 'Guidelines on the Application of Sec 2 para. 1 Cartel Act to Sustainability Cooperations (Sustainability Guidelines)' (Vienna 2022) available at <https://www.bwb.gv.at/fileadmin/user_upload/AFCA_Sustainability_Guidelines_English_final.pdf> (accessed 22 January 2025).

[424] ibid paras 26–28.

[425] ibid para 67.

[426] ibid para 67 (footnote omitted).

[427] ibid para 68.

[428] ibid para 69.

and (3) the existence of 'collateral agreements that are not indispensable for the realisation of its ecological benefits'.[429]

Finally, the guidelines then set out what is meant by the condition of 'contribution to an ecologically sustainable or climate-neutral economy' that the amendment introduced. It explains that

> the undertakings concerned must show the efficiency gain that results from improving the production or distribution of goods or promoting technical or economic progress contributes to an ecologically sustainable or climate-neutral economy, in other words results from ecological benefits (below: 'efficiency gains from ecological benefits'). Should this be the case, it is to be assumed the efficiency gain attained is also beneficial to the general public.[430]
>
> A contribution to ecological sustainability or climate neutrality within the meaning of the [the law] ... is made, in particular, if the efficiency gain delivered by the cooperation contributes to the following aspects of ecological sustainability – which are mentioned in the explanatory remarks to the legislation:
>
> - climate protection,
> - climate change adaptation,
> - transition to a circular economy,
> - reduction of pollution,
> - prevention of harm to the environment,
> - protection and/or restoration of biodiversity and ecosystems.[431]

The guidelines also explain in greater detail what these terms mean[432] and set out that firms must: (1) show to what aspect of sustainability they contribute, (2) what the outcome will be, (3) how and when the benefit will be realized, (4) how the cooperation contributes to the benefits, and (5) and that no other significant damage is done—in line with the do-no-significant-harm principle.[433]

The next condition the guidelines set out is a 'substantiality criterion' contained in the law.

> ... To this end, it is necessary to analyse the positive and negative effects of the cooperation while factoring in the efficiency gains from ecological benefits in their

429 ibid para 74.
430 ibid para 75 (footnotes omitted).
431 ibid para 76.
432 ibid paras 78–84.
433 ibid para 77.

> entirety, in other words from the perspective of the general public. It is then to be assumed consumers enjoy a fair share of the benefits.[434]

It sets out that this means that agreements that do not fully provide benefits for 'consumers on the market in question' can still benefit[435] if the sustainability benefits outweigh the harm.[436]

The guidelines thus open a pathway for environmental sustainability agreements that might otherwise not exist. Yet, this is limited to agreements that only affect the Austrian market. Overall, the changes adopted by the Austrian legislature are aimed at addressing the challenge of translating sustainability matters into the language of competition law. This change in the law, combined with the guidelines, is aimed at increasing legal certainty in the area.[437]

Other jurisdictions also have specific rules that address sustainability-related matters concerning the exception from the general prohibition on anti-competitive agreements. For example, Hungary provides such an exception in Article 17 of the Hungarian Competition Act specifically mentioning the environment:

> An agreement is exempted from the prohibition pursuant to Article 11 provided that
>
> (a) *it contributes to* a more reasonable organization of production or distribution, the promotion of technical or economic progress, or the *improvement* of competitiveness or *of the protection of the environment*;[438]
> (b) it allows trading parties not participating in the agreement a fair share of the resulting benefit;
> (c) the concomitant restriction or exclusion of competition does not exceed the extent necessary to attain economically justified common goals; and
> (d) it does not enable the exclusion of competition in respect of a substantial proportion of the goods concerned.

Thus, some jurisdictions have explicitly decided that it needs to be ensured that the economic analysis of competition authorities when examining restrictions of competition includes sustainability benefits.

434 ibid para 85.
435 ibid para 87.
436 ibid paras 88–93.
437 Whether that actually helps legal certainty can be debated, as there seem now to be different approaches under EU and Austrian competition law. On the issue of diverging approaches in the EU see eg Jurgita Malinauskaite and Fatih Buğra Erdem, 'Competition Law and Sustainability in the EU: Modelling the Perspectives of National Competition Authorities' (2023) 61 *Journal of Common Market Studies* 1211–1234, who highlight the divergent approaches among authorities and questions about legal certainty; in general see also Or Brook, 'Struggling with Article 101(3) TFEU: Diverging Approaches of the Commission, EU Courts, and Five Competition Authorities' (2019) 56 *Common Market Law Review* 121–156.
438 Emphasis added.

VI. Conclusion

In this chapter we explored situations where action by economic actors promote sustainability and how substantive competition law provisions around world deal with such situations. The exploration revealed a variety of options to address actual or perceived conflicts between sustainability and competition. It provides a multitude of options to competition enforcers. The different options presented can be chosen and adapted to the local legal context, allowing agencies to act as public enablers of private sustainability initiatives.

In the first section, we highlighted the fact that not every activity promoting sustainability necessarily restricts competition within the meaning of competition This point seems rather obvious but is often still underappreciated. We noted that it is worth examining any perceived conflict between competition law and sustainability more closely before one asks whether and how a restriction of competition and sustainability benefit should be balanced.

Next, we explored different legal reasons why sustainability measures that appear to be restrictive of competition can fall outside the scope of the competition law prohibitions. These include activities considered non-commercial or non-economic for the purpose of the relevant competition laws, the treatment of collective bargaining and platform models. We also saw how sectoral exemptions exist (most often for the areas of agriculture) that might come into play when actors address sustainability in that sector. Other areas that we examined were state action and compulsion, activities that are designed to ensure compliance with applicable (but not sufficiently enforced laws). In addition, we examined the special treatment of standard-setting, IP pooling, sustainability arrangements that do not substantially affect the parameters of competition, and shareholder agreements concerning sustainability, as one specific example of such agreements.

The next section was dedicated to instances where a conflict between competition (law) and sustainability arrangements does exists. Here, we explored various options for balancing restrictions of competition and sustainability benefits. The central theme was again the overlap between sustainability and concepts such as consumer welfare, as many jurisdictions foresee exemptions for cases where an arrangement provides certain benefits. Thus, we investigated different options for how to balance restrictions of competition and sustainability benefits. First, we examined situations and jurisdictions where an abstract balancing via general or specific public interest clauses takes place. Second, we turned to cases where sustainability benefits are translated into the language of competition laws, thereby allowing the balancing to occur within established economics-based frameworks. Here, we explored different situations—some easier, such as benefits in terms of quality, choice, and innovation. We also identified situations where such balancing raises more challenging questions, namely, where sustainability benefits occur in the future and/or in markets other than those directly affected. To address these challenges, some jurisdictions have adopted the use of broader efficiency measurements. Yet, even these tools are challenged where they are faced with benefits that occur in markets abroad.

Finally, we highlighted how some jurisdictions amended or clarified their competition laws to ensure that elements sustainability can be considered within the economic frameworks they employed. This change can be seen as a reaction to concerns about the competition authorities' mandate and a perceived inability to balance sustainability benefits and restrictions of competition. Thus, the chapter showed that different jurisdictions can draw the area of the overlap between sustainability and benefits derived from a restriction of competition differently. This breadth of overlap depends on whether jurisdictions use a public interest test, or how broad or narrow they construct consumer welfare and other benefits that justify an exception to the prohibition on anti-competitive conduct.

Ujang and Wati and the clearing of rainforest

Ujang and Wati fell victim to deforestation for palm oil plantations, which is a major contributor to the loss of habitat, biodiversity, and CO2 and other emissions. With growing sustainability concerns amongst consumers, there might be questions about whether competition or cooperation might bring about better results in terms of sustainability.

Where cooperation is the way forward, arrangements such as the palm oil pledge raise questions under competition law. The questions will be different depending on the legal framework and the form and governance arrangement chosen. Yet, legally, the questions will, in particular, be whether the arrangement is subject to competition law prohibitions in the first place or whether such a standard fulfils certain conditions and thus operates in a safe harbour. Where an arrangement is subject to competition law, we might ask whether an abstract balancing or a balancing focused on efficiency and consumer welfare might lead the competition authority to find that competition law does not prohibit the arrangement.

5
Process matters

> **Ricarda's struggle with bureaucracy**
>
> Ricarda is the head of legal in a large multinational company that trades beef and raw soy from Brazil's Amazon region, which her company sells in a number of jurisdictions, including the EU. Her company's management and policies strongly support the drive to make the company more sustainable, which is in line with consumer demand that expresses concern over their products' impact on deforestation and CO2 emissions. After advice from leading EU competition lawyers, she is confident that together with like-minded companies, they will be able to set up a standardization scheme that will be compliant with EU competition law and ensure that their beef and soy are sourced only from sustainable sources.
>
> In light of financial reporting standards, the competition assessment of the standard, and with the help of economists and environmental experts, the company can also show the substantive benefits of this standardization agreement.
>
> While she is very sure that the envisioned arrangement is fully in line with EU competition law, she is concerned about the framework the Brazilian competition authority will use to assess the arrangement, whether and how her company could prove the relevant benefits, and whether if things go wrong such an arrangement could expose the company to possibly substantial fines and sanctions.

I. Introduction

Where market players engage in more sustainable practices that might conflict with competition laws in different jurisdictions, what can they expect in terms of enforcement and remedies in different jurisdictions? What other options do competition enforcers have to engage with sustainability? What can be learned from the experiences in other jurisdictions?

This chapter offers a broad menu of options that competition enforcers can choose from and adapt to their local legal environment to foster sustainability. We investigate the relevance of public and private competition law enforcement

Global Antitrust and Sustainability. Julian Nowag, Oxford University Press. © Julian Nowag 2025.
DOI: 10.1093/9780191955013.003.0005

actions in the pursuit of sustainability and how jurisdictions, and in particular, competition agencies have proceeded. These process matters can help policy-makers and competition authorities make sustainability relevant to their work. As such the tools of the enforcement box can be of help to enforcers of competition law even where their substantive laws do not provide as much room for overlaps between competition and sustainability. Ultimately, regulatory tools and enforcement strategies identified herein are for agencies in various jurisdictions to consider and adopt according to whichever best fit the legal context. Enforcement and procedural matters are thus important instruments in fostering sustainability while protecting competition.

In terms of content in this chapter, a range of matters at different stages of the process are addressed. These matters range from objectives of the agency and its priority-setting, to different forms of guidance. Similarly, we explore different models of approval procedures and sandboxing. Moreover, we touch upon relevant evidence, capacity, advocacy, and, more generally, the relationship with other parts of the government. Finally, in this chapter, we study sanctions and remedies, market inquiries, as well as international cooperation. We observe that the toolbox which competition agencies have at their disposal to bring about more sustainability is vast, and that using these tools is often a matter of creativity and political willingness rather than legal possibilities.

II. Objectives and priorities

Where a competition agency wants to engage with the subject of sustainability in its capacity as an enforcer of competition law,[1] the agency's objective and priorities seem a natural starting point because the objectives and priorities of the agency matter.[2]

There are a number of ways in which sustainability can also become relevant in the context of objectives and priorities. On the one hand, areas of the economy or sustainability can be declared a priority at an abstract level. On the other hand, agencies might decide that sustainability-related cases that potentially restrict competition should not be pursued or, more precisely, be de-prioritized. Such a de-prioritization can take the form of a general policy or a decision in an individual

[1] As compared to, for example, their internal staff-related processes and procurement practices.

[2] See, for example, with regard to gender inequality OECD, 'Competition Policy and Gender' (2018) DAF/COMP/GF(2018)4 available at <https://one.oecd.org/document/DAF/COMP/GF(2018)4/en/pdf> (accessed 8 February 2025). The report highlights the critical role of priority-setting and how competition authorities can contribute to the fight against gender inequality when focusing on markets that are particularly critical for women. Similarly, such a prioritization might help in fighting poverty; on this see OECD, 'Competition and Poverty Reduction' DAF/COMP/GF(2013)12 available at <http://www.oecd.org/daf/competition/competition-and-poverty-reduction2013.pdf> (accessed 8 February 2025).

case which is then typically combined with individual guidance. These will be discussed in the next section.[3]

1. Prioritizing sustainability matters/sustainability as an objective for an agency

UK's competition authority when setting its objective for 2020/2021 highlighted:

> in the immediate term ... we propose in 2020/21 to exercise our functions with particular regard to these strategic objectives: ... Climate change—supporting the transition to a low carbon economy: We will develop our understanding of how climate affects markets and consider how, when exercising our functions, we can act in a way that supports the transition to a low carbon economy. We will also consider using our enforcement powers to correct false or misleading statements that affect consumers, for example in the use of 'green' claims.[4]

This was followed in the Annual plan 2022 to 2023 with the aim of 'Supporting the transition to low carbon growth, including through the development of healthy competitive markets in sustainable products and services'.[5] This means the agency will prioritize cases that could impede the UK's net zero goals for a low-carbon economy.[6] The French competition authority also made sustainable development 'a core' of its priorities for 2020[7] and similarly maintained this priority for the period 2023–2024.[8]

Such goals typically lead to prioritizing cases with competitive harms in areas that are relevant for sustainability, like the transition to a low carbon economy. Thus, a competition agency might take a close look at anti-competitive activities hampering sustainable development. This means examining the existence of anti-competitive behaviour in industries relevant to green growth. The European Commission, for example, initiated an in-depth Phase 2 investigation of the *Aurubis/Metallo* merger. In its press statement, the Commission highlighted that

[3] See section III.2.

[4] CMA, 'Corporate Report Annual Plan 2020 to 2021' (19 March 2020) available at <https://www.gov.uk/government/publications/competition-and-markets-authority-annual-plan-2020-to-2021/annual-plan-2020-to-2021> (accessed 8 February 2025).

[5] See CMA, 'Corporate Report Annual Plan 2022 to 2023' (24 March 2022) available at <https://www.gov.uk/government/publications/competition-and-markets-authority-annual-plan-2022-to-2023/annual-plan-2022-to-2023> (accessed 8 February 2025).

[6] ibid para. 2.51.

[7] See Autorité de la Concurrence available at <https://www.autoritedelaconcurrence.fr/fr/communiques-de-presse/lautorite-de-la-concurrence-annonce-ses-priorites-pour-lannee-2020> (accessed 8 February 2025).

[8] See Autorité de la Concurrence available at <https://www.autoritedelaconcurrence.fr/sites/default/files/2023-03/feuille-de-route-2023-2024.pdf?v=1679559101> (accessed 8 February 2025) 4–5.

> Demand for copper is likely to increase, notably also due to the growing importance of electric cars. A well-functioning, competitive copper recycling industry is key to meet the future needs of European industry and to limit the impact on the environment. The Commission will carefully assess the merger between Aurubis and Metallo, the two leading copper scrap refiners in Europe, to ensure the transaction would not negatively affect competition in this important sector.[9]

The press release further highlighted that the major concern for the EU Commission was that the merger might 'disrupt the normal functioning of the copper recycling industry, lowering the incentives for recyclers to collect and sort copper scrap'.[10]

Priority-setting and objectives of agencies can equally come into play concerning matters of inclusive growth and issues affecting poverty,[11] for example by prioritizing cases that have particular negative effects on the poor.

The South African competition agency

> has taken into account the growth and development imperatives of a highly unequal society that is also characterised by high rates of poverty. The Competition Commission's enforcement and advocacy activities are guided by a Prioritisation Framework, which represents the organisation's over-arching strategy.[12] This Framework, adopted in 2008, explicitly incorporates poverty reduction, as it draws on the country's key economic policies that are directed towards the same goal.[13]

The priority areas of the agency are, therefore: 'food and agro-processing; healthcare; intermediate industrial inputs; construction and infrastructure; banking and financial services; banking and financial services; information and communication technology and energy'.[14] In January 2015, the agency also issued a strategic plan for 2015–2020 and announced 'a new emphasis on the developmental role of competition in the economy', using 'merger control and [antitrust] enforcement

[9] EU Commission Press Release Press Mergers: Commission opens in-depth investigation into proposed acquisition of Metallo by Aurubis (Brussels, 19 November 2019) available at <https://ec.europa.eu/commission/presscorner/detail/en/IP_19_6305> (accessed 8 February 2025).

[10] ibid.

[11] See OECD, 'Competition and Poverty Reduction' (n 2); Robert D Anderson and Anna Caroline Müller, 'Competition Policy and Poverty Reduction: A Holistic Approach' (20 February 2013) World Trade Organization Economic Research and Statistics Division Staff Working Paper ERSD-2013-02.

[12] Gertrude Makhaya, Wendy Mkwananzi, and Simon Roberts, 'How Should Your Competition Authorities Approach Competition Enforcement? Reflections on South Africa's Experience' (2012) 19(1) *South African Journal of International Affairs* 43–64.

[13] South African contribution to the OECD Global Forum on Competition, Competition, and Poverty Reduction (January 2013) DAF/COMP/GF/WD(2013)23 available at <https://one.oecd.org/document/DAF/COMP/GF/WD(2013)23/En/pdf> (accessed 8 February 2025).

[14] Competition Commission South Africa, 'Strategic Goals – The Competition Commission' available at <https://www.compcom.co.za/our-strategic-goals/> (accessed 8 February 2025).

to create efficiency gains as well as developmental objectives'.[15] The intent to 'use its regulatory instruments to contribute to a growing and inclusive economy' was inherited in its 2020–2025 plan[16] and its Vision 2030, and those words appear in connection with the Commission's logo and banners.[17] In the judicial dimension, competition and its inclusive mission is even elevated to the constitutional level as a human right in South Africa. In the case *Competition Commission of South Africa v Mediclinic Southern Africa (Pty) Ltd*[18], the Court commented that:

> Colonialism, neo-colonialism and apartheid orchestrated an institutionalised concentration of ownership and control of all things of consequence in our national economy along racial lines. Unsurprisingly, the commanding heights of the corporate sector are seemingly the exclusive terrain of our white compatriots. It is this indisputable reality and our shared commitment to ensuring that South Africa really does get to belong to all who live in it, that the constitutional imperatives, laid out in the Preamble, to improve the quality of life of all citizens and free the potential of each are realised, that the likes of the Competition Act had to and got to see the light of day.[19]
>
> Institutions created to breathe life into these critical provisions of the Act must therefore never allow what the Act exists to undo and to do, to somehow elude them in their decision-making process. The equalisation and enhancement of opportunities to enter the mainstream economic space, to stay there and operate in an environment that permits the previously excluded as well as small and medium-sized enterprises to survive, succeed and compete freely or favourably must always be allowed to enjoy their pre-ordained and necessary pre-eminence.[20]

The Philippines, as a developing country with a high level of poverty and a relatively new competition agency, has also taken an insightful pathway. The Philippine Competition Act, mirroring the Constitution, sets out as in section 2:

[15] Competition Commission South Africa, 'Strategic Plan 2015–2020' available at <http://www.compcom.co.za/wp-content/uploads/2019/10/Strategic-Plan-2015-2020_Signed.pdf> (accessed 8 February 2025).

[16] Competition Commission South Africa, 'Strategic Plan 2020/21–2024/25' available at <https://www.compcom.co.za/wp-content/uploads/2023/09/Competition-Commission-Strategic-Plan-2020.21-to-2024.25.pdf> (accessed 8 February 2025).

[17] See South Africa Competition Commission, 'Overview—The Competition Commission' available at <https://www.compcom.co.za/about-us-2/> (accessed 7 February 2025), see also with more details: Eleanor Fox, 'Good Growth: Competition Policy and Inclusive Growth in The Developing World' in Thomas K Cheng, Julian Nowag, and Dina Waked (eds), *Competition Law in Developing Countries* (forthcoming Edward Elgar 2025).

[18] *Competition Commission of South Africa v Mediclinic Southern Africa (Pty) Ltd* (CCT 31/20) [2021] ZACC 35 (15 October 2021).

[19] ibid para 4.

[20] ibid para 7.

Declaration of Policy.
The efficiency of market competition as a mechanism for allocating goods and services is a generally accepted precept. The State recognizes that past measures undertaken to liberalize key sectors in the economy need to be reinforced by measures that safeguard competitive conditions. The State also recognizes that the provision of equal opportunities to all promotes entrepreneurial spirit, encourages private investments, facilitates technology development and transfer and enhances resource productivity. Unencumbered market competition also serves the interest of consumers by allowing them to exercise their right of choice over goods and services offered in the market.

Pursuant to the constitutional goals for the national economy to attain a more equitable distribution of opportunities, income, and wealth; a sustained increase in the amount of goods and services produced by the nation for the benefit of the people; and an expanding productivity as the key to raising the quality of life for all, especially the underprivileged and the constitutional mandate that the State shall regulate or prohibit monopolies when the public interest so requires and that no combinations in restraint of trade or unfair competition shall be allowed, the State shall:

(a) Enhance economic efficiency and promote free and fair competition in trade, industry and all commercial economic activities, as well as establish a National Competition Policy to be implemented by the Government of the Republic of the Philippines and all of its political agencies as a whole;
(b) Prevent economic concentration which will control the production, distribution, trade, or industry that will unduly stifle competition, lessen, manipulate or constrict the discipline of free markets; and
(c) Penalize all forms of anti-competitive agreements, abuse of dominant position and anti-competitive mergers and acquisitions, with the objective of protecting consumer welfare and advancing domestic and international trade and economic development.

The act thus attached importance to 'a more equitable distribution of opportunities, income, and wealth' and 'to raising the quality of life for all, especially the underprivileged'. To attain these objectives, the agency worked with the National Economic and Development Authority to identify sectors most relevant for poverty reduction and have spillover effects on other parts of the economy. This exercise identified the areas of agriculture, electricity, manufacturing, power generation, telecommunications, and transportation as sectors for the mid-term priority.[21]

[21] For further details see Leni Papa and Raya Teston, 'Competition Policy, Poverty, Inequality: The Philippine Experience' in Julian Nowag (ed), *Research Handbook on Sustainability and Competition Law* (Edward Elgar 2024).

But even in jurisdictions, like the EU, where consumer welfare is an important yardstick, sustainability, including social sustainability, can guide prioritization. For example, the EU Commission can consider the competitive effects of a particular practice on vulnerable consumers' welfare and adjust the corresponding enforcement actions.[22]

2. De-prioritizing cases fostering sustainability

The idea of priority setting can also work in the opposite direction by de-prioritizing certain areas. The European Commission, for example, in its guidance on collective agreements in the gig economy[23] explained that:

> In some cases, solo self-employed persons who are not in a situation comparable to that of workers may nevertheless have difficulties in influencing their working conditions because they are in a weak negotiating position vis-à-vis their counterparty/-ies. Therefore, even if it cannot be assumed that their collective agreements fall outside the scope of Article 101 TFEU, these solo self-employed persons may in fact face difficulties that are similar to those faced by solo self-employed persons in the categories [which do not fall within the scope of Article 101 TFEU[24]]. For this reason, the Commission will not intervene against the following categories of collective agreements:[25]

The Commission then explained in more detail that it will not pursue 'collective agreements concluded by solo self-employed persons with counterparty/-ies that have a certain level of economic strength'[26] and 'collective agreements concluded by self-employed persons pursuant to national or Union legislation'.[27]

The Dutch competition authority has adopted a similar policy with regard to agreements made to comply with binding national, EU, or international legal rules

[22] Francisco Costa-Cabral and Julian Nowag, 'Greedflation, Competition Law, and the Cost-of-Living Crisis' (2023) available at <https://www.socialistsanddemocrats.eu/sites/default/files/2023-06/greedflation-competition-law-and-the-cost-of-living-crisis-report-final.pdf> (accessed 8 February 2025).

[23] Communication from the Commission, Guidelines on the application of Union competition law to collective agreements regarding the working conditions of solo self-employed persons [2022] OJ C 374/2.

[24] These as explained in sections 3.1, 3.2 and 3.3 of the Guidelines are 'economically dependent solo self-employed persons', 'solo self-employed persons working "side-by-side" with workers', and 'solo self-employed persons working through digital labour platforms'.

[25] ibid para 32.

[26] Addressed in paras 33–35.

[27] Addressed in paras 36–40.

on sustainability matters or to so-called 'environmental-damage agreements'.[28,29] While its draft guidelines had set out situations that it thought would warrant the application of Article 101(3) TFEU, it adjusted its approach in light of the EU horizontal guidelines. It now states that

> [a]s an independent supervisor, ACM has discretionary freedom within certain boundaries on how it investigates potential violations or what sanctions it imposes. In [these] two situations, ACM chooses in principle not to investigate. This means that ACM does not take action against undertakings in those cases. Undertakings therefore do not have to fear a fine from ACM.[30]

It then further explains the reasons for this decision. With regard to agreements made to comply with binding national, EU, or international legal rules on sustainability matters, it would not prosecute such cases, 'because ACM does not consider it expedient to protect illicit competition, i.e. competition that would not have existed if binding sustainability rules had been complied with'.[31] And with regard to environmental damages agreements the agency highlights that

> ACM does not consider it expedient to continue investigating an environmental-damage agreement if the initial investigation shows that it is plausible that the agreement is necessary for achieving the environmental benefits and that such benefits sufficiently outweigh the potential competitive disadvantages. It is important that consumers in the relevant market receive an appreciable and objective part of the advantages. This means in any case that the consumers should belong to the group that benefits from the agreement. Furthermore, there should remain a degree of residual competition.[32]

These examples show how discretion by agencies can be used in the sustainability context, both to prioritize or to deprioritize certain areas of the law and thereby foster sustainability.

[28] Defined in para 22 of its Guidelines as 'agreements that contribute efficiently to compliance with an international or national standard or to the achievement of a specific policy objective to prevent environmental damage. In that context, environmental damage can be defined as environmental damage in the production, transport and consumption of goods or services. Environmental damage is caused, for example, by the emission of harmful substances and greenhouse gases, and by the wasting of raw materials. The damage it causes, which is not included in the price, is referred to as negative externalities. This damage is reflected in, for example, atmospheric warming, reduced biodiversity and/or a less healthy living environment.' See ACM, 'ACM's Oversight of Sustainability Agreements: Competition and Sustainability' (4 October 2023) available at <https://www.acm.nl/system/files/documents/Beleidsregel%20Toezicht%20ACM%20op%20duurzaamheidsafspraken%20ENG.pdf> (accessed 8 February 2025).

[29] ibid paras 7–9; 20–24.

[30] ibid para 7.

[31] ibid para 21.

[32] ibid para 23.

III. Openness and formal and informal guidance

While objectives and priorities are important for the general direction of a competition agency. Agencies can also make substantial difference by means of guidance. This will make a particular difference in situations where economic actors aim to promote sustainability, but the exact treatment under competition law is unclear. While the adoption of formal guidelines may have the largest impact as it is taken into account by legal advisers across the board, individual guidance is also relevant. Both forms of guidance are particularly important in the context where economic actors have expressed concerns about the legal treatment of sustainability initiatives.[33] Such guidance can help with situations of over-deterrence and may help to overcome what the EU competition Commissioner has called 'certain level of conservatism in the advisory industry'.[34]

1. Guidelines

In 2020, one of the first agencies to publish general (draft) guidelines[35] in the area of sustainability was the Dutch competition authority, which built upon its earlier 2016 basic principles[36] on how it would conduct oversight of sustainability arrangements and its 2014 vision document.[37] The final version of these guidelines has now been published[38] after the second round of public consultations and consultations with the European Commission, which published its Draft Horizontal Guidelines[39] in March 2022; these also contained a section on sustainability agreements with the final version adopted in June 2023.[40] In addition,

[33] Tomaso Fernando and Claudio Lombardi, 'EU Competition Law and Sustainability in Food Systems: Addressing the Broken Links' (Fair Trade Advocacy Office, February 2019) 32; Thomas Lübbig, 'Sustainable Development and Competition Policy' (2013) 4(1) *Journal of European Competition Law & Practice* 1, Inara Scott, 'Antitrust and Socially Responsible Collaboration: A Chilling Combination?' (2016) 53(1) *American Business* 97–144.

[34] Margrethe Vestager, Keynote speech at Conference 'Sustainability and Competition Policy: Bridging two Worlds to Enable a Fairer Economy', 24 October 2019, available at <https://www.youtube.com/watch?v=7mpWAOhkQbY> (accessed 8 February 2025).

[35] ACM, Draft Guidelines 'Sustainability Agreements' (9 July 2020), available at <https://www.acm.nl/en/publications/draft-guidelines-sustainability-agreements> (accessed 8 February 2025).

[36] ACM, 'ACM Sets Basic Principles for Oversight of Sustainability Arrangements' (2 December 2016) available at <https://www.acm.nl/en/publications/publication/16726/ACM-sets-basic-principles-for-oversight-of-sustainability-arrangements> (accessed 8 February 2025).

[37] ACM, 'Vision Document on Competition and Sustainability' (9 May 2014) available at <https://www.acm.nl/en/publications/publication/13077/Vision-document-on-Competition-and-Sustainability> (accessed 8 February 2025).

[38] ACM (n 28).

[39] European Commission, 'Public Consultation on the Draft Revised Horizontal Block Exemption Regulations and Horizontal Guidelines' (2022) available at <https://competition-policy.ec.europa.eu/public-consultations/2022-hbers_en> (accessed 8 February 2025).

[40] European Commission, 'Guidelines on the Applicability of Article 101 of the Treaty on the Functioning of the European Union to Horizontal Cooperation Agreements' [2023] OJ C 259/1,

the EU has also published specific guidelines on agricultural and competition law.[41]

There are other examples from around the EU. The Austrian competition authority published guidelines[42] in September 2022 after being asked to do so by the legislator. The Greek competition agency, while not adopting guidelines, has published a Staff Discussion Paper on Sustainability Issues and Competition Law;[43] similarly the German competition authority followed in October 2020 by publishing a background paper on the matter.[44] Portugal has also adopted a form of guidance document, called best practice,[45] which follows closely the EU guidance but seems more accessible and hands-on for businesses.

Outside the EU, the UK as a former EU member state where the text of competition law provisions remains similar to EU competition, adopted an information sheet in 2021[46] and has in October 2023 published guidelines on 'Green Agreements'.[47] The UK also addresses sustainability in its merger guidelines,[48]

available at <https://eur-lex.europa.eu/legal-content/EN/TXT/PDF/?uri=CELEX:52023XC0721(01)> (accessed 8 February 2025).

[41] European Commission, Commission Guidelines on the Exclusion from Article 101 of the Treaty on the Functioning of the European Union for Sustainability Agreements of Agricultural Producers Pursuant to Article 210a of Regulation (EU) No 1308/2013 (C/2023/8306 final) available at <https://eur-lex.europa.eu/legal-content/EN/ALL/?uri=PI_COM:C(2023)8306> (accessed 8 February 2025).

[42] Bundeswettbewerbsbehörde, 'Leitlinien zur Anwendung von § 2 Abs 1 KartG auf Nachhaltigkeitskooperationen (Nachhaltigkeits-LL)' (Vienna, September 2022) available at <https://www.bwb.gv.at/fileadmin/user_upload/Leitlinien_zur_Anwendung_von____2_Abs_1_KartG_auf_Nachhaltigkeitskooperationen__Nachhaltigkeits-LL__Stand_9_2022.pdf> (accessed 8 February 2025).

[43] Hellenic Competition Commission, 'Staff Discussion Paper on Sustainability Issues and Competition Law' available at <https://www.epant.gr/en/information/publications/research-publications/item/2706-staff-discussion-paper-on-sustainability-issues-and-competition-law.html> (accessed 8 February 2025).

[44] Bundeskartellamt, 'Offene Märkte und nachhaltiges Wirtschaften – Gemeinwohlziele als Herausforderung für die Kartellrechtspraxis Virtuelle Tagung des Arbeitskreises Kartellrecht' (1 October 2020) available at <https://www.bundeskartellamt.de/SharedDocs/Publikation/DE/Diskussions_Hintergrundpapier/AK_Kartellrecht_2020_Hintergrundpapier.pdf?__blob=publicationFile&v=2> (accessed 8 February 2025).

[45] Portuguese Competition Authority, 'Best Practices Guide on Sustainability Agreements' (2024) available at <https://www.concorrencia.pt/sites/default/files/documentos/guias-promocao-da-concorrencia/Best%20Practices%20Guide%20on%20Sustainability%20Agreements%20-%20Final%20Version.pdf> (accessed 8 February 2025).

[46] Competition and Markets Authority, 'Guidance—Environmental Sustainability Agreements and Competition Law' (27 January 2021), available at <https://www.gov.uk/government/publications/environmental-sustainability-agreements-and-competition-law/sustainability-agreements-and-competition-law> (accessed 8 February 2025).

[47] Competition and Markets Authority, 'Green Agreements Guidance: Guidance on the application of the Chapter I prohibition in the Competition Act 1998 to environmental sustainability agreements' (October 2023) CMA 185 12 October 2023' available at <https://assets.publishing.service.gov.uk/media/6526b81b244f8e000d8e742c/Green_agreements_guidance_.pdf> (accessed 8 February 2025).

[48] Competition and Markets Authority, 'Merger Assessment Guidelines' (March 2021) CMA129, available at <https://assets.publishing.service.gov.uk/government/uploads/system/uploads/attachment_data/file/1051823/MAGs_for_publication_2021_--_.pdf> (accessed 8 February 2025).

highlighting that sustainability can be an important (possibly the main) competition parameter.[49]

Outside Europe, the competition authority of New Zealand adopted 'Collaboration and Sustainability Guidelines'.[50] In December 2024, the Australian competition authority also published its finalized guide for businesses on sustainability collaborations and competition law.[51] This guidance document also contains a succinct business-friendly five-step checklist that has been adopted for businesses considering collaboration on sustainability matters.[52] The Japanese competition authority had already in 2001 established specific guidelines for joint recycling activities[53] and in March 2023 adopted more general guidelines (revised in April 2024).[54] These guidelines have possibly the broadest coverage of any guidelines in the field. They cover not only cooperation between businesses but equally address vertical restrictions, abuses of superior bargaining power, mergers, and consultation with the agency. While these guidelines primarily address the 'green transition', the agency highlights 'that the analysis framework and other matters indicated in the Guidelines can [most likely] also be applied to the activities of enterprises, etc. toward the achievement of the Sustainable Development Goals ("SDGs") implemented similarly for socially and publicly desirable objectives, considering the characteristics of acts conducted as such activities'.[55] Similarly, the Competition and Consumer Commission of Singapore published its Guidance Note on Business Collaborations Pursuing Environmental Sustainability Objectives in March 2024.[56] Along this developmental trajectory, in Brazil scholars have also called for guidelines along the EU model.[57]

49 ibid para 2.5.

50 New Zealand Commerce Commission, 'Collaboration and Sustainability Guidelines' (November 2023) available at <https://comcom.govt.nz/__data/assets/pdf_file/0033/335985/Collaboration-and-Sustainability-Guidelines-30-November-2023.pdf> (accessed 8 February 2025).

51 Australian Competition and Customer Commission, 'Sustainability Collaborations and Australian Competition Law A Guide for Business' (18 December 2024) available at < https://www.accc.gov.au/system/files/sustainability-collaborations-and-australian-competition-law-guide_1.pdf> (accessed 8 February 2025)

52 ibid Attachment A.

53 JFTC, 'Guidelines Concerning Joint Activities for Recycling under the Antimonopoly Act' (26 June 2001, last amended 1 January 2010) available at <https://www.jftc.go.jp/en/legislation_gls/imonopoly_guidelines_files/recycle.pdf> (accessed 8 February 2025).

54 Japan Fair Trade Commission, 'Guidelines Concerning the Activities of Enterprises, etc. Toward the Realization of a Green Society Under the Antimonopoly Act' (31 March 2023, revised 24 April 2024) available at <https://www.jftc.go.jp/en/pressreleases/yearly-2024/April/240424EN2.pdf> (accessed 8 February 2025).

55 ibid 3.

56 Competition and Consumer Commission of Singapore, 'Guidance Note on Business Collaborations Pursuing Environmental Sustainability Objectives' (1 March 2024) (Guidance Note) <https://www.cccs.gov.sg/-/media/custom/ccs/files/media-and-publications/media-releases/environment-sustainability-guidance-note-1-mar-24/cccs-environmental-sustainability-collaboration-guidance-note_full.ashx> (accessed 8 February 2025).

57 Leonardo Rocha e Silva and Paula Susanna Amaral Mello, 'Cooperation Agreements between Competitors to Promote Sustainable Development Measures: What Should Cade's Role Be?' *Migalhas, Law News Blog* (6 August 2020) available at <http://dx.doi.org/10.2139/ssrn.4346195> (accessed 8 February 2025).

2. Openness, informal guidance for individual cases

Nearly all of the above-mentioned guidelines and documents explain that agencies are open to be approached when questions about the interaction between competition law and sustainability[58] arise.[59] For example, the EU's agricultural and competition law guidelines[60] and Article 210a(6) of its relevant regulation[61] allow producers or associations of producers to request an opinion from the Commission on the compatibility of their sustainability agreements. Parties to the agreement can also join the request.

The UK announced an open-door policy for sustainability agreements in its last guidelines. In this regard, openness of agencies to such informal guidance, comfort letters, and official statements by the authorities, for example, the Dutch[62] and UK[63] competition authorities, to approach them where questions arise might go a long way.

Since the announcement, the Dutch competition authority has received numerous request and has provided informal guidance. One project, for example, concerned the collaboration between Shell and Total Energies to establish storage in empty natural gas fields for captured CO2.[64] Their collaboration sought to shoulder the substantial investment cost for the first 20 per cent of the capacity together, and competition would only take place for the other 80 per cent. Another case concerned a scheme by garden centres where they would warn and ban plant sellers who used illegal pesticides.[65]

[58] For a suggestion that guidance should adopt a differentiation between high-risk and low-risk collaboration and the corresponding responses by agencies, see Daniela Bove, 'Sustainability Considerations in the Antitrust Mandate: A Green Evolution or a Prioritisation of Sustainable Development Goals?' *Competition Commission of South Africa* (1 August 2024) available at <https://www.compcom.co.za/wp-content/uploads/2024/08/Daniela-Bove-Sustainability-considerations-in-the-antitrust-mandate.pdf> (accessed 8 February 2025).

[59] Some have suggested that the exceptional guidance given during Covid by the EU Commission could be extended to sustainability issues and be further extended to other public policies or social initiatives; see Ben Van Rompuy, 'How to Green-Light Sustainability Agreements?' (2020) 4 *European Competition & Regulation Law Review* 257, 258–259.

[60] European Commission (n 41).

[61] Regulation (EU) No 1308/2013 of the European Parliament and of the Council of 17 December 2013 establishing a common organisation of the markets in agricultural products and repealing Council Regulations (EEC) No 922/72, (EEC) No 234/79, (EC) No 1037/2001 and (EC) No 1234/2007 OJ L 347/671.

[62] Which already appeared in the ACM, 'Draft Guidelines "Sustainability Agreements"' (n 35) para 61; now in ACM, 'ACM's Oversight of Sustainability Agreements: Competition and Sustainability' (n 28) section 4.

[63] CMA (n 47) section 7.

[64] ACM Press Release, 'ACM: Shell and TotalEnergies can collaborate in the storage of CO2 in empty North Sea gas fields' (27 June 2022) available at <https://www.acm.nl/en/publications/acm-shell-and-totalenergies-can-collaborate-storage-co2-empty-north-sea-gas-fields> (accessed 8 February 2025).

[65] ACM Press Release, 'ACM agrees to arrangements of garden centers to curtail use of illegal pesticides' (27 June 2022) available at <https://www.acm.nl/en/publications/acm-agrees-arrangements-garden-centers-curtail-use-illegal-pesticides> (accessed 8 February 2025). The scheme also included guarantees to ensure due process and readmission.

The French competition authority has also set up a framework allowing undertakings to request informal guidance from them[66] under which informal guidance has been issued.[67] The German competition authority, beyond its non-binding discussion paper, has also provided informal guidance in a number of cases. It advised the participants on whether or not it would take action against the initiatives, based on its priority-setting authority.[68] The cases concern, for example, the Fairtrade label, where the agency decided not to take up the case. It found the arrangement would likely not fall under Article 101(1) TFEU or that they could at least be exempted under Article 101(3) TFEU. The case of the animal welfare improvement fund is another interesting example. In this case, a fund was created by retailers who agreed to pay a premium per kilo for pork and chicken. The funds would be used to improve the living conditions of pigs and chickens on the farms that joined the scheme. The agency was engaged twice with the initiative and held that it would not intervene for 2014–2018. After agreeing to alterations, the agency again gave a clean bill of health for 2018–2020.[69]

The US Department of Justice (DoJ) had already sent a business review letter in a similar case,[70] the Fair Factories Clearinghouse Information Sharing Program, back in 2000.[71] This case concerned a supply chain, in which a central body in the apparel and footwear supply chain was set up. It collected and shared information on forced labour and workers' rights, child labour, as well as health and safety matters; it even included information on factories' wages and working hours. The DoJ highlighted that it did not find major antitrust problems because the programme followed safe harbour rules for standards, only dealt with de minimis[72] matters, and the body had an antitrust compliance programme in place.

[66] Autorité de la concurrence, 'Notice on Informal Guidance from the Autorité in the Area of Sustainability' available at <https://www.autoritedelaconcurrence.fr/sites/default/files/2024-05/20240527-communique-orientations-informelles-en.pdf> (accessed 8 February 2025).

[67] See, eg, Autorité de la concurrence, 'Informal Guidance 24-DD-01 of 14 June 2024 on a Standardised Methodology for Calculating Products' Environmental Footprint in the Animal Nutrition Sector' available at <https://www.autoritedelaconcurrence.fr/sites/default/files/2024-07/24-0021DD%20-%20Lettre%20orientations%20informelles%202.pdf> (accessed 8 February 2025).

[68] For an overview, see Felix Engelsing and Moritz Jakobs, 'Nachhaltigkeit und Wettbewerb' [2019] *Wirtschaft und Wettbewerb* 16–22.

[69] The authority looked at the evolution of the market conditions and highlighted the non-discriminatory access to the scheme and that it was ensured that no sensitive information would be exchanged.

[70] For a comparison of the practice of US business review letters and EU comfort letters see Giorgio Monti, 'Business Cooperation in Times of Emergency: The Role of Competition Law' (2020) available at <https://www.competitionpolicyinternational.com/business-cooperation-in-times-of-emergency-the-role-of-competition-law> (accessed 8 February 2025) who highlights that the greater detail found in the US letters is more helpful in providing guidance.

[71] DoJ, Letter from Joel I Klein, Assistant Attorney General, US Dep't of Justice, Antitrust Div, to Kenneth A Letzler and Richard M Lucas (7 April 2000) available at <http://www.justice.gov/atr/public/busreview/4513.pdf> (accessed 8 February 2025).

[72] The agreement affected the final retail price by up to 0.5 per cent for foreign-produced footwear and apparel and up to 3 per cent for US-produced goods.

In Asia, Singapore's Competition and Consumer Commission (CCCS) has published a guidance note along its streamlined notification process, which is designed to provide quicker decisions on business collaborations pursuing environmental sustainability. In brief, businesses can notify CCCS on their potential collaborations, and the CCCS takes a two-phase approach in its assessment, with Phase 1 being a thirty-working-day review for simple cases and (additional) Phase 2 of 120 days for complicated cases. Businesses can also initiate pre-notification discussions with CCCS, particularly on the content and timing of their notification.[73]

In some countries, such informal advice is available more generally. The Japanese competition authority also operates a general consultation service that guided a city initiative involving all retailers and consumers.[74] The aim was to reduce the use of plastic shopping bags via a small charge for them. The agencies advised the participants that the restriction was only ancillary, moreover, it was proportionate to reduce plastic waste. More recently, the JFTC's guidelines have restated that its consultation process is also open for sustainability cases.[75] It offers to provide more *ad hoc*-based advice orally, or more formal advice where a standard form is submitted. The advice given and the companies involved will then also be published.

3. Informal guidance and publicity

While informal guidance is an important way to achieve legal certainty and clarity regarding the agency's views in an individual case, it is not a panacea.

In fact, informal guidance might be problematic when it is not published because it does not address legal certainty issues in jurisdictions where private enforcement exists.[76] Parties and courts involved in private enforcement cases will often need to learn the views of agencies provided in the form of individual informal guidance. Thus, agencies should publish their informal guidance as far as possible. Such publication ensures that courts and parties can access the information and allows other interested parties to work with these publications, providing inspiration for further inquiries with the agencies. The German agency's practice

[73] Competition and Consumer Commission of Singapore: Guidance Note on Business Collaborations Pursuing Environmental Sustainability Objectives (1 March 2024) <https://www.cccs.gov.sg/-/media/custom/ccs/files/media-and-publications/media-releases/environment-sustainability-guidance-note-1-mar-24/cccs-environmental-sustainability-collaboration-guidance-note_full.ashx> (accessed 8 February 2025).

[74] As reported in OECD, 'Horizontal Agreements in the Environmental Context' (2010) <https://www.oecd.org/en/publications/horizontal-agreements-in-the-environmental-context_c788a7fb-en.html> (accessed 8 February 2025) 70–72.

[75] JFTC (n 54) 1, 4, 69–70.

[76] See more generally on this risk in Europe Or Brook, *Non-Competition Interests in EU Antitrust Law: An Empirical Study of Article 101 TFEU* (CUP 2022) ch 7, 'Enforcement discretion'.

of publishing case reports covering individual guidance on sustainability matters[77] is thus to be commended.

Yet, it should be noted that informal guidance in individual cases, whether published or not, is often not binding on the courts in private enforcement cases.[78] Moreover, others like the EU Commission could take up the case, where a national agency gives such informal guidance because they are not bound by it. The non-binding nature is, for example, specifically mentioned in Article 37a of the Greek Competition Act. Article 37a(1) allows the president to issue letters of non-action because the arrangement is not restrictive of competition or justified, 'or on public interest grounds, such as the implementation of sustainable development objectives'. Yet Article 37a(4) clarifies: 'The no-action letter has no binding effect on the Competition Commission and the courts.' More formal guidance by means of guidelines might be more helpful.[79] Such guidance may have more persuasive force in cases before a court or might even be formally binding on courts in some jurisdictions.[80] Ultimately, legislative action might be called for to address the remaining issues of legal certainty.

IV. Approval/exemption procedures and sandboxing

Having seen the importance of individual guidance, as well as the possible problems in terms of legal certainty, we now turn the focus on the means that provide a greater level of legal certainty for the actors involved.

The two main areas that can help with serious legal certainty issues faced by sustainability initiatives are approval/exemption proceedings. These provide a binding decision by the agency. A second tool that can also help with legal certainty issues but is less often encountered is sandboxing.

1. Approval/exemption procedure

An approval or exemption procedure provides legal certainty by means of an *ex ante* procedure that concludes with a binding decision. Such a system has been in

[77] See the case report published by the Bundeskartellamt available at <https://www.bundeskartellamt.de/SharedDocs/Meldung/DE/AktuelleMeldungen/2022/08_03_2022_Fallberichte_Nachhaltigkeit.html> (accessed 8 February 2025).

[78] See also Giorgio Monti, 'Four Options for a Greener Competition Law' (2020) 11(3–4) *Journal of European Competition Law & Practice* 131.

[79] See eg Jordan Ellison, 'A Fair Share: Time for the Carbon Defence?' (21 February 2020) available at <https://ssrn.com/abstract=3542186> (accessed 8 February 2025).

[80] See for example Clement Mifsud-Bonnici's contribution on Malta in Bruce Kilpatrick, Pierre Kobel, and Pranvera Këllezi (eds), *Competition Law and Sustainability* (forthcoming Springer 2024), who explains how the EU Commission's guidelines bind the Maltese courts.

place in a number of jurisdictions around the globe. For example, before the implementation of Regulation 1/2003,[81] which introduced the decentralized application of the EU competition rules, it was a standard procedure in the EU. Regulation 17[82] provided that companies need to notify any restriction of competition within the meaning of Article 101(1) TFEU to the EU Commission. The Commission had the power to find that Article 101(1) TFEU did not apply (negative clearance under Article 2 of Regulation 17), or decide that the exemption conditions of Article 101(3) TFEU were fulfilled.

The Commission used this power to exempt a number of agreements with environmental impacts.[83] Amongst them, the possibly most famous decision in this area is the *CECED*[84] decision.

CECED (EU)[85]

This exemption decision from 1999 concerned an agreement between washing machine producers and importers to phase out the production and import of washing machines with the lowest energy efficiency (categories D to G).

Findings of the competition agency

The Commission identified that the agreement restricted competition by removing certain (legal) washing machines from the market, limiting consumer choice to a narrow range of energy efficiency ratings. In its exemption decision of the agreement the Commission declared that the agreement would fulfil the condition of Article 101(3) TFEU as it would foster economic and technical progress. It found that

> The agreement is designed to reduce the potential energy consumption of new washing machines by at least 15 to 20% [and] 7.5 TWh would be saved in 2015 ...[86]
>
> Washing machines which ... consume less electricity are objectively more technically efficient. Reduced electricity consumption indirectly leads to reduced pollution from electricity generation. The future operation of the total

[81] EU Council Regulation (EC) No 1/2003 of 16 December 2002 on the implementation of the rules on competition laid down in Articles 81 and 82 of the Treaty OJ [2003] OJ L 1/1.
[82] Regulation No 17: First Regulation implementing Articles 85 and 86 of the Treaty [1962] OJ 13, English special edition Series [1959–1962] I Vol 87.
[83] For an overview see Julian Nowag, *Environmental Integration in Competition and Free-Movement Laws* (OUP 2017) 225–230.
[84] *CECED* (IV.F.1/36.718) Commission Decision 2000/475/EC [2000] OJ L187/47.
[85] ibid.
[86] ibid para 47.

of installed machines providing the same service with less indirect pollution is more economically efficient than without the agreement. . . .[87]

[T]he pollution avoided [is estimated] at 3.5 million tons of carbon dioxide, 17,000 tons of sulphur dioxide and 6,000 tons of nitrous oxide per year in 2010 . . . Although such emissions are more efficiently tackled at the stage of electricity generation, the agreement is likely to deliver both individual and collective benefits for users and consumers.[88] (para 51)

The Commission also found that on the one hand, the typical consumer would be able to recoup higher purchases in a period of between nine and forty months due to the increased energy-efficiency.[89] On the other hand, there were collective environmental benefits:

According to Article [191 TFEU], environmental damage should be rectified at source. The [Union] pursues the objective of a rational utilisation of natural resources, taking into account the potential benefits and costs of action. Agreements like CECED's must yield economic benefits outweighing their costs and be compatible with competition rules. Although electricity is not a scarce resource and consumption reductions do not tackle emissions at source, account can also be taken of the costs of pollution. . . .[90]

The Commission reasonably estimates the saving in marginal damage from (avoided) carbon dioxide emissions (the so- called 'external costs') at EUR 41 to 61 per ton of carbon dioxide. On a European scale, avoided damage from sulphur dioxide amounts to EUR 4000 to 7000 per ton and EUR 3000 to 5000 per ton of nitrous oxide. On the basis of reasonable assumptions, the benefits to society brought about by the CECED agreement appear to be more than seven times greater than the increased purchase costs of more energy-efficient washing machines. Such environmental results for society would adequately allow consumers a fair share of the benefits even if no benefits accrued to individual purchasers of machines.[91]

In conclusion, the EU Commission stated that:

The expected contribution to furthering energy efficiency both within the current technological limits of categories A to C and beyond the limits of category A, the cost-benefit ratio of the standard and the return on investment

[87] ibid para 48.
[88] ibid para 51.
[89] And there would potentially be stronger competition in the remaining energy efficiency categories, A–C. Ibid paras 52–53.
[90] ibid para 55 (footnote omitted).
[91] ibid para 56 (footnote omitted).

> for individual users point to the conclusion that the agreement is likely to contribute significantly to technical and economic progress whilst allowing users a fair share of the benefits.[92]
>
> And after examining the other conditions it concluded:
>
> that the cumulative conditions of Articles 81(3) of the EC Treaty and 53(3) of the EEA Agreement are fulfilled. . . .[93]
>
> Pursuant to Article 8(1) of Regulation No 17, a decision in application of Article [101](3) is to be issued for a specific period. As notified, the obligations agreed by the parties remain binding upon them until 31 December 2001. It is therefore appropriate to define the duration of this exemption accordingly.[94]

The EU Commission took a similar exemption decision in *EACE*.[95] However, with the abolition of the exemption regime in the EU, such legal certainty no longer exists in the same form in the EU.

Yet, other jurisdictions still have systems that provide such legal certainty. An example in the environmental sustainability context is the Australian authorization system under which the Australian competition authority authorized the Battery Stewardship Council.[96] As we saw in the previous chapter, the scheme which was established to ensure the recycling of batteries was granted authorization because:

> For the reasons outlined in this determination, and subject to the condition below, the ACCC is satisfied, in all the circumstances, that the Proposed Conduct would be likely to result in a benefit to the public and the benefit to the public would outweigh the detriment to the public that would result or be likely to result from the Proposed Conduct, including any lessening of competition.[97]

The authorization was granted for five years until 2025, but some conditions were imposed on the parties, including establishing an advisory committee. In similar fashion, New Zealand has also applied an authorization system.[98]

[92] ibid para 57.
[93] ibid para 67.
[94] ibid para 68.
[95] European Commission, *XXVIIIth Report on Competition Policy 1998* (Office for Official Publications of the European Communities 1999) 152.
[96] See ACCC, 'Determination Application for authorisation AA1000476 lodged by Battery Stewardship Council in respect of the Battery Stewardship Scheme' (5 October 2020) Authorization number: AA1000476 available at <https://www.accc.gov.au/public-registers/authorisations-and-notifications-registers/authorisations-register/battery-stewardship-council> (accessed 8 February 2025).
[97] ibid para 5.3.
[98] See Commerce Commission New Zealand, 'Authorization Guidelines' <https://comcom.govt.nz/__data/assets/pdf_file/0012/91011/Authorisation-Guidelines-June-2023.pdf> (accessed 8 February 2025).

These authorization and exemption decisions show us how this procedural tool can be used to increase legal certainty in the area of sustainability and antitrust.

2. Sandbox and ongoing supervision

Another less well-known tool in the area of antitrust is sandboxing.[99] The Greek competition authority had suggested the use of this tool, known from other areas of regulation, with regard to antitrust, particularly sustainability and antitrust.[100] The sandbox environment means that the companies taking part have been briefed about the general principles but can experiment with different setups. The whole process takes place under the supervision of the competition authority. When the agency spots problems, it will engage with the companies instead of punishing an otherwise possibly punishable violation. The Greek competition authority started its sustainability sandbox as a secure online platform.[101] In general, the sandbox procedure allows the companies to apply to the agency to take part in the sandbox scheme. The parties must submit an application that follows a specific form and contains the relevant information regarding competition law. After evaluating the application, the companies can implement their proposal and are supervised. An *ex-post* evaluation will also take place.

While not as institutionalized as sandboxing, competition authorities might also engage in other forms of ongoing supervision and engagement. For example, the above-mentioned[102] cases from Germany involved continued engagement by the German competition authority. It provided guidance to the initiative and issued a non-enforcement letter for a certain period. At the end of the period, the agency and the initiative re-engaged, and changes were implemented after the advice from the agency, which then issued another non-enforcement letter.

In all these cases, enforcement costs in terms of supervision are an important consideration for an agency. Thus, it needs to be ensured that the monitoring costs for the agency are low and that the firms involved have to report to the agency actively.[103]

[99] In general, on regulatory sandboxes see eg Hilary J Allen, 'Regulatory Sandboxes' (2019) 87 *George Washington Law Review* 579–645.

[100] Hellenic Competition Commission (n 43) para 114.

[101] Available at <https://sandbox.epant.gr/en/> (accessed 8 February 2025); see also the consultation which explained in more detailed the reasoning and envisioned procedure and results, available at < https://www.epant.gr/en/information/sustainability/sandbox.html> (accessed 8 February 2025).

[102] See text to (n 68f).

[103] See also Giorgio Monti, 'Implementing a Sustainability Agenda in Competition Law and Policy' in Julian Nowag (ed), *Research Handbook on Sustainability and Competition Law* (Edward Elgard 2024).

V. Evidence, capacity, cooperation, and advocacy

When sustainability matters are at issue, questions around evidence and the capacity to deal with such evidence are particularly important. On the one hand, businesses and agencies need to clearly understand what type of evidence is acceptable in the legal system governing the case. On the other hand, where evidence and questions regarding sustainability are raised, the capacity and available skills of the agency and courts dealing with the case are relevant to critically evaluate these issues.

1. Evidence and burden of proof

In terms of evidence in sustainability cases, we can look at the kind of evidence that is acceptable and how the burden of proof might be structured.

a) The evidence

The type of evidence that is acceptable naturally depends on the nature of the claim in question. Thus, the evidence might be more or less the same in sustainability cases as in non-sustainability cases, where the harm or benefit is based on more orthodox theories of harms or benefits.[104] Where specific environmental benefits are at issue, insights from environmental economics can be helpful.[105] In the context of the evidence for the benefits of horizontal agreements,[106] the European Commission established the distinction between use benefits, non-use benefits, and collective benefits.[107] The first two benefits are typically examined using quantitative evidence based on traditional tools, such as willingness to pay,[108] while being mindful of measuring the actual consumer preferences. For example, there can be differences between stated preferences and actual buying behaviour.

> This may indicate that consumers' declared preferences either over-estimate or under-estimate their true preferences. To mitigate such biases, which often result from hypothetical questions in consumer surveys, such surveys should provide

[104] See for example Chapter 4, section IV. 2. a) and b).

[105] See Adina Claici and Jasper Lutz, 'Beyond the Policy Debate: How to Quantify Sustainability Benefits in Competition Cases' (2021) 5(3) *European Competition and Regulatory Law Review* 200–209.

[106] With regard to the burden of proof in mergers and how this could be changed in the context of sustainability see Simon Holmes and Michelle Meagher, 'A Sustainable Future: How Can Control of Monopoly Power Play a Part? Part III: Using Merger Control to Intervene Before the Problem Arises or Gets Worse' (2023) 44(4) *European Competition Law Review* 158–159.

[107] For the details see Chapter 4, section IV. 2. f).

[108] European Commission Guidelines (n 40) para 9.4.3.

appropriate context. In addition, the questions posed should take into account societal norms, consumer knowledge and habits, and expectations about the behaviour of others.[109]

With regard to collective benefits the Commission's guidelines highlight that:

> [t]he parties should be able to:
> (a) describe clearly the claimed benefits and provide evidence that they have already occurred or are likely to occur;[110]
> (b) define clearly the beneficiaries;
> (c) demonstrate that the consumers in the relevant market substantially overlap with the beneficiaries or form part of them;[111] and
> (d) demonstrate that the share of the collective benefits that accrues to the consumers in the relevant market, possibly together with individual use and non-use value benefits accruing to those consumers, outweighs the harm suffered by those consumers as a result of the restriction.
>
> Evidence for collective benefits contained in public authorities' reports or in reports prepared by recognized academic organizations may be of particular value for this assessment.
>
> Where there is no available data that allows for a quantitative analysis of the benefits of the agreement, other evidence may be considered, provided that it shows a clearly identifiable positive impact on consumers in the relevant market, not a marginal one. As there is currently little experience with measuring and quantifying collective benefits, the Commission aims to provide more guidance on this issue when it has gained sufficient experience of dealing with concrete cases, which may enable it to develop methodologies of assessment.[112]

In other words, an insistence on quantitative evidence might hinder pro-competitive sustainability activities. Thus, the Dutch competition authority had equally clarified in their draft guidelines that qualitative evidence is permissible where quantification is impossible.[113]

The European Commission has accepted that certain out-of-market and future benefits have to be considered in Article 101(3) TFEU.[114] In this regard, just as in

[109] ibid para 579.
[110] It adds in fn 408 that: 'Benefits that will materialise in the future may be taken into account to the extent that they will accrue to consumers in the relevant market.'
[111] It adds in fn 409 that: 'in cases where collective benefits are dispersed among a large section of society, it is less likely that the overlap with the consumers in the relevant market will be substantial.'
[112] ibid paras 587–589.
[113] ACM, 'Draft Guidelines' (n 35) paras 31–35.
[114] See discussion in Chapter 4, section IV. 2. e).

mergers, a discount rate for environmental impacts and its correlation with the normal discount rate used in business/project appraisal has been suggested.[115]

b) Burden of proof

Another relevant question regarding evidence is related to the burden of proof, and specifically questions around presumptions. Under EU competition law, the burden of proof comes into play in questions of whether an agreement restricts competition by object or effect, or whether the agreement needs to be examined.[116] In effect cases, the EU Commission or claimant must provide more evidence showing an actual restriction of competition. In contrast, in cases of an object restriction, the effects are presumed.

Whether an agreement restricts competition by object needs to be assessed, taking into account 'relevant aspects—having regard, in particular, to the nature of the services at issue, as well as the real conditions of the functioning and structure of the markets—of the economic or legal context'.[117] The EU Commission also discussed this matter with regard to sustainability agreements in its guidelines and explained that within this analysis of the context, the sustainability objective can be taken into account. If the parties can show that they pursue a genuine sustainability objective, this can raise doubt as regards the object restriction of the agreement, even where it concerns matters such as price fixing, market or customer allocation, limitation of output or innovation. In these situations, the case will be assessed under the effects standard.[118]

Similarly, questions concerning the burden of proof might arise when parties claim sustainability benefits. In many jurisdictions, concerns about the ability of agencies or judges to calculate such benefits are addressed by burden of proof rules. In the EU, as in many other jurisdictions, it is for the defendant, rather than the competition agency, to provide evidence of any claimed benefits, including valuations and supporting evidence.[119]

2. Capacity and skills, cooperation, and advocacy

The capacity and skills of agency personnel and judges are always a consideration in competition law matters, whether these are questions of economics and functioning of markets, understanding technology, or evaluating sustainability matters.

115 Matthew Johnson, 'The Role of Sustainability in Merger Control' *Oxera* (16 April 2021) <https://www.oxera.com/insights/agenda/articles/the-role-of-sustainability-in-merger-control/> (accessed 8 February 2025).

116 On the distinction between object and effect, see eg European Commission, Guidelines (n 40) paras 532–536.

117 Case C-228/18 *Budapest Bank* EU:C:2020:265 para 67.

118 European Commission, Guidelines (n 40) paras 532–536.

119 See Monti (n 78) 129 and Nowag (n 83) 236–238.

Think, for example, about the challenge that the Dutch competition agency faced in the *coal power* case[120] which we discussed earlier.[121] Here, the agency calculated the possible overall benefit to society[122] which can then be divided to calculate the individual benefit.

This suggests that it is valuable for agencies to strengthen and broaden their capacities in sustainability matters, a broad -possibly all encompassing- field covering environmental, economic, and social matters. This capacity is a challenge for many agencies. Even more so for agencies in developing countries, which may lack the capacity and resources to have teams of lawyers and economists working on an individual case for months.

However, beyond hiring people with the relevant expertise[123] or outsourcing such tasks, there are other ways to strengthen capacity. For example, dedicated units can be set up to deal with such matters whenever they arise. The Swiss and the UK competition authorities have for example set up such task forces.[124]

Another way to address capacity is by cooperation with other regulators and stakeholders including civil society organizations and internationally with other agencies. For example, setting up joint units with other government parts might help to better understand sustainability matters, as the Greek competition authority highlights.[125] Similarly, the French competition authority has set up a working group together with different French sector regulators[126] with a particular view to climate urgency. In the Philippines, the competition authority has closely worked with the national development commission to better understand the developmental challenges in the Philippines.[127] To address capacity, the Dutch competition authority in its *coal power* case[128] brought in outside help in the form of a study by the Netherlands Bureau for Economic Policy Analysis, an independent research institute.

[120] ACM, 'Notitie ACM over sluiting 5 kolencentrales in SER Energieakkoord' (26 September 2013) available at <https://www.acm.nl/nl/publicaties/publicatie/12033/Notitie-ACM-over-sluiting-5-kolencentrales-in-SER-Energieakkoord> (accessed 8 February 2025).

[121] See in this regard Chapter 4, section IV. 2. e).

[122] See also the EU Commission's *CECED* decision (n 84), which looked at the 'collective environmental benefits' and calculated them in economic terms by placing a monetary value upon the saved carbon dioxide, sulphur dioxide, and nitrous oxide.

[123] See also Monti (n 103) text after fn 25ff.

[124] Note, that the only the UK authority has officially announced the establishment, see <https://www.gov.uk/government/news/cma-publishes-environmental-sustainability-advice-to-government> (accessed 30 November 2023).

[125] Hellenic Competition Commission (n 43) para 113,

[126] This group is comprised of AMF, CSA, ARCEP, CNIL, Hadopi, ART, CRE, and Arjel, see press release (19 December 2019) 'Independent public and administrative authorities develop their collaboration on the challenges of climate warming' available at <https://www.autoritedelaconcurrence.fr/en/press-release/independent-public-and-administrative-authorities-develop-their-collaboration> (accessed 8 February 2025).

[127] See Papa and Teston (n 21).

[128] ACM (n 120).

Capacity is an important consideration in this field. The ICN report on sustainability and competition law[129] that collected answers from different competition authorities around the world showed that

> while a limited number of CA [competition agencies] have already taken action to deal with an expertise gap, a much larger portion of CAs are planning to do so. ... [Many agencies have the] view that sharing experience via co-operation with foreign CAs is key, especially at the early stage, but if the issue is longer term, CAs want to internalise knowledge through some form of capacity building. Similarly, a large portion of respondent NGAs find the topic challenging, and an overwhelming majority of NGAs are planning preparations in the topic.[130]

On the one hand, cooperation with other actors is closely linked to capacity as it helps competition agencies in dealing with matters where they are not experts. On the other hand, cooperation is an important element in competition advocacy.[131]

In sustainability-related matters, advocacy can come in different forms and shapes. In developing[132] but also in developed countries, advocacy can focus on legal, structural, or behavioural barriers that prevent small and micro businesses from entering markets, whether such obstacles result from new or existing laws and government programmes.[133] Such activities should increase or protect existing competition from such small and micro enterprises which can play an important role in the fight against poverty. Moreover, in particular in developed countries, advocacy might also take aim at anti-competitive practices that might otherwise not be illegal. For example, export cartels might be legal because they primarily affect markets abroad. Yet, such cartels might have substantial effects on poverty in developing countries and may, thus, be an appropriate focus for advocacy efforts by agencies.[134] Competition agencies can also become active in advising on market designs relevant to sustainability. In other words, they can help the legislator or

[129] Hungarian Competition Authority, 'Sustainable Development and Competition Law – Survey Report (Special Project for the 2021 ICN Annual Conference)' (30 September 2021) available at <https://www.gvh.hu/pfile/file?path=/en/gvh/Conference/icn-2021-annual-conference/sustainability_survey_REPORT_3rdEd_2021_09_30_final_PUBLIC.pdf1&inline=true> (accessed 30 November 2023).

[130] ibid 11 (references omitted).

[131] Competition advocacy covers a huge variety of activities by agencies aimed at promoting a competitive market environment. On the topic in general see eg Irina Knyazeva, 'Competition Advocacy: Soft Power in Competitive Policy' (2013) 6 *Procedia Economics and Finance* 280–287.

[132] With regard developing countries in particular see eg John Clark, 'Competition Advocacy: Challenges for Developing Countries' (2005) 6(4) *OECD Journal: Competition Law and Policy* 69–80; Allan Fels and Wendy Ng, 'Rethinking Competition Advocacy in Developing Countries' in Daniel D Sokol, Thomas K Cheng, and Ioannis Lianos (eds), *Competition Law and Development* (Stanford University Press 2013) 182–198.

[133] OECD (n 2) 216.

[134] ibid 417.

other regulators in the functioning of markets. In this way, they can help ensure that the competition can deliver its possible benefits for sustainability.[135] An example might be the work of the Mexican competition authority. It advised on the design of the energy market that aimed to transition the energy system by means of clean energy certificates. In its report on the market design,[136] the Mexican competition authority made fifty-one specific recommendations, ensuring in particular that competition is not reduced, so that clean energy projects are not discouraged and their financing is not hampered.

VI. Market inquiries and procedure

Another crucial area to explore is market enquiries/investigations/studies and questions of procedure, including private enforcement, and how they might help promote sustainability.

1. Market inquiries/studies/investigations

Market inquiries, sometimes also called market studies or market investigations,[137] allow competition agencies to target areas of particular relevance to sustainability. Such an inquiry allows the agency not only to obtain different input and evidence from a variety of stakeholders and market participants, but it may also—depending on the jurisdiction and system—allow the agency to adopt remedies to issues that hinder competition from contributing to increased sustainability.

The UK competition authority has gone down that road.[138] It has a rather sophisticated system at its disposal that allows the agency not only to require companies to provide information but also to impose behavioural and even structural remedies. Due to its wider mandate (also including consumer protection), the agency examines whether the working of the market has 'effects adverse to the interests of consumers'.[139] In its market inquiries, the competition authority

[135] See on the relationship between competition and sustainability Chapter 2.

[136] Comisión Federal de Competencia Económica, 'Transición Hacia Mercados Competidos de Energía: Los Certificados de Energías Limpias En La Industria Eléctrica Mexicana' (2021) available at <https://www.cofece.mx/transicion-hacia-mercados-competidos-de-energia-los-certificados-de-energias-limpias-en-la-industria-electrica-mexicana > (accessed 8 February 2025).

[137] Sometimes jurisdictions also distinguish between studies and investigations, etc where one involves a more in-depth examination with the potential for further-reaching remedies.

[138] For a discussion see also Simon Holmes, 'Climate Change, Sustainability and Competition Law' (2020) 8(2) *Journal of Antitrust Enforcement* 392–393 and Nicole Kar and Emma Cochrane, 'Sustainability and Competition in the UK after Brexit' in Julian Nowag (ed), *Research Handbook on Sustainability and Competition Law* (Edward Elgar 2024) 455.

[139] Section 130A Enterprise Act 2002.

examines regulatory, economic drivers, and consumer and business behaviour and how they interact.[140]

The UK competition authority used this power to conduct an inquiry into electric vehicle charging stations and followed up with an investigation into anti-competitive behaviour in that field, but also committed itself to initiate another market inquiry into a sector relevant for climate change.[141]

The market study was concluded in 2021 and identified a number of issues. To address these, the agency:

a) made specific recommendations to the government to increase its efforts for the roll-out of a comprehensive charging network across the UK;
b) initiated an investigation into exclusivity agreement concerning charging stations along motorways which were particularly long.[142]

Another case where the UK authority has used this tool in a sustainability-related market is the study into social care for children. This study, which was concluded in 2022[143] was carried out because 'the case for a market study in this area was particularly strong due to the profound impact that any problems would have on the lives of children in care ... and in particular the deep impact that outcomes in this market can have on the lives of children'.[144] It concluded that there were substantial issues with placements of children and the authority summaries these as:

- a lack of placements of the right kind, in the right places, means that children are not consistently getting access to care and accommodation that meets their needs;

[140] For details see CMA, 'Guidance on the CMA's Investigation Procedures in Competition Act 1998 cases: CMA8' (31 January 2022) available at <https://www.gov.uk/government/publications/guidance-on-the-cmas-investigation-procedures-in-competition-act-1998-cases/guidance-on-the-cmas-investigation-procedures-in-competition-act-1998-cases#issuing-the-cmas-provisional-findings--the-statement-of-objections-and-draft-penalty-statement> (accessed 8 February 2025).

[141] See CMA, 'Correspondence: Environmental Sustainability and the UK Competition and Consumer Regimes: CMA Advice to the Government' (March 2022) available at <https://www.gov.uk/government/publications/environmental-sustainability-and-the-uk-competition-and-consumer-regimes-cma-advice-to-the-government/environmental-sustainability-and-the-uk-competition-and-consumer-regimes-cma-advice-to-the-government> (accessed 8 February 2025).

[142] This investigation ended with commitment in 2022 where the parties agreed to abandon the exclusivity provisions. See CMA, Case number 51050, 'Decision to accept binding commitments in relation to certain exclusive arrangements for the supply of electric vehicle charging points' (8 March 2022) available at <https://assets.publishing.service.gov.uk/media/622634d28fa8f5490d52ef91/EV_decision_to_accept_commitments_V2_070322.pdf> (accessed 8 February 2025).

[143] CMA 'Final Report into its Market Study into Children's Social Care Provision' (10 March 2022) available at <https://www.gov.uk/government/publications/childrens-social-care-market-study-final-report> (accessed 8 February 2025).

[144] ibid para 2.

- the largest private providers of placements are making materially higher profits, and charging materially higher prices, than we would expect if this market were functioning effectively; and
- some of the largest private providers are carrying very high levels of debt, creating a risk that disorderly failure of highly leveraged firms could disrupt the placements of children in care.[145]

The relevant ministry in charge of children's welfare (the Department of Education) accepted the authority's recommendations.

Outside the UK, in Latin America, along similar terms, an enforcement agenda has been suggested for mining and the food sector to ensure the green transition in Latin America, regulate mining of crucial material for the transition, and address hydrogen and deforestation issues.[146]

2. Procedure

However, not all jurisdictions and authorities have such sophisticated and far-reaching tools at their disposal.[147] Yet, even in the context of rather standard investigations into anti-competitive behaviour or mergers, procedural rules can make a difference in terms of sustainability.

First and foremost, informational input into investigations is key to understanding any interaction between competition and sustainability impacts. Procedures that allow inputs from a diverse range of stakeholders and market participants are important[148] and can be guaranteed by ensuring that third parties are permitted to make submissions and provide evidence in competition proceedings.

In South Africa, the competition tribunal set a precedent in 2011[149] when it allowed the participation of environmental NGOs in the context of a merger case concerning seed companies, that had potential implications for sustainability.

[145] ibid para 4.

[146] Francisco Beneke, 'Competition Law in Latin America and Global Greenhouse Gas Emissions – The Way Forward' (25 June 2024). Max Planck Institute for Innovation & Competition Research Paper No. 24-12, available at <http://dx.doi.org/10.2139/ssrn.4875740> (accessed 8 February 2025).

[147] See also Aydin Umut and Tim Büthe, 'Competition Law and Policy in Developing Countries: Explaining Variations in Outcomes; Exploring Possibilities and Limits' (2016) 79(4) *Law and Contemporary Problems* 1–36; Dina Waked, 'Antitrust Enforcement in Developing Countries: Reasons for Enforcement and Non-Enforcement Using Resource-Based Evidence' 5th Annual Conference on Empirical Legal Studies Paper (12 July 2010) available at <http://dx.doi.org/10.2139/ssrn.1638874> (accessed 8 February 2025); and in general Thomas K Cheng, *Competition Law in Developing Countries* (OUP 2020).

[148] See in this regard Maria Ioannidou, '"Responsive" Remodelling of Competition Law Enforcement' (2020) 40(4) *Oxford Journal of Legal Studies* 846–877.

[149] *Pioneer Hi-Bred International, Inc/Pannar Seed (Pty) Ltd* IM083Dec10 (14 Oct 2011).

Pioneer Hi-Bred International, Inc/Pannar Seed (Pty) Ltd[150]

The case concerns a proposed merger between Pioneer Hi-Bred International, a subsidiary of the US Dupont company, and Pannar Seed, which was the largest independent company in the seed business in South Africa. The Competition Tribunal allowed two environmental NGOs, Biowatch and the African Centre for Biodiversity (ACB), as interveners. While the tribunal initially prohibited the merger, after an appeal the merger was allowed, subject to conditions.

Background

The two NGO intervenors were concerned with protecting the sustainability of food supplies, the impact on small and subsistence farmers, and in particular the effects on pricing and the availability of alternative products. ACB, one of the interveners, provided extensive evidence that an agricultural economist had collected working in close cooperation with small and subsistence farmers.

Overall, the

> ACB argued that a small but significant increase in maize seed prices as a result of the proposed deal would have a detrimental effect on small-scale commercial and subsistence farmers in South Africa.[151]

Decision

Based on the ACB's submissions the Tribunal found that

> the public interest issues raised by ACB are premised on the assumption that the proposed merger would lead to a small but significant increase in price of hybrid maize seeds. We found that such price increases are indeed likely as a result of the proposed merger. The concerns of ACB therefore our merger specific since they stem directly from the price increase is likely to be brought about by the merger itself.[152]

And after weighing the evidence provided by the NGO, the Tribunal concluded:

> Therefore we find that a small but significant post-merger increase in the price of hybrid maize seeds would have a severe adverse effect on those small scale

[150] ibid.
[151] ibid para 59.
[152] ibid para 406.

> commercial and subsistent farmers who currently use hybrid seeds. Hybrid seed at present represent a minimum of 15% of the seed used by 1.2 million of these farmers and this figure, according to Van Rooyan's testimony, is expected to increase after the proposed merger.[153]

The case shows how the submissions by these NGOs provided further important information on the merger's impact on small and subsistence farmers.

The fact that such informational input is crucial is also recognized by the Australian competition authority. Whenever an application for authorization on public interest grounds is submitted, the agency will undertake a public consultation on the application.[154] This process takes place once the agency has come up with a draft decision on the application and any interested person can participate. According to section 90A(12) of the Competition and Consumer Act 2010, an interested person is someone who has notified the competition authority of its interest in the application and has a real and substantial interest in the outcome of the process.

3. Rights to private action

While we have already discussed the option of interested parties to participate in proceedings before the competition authority or in subsequent court proceedings, private enforcement is also an interesting avenue in sustainability matters. While only some jurisdictions foresee private enforcement, even in those countries that foresee such possibilities, it is not always clear whether parties affected by the sustainability effects could bring competition proceedings. We might think of examples like a merger or anti-competitive agreement leading to more significant pollution because it hinders sustainable innovation, or of a case like the just-discussed South African case *Pioneer/Pannar Seed* with impacts on small and subsistence farmers.

In these cases, civil procedure rules and realities of financial abilities and possibly small individual damages caused will impact the ability to obtain relief and access to justice. This problem is also known in competition cases in terms of consumer damages actions.[155] In the EU it is in part addressed by the EU directive on

[153] ibid para 425.

[154] For further details, see the discussion of Georgina Foster, 'Australia: Sustainability as a Public Benefit to be Weighed Against the Anti-Competitive Detriments of Competitor Collaborations' in Julian Nowag (ed), *Research Handbook on Sustainability and Competition Law* (Edward Elgar 2024) 483.

[155] See in general also Maria Ioannidou, *Consumer Involvement in Private EU Competition Law Enforcement* (OUP 2015).

collective redress.[156] Just as in such consumer cases, questions around representative and collective actions will be key in the described sustainability scenarios. It is unlikely that a subsistence farmer will have the financial means and abilities to challenge a multimillion-dollar merger. The environmental damage of increased pollution also creates problems with standing and questions about who is representing nature in such cases. Thus, the availability of collective and representative actions is crucial in the sustainability context, whether it is concerned with stopping anti-competitive activity or compensating for damages incurred.

VII. Sanctions and remedies

Sanctions and remedies are also closely related to procedural matters. These can equally be important when discussing sustainability matters in competition law. On the one hand, fines might be lowered or increased in sustainability-related cases. On the other hand, we might see remedies that address specific sustainability matters.

1. Fines and sanctions

In Europe, a number of agencies have adopted changes to their fining policies related to their overall amendments to address sustainability matters, in particular with regard to horizontal cooperation matters. In this context, authorities were concerned about over-deterrence with regard to sustainability initiatives, particularly after it had been reported that a number of companies abstained from cooperating on sustainability initiatives as they feared fines.[157]

The Dutch competition agency suggested in its draft sustainability guidelines that it would not impose fines if the following cumulative conditions were met:

1. the parties followed the agency's guidelines or informal guidance in good faith;
2. … the details of the agreement [were published] openly;
3. … the arrangement [was adjusted] after [the] agency notified them of the objection.[158]

[156] Directive (EU) 2020/1828 of the European Parliament and of the Council of 25 November 2020 on representative actions for the protection of the collective interests of consumers and repealing Directive 2009/22/EC (Text with EEA relevance) [2020] OJ L 409/1.
[157] Linklater Study, 'Competition Law Needs to Cooperate: Companies Want Clarity to Enable Climate Change Initiatives to be Pursued' available at <https://www.linklaters.com/en/insights/blogs/linkingcompetition/2020/esg/competition-and-sustainability> (accessed 8 February 2025).
[158] ACM (n 35) para 61.

This section was in the final version partly adjusted.[159] In a certain way the agency set a trend that has been followed by the Austrian[160] and the UK competition agencies. The UK agency also adopted this approach shortly after and explained that it would not impose fines where an agreement had been discussed with the agency and all relevant facts were disclosed to the agency.[161] The European Commission followed the same approach but placed it on a more general basis regarding guidance letters on unilateral or collaborative actions. It will not impose fines where the informal guidance set out in its guidance letter is followed in good faith.[162]

Overall, these examples concern situations where the companies aimed at fostering sustainability but still run afoul of competition rules. However, we can equally imagine the opposite situation, where an agency uses its powers to tackle actions by companies that harm sustainability. For example, it has been suggested that such negative effects could serve as an aggregating factor in the fine-setting process, particularly where the harmful collusion occurred due to an initiative, such as a standard-setting initiative, that was designed to increase sustainability.[163] One such example that may fall into this category is are the decisions by Italian competition authority in *Corepla*[164] and *Google/Enel X*.[165] In *Corepla* a fine of 27 million euros was imposed for an abuse of a dominant position in the market for the recovery and recycling of plastic packaging for food use. *Corepla* had implemented an articulated strategy aimed at hindering the operation of its competitor, Coripet. The authority highlighted that its decision prevented harm to competition, and contributed to the achievement of sustainability, including recycling and waste management, and might have been a contributing factor in the fining

[159] ACM (n 28) para 40.

[160] See Bundeswettbewerbsbehörde, Guidelines on the Application of Sec 2 para 1 Cartel Act to Sustainability Cooperations (Sustainability Guidelines) (September 2022) available at <https://www.bwb.gv.at/fileadmin/user_upload/AFCA_Sustainability_Guidelines_English_final.pdf> (accessed 8 February 2025) para 104, which explains that fines would only be issued if companies that had received informal guidance had not suspended their agreement or consulted with the agency after a material change in circumstances.

[161] UK draft guidance on the application of the Chapter I prohibition in the Competition Act 1998 to environmental sustainability agreements—CMA177 (28 February 2023) available at < https://assets.publishing.service.gov.uk/media/63fde435e90e0740de2669e7/Draft_Sustainability_Guidance_document__.pdf> (accessed 8 February 2025) para 7.12; This was also retained in the finalized version of the guidelines, see section 7.

[162] Commission Notice on informal guidance relating to novel or unresolved questions concerning Articles 101 and 102 of the Treaty on the Functioning of the European Union that arise in individual cases (guidance letters) (2022/C 381/07) [2022] OJ C 381/9 para 25, this is also subject to providing full, accurate, and truthful information to the Commission in the first place, as well as a material change clause—see para 26.

[163] See Monti (n 103).

[164] Autorita' Garante della Concorrenza e del Mercato, Press Release A531 'ICA: sanction of €27 million to Corepla for abuse of dominant position in the recovery of pet plastic packaging' available at <https://en.agcm.it/en/media/press-releases/2020/11/A531> (accessed 8 February 2025).

[165] Autorita' Garante della Concorrenza e del Mercato, Press Release A529 'ICA: Google fined over 100 million for abuse of dominant position' available at <https://en.agcm.it/en/media/press-releases/2021/5/A529> (accessed 8 February 2025).

decision. In *Google/Enel X* the agency was more explicit. The environmental harm was considered as an aggravating factor when fines were imposed on Google, in respect of its refusal to include the *Enel X* app, which facilitates the recharging of electric vehicles, on Android Auto. At the end, a €100 million fine was imposed, taking into account the 'possible negative effects [which] could occur to the diffusion of electric vehicles, to the use of "clean" energy and to the transition towards a more environmentally sustainable mobility'.[166]

2. Remedies

When imposing or considering remedies proposed by the parties, sustainability consideration may also play a role.[167] Remedies can also be likened closely to the issuance of fines. For example, the Hungarian competition authority takes a similar approach to the one we have just examined in the context of fines. Yet, it places this approach within the broader context of remedies. In its fining guidelines, the agency sets out in it that it will take into account 'cooperative conduct that facilitates the proceedings'[168] and that

> fines, besides functioning as an instrument of general and special prevention, also promote the detection and prevention of infringements, the protection of the interests of consumers and undertakings that are in a disadvantaged position due to the damage caused by infringements, and the efficient use of available resources. In order to facilitate the achievement of these policy objectives, the [agency] aims to encourage undertakings to cooperate in proceedings by providing them with the possibility of obtaining a (further) fine reduction. This cooperation can take several forms, such as the leniency policy, settlement agreement, proactive reparation, compliance efforts and other means of cooperation.[169]

It then further explains that 'proactive reparation' means compensation and explains that when examining the compensation offered by the undertaking, it would consider:

[166] ibid.

[167] See also Holmes and Meagher (n 106).

[168] Hungarian Competition Authority, 'Notice No 1/2020 of the President of the Hungarian Competition Authority and the Chair of the Competition Council of the Hungarian Competition Authority on the method of setting fines for infringements of antitrust type of prohibitions amended by Notice No 1/2021' available at < https://www.gvh.hu/pfile/file?path=/en/for_professional_users/notices/1_2020_antitroszt-kozlemeny_egyseges-szerkezetben_1_2021_modositassal_a&inline=true#page=4.38> (accessed 8 February 2025), para 24.

[169] ibid.

i. whether the proactive reparation offered is directly related to the issue subject to the competition supervision proceeding;
ii. whether the commitment is specifically intended to remedy the competition issue subject to the proceeding and is not a measure that has already been decided and will be taken in any case;
iii. how the value, cost (or fiscal effects) of the measure (e.g., investment) relates to the amount of the calculated fine;
iv. whether proactive reparation directly benefits a wide range of consumers (and at least those affected by the infringement);
v. the impact of the commitment on job creation, market access, foreign trade and tax revenues;
vi. whether *the commitment contributes to sustainability or environmental protection, thereby increasing consumer welfare*;
vii. whether the commitment is sufficiently substantiated when the proactive reparation is offered, whether the benefits to be achieved by the commitment can be substantiated by data or analysis and after its implementation, whether the effects of the commitment can be verified by audited results and thus accounted for.[170]

Thus, remedies and their interaction with sustainability may be considered when determining the level of fines.

However, remedies might also be specifically designed to address sustainability concerns, for example, in the context of mergers. An example of such an approach might be the conditional approval of a merger subject to conditions that ensure that concerns regarding sustainability are addressed. We might mention the EU Commission cases of *Schwarz Group/Suez Waste Management Companies*[171] or *GE/Alstom*[172] in this context. In the first case, a divesture requirement ensured that consumers would be able to continue to have less polluting lightweight packaging sorting services available. *GE/Alstom* concerned an innovation heavy-duty gas turbine business that Alstom had developed with environmental benefits which would not be commercialized by GE.[173] Other formulations of remedies include making data available so that greener energy providers could target the dominant companies' customers.[174] The creative remedy imposed in the French *Gaz de*

[170] ibid para 33 (emphasis added).
[171] Case M.10047 *Schwarz Group/Suez Waste Management Companies* [2021] C(2021) 2689 final.
[172] Case M.7278 *GE/Alstom* [2015] C(2015) 6179 final.
[173] This business was subsequently bought by Ansaldo Energia, which finalized the development of the turbine and further innovated by allowing the use of hydrogen, an important technology for decreasing CO2 emission.
[174] Christophe Lemaire, 'French Competition Authority Fines EDF €300 Million for Abuse of Dominance' *Ashurst* (19 April 2022) available at <https://www.lexology.com/library/detail.aspx?g=abcb4740-23a8-45e1-ab8a-51d8cdae70ee> (accessed 12 January 2025).

Bordeaux[175] case goes in a similar direction of allowing (also greener) competitors to target customers. The case concerned an abuse of a dominant position by a supplier of natural gas. It withdrew the regulated tariff from its customers and systematically promoted its own market offers on its website and through its telephone helpline. Apart from imposing a fine, the French Competition Authority mandated the supplier to publish a summary of the case decision on its website for three months so as to incentives customers to switch to cheaper and greener competitors.[176] Where jurisdictions have public interest clauses the remedies might be going even further. For example, the South African competition tribunal in *Anheuser-Busch/SABMiller*[177] approved conditions on the merger that required active measures by the merging parties to make contributions to the development of agricultural and smaller enterprises in South Africa.

Injunctions are obviously also a tool that can be useful in the toolbox to foster sustainability. The question of how far such injunctions can be used to move into more sustainable directions is one of the facts of the case but equally of the relevant legal framework. In other words, it is context-dependent. The *US Car Emissions* case[178] is one where a number of plaintiffs could prove an antitrust violation but failed to mandate the installation of more efficient cleaning systems in cars by means of an injunction, yet obtained reimbursement in the form of damages for the installation of such devices.

US Car Emissions Case[179]

In a case from the 1970s,[180] the four largest automobile manufacturers in the US were charged with conspiring through their trade association to suppress the development of automobile anti-pollution technology, which resulted in millions of automobiles being driven without effective emission control devices. Upon the parties' consent, a consent judgment was entered into and the manufacturers agreed to terminate their cooperative anti-competitive efforts.

[175] Autorité de la concurrence Press Release, 'Gas supply: the Autorité de la concurrence hands out fines worth one million euro to Gaz de Bordeaux and its parent companies for abusing the resources at its disposal as a public service to develop its competitive activity' available at <https://www.autoritedelaconcurrence.fr/en/press-release/gas-supply-autorite-de-la-concurrence-hands-out-fines-worth-one-million-euro-gaz-de> (accessed 8 February 2025).

[176] Autorité de la concurrence, 'Decision 22-D-17 of October 11, 2022 regarding practices implemented by Gaz de Bordeaux company in the gas sector' available at <https://www.autoritedelaconcurrence.fr/sites/default/files/integral_texts/2022-10/22d17.pdf> (accessed 8 February 2025).

[177] *Anheuser-Busch InBev/SAB Miller* Case No LM211Jan16.

[178] *Re Multidistrict Vehicle Air Pollution*, 538 F 2d 231 (9th Cir 1976).

[179] ibid.

[180] *United States v Automobile Manufacturers Ass'n*, 307 F Supp. 617 (CD Cal 1970).

Background

In light of the antitrust violation and the lack of pollution control devices in the driven vehicles, the applicants applied the injunction with the aim of 'retrofitting', without charge or at a reduced charge, their automobiles, and sought restitution payment, to those persons who had already had their vehicles retrofitted, for the relevant costs incurred in retrofitting.

Decision

The Court rejected the application for injunctive relief, as paragraph 16 of the Clayton Act does not permit affirmative relief for past conduct for the purpose of achieving goals that are not related to the purposes of the antitrust laws. The Court note that

> major antitrust functions which injunctive relief granted under § 16 might serve: (1) putting an end to the illegal conduct, (2) depriving violators of the benefits of their illegal conduct, and (3) restoring competition in the market place. ... We do not overlook a fourth function—to make whole those who have been injured by the conduct of the violators. That function is usually served by the § 4 remedy of treble damages.

In some scenarios, the Court recognized that injunctive relief is possible if found:

> Similarly, the Sixth Circuit has held that a conspiracy by a board of realtors to exclude Blacks from purchasing homes in certain areas may be enjoined under § 16. An effect of an injunction would be to further civil rights policy, but the complaint charged impediments to the flow in interstate commerce of persons, mortgage financing and building materials. *Bratcher v. Akron Area Board of Realtors*, 6 Cir., 1967, 381 F.2d 723....
>
> [T]he cases stand only for the proposition that § 16 provides relief which may have effects other than restoring competition when that relief has the effect of ending an ongoing antitrust violation, one of the functions of the antitrust laws....
>
> [T]he hybrid remedy sought here—affirmative equitable relief not involving ongoing violations and for the purpose of alleviating injury to something other than the competitive system—serves no antitrust purpose ... Here, there are no ongoing violations to be ended.

However, on the relief for reimbursement, the Court held that

> While restitution is indeed an equitable remedy, § 16 [of the Clayton Act] limits the equitable remedies available under its terms to those against

> 'threatened loss or damage'. Here, the 'reimbursement' would be awarded for the loss which has already occurred, at the time the car owner paid to have his vehicle retrofitted; it would not be relief 'against threatened loss or damage'. Recovery for past losses is properly covered under § 4; it comes under the head of 'damages'. See *Greenwood County v. Duke Power Co.*, 4 Cir., 1939, 107 F.2d 484, 487. What plaintiffs seek is not 'restitution' in the sense in which that term is usually used. Defendants have not received from the car owners any money to which they are not entitled; plaintiffs do not claim that they have. Thus, whether payments which appellants seek for some of their citizens is 'equitable' or not is of no consequence because § 16 does not allow the claimed relief for past loss.

VIII. International cooperation

Against the background of sustainability and competition law as an emerging field, international cooperation is crucial. In a survey for the International Competition Network, most competition agencies said that sustainability and its interaction with competition should be amongst the top five topics for international organizations.[181]

International cooperation is important for at least two reasons. On the one hand, it may help in managing divergent approaches. On the other hand, it helps in terms of learning and the exchange of knowledge.

Divergence can occur, for example, if sustainability initiatives are not illegal in some jurisdictions, but others take a more critical approach. Two initiatives to prevent deforestation of the primary rain forests exemplify this. One example concerns an international initiative that was launched under the auspices of the UN's climate conference concerning the sale of palm oil from newly deforested lands in Indonesia. Indonesia's competition agency, after initially not raising objections, faced pressure to prohibit a private standard for palm oil that reduced deforestation.[182] Even without initiating a formal investigation, the expression of

[181] Hungarian Competition Agency, ICN report (n 129) 56. Also highlighting the need for more cooperation (even within the EU), Jurgita Malinauskaite, 'Competition Law and Sustainability: EU and National Perspectives' (2022) 13(5) *Journal of European Competition Law & Practice* 336–348; and in general Antonio Capobianco, John Davies, and Sean F Ennis (2016) 'Implications of Globalisation for Competition Policy: The Need for International Cooperation in Merger and Cartel Enforcement', E15 Expert Group on Competition Policy and the Trade System, available at <https://papers.ssrn.com/sol3/papers.cfm?abstract_id=2450137> (accessed 8 February 2025).

[182] The Indonesian competition authority KPPU threatened to fine palm-oil traders who had decided not to buy palm oil from farmers that engaged in illegal deforestation, giving in to political pressure after initially endorsing the initiative. See <https://www.straitstimes.com/asia/se-asia/palm-oil-companies-ditch-landmark-indonesian-zero-deforestation-pact> (accessed 8 February 2025).

concerns by the agency was enough for the parties to abandon the standard.[183] A similar private initiative concerning agricultural products which aimed at reducing deforestation in Brazil was abandoned after powerful agricultural landowners in the Amazon region threated proceedings before the Brazilian competition authority.[184] These cases show why cooperation and comity is advisable.

The interaction with government regulation and trade also becomes clear in this area of private standards. Where private initiatives fail, states might step in. In the Indonesian case, the private standard was replaced by a nearly identical law of the Indonesian state.[185] Another example is the recent EU deforestation regulation that imposed extensive due diligence obligations for products stemming from wood, palm oil, cattle, soya, cocoa, coffee, and rubber.[186] Similarly, the import of certain palm oil products has recently been banned in the US for reasons of forced labour.[187]

Cooperation is also important as it helps in dealing with this new area of sustainability and competition where many agencies still deal with gaps in their expertise.[188] In this area, individual cooperation but also multilateral exchange of ideas and expertise at fora such as UCTAD, OECD, or the International Competition Network are important.

IX. Conclusion

In this final chapter, we looked at what competition enforcement can do beyond the substantive competition rules when they want to make a difference in terms of sustainability. Enforcement and procedural matters are important instruments to foster sustainability while protecting competition, even where the substantive provisions of competition law do not allow as much for overlaps. The chapter thus provided a range of options to engage with sustainability in competition law enforcement which enforcers can employ and adapt to their local needs and their specific legal framework. In the chapter, we discussed different ways how prioritizing

[183] The private standard was then replaced by a nearly identical standard by the Indonesian state. However, one might wonder whether the enforcement of this public standard would have the same effectiveness as a private standard in particular in the remote areas where public law enforcement in general is not the strongest.

[184] For details see Juan David Gutiérrez and Sebastián Solarte-Caicedo, 'Environmental Sustainability and Competition in Latin American Jurisdictions' in Julian Nowag (ed), *Research Handbook on Sustainability and Competition Law* (Edward Elgar 2024) 528.

[185] Note again, that the effectiveness of enforcing this public standard, especially in remote areas, in comparison to the private standard, can be questioned..

[186] Regulation (EU) 2023/1115 of the European Parliament and of the Council of 31 May 2023 on the making available on the Union market and the export from the Union of certain commodities and products associated with deforestation and forest degradation and repealing Regulation (EU) No 995/2010 [2023] OJ L 150/206.

[187] BBC, 'US bans Malaysian palm oil producer over forced labour' (1 October 2020) available at <https://www.bbc.co.uk/news/business-54366607> (accessed 8 February 2025).

[188] Hungarian Competition Agency, ICN report (n 129) 11.

some areas and de-prioritizing other areas could help in this regard. Then, we explored the important area of guidance by competition agencies. On the one hand, we saw how a number of competition agencies have now adopted guidelines for sustainability matters or how more general guidelines include sections on sustainability. On the other hand, we saw agencies adopting a policy of more informal guidance for businesses where the agency provides advice in individual cases and how some agencies have specifically announced an 'open door policy' for sustainability initiatives for the business world. After this guidance-based approach, we explored different forms of more formal approval and exemption procedures that provide more legal certainty to individual parties and how sandboxing and ongoing supervision might be used in the sustainability context. This marked the start of more procedural elements in this chapter. We examined questions of evidence, capacity, and cooperation with other agencies, as well as advocacy matters. We also covered market inquiries, procedural participation by third parties, and rights to private action. As the last part of the long competition procedures, we addressed how fines, sanctions, and remedies might play a role. Finally, we looked at international cooperation to reduce divergent outcomes and to improve skills and knowledge in this vital area.

Ricarda's struggle with bureaucracy

Ricarda will be disappointed and will have to continue her struggle with bureaucracy. In particular, the assessment principles used by the Brazilian competition authority for such actions have yet to be fully set out in guidelines.

However, not all is bleak. Many competition authorities offer the option to contact them and discuss proposals on sustainability matters with them. There is, moreover, an emerging discussion and learning of different competition authorities, possibly even a consensus. Thus, while not making local legal advice obsolete, clear compliance with the EU rules may go a long way. Similarly, the help of economists and environmental experts to exemplify the benefits of the standard will certainly improve any submissions where they are required.

Yet, as with many business transactions, this transaction is also certainly not risk-free. But with the help of competition lawyers and open and transparent interaction with the relevant agencies, risks can be minimized.

6
Conclusion

I. Overall contribution

This book shows that the areas of sustainability and antitrust are not two separate spheres: they overlap to a smaller or larger extent in different jurisdictions. The identification of this overlap can, on the one hand, involve the enforcement of competition law to foster sustainability, thus making competition enforcers guardians of sustainability. On the other hand, it can mean that agencies enable or allow private actors to foster sustainability. This enabling of private sustainability action *may* involve a (more or less controversial) balancing between competition and sustainability. However, in many cases, the overlap does not involve such balancing.

The hope is that this book is able to provide enforcers and policymakers food for thought and new insights by identifying diverse tools used in different jurisdictions to handle the matter. These insights will hopefully allow enforcers and policymakers to think more creatively about the interplay between sustainability and antitrust. We need creativity and innovation to ensure that competition policy contributes to a more sustainable world. However, in the end, this book can only provide possible pathways to engage with the sustainability and competition law interplay. Whether an enforcer does engage is a policy question and possibly a political question. Yet, in some jurisdictions, the law might force the enforcer into a specific direction.[1]

II. A brief recap

In the course of the book, we briefly introduced the interaction between sustainability and antitrust before we explored the concept of sustainability in more detail.

1. Sustainability

Examining the history of sustainability and the three core tenets of environmental, social, and economic sustainability, it became clear how economic

[1] See in this regard Chapter 1, section IV.

Global Antitrust and Sustainability. Julian Nowag, Oxford University Press. © Julian Nowag 2025.
DOI: 10.1093/9780191955013.003.0006

development—and thus productive and dynamic efficiency—is central to achieve social sustainability. In turn, social sustainability, with its focus on poverty reduction and other equity improvements for people, is the basis to ensure that nature is protected. Environmental protection and thus environmental sustainability sets the outer boundaries for any economic and social development, as we need to stay within the planetary boundaries to ensure that future generations will be able to meet their needs.

The key challenges in the context of environmental sustainability are climate change, loss of biodiversity, deforestation and changes in land use, as well as pollution. In the 1990s the sustainability debate shifted, broadening the previous focus on government action to achieve sustainability. Corporate conduct in the form of sustainable and unsustainable business practices became an additional point of attention, and questions about the interaction between sustainability and competition arose more prominently. At the same time, numerous constitutions around the world require states and their administrations to consider sustainability in their action. Considering sustainability impacts, such as effects on climate change goals, is also required by specific legislation, via directly applicable international law and in some jurisdictions, competition laws.

2. Economics, competition, and sustainability

This background chapter provided us with a basic understanding to explore the relationship between sustainability and competition from an economics perspective. We gathered insights from economic theory and also examined more practical economic studies. From a theoretical perspective, the chapter showed how sustainability concerns and competition often overlap. On the one hand, a positive relationship exists such that increased competition leads to increased sustainability. On the other hand, there are cases where reduced competition has increased sustainability, as competition induces unsustainable business practices.

We, then, explored the underlying assumptions of these theoretical models, which might not apply in a specific real-world case. The theoretical findings are also supported by practical insights and case studies. Competition—where sustainability is a competition parameter—increases sustainability, although there are also studies that suggest the opposite. We also saw how the measurement of relevant consumer benefits in antitrust could be updated to better take into account sustainability benefits and how important well-crafted consumer questionnaires are. Then, we compared state action with action by firms in achieving more sustainable market outcomes. We examined important instruments in state's toolboxes in particular taxation, financial support, regulation, competition advocacy, and competition law enforcement as a pre-distributive tool. These tools are theoretically superior to firms restricting competition. However, only in theory, governments are prefect and many practical limitations on government action (eg, jurisdictional) are not considered when comparing private and public action theoretically. Overall, in studying the economics of sustainability and competition it became clear that three interrelated variables affect sustainability outcomes: state regulation, competition, and cooperation/market power. The optimal balance between these three variables is difficult to establish in the abstract and needs to be considered in the specific context. In other words, to achieve more sustainable outcomes we need to ask first whether the state or the market is better placed in specific situations, and if the market is better placed, does competition or cooperation/monopoly provide superior outcomes? Overall, the chapter and its economic insights provided us with the foundation to delve deeper into identifying the overlap between competition and sustainability in the subsequent chapters on substantive competition law.

3. Competition authorities as guardians of sustainability

In Chapter 3, we considered the question of how the enforcement of the antitrust rules against restrictions of competition can foster sustainability. In other words, how competition authorities can act as guardians of sustainability by using competition law as a sword to fight unsustainable practices. In these situations, sustainability is fostered by maintaining competition. Competition authorities can achieve such results by using the traditional tools even in the most orthodox way. Yet, more can be achieved when sustainability is protected as a parameter of competition, for example as quality or (sustainable) innovation.

While quality and innovation fall within the more traditional variables considered in competition law enforcement, they provide a pathway to consider sustainability elements, where a particular practice affects these. We have also seen that some jurisdictions are able to go further by making use of their provisions on exploitative business practices. The consideration of exploitative abuses by firms in a dominant position seems an idea that is particularly apt to be used in the context of activities that harm sustainability. The chapter, however, also cautioned against using an expansive interpretation to cover unsustainable business practices. Some jurisdictions have specific rules addressing, for example, buyer power so that an expansive interpretation might not be necessary. Moreover, we saw how an expansive interpretation also risks going beyond the 'proper role' of competition law. Although it is difficult to make broad and general statements about the proper role of competition law, given the need to take account of the specific legal and institutional context, the risk should not be disregarded. Overall, the chapter showed how competition policy can be instrumental in the broader debate surrounding sustainability.

4. Competition authorities as public enablers of private sustainability

We explored the opposite situation in Chapter 4, the second chapter on substantive antitrust law. The chapter was dedicated to situations where economic actors promote sustainability and how these are treated by the substantive competition law provisions around the world. The first part of that chapter was dedicated to situations where the specific competition rules operate in such a way that the action is not covered by the relevant rules. In particular, we showed that not every activity promoting sustainability is subject to the prohibition of restrictions on competition. While a rather obvious point, it is nonetheless sometimes overlooked. Thus, it was noted that any perceived conflict between sustainability and antitrust deserves a closer examination before we ask whether and how a restriction of competition and sustainability benefit should be balanced. In this part of the chapter, we saw that numerous measures that may foster sustainability fall outside the scope of competition law. For example, competition laws often only cover commercial/economic activities so that non-commercial/non-economic sustainability activities are not subjected to the competition law prohibitions.

Moreover, we saw that where sustainability is promoted by means of collective bargaining or as part of platform models, competition law may not apply. In the agricultural sector and other sectors, sectoral exemption to antitrust may equally ensure that sustainability action is not prohibited by competition law. It was also highlighted how another group of activities that may promote sustainability could be outside the scope of the antitrust prohibitions. This group of activities included action that results from 'state action' or 'state compulsion', activities designed to ensure compliance with applicable laws and regulations, standard-setting activities where certain conditions are fulfilled, and IP pooling.

Finally, we focused on sustainability arrangements that do not restrict competition because they do not substantially affect the parameters of competition with shareholder agreements regarding voting on sustainability motions at annual general meetings as one example. While this first part of the chapter covered cases where a conflict and a subsequent balancing between the restriction of competition and sustainability can be avoided, the second part of the chapter examined exactly this kind of balancing. However, we also saw how this balancing can take different forms and can be more or less controversial. It was highlighted how a general distinction can be drawn between a form of abstract, more legal, balancing, and balancing that takes the place within economics-based competition law frameworks that may focus on matters such as on consumer welfare.

Abstract balancing typically involves a balancing as part of general public interest clauses, or public interest clauses that exist for specific public interests or situations. The chapter showed how sustainability may well fit within these abstract balancing clauses which often use a kind of proportionality test to balance matters. We, then, turned to situations where sustainability benefits are translated into the language of competition laws to use balancing within established economic frameworks. This part of the chapter explored cases where sustainability fits rather easily into established frameworks, by using concepts such as quality, choice, and innovation. But we also surveyed situations that are more challenging, situations where sustainability benefits occur in the future and/or in markets that are different from the market(s) where the restriction arose. In this context, the chapter also considered the options and challenges of tools to address such sustainability benefits, in particular broader efficiency measurements.

The final part of the chapter was dedicated to reactions in some jurisdictions to concerns about the mandate of competition authorities and their perceived inability to balance sustainability benefits and restrictions of competition. These jurisdictions addressed this challenge by changing or clarifying their competition laws to ensure that sustainability can be considered by the decision-makers.

5. Process matters

In Chapter 5, we turned away from the substantive law and focused on procedural matters. The chapter examined how antitrust enforcers could use procedural tools to make a difference in terms of sustainability. An important tool in this regard was priority-setting, where sustainability-relevant enforcement action is prioritized and/or where sustainability initiatives that may potentially be problematic under competition law are de-prioritized if they have positive effects on sustainability and produce only minor effects on competition. Moreover, we saw how legal certainty can be improved by individual guidance, in particular where it is subsequently published, and guidelines issued by agencies. Individual guidance and guidelines are particularly important where a concern exists that private actors are discouraged from engaging in sustainability activities due to fears about competition law. We also observed how different agencies either adopted specific sustainability guidelines or decided to include a sustainability chapter in more general guidelines. As far as guidance is concerned, an important instrument might also be the announcement of an 'open door policy' for sustainability initiatives. Such a policy enables the private sector to engage with the competition agency and obtain insights in the agency's thinking and concerns before particular initiatives are put into action.

The chapter then moved on to explore different and more formal approval and exemption procedures. These provide an even higher degree of legal certainty to individual parties. Moreover, we showed how 'sandboxing', with its ongoing supervision, might be used in the sustainability context. We then turned to other more procedural matters that come into play once an agency is engaged in examining a sustainability-related case. In that context, we examined questions of evidence, capacity, and cooperation with other agencies, as well as advocacy activities by agencies. As part of the broader gathering of input and information in sustainability matters, we also covered market inquiries and procedural participation by third parties, as well as private enforcement. The chapter also covered the final stages of competition proceedings, in this context we investigated how sustainability matters could be considered in setting fines and how sanctions and remedies might be influenced by taking into account sustainability. In the final part of this last chapter, we saw the importance of international cooperation which assists in reducing divergent outcomes between jurisdiction and helps in improving skills and knowledge about the interaction between sustainability and antitrust.

III. Outlook

Overall, we hope that the book has provided numerous thought-provoking insights and showed how sustainability and consumer welfare overlap. More importantly, while there are hard cases in the sustainability and competition debate, not every sustainability case is a hard one. We have seen several ways in which different jurisdictions deal also with the hard cases, but we also saw how the vast majority of sustainability cases can readily fit within established categories. The cases and approaches explored in this book should allow decision-makers to look at and select a suitable approach amongst a wide variety of options. The aspiration is that, by being equipped with a wide range of tools and approaches, decision-makers can take the right steps in ensuring a more sustainable future without compromising core tenets of antitrust law.

Index

For the benefit of digital users, indexed terms that span two pages (e.g., 52–53) may, on occasion, appear on only one of those pages.